17th Conference of the European Chapter of the Association for Computational Linguistics (EACL 2023)

Student Research Workshop

Dubrovnik, Croatia
2-4 May 2023

ISBN: 978-1-7138-7376-1

Printed from e-media with permission by:

Curran Associates, Inc.
57 Morehouse Lane
Red Hook, NY 12571

Association for Computational Linguistics
209 N. Eighth Street
Stroudsburg, Pennsylvania 18360

Phone: 1-570-476-8006
Fax: 1-570-476-0860

acl@aclweb.org

Additional copies of this publication are available from:

Curran Associates, Inc.
57 Morehouse Lane
Red Hook, NY 12571 USA
Phone: 845-758-0400
Fax: 845-758-2633
Email: curran@proceedings.com
Web: www.proceedings.com

EACL 2023

The 17th Conference of the European Chapter of the Association for Computational Linguistics

Proceedings of the Student Research Workshop

May 2-4, 2023

Introduction

Welcome to the EACL 2023 Student Research Workshop!

The EACL 2023 Student Research Workshop (SRW) is a forum for students in the field of Computational Linguistics and Natural Language Processing to come together to discuss and advance their research with help from more experienced researchers from both academia and industry.

Following the tradition of the previous student research workshops, we have two tracks: research papers and thesis proposals. The research paper track is a venue for PhD students, Master's students, and advanced undergraduate students to describe completed work or work-in-progress along with preliminary results. The thesis proposal track is offered for students who have decided on a thesis topic and are interested in receiving feedback for their proposal with suggestions for both making the ideas achievable, as well as discussions related to future directions for their work.

The student research workshop has received considerable attention, and papers have addressed research questions in various areas and in several different languages. After excluding the withdrawn submissions, we received 40 submissions in total: 7 thesis proposals and 33 research papers. We accepted 6 thesis proposals and 13 research papers, resulting in an overall acceptance rate of $\approx 48\%$. Excluding non-archival papers, 16 papers appear in these proceedings. All the accepted papers will be presented as part of the EACL conference.

Mentoring is a core part of the SRW. In keeping with previous years, we organized pre-submission mentoring to improve the writing style and presentation of submissions. A total of 8 papers participated in this program. It offered students the opportunity to receive guidance from an experienced researcher before their submission was peer-reviewed for acceptance. We also offered post-submission mentorship for improving the quality of the poster presentation of accepted papers. A total of 13 submissions participated in this program.

We thank our program committee members for providing careful and comprehensive reviews for the papers, and all of our mentors for donating their time to provide feedback to our student authors. Thanks to our faculty advisors, Valerio Basile and Natalie Schluter, for the essential advice and suggestions, and to the EACL 2023 organizing committee for their support in the entire process. Finally, we would like to thank all the authors whose participation has made the workshop a success!

Program Committee

Organizers

Elisa Bassignana, IT University of Copenhagen
Matthias Lindemann, University of Edinburgh
Alban Petit, Université Paris-Saclay

Faculty advisers

Valerio Basile, University of Turin
Natalie Schluter, IT University of Copenhagen, Apple Inc.

Program Committee

Gavin Abercrombie, Heriot Watt University
Manex Agirrezabal, University of Copenhagen
Ilseyar Alimova, Kazan Federal University
Miguel A. Alonso, Universidade da Coruña
Mithun Balakrishna, Amazon.com Inc
Maria Barrett, IT University of Copenhagen
Pierpaolo Basile, Department of Computer Science, University of Bari Aldo Moro
Chris Biemann, Universität Hamburg
Russa Biswas, FIZ Karlsruhe - Leibniz Institute for Information Infrastructure, AIFB Institute, KIT
Gerlof Bouma, University of Gothenburg
Johan Boye, KTH
Davide Buscaldi, LIPN, Université Sorbonne Paris Nord
Ruken Cakici, METU, Ankara
Burcu Can, University of Stirling
Giovanni Cassani, Tilburg University
Li-hsin Chang, University of Turku
Lin Chen, Engineering Manager, Meta Platform Inc.
Alexandra Chronopoulou, LMU Munich
Juan Manuel Coria, Université Paris-Saclay CNRS, LISN
Ruixiang Cui, University of Copenhagen
Verna Dankers, University of Edinburgh
Dana Dannélls, Språkbanken Text, Dept. of Swedish, University of Gothenburg
Orphee De Clercq, LT3, Ghent University
Iria De-dios-flores, Universidade de Santiago de Compostela. CiTIUS center on Intelligent Technologies.
Roberto Dessì, Facebook AI Research / Universitat Pompeu Fabra
Mattia Di Gangi, AppTek GmbH
Elisa Di Nuovo, European Parliament
Antoine Doucet, University of La Rochelle
Mahmoud El-haj, Lancaster University
Desmond Elliott, University of Copenhagen
Dayne Freitag, SRI International

Saadia Gabriel, University of Washington
Björn Gambäck, Norwegian University of Science and Technology
Marcos Garcia, Universidade de Santiago de Compostela
Aina Garí Soler, LTCI, Télécom-Paris, Institut Polytechnique de Paris
Filip Ginter, University of Turku
Jonas Groschwitz, Saarland University
Katharina Haemmerl, Center for Information and Language Processing, LMU
Jiatong Han, National University of Singapore
Helmut Horacek, German Research Center for AI (DFKI)
Md.murad Hossain, PhD student
Dirk Hovy, Bocconi University
Filip Ilievski, USC Information Sciences Institute
Ashwin Ittoo, ULiege
Tommi Jauhiainen, University of Helsinki
Richard Johansson, University of Gothenburg
Katharina Kann, University of Colorado Boulder
Alina Karakanta, Fondazione Bruno Kessler (FBK), University of Trento
Amr Keleg, The University of Edinburgh
Najoung Kim, Boston University
Florian Kunneman, Vrije Universiteit Amsterdam
Andrey Kutuzov, University of Oslo
Els Lefever, LT3, Ghent University
Jens Lemmens, University of Antwerp
Hongmin Li, California State University, East Bay
Sheng Liang, Center for Information and Language Processing, LMU Munich
Lucy Lin, Spotify
Kevin Lin, Microsoft
Xinyuan Lu, National University of Singapore
Enrique Manjavacas Arevalo, University of Leiden
Alessandro Mazzei, Università degli Studi di Torino
Louise Mcnally, Universitat Pompeu Fabra
Syed Mehtab Alam, CIRAD, TETIS
Paola Merlo, University of Geneva
Nada Mimouni, CNAM Paris
Gosse Minnema, University of Groningen
Aditya Mogadala, Amazon
Olof Mogren, RISE Research institutes of Sweden
Adib Mosharrof, University of Kentucky
Max Müller-eberstein, IT University of Copenhagen
Costanza Navarretta, University of Copenhagen
Massimo Nicosia, Google
Anna Nikulásdóttir, Grammatek ehf
Joakim Nivre, Research Institutes of Sweden
Stefan Olafsson, Reykjavik University
Patrizia Paggio, University of Copenhagen and University of Malta
Alexander Panchenko, Skolkovo Institue of Science and Technology
Ludovica Pannitto, CIMeC - University of Trento
Lucia Passaro, University of Pisa
Stellan Petersson, University of Gothenburg
Marco Polignano, University of Bari
Yanxia Qin, School of Computing, National University of Singapore

Taraka Rama, Walmart Global Tech
Abhinav Ramesh Kashyap, ASUS AICS
Paul Rayson, Lancaster University
Lina M. Rojas Barahona, Orange Innovation Research
Sepideh Sadeghi, Google Inc.
Manuela Sanguinetti, University of Cagliari, Department of Mathematics and Computer Science
David Sasu, IT University of Copenhagen
Yves Scherrer, University of Helsinki
Sina Sheikholeslami, KTH Royal Institute of Technology
Manish Shrivastava, International Institute of Information Technology Hyderabad
Vered Shwartz, University of British Columbia
Kairit Sirts, University of Tartu
Pia Sommerauer, Vrije Universiteit Amsterdam
Marco Antonio Stranisci, University of Turin
Sara Stymne, Uppsala University
Alane Suhr, AI2
Alberto Testoni, University of Trento
Arda Tezcan, LT3, Language and Translation Technology Team, Ghent University
Isabel Trancoso, INESC-ID / IST Univ. Lisbon
Enrica Troiano, Vrije Universiteit
Dennis Ulmer, IT University of Copenhagen
Sowmya Vajjala, National Research Council
Antal Van Den Bosch, Utrecht University
Rob Van Der Goot, IT University of Copenhagen
Bonnie Webber, University of Edinburgh
Xinnuo Xu, University of Edinburgh
Mike Zhang, IT University of Copenhagen
Shiyue Zhang, The University of North Carolina at Chapel Hill
Heike Zinsmeister, Universität Hamburg

Mentors

Gavin Abercrombie, Heriot Watt University
Maria Barrett, IT University of Copenhagen
Burcu Can, University of Stirling
Orphee De Clercq, LT3, Ghent University
Jonas Groschwitz, Saarland University
Dirk Hovy, Bocconi University
Florian Kunneman, Vrije Universiteit Amsterdam
Costanza Navarretta, University of Copenhagen
Yves Scherrer, University of Helsinki
Vered Shwartz, University of British Columbia
Pia Sommerauer, Vrije Universiteit Amsterdam
Antal Van Den Bosch, Utrecht University
Rob Van Der Goot, IT University of Copenhagen
Bonnie Webber, University of Edinburgh

Table of Contents

Revealing Weaknesses of Vietnamese Language Models Through Unanswerable Questions in Machine Reading Comprehension

Son Quoc Tran[1,4], Phong Nguyen-Thuan Do[4], Kiet Van Nguyen[2,3,4], Ngan Luu-Thuy Nguyen[2,3,4]

[1]Denison University, Granville, OH, USA

[2]University of Information Technology, Ho Chi Minh City, Vietnam

[3]Vietnam National University, Ho Chi Minh City, Vietnam

[4]The UIT NLP Group, Vietnam National University, Ho Chi Minh City

tran_s2@denison.edu, phongdntvn@gmail.com, {kietnv, ngannlt}@uit.edu.vn

Abstract

Although the curse of multilinguality significantly restricts the language abilities of multilingual models in monolingual settings, researchers now still have to rely on multilingual models to develop state-of-the-art systems in Vietnamese Machine Reading Comprehension. This difficulty in researching is because of the limited number of high-quality works in developing Vietnamese language models. In order to encourage more work in this research field, we present a comprehensive analysis of language weaknesses and strengths of current Vietnamese monolingual models using the downstream task of Machine Reading Comprehension. From the analysis results, we suggest new directions for developing Vietnamese language models. Besides this main contribution, we also successfully reveal the existence of artifacts in Vietnamese Machine Reading Comprehension benchmarks and suggest an urgent need for new high-quality benchmarks to track the progress of Vietnamese Machine Reading Comprehension. Moreover, we also introduced a minor but valuable modification to the process of annotating unanswerable questions for Machine Reading Comprehension from previous work. Our proposed modification helps improve the quality of unanswerable questions to a higher level of difficulty for Machine Reading Comprehension systems to solve.

1 Introduction

Machine Reading Comprehension (MRC) is a challenging research field in Natural Language Processing, in which systems learn to predict answers for the questions inputted by users given a relevant context. MRC has many real-world applications such as Open Domain Question Answering (Chen et al., 2017) and conversational Question Answering (Reddy et al., 2019). Thanks to the rapid development of pre-trained large language models, performances of MRC systems show substantial progress. Pre-trained large language models are typically deep learning models designed based on the architecture of the Transformers model (Vaswani et al., 2017). These models are pre-trained on very large text corpora using unsupervised tasks such as Masked Language Model and Next Sentence Prediction (Devlin et al., 2019). After the pre-training phase, researchers can leverage the language understanding of these models by fine-tuning them on downstream tasks such as MRC. After being fine-tuned, these language models can achieve state-of-the-art performances on many benchmarks.

Researchers also pre-train multilingual models which are transformers-based models pre-trained with text corpora in over 100 languages Conneau et al. (2020); Devlin et al. (2019). Although multilingual models do not rely on direct cross-lingual supervision while being pre-trained, they can achieve surprisingly high performances on different tasks in multilingual settings. Besides, these multilingual models also excel in monolingual settings, especially in low-resource languages, where the number of high-quality works in developing monolingual language models is still limited. However, the abilities of multilingual language models are restricted by the curse of multilinguality (Conneau et al., 2020): pre-training a multilingual model with a fixed capacity on an increasing number of languages only improves its performances up to a certain point. Therefore, pre-trained multilingual models often show many language weaknesses compared to monolingual counterparts in monolingual settings.

Following the success of pre-trained models in English (Devlin et al., 2019; Zhuang et al., 2021), researchers all over the world carry out many high-quality works in pre-training monolingual language models such as CamemBERT (Chan et al., 2020) in French, GELECTRA (Martin et al., 2020) in German, and PhoBERT (Nguyen and Tuan Nguyen,

Proceedings of the 17th Conference of the European Chapter of the Association for Computational Linguistics: Student Research Workshop, pages 1–13
May 2-4, 2023 ©2023 Association for Computational Linguistics

2020) in Vietnamese. These monolingual models also achieve state-of-the-art performance on numerous benchmarks, directly empowering the field of Natural Language Processing to develop in their respective languages.

Facilitated by the development of pre-trained language models, MRC has recently also shown great progress in many languages. For example, RoBERTa (Liu et al., 2019), CamemBERT (Martin et al., 2020) and GELECTRA (Chan et al., 2020) achieve near human performances on SQuAD (Rajpurkar et al., 2018), FQuAD (d'Hoffschmidt et al., 2020; Heinrich et al., 2021) and GermanQuAD (Möller et al., 2021), respectively. However, for other low-resource languages, such as Vietnamese, the performances of pre-trained language models are significant far lower than that of humans (Nguyen et al., 2022). We can explain these difficulties in research by the underdevelopment of Vietnamese monolingual language models. As a result, most researchers (Nguyen et al., 2021a; Hai et al., 2021; Nguyen and Do, 2021; Nguyen et al., 2020c) in Vietnamese MRC have to use multilingual models, which have many limitations in monolingual settings, as the cores of their MRC systems.

The difficulties that Vietnamese MRC researchers encounter, together with the limited number of works on Vietnamese monolingual models, suggest that more high-quality research into Vietnamese monolingual models is urgently needed. Therefore, in order to suggest new directions for these future works, we attempt to reveal the language weaknesses of monolingual models by analyzing the performances of monolingual models in comparison with those of multilingual ones.

In this work, we choose to investigate the performances of models on MRC because it is a suitable task for exploring the weaknesses of language models from multiple linguistic aspects. MRC allows us to examine the performance of models on lexical aspects, single-sentence level aspects, and multi-sentence level aspects of natural language. For instance, in order to answer "Who" questions, MRC models must be competent in recognizing the person's name in a sentence, demonstrating their proficiency in Named Entity Recognition. Besides, to fully understand the given context, MRC models are expected to acquire extraordinary Reading Comprehension skills such as coreference resolution and bridging, which are part of the multi-sentence level aspects of language understanding.

We focus our analysis on unanswerable questions because unanswerable questions proposed by Nguyen et al. (2022) are much more challenging than answerable questions in the same dataset, which directly creates more materials for us to reveal the language weaknesses of models. Additionally, since Nguyen et al. (2022) proposed a novel method for annotating unanswerable questions, which involves instructing annotators to use various techniques to transform answerable questions into unanswerable ones instead of generating unanswerable questions from scratch, UIT-ViQuAD 2.0 has successfully introduced many new types of unanswerable questions. Therefore, we have a more diverse range of language aspects to analyze the performances of models on.

we initially examine the performance of monolingual and multilingual models on the UIT-ViQuAD 2.0 development set. However, we concern that the development set of UIT-ViQuAD 2.0 may not be sufficiently challenging to expose the language weaknesses of models on specific language aspects. Hence, we annotate a new set of high-quality unanswerable questions on an out-of-domain corpus to further analyze the language proficiency of both monolingual and multilingual models.

Our contributions are summed as follows:

1. Our work successfully discovers different language weaknesses and strengths of Vietnamese monolingual models. Results from our work provide good directions for future works on more robust Vietnamese monolingual models.

2. To more accurately assess the language abilities of models, we propose a new method for annotating high-quality unanswerable questions that successfully further challenge current systems in MRC.

3. Results from our analysis reveal that new high-quality Vietnamese Machine Reading Comprehension benchmarks are urgently needed.

2 Related Work

Unanswerable Questions. Unanswerable questions in MRC draw much attention from the research community after the publication of SQuAD 2.0 (Rajpurkar et al., 2018). Following the guidelines proposed by Rajpurkar et al. (2018), unanswerable questions in MRC are introduced in MRC of other languages such as French in FQuAD 2.0 (Heinrich et al., 2021) and Vietnamese in UIT-ViQuAD 2.0 (Nguyen et al., 2022). The research community commonly refers to unanswerable questions in SQuAD, FQuAD, and UIT-ViQuAD as "artificial unanswerable questions" because annotators are instructed to intentionally create questions that cannot be answered using the information provided in the given context. On the other hand, unanswerable questions that naturally arise are also introduced recently in Natural Questions (Kwiatkowski et al., 2019) and TyDi QA (Clark et al., 2020), in which the evidence documents are provided after the questions are written by annotators.

Multilingual versus Monolingual Models. Vulić et al. (2020) probe an empirical analysis on monolingual BERTs and mBERT across six languages and five different lexical tasks. They show that Monolingual BERT encodes significantly more lexical information than mBERT.

Besides, Rust et al. (2021) compare pre-trained multilingual language models with monolingual counterparts regarding their monolingual task performances in nine languages and five tasks to reveal the reason for the gap between the performances of monolingual models and multilingual models. This comprehensive analysis later reveals that while pre-training data size played a vital role in the performances of language models on downstream tasks, the monolingual tokenizers designed by native speakers are also an important reason for the high performances of monolingual models in single-language settings. Results from this analysis show that Nguyen and Tuan Nguyen (2020) significantly contributed to the development of Vietnamese language models with a high-quality tokenizer that is suitable for the unique linguistic features of Vietnamese.

3 Models and Analysis Method

3.1 Models

In this work, to highlight the weaknesses of Vietnamese language models, we compare the performances of two Vietnamese monolingual language models with those of two multilingual language models.

Multilingual Language Models. We choose mBERT (Devlin et al., 2019) and XLM-RoBERTa (Conneau et al., 2020) as two multilingual models. Because we are investigating the weaknesses of existing models of each language model type, we decide to use XLM-RoBERTa$_{\text{LARGE}}$, which outperforms XLM-RoBERTa$_{\text{BASE}}$ in almost all tasks of natural language processing. XLM-RoBERTa$_{\text{LARGE}}$ has 24 transformer-based layers with 560M parameters and was trained on 2394.3 GiB of text in 100 languages, in which 137.3 GiB of 24.7 billion word tokens is Vietnamese text. On the other hand, mBERT has 12 transformer-based layers with 178M parameters and was trained in 104 languages, including Vietnamese.

Monolingual Language Models. We choose the large version of PhoBERT (Nguyen and Tuan Nguyen, 2020), and Vietnamese WikiBERT (Pyysalo et al., 2021) as two competitive monolingual models against multilingual counterparts. PhoBERT$_{\text{LARGE}}$ is a transformer-based model with 370M parameters and is trained with 20GiB of 3 billion Vietnamese word tokens. The critical difference of PhoBERT from multilingual models is that PhoBERT segments Vietnamese words before applying the Byte-Pair encoding methods (Sennrich et al., 2016) to the pre-training data. For example, while multilingual models tokenize the word "học sinh"(*student*) as two tokens, "học" and "sinh", PhoBERT treats this whole word as a single token "học_sinh" This is because white space in Vietnamese is used to separate the syllables instead of words.

On the other hand, Vietnamese WikiBERT has 101M parameters and is trained with 172M Vietnamese tokens. Because researchers developing Vietnamese WikiBERT are not Vietnamese native speakers, they do not acknowledge the unique linguistic features of the Vietnamese language as Nguyen and Tuan Nguyen (2020) do.

In this paper, for simplicity, we will refer to PhoBERT$_{\text{LARGE}}$, XLM-RoBERTa$_{\text{LARGE}}$ and Vietnamese WikiBERT as PhoBERT, XLM-RoBERTa, and WikiBERT, respectively.

3.2 Analysis Method

Following previous works (Rajpurkar et al., 2016, 2018; Nguyen et al., 2020a), we use two metrics, Exact Match (EM) and F1-score, to evaluate the overall performances of different models on Reading Comprehension task.

- **EM**: (Exact Match) The percentage of answers predicted by the MRC system match exactly any one of the gold answer(s) annotated by the human reader.

		EM(%)	F1(%)	$\text{Recall}_{\text{unanswerable}}(\%)$	$\text{Recall}_{\text{answerable}}(\%)$
monolingual	WikiBERT	46.51	55.84	50.68	74.37
	PhoBERT	63.52	75.87	73.37	**89.21**
multilingual	$\text{mBERT}_{\text{our}}$	57.66	66.84	65.84	80.47
	$\text{mBERT}_{\text{VLSP}}$	53.55	63.03	-	-
	XLM-RoBERTa	**67.84**	**78.15**	**75.86**	88.81

Table 1: Performance of models on the UIT-ViQuAD 2.0 Development set

- **F1**: F1-score measured the average overlap between predicted answers with those in the gold answers. For each question, we calculate the F1 score of predicted answer with each gold answer, and take the maximum F1 as the F1 of the corresponding question.

Because we carry out our analysis on the test set that requires models having abilities to recognize unanswerable questions, we also take into consideration the performances of models in classifying answerable and unanswerable questions. Performances on classification tasks are reported in our analysis as Recall on answerable questions and unanswerable questions.

- $\textbf{Recall}_{\textbf{unanswerable}}$: The percentage of unanswerable questions that the model correctly predicts as not having the answer in the given context.

- $\textbf{Recall}_{\textbf{answerable}}$: The percentage of answerable questions that model attempt to answer. In order to focus on the classification task, this metric does not consider whether the model predicts the correct answer.

Then, in order to analyze the performances of models on different language aspects, we annotate each unanswerable question into one of 7 unanswerable types, most of which are inspired by (Nguyen et al., 2022).

Besides, as we focus on suggesting new directions for works in developing Vietnamese monolingual models, instead of pointing out the weaknesses of any single model, we focus on determining different hard language aspects that are challenging for all investigated Vietnamese language models. Thus, we define two new concepts for this purpose:

- **Monolingual hard unanswerable questions**: Unanswerable questions that both WikiBERT and PhoBERT attempt to answer.

- **Multilingual hard unanswerable questions**: Unanswerable questions that both mBERT and XLM-RoBERTa attempt to answer.

These concepts of monolingual and multilingual hard unanswerable questions empower us to focus on the language weaknesses that both monolingual models have compared to the weaknesses of both mBERT and XLM-RoBERTa. Thus, we can encourage future research to follow effective methods from previous works and develop new methods to deal with the existing weaknesses. To compare the results between different experiments, we calculate the percentage of monolingual and multilingual hard unanswerable questions over the total number of unanswerable questions in each unanswerable type.

3.3 Experimental Settings

All models are trained with 28,457 questions in training set of UIT-ViQuAD 2.0 (Nguyen et al., 2022) in 2 epochs. We use Adam optimizer (Kingma and Ba, 2015) with learning rate of $2 \cdot 10^{-5}$, $\beta_1 = 0.9$, $\beta_2 = 0.999$, and 100 warm-up steps for all 4 models. We fine-tuned all four models on a single NVIDIA Tesla K80 provided by Google Colaboratory. Due to these limited resources in computation, we have to fine-tune our models with a small number of samples per batch. The fine-tuning batch size we use for XLM-RoBERTa, mBERT, WikiBERT is 4, while 8 is the batch size in fine-tuning PhoBERT. We then evaluate models on the development set of UIT-ViQuAD 2.0 in Section 4 and Parallel UIT-VinewsQA in Section 5.

4 Analysis on UIT-ViQuAD 2.0

4.1 Overall Performance

Table 1 shows the performance of models on the development set of UIT-ViQuAD 2.0 (Nguyen et al., 2022). XLM-RoBERTa out-

	# Unanswerable questions in developement set	Monolingual hard unanswerable questions (%)	Multilingual hard unanswerable questions(%)
Antonym	80	**15.00**	16.25
Overstatement & Understatement	68	**8.82**	14.71
Entity Swap	360	14.17	**6.39**
Normal Word Swap	383	**15.67**	16.97
Relation Reverse	138	28.99	**13.04**
Adverbial Clause Swap	21	38.10	**33.33**
Modifiers Swap	91	**13.19**	19.78
Dataset Noise	27	40.74	33.33
Total	1,168	17.20	**14.00**

Table 2: Number of monolingual and multilingual hard unanswerable questions alongside with the number of unanswerable questions in the the full development set by types

performs other three models on EM, F1 and $\text{Recall}_{\text{unanswerable}}$ while slightly underperforms PhoBERT on $\text{Recall}_{\text{answerable}}$.

The development set of UIT-ViQuAD 2.0 was used as the public test for VLSP2021: Machine Reading Comprehension (Nguyen et al., 2022). Based on the results published after the shared task, our fine-tuned mBERT substantially outperforms the mBERT baseline of the organizers.

4.2 Performance on Unanswerable Questions

We then analyze the performances of models on different unanswerable types of unanswerable questions (see Table 7 in A.1 for examples). We closely follow unanswerable question types defined by Nguyen et al. (2022). However, based on our observation, when using *Entity Swap* for creating unanswerable questions, annotators might unintentionally reverse the relation of entities in the original questions. Therefore, in order to exploit these important questions for revealing language weaknesses of monolingual models, we define *Relation Reverse* as a new unanswerable type for our analysis and analyze it separately from *Entity Swap* type. Results from our analysis (Table 2) show that questions of *Relation Reverse* type are much more challenging for models than those of *Entity Swap* type.

Results from our analysis successfully reveal some language weaknesses of monolingual models. As reported in Table 2, the performances of Vietnamese monolingual models on *Entity Swap* and *Relation Reverse* types are significantly lower than those of multilingual models. This result shows us that the ability to represent the relationships between different entities in the context of Vietnamese monolingual models are significantly inferior than multilingual models.

However, monolingual models show strong performances on *Modifiers Swap type* which requires language models to have a good ability in understanding the modified relationships between different words in the sentence. In other words, Vietnamese monolingual models acquire a better ability in low-level lexical and grammatical features of Vietnamese than multilingual counterparts do. We hypothesize that the unusual characteristics of the Vietnamese language pose significant challenges for multilingual models. If an adjective is used as a noun modifier in Vietnamese, the adjective must go after the main noun instead of before, as in English and many other resource-rich languages.

On the other hand, monolingual and multilingual models show little difference in their performances on unanswerable question types of *Antonym*, *Overstatement & Understatement*, and *Adverbial Clause Swap*. However, we are concerned that the number of high-quality unanswerable questions of those types in the development set of UIT-ViQuAD 2.0 is not enough to reveal weaknesses of language models in these aspects of language. Therefore, we annotate a new small high-quality benchmark on the corpus of UIT-VinewsQA (Nguyen et al., 2020b), which is another high-quality Vietnamese MRC dataset.

5 Analysis on Parallel UIT-VinewsQA

	# entities	# paragraphs	# sentences	# tokens
UIT-VinewsQA	4,465	500	8,131	159,857
UIT-ViQuAD	6,476	557	3,208	78,628

Table 3: Number of entities, paragraphs, sentences and tokens of UIT-VinewsQA and UIT-ViQuAD development sets predicted by Trankit, a light-weight Transformer-based toolkit for multilingual natural language processing (Nguyen et al., 2021b)

UIT-VinewsQA is an extractive question answer-

		EM(%)	F1(%)	$F1_{answerable}$(%)	$Recall_{unanswerable}$(%)	$Recall_{answerable}$(%)
monolingual	WikiBERT	36.61	48.12	61.61	34.64	81.79
	PhoBERT	40.54	56.86	80.16	33.57	**95.71**
multilingual	mBERT	41.61	52.35	65.06	38.64	83.21
	XLM-RoBERTa	**49.64**	**62.50**	**81.80**	**43.21**	95.00

Table 4: Performances of models on Parallel UIT-VinewsQA

ing dataset on Vietnamese healthcare news articles, most of which are narrative articles instead of informative like articles on the Wikipedia platform. Moreover, healthcare articles in UIT-VinewsQA are written for people with different education levels, so the sentence structure used in these articles must be simpler than that of Wikipedia articles. Therefore, as presented in Table 3, UIT-VinewsQA has some linguistic differences from UIT-ViQuAD, such as

- UIT-VinewsQA has fewer entities per sentence than UIT-ViQuAD. This significantly reduces the challenging level of recognizing relations between entities in the given context of extractive question answering task. Therefore, unanswerable questions of types such as *Entity Swap* and *Relation Reverse* are not as challenging for language models in UIT-VinewsQA compared to UIT-ViQuAD 2.0.
- UIT-VinewsQA has fewer tokens per sentence than UIT-ViQuAD, which leads to simpler sentence structures across the corpus.

5.1 Benchmark Annotations

When annotating new unanswerable questions on UIT-VinewsQA, we strictly follow the procedure proposed by Nguyen et al. (2022): we transform answerable questions extracted from the development set of UIT-VinewsQA into unanswerable questions. However, to promote the diversity of unanswerable questions, we intentionally sample our answerable questions based on their reasoning skills inspired by Nguyen et al. (2020b) (word matching, paraphrasing, single-sentence reasoning, multiple-sentence reasoning). For each answerable reasoning skill - unanswerable question type pair, we annotated ten unanswerable questions. Therefore, we have a benchmark of 280 unanswerable questions of four answerable reasoning skills and seven unanswerable question types in addition to 280 answerable questions extracted from the UIT-VinewsQA development set. We name this benchmark Parallel UIT-VinewsQA because each answerable question in the benchmark is accompanied by a corresponding unanswerable question.

Besides, during the annotating process, we do not show our annotators the answers to the original (answerable) questions and ask them to annotate answers for these questions before transforming original questions into unanswerable ones. We only include an unanswerable question into our benchmark if the annotator correctly answers the corresponding answerable question. This helps us strictly require our annotators to grasp a "big picture" of the given context instead of merely focusing on the sentences containing answers to the original questions. In later analysis, we find out that this process significantly improves the quality of questions of all unanswerable types.

5.2 Performance on Parallel UIT-VinewsQA

Table 4 show that all considered models achieve only from 33.57% to 43.21% on $Recall_{answerable}$ when evaluated on the 280 newly annotated unanswerable questions. his cannot be attributed solely to the out-of-domain context, as the models performed well on the 280 answerable questions extracted from UIT-ViNewsQA, achieving the highest F1 score of 81.80% among the four models. This result indicates that while UIT-VinewsQA is considered one of the high-quality Vietnamese MRC datasets, it does not fully reveal the existing weaknesses of MRC systems.

Our newly generated unanswerable questions thus give us much more materials to analyze the weaknesses and strengths of monolingual models in MRC. We then analyze the weaknesses of language models by examining the percentage of monolingual and multilingual hard unanswerable questions out of the total number of unanswerable questions.

Due to the linguistic features of the UIT-VinewsQA corpus shown in Table 3, *Entity Swap* and *Relation Reverse* types of unanswerable questions are no longer challenging as they are in UIT-ViQuAD. On the other hand, the most notable result

	# Unanswerable questions in Parallel UIT-VinewsQA	Monolingual hard unanswerable questions (%)	Multilingual hard unanswerable questions (%)
Antonym	40	55.00	**37.50**
Overstatement & Understatement	40	50.00	**45.00**
Entity Swap	40	25.00	**22.50**
Normal Word Swap	40	45.00	**35.00**
Relation Reverse	40	**35.00**	37.50
Adverbial Clause Swap	40	72.50	**62.50**
Modifiers Swap	40	**55.00**	57.50
Total	280	48.21	**42.50**

Table 5: Number of monolingual and multilingual hard unanswerable questions alongside with the number of unanswerable questions in the Parallel UIT-VinewsQA by types

from our analysis is that *Antonym* type is significantly more challenging for monolingual models than for multilingual models. As the unanswerable questions of *Antonym* type in SQuAD 2.0 (Nguyen et al., 2020a) often require language models good lexical knowledge to correctly recognize, monolingual models are believed to have advantages over multilingual counterparts. This is because (Vulić et al., 2020) show that monolingual models often encode significantly more lexical information than monolingual models. However, because we are following the process of annotating unanswerable questions proposed by Nguyen et al. (2022) on a different corpus, we hypothesize that there may be some significant changes in unanswerable questions of *Antonym* type in our benchmark.

5.3 Analysis on Antonym Type

Closely examining the performances of models on each unanswerable question of *Antonym* type, we see that monolingual models often fail to recognize an unanswerable question when the antonym used to create that question does not explicitly contradict the context. Based on this observation, we believe that these questions should be analyzed separately from other questions of *Antonym* type to understand the language weaknesses of monolingual models fully. We then divide *Antonym* type into two new types of *Implicit Antonym* and *Explicit Antonym* to further explore the effects each type have on two types of language models (see Figure 1 in A.2 for examples). In short, language models can correctly predict unanswerable questions of *Explicit Antonym* using only lexical knowledge. However, to recognize an unanswerable question of *Implicit Antonym*, models must acquire an adequate amount of high-level semantic knowledge.

Our analysis (Table 6) reveals that while monolingual models show comparable performance on *Explicit Antonym* type to multilingual models, *Implicit Antonym* type is significantly more challenging for monolingual models than for multilingual models. This result proves that monolingual models lack skills in representing the relations between context and the adjective describing the context, which is part of high-level semantic knowledge.

6 Conclusion

In this paper, we present the first comprehensive analysis to reveal the weaknesses of state-of-the-art Vietnamese language models. Our experiments show that while Vietnamese language models demonstrate good lexical and grammatical abilities in Vietnamese, they show inferior performances when questions require high-level semantic knowledge to successfully identify the unanswerability. This general result from our analysis shows that the inferior performances of Vietnamese language models on Machine Reading Comprehension task are mainly due to its inferior ability in grasping the big "picture" of the given context.

Besides, our analysis also show that Vietnamese MRC benchmarks overestimate the comprehension skills of models in some language aspects, so state-of-the-art performances on MRC benchmarks does not accurately reflect the progress of Vietnamese Machine Reading Comprehension.

7 Future Directions

Based on the results from our analysis, we suggest several future directions for both Vietnamese monolingual language models and Vietnamese MRC benchmarks.

7.1 Language Models

Our analysis shows that monolingual models, especially PhoBERT, acquire comparable abilities in recognizing the differences in lexical information between unanswerable questions and the given con-

	Full Benchmark	Hard Monolingual Unanswerable questions (%)	Hard Multilingual Unanswerable questions (%)
Explicit Antonym	25	40.00	**32.00**
Implicit Antonym	15	80.00	**46.67**

Table 6: Number of monolingual and multilingual hard unanswerable questions alongside with the number of unanswerable questions in the Parallel UIT-VinewsQA in Implicit and Explicit Antonym types

text. However, monolingual models show poor performances when encountering unanswerable questions that require the ability to comprehend a bigger "picture". For example, while monolingual models perform very well on unanswerable questions that use explicit antonyms, they often have difficulties in recognizing unanswerable questions when these questions are created using implicit antonyms. We explain this phenomenon by the findings of Zhang et al. (2021) as pre-training language models on larger text copora results in significant improvement on downstream tasks that require high-level semantic and factual knowledge such as Machine Reading Comprehension. Therefore, when encountering unanswerable questions that require ability to grasp big "picture," models pre-trained with smaller text corpora will show lower performances. Hence, the small size of pre-training corpora of PhoBERT and WikiBERT may be the main reason for their poor performances in MRC.

Scaling the pre-training data size of PhoBERT will further develop this model and empower it to achieve state-of-the-art performances on different benchmarks of Machine Reading Comprehension. Besides, we believe that introducing a new unsupervised task for the pre-training phase that focuses on improving the high-level semantic and factual knowledge of pre-trained models also plays an integral role in developing language models in the future.

7.2 Benchmarks

Unanswerable Questions. Although UIT-ViQuAD 2.0 successfully further introduced new types of artificially unanswerable questions, our work in Section 5 shows that current unanswerable questions in the development test of UIT-ViQuAD 2.0 are still not challenging enough. In order to increase the challenging levels of unanswerable questions, we believe that more high-quality works on adversarial human annotation for unanswerable questions are needed. These works can follow the guidelines of adversarial human annotation for unanswerable questions (Bartolo et al., 2020). Results of these works can reveal different techniques to annotate hard unanswerable questions and therefore be valuable for improving the guidelines for unanswerable questions annotation for Machine Reading Comprehension.

Quality of Benchmark. On the other hand, as we have shown in section 5, although PhoBERT and XLM-RoBERTa achieve high performances on the UIT-VinewsQA development set, our unanswerable questions reveal that these two models do not truly understand the context to give the correct answer for questions in the original development set. We hypothesize that questions in UIT-VinewsQA enable machine reading comprehension systems with shortcut learning knowledge (Lai et al., 2021) to achieve high performance due to biases in annotating process. Therefore, we believe that studies on how Vietnamese machine reading comprehension systems are currently evaluated are important for tracking the progress of Vietnamese language systems.

References

Max Bartolo, Alastair Roberts, Johannes Welbl, Sebastian Riedel, and Pontus Stenetorp. 2020. Beat the AI: Investigating adversarial human annotation for reading comprehension. *Transactions of the Association for Computational Linguistics*, 8:662–678.

Branden Chan, Stefan Schweter, and Timo Möller. 2020. German's next language model. In *Proceedings of the 28th International Conference on Computational Linguistics*, pages 6788–6796, Barcelona, Spain (Online). International Committee on Computational Linguistics.

Danqi Chen, Adam Fisch, Jason Weston, and Antoine Bordes. 2017. Reading Wikipedia to answer open-domain questions. In *Proceedings of the 55th Annual Meeting of the Association for Computational Linguistics (Volume 1: Long Papers)*, pages 1870–1879, Vancouver, Canada. Association for Computational Linguistics.

Jonathan H. Clark, Eunsol Choi, Michael Collins, Dan Garrette, Tom Kwiatkowski, Vitaly Nikolaev, and

Jennimaria Palomaki. 2020. TyDi QA: A benchmark for information-seeking question answering in typologically diverse languages. *Transactions of the Association for Computational Linguistics*, 8:454–470.

Alexis Conneau, Kartikay Khandelwal, Naman Goyal, Vishrav Chaudhary, Guillaume Wenzek, Francisco Guzmán, Edouard Grave, Myle Ott, Luke Zettlemoyer, and Veselin Stoyanov. 2020. Unsupervised cross-lingual representation learning at scale. In *Proceedings of the 58th Annual Meeting of the Association for Computational Linguistics*, pages 8440–8451, Online. Association for Computational Linguistics.

Jacob Devlin, Ming-Wei Chang, Kenton Lee, and Kristina Toutanova. 2019. BERT: Pre-training of deep bidirectional transformers for language understanding. In *Proceedings of the 2019 Conference of the North American Chapter of the Association for Computational Linguistics: Human Language Technologies, Volume 1 (Long and Short Papers)*, pages 4171–4186, Minneapolis, Minnesota. Association for Computational Linguistics.

Martin d'Hoffschmidt, Wacim Belblidia, Quentin Heinrich, Tom Brendlé, and Maxime Vidal. 2020. FQuAD: French question answering dataset. In *Findings of the Association for Computational Linguistics: EMNLP 2020*, pages 1193–1208, Online. Association for Computational Linguistics.

Nam Le Hai, Duc Nguyen Sy, Quan Chu Quoc, and Vi Ngo Van. 2021. Vc-tus at vlsp 2021 - vimrc challenge: Improving retrospective reader for vietnamese machine reading comprehension. In *Proceedings of the 8th International Workshop on Vietnamese Language and Speech Processing (VLSP 2021)*.

Quentin Heinrich, Gautier Viaud, and Wacim Belblidia. 2021. Fquad2.0: French question answering and knowing that you know nothing.

Diederik P Kingma and Jimmy Ba. 2015. Adam: A method for stochastic optimization. In *ICLR (Poster)*.

Tom Kwiatkowski, Jennimaria Palomaki, Olivia Redfield, Michael Collins, Ankur Parikh, Chris Alberti, Danielle Epstein, Illia Polosukhin, Jacob Devlin, Kenton Lee, Kristina Toutanova, Llion Jones, Matthew Kelcey, Ming-Wei Chang, Andrew M. Dai, Jakob Uszkoreit, Quoc Le, and Slav Petrov. 2019. Natural questions: A benchmark for question answering research. *Transactions of the Association for Computational Linguistics*, 7:452–466.

Yuxuan Lai, Chen Zhang, Yansong Feng, Quzhe Huang, and Dongyan Zhao. 2021. Why machine reading comprehension models learn shortcuts? In *Findings of the Association for Computational Linguistics: ACL-IJCNLP 2021*, pages 989–1002, Online. Association for Computational Linguistics.

Yinhan Liu, Myle Ott, Naman Goyal, Jingfei Du, Mandar Joshi, Danqi Chen, Omer Levy, Mike Lewis, Luke Zettlemoyer, and Veselin Stoyanov. 2019. Roberta: A robustly optimized bert pretraining approach.

Louis Martin, Benjamin Muller, Pedro Javier Ortiz Suárez, Yoann Dupont, Laurent Romary, Éric de la Clergerie, Djamé Seddah, and Benoît Sagot. 2020. CamemBERT: a tasty French language model. In *Proceedings of the 58th Annual Meeting of the Association for Computational Linguistics*, pages 7203–7219, Online. Association for Computational Linguistics.

Timo Möller, Julian Risch, and Malte Pietsch. 2021. GermanQuAD and GermanDPR: Improving non-English question answering and passage retrieval. In *Proceedings of the 3rd Workshop on Machine Reading for Question Answering*, pages 42–50, Punta Cana, Dominican Republic. Association for Computational Linguistics.

Dat Quoc Nguyen and Anh Tuan Nguyen. 2020. PhoBERT: Pre-trained language models for Vietnamese. In *Findings of the Association for Computational Linguistics: EMNLP 2020*, pages 1037–1042, Online. Association for Computational Linguistics.

Kiet Nguyen, Nhat Nguyen, Phong Do, Anh Nguyen, and Ngan Nguyen. 2021a. Vireader: A wikipedia-based vietnamese reading comprehension system using transfer learning. *Journal of Intelligent and Fuzzy Systems*, 41:1–19.

Kiet Nguyen, Vu Nguyen, Anh Nguyen, and Ngan Nguyen. 2020a. A Vietnamese dataset for evaluating machine reading comprehension. In *Proceedings of the 28th International Conference on Computational Linguistics*, pages 2595–2605, Barcelona, Spain (Online). International Committee on Computational Linguistics.

Kiet Nguyen, Son Quoc Tran, Luan Thanh Nguyen, Tin Van Huynh, Son T. Luu, and Ngan Luu-Thuy Nguyen. 2022. Vlsp 2021 shared task: Vietnamese machine reading comprehension.

Kiet Nguyen, Tin Van Huynh, Duc-Vu Nguyen, Anh Gia-Tuan Nguyen, and Ngan Luu-Thuy Nguyen. 2020b. New vietnamese corpus for machine reading comprehension of health news articles. *arXiv preprint arXiv:2006.11138*.

Kiet Van Nguyen, Khiem Vinh Tran, Son T. Luu, Anh Gia-Tuan Nguyen, and Ngan Luu-Thuy Nguyen. 2020c. Enhancing lexical-based approach with external knowledge for vietnamese multiple-choice machine reading comprehension. *IEEE Access*, 8:201404–201417.

Minh Van Nguyen, Viet Dac Lai, Amir Pouran Ben Veyseh, and Thien Huu Nguyen. 2021b. Trankit: A light-weight transformer-based toolkit for multilingual natural language processing. In *Proceedings of the 16th Conference of the European Chapter of the Association for Computational Linguistics: System Demonstrations*, pages 80–90, Online. Association for Computational Linguistics.

Nhat Duy Nguyen and Phong Nguyen-Thuan Do. 2021. Uitsunwind at vlsp 2021 - vimrc challenge: A simply self-ensemble model for vietnamese machine reading comprehension. In *Proceedings of the 8th International Workshop on Vietnamese Language and Speech Processing (VLSP 2021)*.

Sampo Pyysalo, Jenna Kanerva, Antti Virtanen, and Filip Ginter. 2021. WikiBERT models: Deep transfer learning for many languages. In *Proceedings of the 23rd Nordic Conference on Computational Linguistics (NoDaLiDa)*, pages 1–10, Reykjavik, Iceland (Online). Linköping University Electronic Press, Sweden.

Pranav Rajpurkar, Robin Jia, and Percy Liang. 2018. Know what you don't know: Unanswerable questions for SQuAD. In *Proceedings of the 56th Annual Meeting of the Association for Computational Linguistics (Volume 2: Short Papers)*, pages 784–789, Melbourne, Australia. Association for Computational Linguistics.

Pranav Rajpurkar, Jian Zhang, Konstantin Lopyrev, and Percy Liang. 2016. SQuAD: 100,000+ questions for machine comprehension of text. In *Proceedings of the 2016 Conference on Empirical Methods in Natural Language Processing*, pages 2383–2392, Austin, Texas. Association for Computational Linguistics.

Siva Reddy, Danqi Chen, and Christopher D. Manning. 2019. CoQA: A conversational question answering challenge. *Transactions of the Association for Computational Linguistics*, 7:249–266.

Phillip Rust, Jonas Pfeiffer, Ivan Vulić, Sebastian Ruder, and Iryna Gurevych. 2021. How good is your tokenizer? on the monolingual performance of multilingual language models. In *Proceedings of the 59th Annual Meeting of the Association for Computational Linguistics and the 11th International Joint Conference on Natural Language Processing (Volume 1: Long Papers)*, pages 3118–3135, Online. Association for Computational Linguistics.

Rico Sennrich, Barry Haddow, and Alexandra Birch. 2016. Neural machine translation of rare words with subword units. In *Proceedings of the 54th Annual Meeting of the Association for Computational Linguistics (Volume 1: Long Papers)*, pages 1715–1725, Berlin, Germany. Association for Computational Linguistics.

Ashish Vaswani, Noam Shazeer, Niki Parmar, Jakob Uszkoreit, Llion Jones, Aidan N Gomez, Ł ukasz Kaiser, and Illia Polosukhin. 2017. Attention is all you need. In *Advances in Neural Information Processing Systems*, volume 30. Curran Associates, Inc.

Ivan Vulić, Edoardo Maria Ponti, Robert Litschko, Goran Glavaš, and Anna Korhonen. 2020. Probing pretrained language models for lexical semantics. In *Proceedings of the 2020 Conference on Empirical Methods in Natural Language Processing (EMNLP)*, pages 7222–7240, Online. Association for Computational Linguistics.

Yian Zhang, Alex Warstadt, Xiaocheng Li, and Samuel R. Bowman. 2021. When do you need billions of words of pretraining data? In *Proceedings of the 59th Annual Meeting of the Association for Computational Linguistics and the 11th International Joint Conference on Natural Language Processing (Volume 1: Long Papers)*, pages 1112–1125, Online. Association for Computational Linguistics.

Liu Zhuang, Lin Wayne, Shi Ya, and Zhao Jun. 2021. A robustly optimized BERT pre-training approach with post-training. In *Proceedings of the 20th Chinese National Conference on Computational Linguistics*, pages 1218–1227, Huhhot, China. Chinese Information Processing Society of China.

A Supplementary material

A.1 Unanswerable Types Examples

Table 7 shows examples of the unanswerable types that we focus our analysis on. Most unanswerable types in our work are inspired by the original work of Nguyen et al. (2022).

A.2 Implicit and Explicit Antonym

Figure 1 shows examples for Implicit Antonym and Explicit Antonym, which are defined in Section 5 of our analysis.

Reasoning	Description	Example
Antonym	Antonym used	**Sentence**: Vào năm 1171, Richard khởi hành đến Aquitaine với mẹ mình và Henry phong ông là Công tước xứ Aquitaine theo yêu cầu của Eleanor. (*In 1171, Richard departed to Aquitaine with his mother and Henry, who had appointed him as the Duke of Aquitaine at the request of Eleanor.*) **Original question**: Richard khởi hành đến Aquitaine với mẹ vào năm nào? (*In what year did Richard depart to Aquitaine with his mother?*) textbfUnanswerable question: Richard khởi hành từ Aquitaine với mẹ vào năm nào? (*In what year did Richard depart from Aquitaine with his mother?*)
Overstatement	Word that has similar meaning but with a higher shades of meaning is used	**Sentence**: Ngày 9 tháng 11 năm 1989, vài đoạn của Bức tường Berlin bị phá vỡ, lần đầu tiên hàng ngàn người Đông Đức vượt qua chạy vào Tây Berlin và Tây Đức. (*On November 9, 1989, several parts of the Berlin Wall were collapsed, and for the first time thousands of East Germans crossed into West Berlin and West Germany.*) **Original question**: Bức tường Berlin đã bị sụp đổ một vài đoạn vào ngày nào? (*On which date were some parts of Berlin Wall collapsed?*) **Unanswerable question**: Bức tường Berlin đã bị sụp đổ hoàn toàn vào ngày nào? (*On which date was Berlin Wall completely collapsed?*)
Understatement	Word that has similar meaning but with a lower shades of meaning is used	**Sentence**: Quân đội Nhật Bản chiếm đóng Quảng Châu từ năm 1938 đến 1945 trong chiến tranh thế giới thứ hai. (*The Japanese army occupied Guangzhou from 1938 to 1945 during the second world war.*) **Original question**: Khi Chiến tranh Thế giới thứ hai xảy ra thì Quảng Châu bị nước nào chiếm đóng? (*During the World War II, Guanzong was occupied by which country?*) **Unanswerable question**: Khi Chiến tranh Thế giới thứ hai xảy ra thì Quảng Châu bị nước nào đe dọa? (*During the World War II, Guanzong was attacked by which country?*)
Entity Swap	Entity replaced by other entity	**Sentence**: Là cảng Trung Quốc duy nhất có thể tiếp cận được với hầu hết các thương nhân nước ngoài, thành phố này đã rơi vào tay người Anh trong chiến tranh nha phiến lần thứ nhất. (*As the only Chinese port accessible to most foreign merchants, the city fell to the British during the First Opium War.*) **Original question**: Trong cuộc chiến nào thì Anh Quốc đã chiếm được Quảng Châu? (*In which war did Britain occupy Guangzhou?*) **Unanswerable quetion**: Trong cuộc chiến nào thì Nhật đã chiếm được Quảng Châu? (*In which war did Japan occupy Guangzhou?*)
Relation Reverse	Reverse the relation between two entities	**Sentence**: Một lần nữa, Gandhi bị bắt giam, và chính quyền tìm cách đập tan ảnh hưởng của ông bằng cách cách li hoàn toàn ông và các người đi theo ủng hộ. (*Once again, Gandhi was imprisoned, and the government sought to crush his influence by completely isolating him from his followers.*) **Original question**: Chính quyền làm cách nào để đập tan ảnh hưởng của Gandhi?(*How does the government crush Gandhi's influence?*) **Unanswerable question**: Gandhi làm cách nào để đập tan ảnh hưởng của Chính quyền?(*How does Gandhi crush the influence of the government?*)
Normal Word Swap	A normal word replaced by another normal word	**Sentence**: Sự phát hiện của Hofmeister năm 1851 về các thay đổi xảy ra trong túi phôi của thực vật có hoa [...] (*Hofmeister's discovery in 1851 of changes occurring in the embryo sac of flowering plants [...]*) **Original question**: Năm 1851 nhà sinh học Hofmeister đã tìm ra điều gì ở thực vật có hoa? (*What did the biologist Hofmeister discover in flowering plants in 1851?*) **Unanswerable question**: Năm 1851 nhà sinh học Hofmeister đã công nhận điều gì ở thực vật có hoa? (*What did the biologist Hofmeister accept in flowering plants in 1851?*)
Adverbial Clause Swap	Adverbial clause replaced by another adverbial clause related to the context	**Sentence**: Trước đó Phạm Văn Đồng từng giữ chức vụ Thủ tướng Chính phủ Việt Nam Dân chủ Cộng hòa từ năm 1955 đến năm 1976. Ông là vị Thủ tướng Việt Nam tại vị lâu nhất (1955–1987). Ông là học trò, cộng sự của Chủ tịch Hồ Chí Minh. (*Pham Van Dong previously held the position of Prime Minister of the Democratic Republic of Vietnam from 1955 to 1976. He was the longest-serving Prime Minister of Vietnam (1955-1987). He was a student and collaborator of President Ho Chi Minh.*) **Original question**: Giai đoạn năm 1955-1976, Phạm Văn Đồng nắm giữ chức vụ gì? (*What position did Pham Van Dong hold during the period from 1955 to 1976?*) **Unanswerable question**: Khi là cộng sự của chủ tịch Hồ Chí Minh, Phạm Văn Đồng nắm giữ chức vụ gì? (*As a collaborator of President Ho Chi Minh, what position did Pham Van Dong hold?*)
Modifiers Swap	Modifier of one word in the given context is used for another word	**Sentence**: Các phần mềm giáo dục đầu tiên trong lĩnh vực giáo dục đại học (cao đẳng) và tập trung được thiết kế chạy trên máy tính đơn (hoặc các thiết bị cầm tay). Lịch sử của các phần mềm này được tóm tắt trong SCORM 2004 2nd edition Overview (phần 1.3) (*The first educational software in the field of higher education (college) and concentration was designed to run on a single computer (or portable devices). The history of these software is summarized in SCORM 2004 2nd edition Overview (section 1.3).*) **Original question**: Lịch sử của các phần mềm giáo dục đầu tiên trong lĩnh vực giáo dục đại học (cao đẳng) được tóm tắt, ghi nhận ở đâu? (*Where did the history of the first educational software in the field of higher education (college) was summarized and recorded?*) **Unanswerable quetion**: Lịch sử của các phần mềm giáo dục trong lĩnh vực giáo dục đại học (cao đẳng) được tóm tắt, ghi nhận đầu tiên ở đâu? (*Where did the history of the educational software in the field of higher education (college) was first summarized and recorded?*)

Table 7: Categories of unanswerable questions in UIT-ViQuAD 2.0. Most of categories are inspired by and adopted from Nguyen et al. (2022)

Context: Uống rượu pha với nước có ga, dạ dày phải tiết nhiều chất nhờn mà không hình thành axit chlorhydric, lâu dài làm giảm khả năng tiêu hóa của dạ dày. (*When we drink alcohol mixed with carbonated water, the stomach must secrete a lot of mucus without forming hydrochloric acid, which reduces the digestive ability of the stomach in the long run.*)

Answerable question: Uống rượu pha với nước có ga có tác hại như thế nào? (*What are the harmful effects of drinking alcohol mixed with carbonated water?*)
Unanswerable question: Uống rượu pha với nước có ga có lợi ích như thế nào? (*What are the benefits of drinking alcohol mixed with carbonated water?*)

Implicit Antonym: "giảm khả năng tiêu hóa của dạ dày" (*reduces the digestive ability of the stomach*) and "lợi ích" (*benefits*)

Context: Đọc sách vào ban đêm có thể giúp bạn ngăn ngừa một số bệnh. Đặc biệt làm giảm nguy cơ bệnh Alzheimer (mất trí nhớ). (*Reading at night can help prevent some diseases. Especially reduces the risk of Alzheimer's disease (dementia).*)

Answerable question: Việc đọc sách vào ban đêm đặc biệt làm giảm nguy cơ về bệnh gì? (*Reading at night especially reduces the risk of what disease?*)
Unanswerable question: Việc đọc sách vào ban ngày đặc biệt làm giảm nguy cơ về bệnh gì? (*Reading during the day especially reduces the risk of what diseases?*)

Explicit Antonym: "ban đêm" (night) and "ban ngày" (day)

Figure 1: Example of Implicit and Explicit Antonym

Incorporating Dropped Pronouns into Coreference Resolution: The case for Turkish

Tuğba Pamay Arslan and **Gülşen Eryiğit**
İTÜ NLP Research Group
Department of AI&Data Engineering
Faculty of Computer&Informatics
Istanbul Technical University
[pamay, gulsen.cebiroglu]@itu.edu.tr

Abstract

Representation of coreferential relations is a challenging and actively studied topic for pro-drop and morphologically rich languages (PD-MRLs) due to dropped pronouns (e.g., null subjects and omitted possessive pronouns). These phenomena require a representation scheme at the morphology level and enhanced evaluation methods. In this paper, we propose a representation & evaluation scheme to incorporate dropped pronouns into coreference resolution and validate it on the Turkish language. Using the scheme, we extend the annotations on the only existing Turkish coreference dataset, which originally did not contain annotations for dropped pronouns. We provide publicly available pre and post processors to enhance the prominent CoNLL coreference scorer also to cover coreferential relations arising from dropped pronouns. As a final step, the paper reports the first neural Turkish coreference resolution results in the literature. Although validated on Turkish, the proposed scheme is language-independent and may be used for other PD-MRLs.

1 Introduction

Coreference resolution (CR) is a semantic-level natural language processing (NLP) task and aims to determine sets of mentions which describe the same real-world entity (e.g., a person, a place, a thing, an event). An end-to-end CR system has two sequential steps: mention detection and mention clustering. The mention detection stage focuses on identifying all possible coreferential mentions referring to a real-world entity within a text. In the next step, the mention clustering stage collects mentions referring to the same real-world entity under the same cluster, resolving which extracted mentions are coreferential.

Although CR is an NLP subject that has been studied for quite a long time (Ng and Cardie, 2002; Sukthanker et al., 2020), studies on PD-MRLs are still in their infancy, and Turkish is one of them.

In MRLs, words may appear under different surface forms taking different types of affixes. In some languages, the richness level may be very high so that most syntactic information is carried at the morphological level leading to the possibility of dropping some functional words and pronouns. An example from the Turkish language (a highly rich MRL) is provided below[1], where verbal agreement and possessive suffixes[2] allow the drop of personal and possessive pronouns. Morphemes emphasized with bold font describe the dropped pronouns: '-im' holds for the pronoun 'benim' (*me*) and '-n' holds for 'sen' (*you*). However, the sentence is naturally made as exemplified below in the second line without personal and possessive pronouns.

Sen benim geldiğ**im**i gördü**n** mü?
~~Sen benim~~ geldiğ**im**i gördü**n** mü?
You I came see did
Did you see that I came?

The pro-drop nature of such languages reveals the need for mention annotation on other tokens (i.e., artificially inserted (Pradhan et al., 2012a; Nedoluzhko et al., 2022) or existing tokens (Rodrıguez et al., 2010; Klemen and Žitnik, 2021) other than the dropped pronouns, such as verbs carrying personal suffixes). The morphological richness in these languages may reveal the appearance of multiple coreference relations on a single token which is illustrated below. The word 'annemin' (*of my mother*) in the below example carries multiple coreferential relations[3] to different people: *me* and *my mother*.

[1] Color codes are used to indicate mentions referring to the same entity.

[2] One should note that personal and possessive suffixes differ from the phenomena called clitic pronouns in Romance languages (e.g. French, Portuguese, Italian) in two ways: 1) These suffixes always appear at the morphology level of a verb or noun although an overt pronoun depicting the same entity exist within the sentence. 2) They always appear as suffixes whereas clitic pronouns in Romance languages are written either as a separate word or as an attachment via a hyphen.

[3] '-m' holds for the pronoun 'benim' (*my*) and the word 'annem' (*my mother*) is a mention itself.

Proceedings of the 17th Conference of the European Chapter of the Association for Computational Linguistics: Student Research Workshop, pages 14–25
May 2-4, 2023 ©2023 Association for Computational Linguistics

Sen [benim] [anne[m]in] geldiğ[**i**]ni gördün mü?
~~Sen~~ ~~benim~~ **annemin** geldiğ**i**ni gördü**n** mü?
You my mother came see_did
Did you see the coming of my mother?

Unfortunately, existing coreference evaluators (Pradhan et al., 2014), originally developed for nonprodrop languages (e.g., English), do not support multiple coreferential relations on a single token. On the other hand, representations relying on artificially inserted tokens have their deficiencies, although eliminating the multiple coreference issue:

1. difficulty in determining the most accurate and natural position of the artificial token in the sentence,
2. extra burden during manual annotations,
3. corruption of the original sentence flow,
4. extra coding of the already available information easily deducible from morphology.

In this paper, we propose a representation & evaluation scheme using existing tokens to incorporate dropped pronouns into coreference resolution and validate it on Turkish. Using this scheme, we extend the annotations on the only existing Turkish coreference dataset (Schüller et al., 2017; Pamay and Eryiğit, 2018), which originally did not contain annotations for dropped pronouns. We provide publicly available pre and post processors[4] to enhance the prominent CoNLL coreference scorer[5] (Pradhan et al., 2014) to also cover multiple coreferential relations arising from dropped pronouns. As a final step, the paper reports the first neural Turkish coreference resolution results in the literature providing a strong baseline for future studies in this field. The preliminary results are reported on a neural coreference resolution model with a mention-ranking approach (Klemen and Žitnik, 2021), which was introduced for Slovene, another PD-MRL. Since the coreference information is coded at the morphology level, we investigate the impact of different word embeddings (Mikolov et al., 2013a,b; Grave et al., 2018), neural language models (Peters et al., 2018; Devlin et al., 2018; Schweter, 2020), and the inclusion of hand-crafted features used in previous studies (Schüller et al., 2017; Pamay and Eryiğit, 2018) to analyze their representation power for morphological richness. Although validated on Turkish, the proposed scheme is language-independent and may be used for other PD-MRLs.

The paper is structured as follows: Section 2 gives the related work, Section 3 introduces the representation of dropped pronouns on existing data sets in the literature, Section 4 presents the proposed representation & evaluation scheme for dropped pronouns, Section 5 presents the experimental setup and results, and Section 6 gives the conclusion.

2 Related Work

Machine learning methods requiring hand-crafted features have been used in the CR literature for a long time. Generally, learning-based CR models are collected under three main categories: mention-pair (Ng, 2005; Ji et al., 2005; Nicolae and Nicolae, 2006; Yang et al., 2006; Denis and Baldridge, 2007a; Haponchyk and Moschitti, 2017), entity-mention (McCallum and Wellner, 2005; Denis and Baldridge, 2007a; Culotta et al., 2007), and ranking mechanisms (Denis and Baldridge, 2007b; Rahman and Ng, 2009, 2011). Deep neural networks have been frequently used in recent studies: mention-pair (Martschat and Strube, 2015), entity-mention (Clark and Manning, 2015), mention-ranking (Fernandes et al., 2012; Durrett and Klein, 2013; Björkelund and Kuhn, 2014; Wiseman et al., 2015, 2016). Recently, several neural end-to-end systems which focus on determining the mentions automatically before or in line with the coreference resolution stage have been also introduced (Lee et al., 2017; Joshi et al., 2020; Liu et al., 2020; Xu and Choi, 2020).

Besides the above-mentioned studies on English, the CR studies focusing on pro-drop languages have been increasing. Kong and Ng (2013) improved the CR performance reported in (Pradhan et al., 2012a) by exploiting zero-pronouns (i.e. elided pronouns) on Chinese with traditional machine learning methods. Chen and Ng (2013) enhanced the available approach (Zhao and Ng, 2007) with a richer feature set and also incorporated the dropped pronouns as a referential mention. Neural CR architectures were also employed in the Chinese CR studies (Chen and Ng, 2016; Yin et al., 2016). For Korean, Park et al. (2020) proposed a neural architecture using pointer networks to reduce the computational complexity of an available end-to-end model (Joshi et al., 2019). Guarasci et al. (2021) used ELECTRA (Clark et al., 2020) on the neural structure (Lee et al., 2018) for Italian.

[4]Available from `https://github.com/TugbaP/processors-for-conll-coreference-scorer`

[5]`http:/github.com/conll/reference-coreference-scorers`

Klemen and Žitnik (2021) proposed a neural CR model focusing on only mention clustering stage for Slovene.

Evaluation of CR systems is a challenging topic which resulted with several evaluation metrics in the literature: MUC (Vilain et al., 1995), B-Cubed (Bagga and Baldwin, 1998), mention-based & entity-based CEAF (Luo, 2005), BLANC (Recasens and Hovy, 2011), the averaged CoNLL score (Denis and Baldridge, 2009; Pradhan et al., 2014). Each metric evaluates a CR system from different perspectives and has pros and cons. A widely used evaluator (from now on referred to as the CoNLL scorer (Pradhan et al., 2014)) outputs CR performances via all these metrics.

Previous works on Turkish CR are based on traditional machine learning algorithms (Yıldırım and Kılıçaslan, 2007; Yıldırım et al., 2007; Kılıçaslan et al., 2009; Küçük and Yöndem, 2015; Schüller et al., 2017; Pamay and Eryiğit, 2018). The most recent Turkish coreference dataset (MTCC - Marmara Turkish Coreference Corpus) is from Schüller et al. (2017), and consists of a document subset extracted from METU Turkish Corpus (MTC) (Say et al., 2002). The dataset had been later extended by morpho-syntactic features by Pamay and Eryiğit (2018) using an automated Turkish NLP pipeline (Eryiğit, 2014). This dataset does not contain annotations for dropped pronouns.

3 Representation of Dropped Pronouns on Existing Data Sets

The CR literature has annotated datasets supporting various languages: MUC (Hirschman and Chinchor, 1998; Chinchor, 2001; Chinchor and Sundheim, 2003), ACE (Doddington et al., 2004), SemEval2010 (Recasens et al., 2010), OntoNotes (Pradhan et al., 2007, 2012b). The MUC covers coreference relation only for English which is not a pro-drop language. The ACE focuses on only seven pre-defined type entities, therefore, dropped pronouns were excluded in the annotation process for Arabic (a pro-drop language). Although the SemEval2010 includes pro-drop languages (e.g. Catalan, Spanish (Recasens and Martí, 2010)), dropped pronouns were not covered during the annotation. Compared with these datasets, the OntoNotes is more comprehensive and contains gold-standard coreferential relations of dropped pronouns for Chinese and Arabic.

In the OntoNotes, dropped pronouns are represented by a unique artificial token: (“`*pro*`” for Chinese and “`*`” for Arabic), which is inserted into the correct position where the subject or object is omitted in a sentence during the annotation. This token indicates that a pronoun has been dropped from this location in the sentence. Example 1 shows how a dropped pronoun is represented for Chinese.

> (Zh.) 吉林省主管经贸工作的副省长全哲洙说：“**(*pro*)** 欢迎国际社会同 **(我们)** 一道，共同推进图门江开发事业，促进区域经济发展，造福东北亚人民。”
>
> (En.) *Quan Zhezhu, Vice Governor of Jinlin Province who is in charge of economics and trade, said: “**(*pro*)** Welcome international societies to join **(us)** in the development of Tumen Jiang, so as to promote regional economic development and benefit people in Northeast Asia”.*

Example 1: Annotation of dropped pronouns with artificial **(*pro*)** token in Chinese (Pradhan et al., 2012b)

Chinese and English translations of the same sentence are shown in the Example 1. In Chinese, `*pro*` is inserted for an omitted subject pronoun, which is referential with another pronoun: (我们) (‘us’ in English).

A recent study (Nedoluzhko et al., 2022) proposed a similar representation scheme as in the OntoNotes, built on top of the CoNLL-UD framework (Nivre et al., 2016, 2017), called the CorefUD. Dropped pronouns are represented by inserted tokens, called empty nodes (i.e. zeros), and they are related to their syntactic heads (hereinafter referred to as ‘owner’) by dependency relations. The CorefUD introduces how the inserted tokens should be represented (with a sub-indexed token number i.e. <tokenID>.<subIndex>); however, there is no standard on where to add them across different languages. In Hungarian, they are added immediately after their owners in the sentence (with some minor exceptions due to punctuations). In Czech, Spanish and Catalan, there is no strict rule about their positions except that empty nodes are almost always placed before their owners. The decisions about their positions seem to be affected by the fact that they will have an influence on the dependency trees of the related language.

Besides the explained representation above, Iida and Poesio (2011) introduced another approach and applied it on the Italian CR dataset. Italian is a partial PD-MRL, allowing only omitted subjects, called null-subjects. In this approach, instead of an artificially inserting token, dropped subject pronouns are directly annotated on the verbs. Example 2 shows how a dropped subject pronoun is represented for Italian.

> (It.) **(Pahor)** è nato a Trieste, allora porto principale dell'Impero Austro-Ungarico. A sette anni **(vide)** l'incendio del Narodni dom.
> (En.) ***(Pahor)*** *was born in Trieste, then the main port of the Austro-Hungarian Empire. At the age of seven* ***(he)*** *saw the fire of the Narodni dom.*

Example 2: Annotation of dropped subject pronoun in Italian (Iida and Poesio, 2011)

Italian and English translations of the same sentence are shown in Example 2. In this approach, each verb is considered as a potential coreferential mention. Mentions existing before this verbal mention in a text are considered antecedents of the verb. In the example, the predicate of the second Italian sentence, `vide`, has a coreference relation with `Pahor` in the first sentence. Since English is not a pro-drop language, the subject of the second sentence, `he`, is explicitly defined, and the coreference relation are made between `he` and `Pahor`. Slovenian CR dataset (Klemen and Žitnik, 2021) used the same representation approach for null-subjects as in Italian.

Both the OntoNotes and CorefUD approaches propose inserting new tokens to represent dropped pronouns, but from different perspectives. In the OntoNotes, all type of dropped pronouns are represented with the same artificial token which could be easily adapted to various languages. However, each dropped pronoun is represented with the same surface form creating ambiguity for automated CR systems. On the other hand, the CorefUD proposes inserting an empty token according to pronominal information at the morphology level, not a unique token for all dropped pronouns; however, it requires extra coding of the already available information easily deducible from the owner's morphology information. These approaches harm the original sentence flow, reduce human readability and also cause an extra burden to the annotation process from the perspective of determining the most accurate and natural position of the these newly inserted tokens in the sentence. However, they both allow direct use of existing evaluation tools, which may be considered as an advantage of these approaches.

Moreover, the Universal Dependencies (UD)[6] (Nivre et al., 2016, 2017) initiative suggests to reduce the use of additional artificial tokens (i.e., inflectional groups) even in case of derivational suffixes/cases requiring a new sub-token group. However, the above-mentioned approaches propose inserting extra nodes based on morphological suffixes, which may be treated as contradictory.

Using existing tokens to represent coreferential relations of dropped pronouns overcomes these drawbacks. However, in extreme PD-MRLs, dropping may occur in cases other than null-subjects; e.g., dropped possessive pronouns. The morphological richness in these languages may reveal the appearance of multiple coreference relations on a single token; e.g., a nominal as exemplified in the introduction section. This is a barrier in front of using existing evaluation tools for such kind of representations.

4 The Proposed Scheme

This section introduces our representation and evaluation scheme and its validation.

4.1 Dataset Representation

Morphologically rich languages allow nouns and verbs to contain pronominal markers in their morphological analyses. A pronominal marker may be a possessive marker for nouns or a personal marker for verbs. These markers carry information about the related person who did the action (or was affected by the action passively) or specify the properties of a pronominal possessor of a noun/noun phrase. In PD-MRLs, information about the omitted pronouns can be reached by these markers. The proposed scheme considers the pronominal markers in existing nouns/verbs as a coreferential mention and allows a coreferential relation between these markers and other mentions of the same entity. Example 3 shows coreferential relations between pronominal markers and mentions for a sample Turkish sentence with its English translation. Please refer to Figure 1 for the literal translation.

> (Tr.) Ahmet bugün yeni **okulunda** öğretmenliğe başladı. **Okulunu** çok sevmiş.
> (En.) *Ahmet started teaching at his new school today. He liked his school very much.*

Example 3: Representation of dropped pronouns in Turkish.

The nominal word, `okulunda`, has a morphological analysis as `okul+Noun+A3sg+P3sg+Loc` with

[6]UD aims to create a common framework for annotation of grammar (parts of speech, morphological features, and syntactic dependencies) across different human languages.

<table>
<tr><td colspan="10">#sntNo: 00002213_102</td></tr>
<tr><td>1</td><td>Ahmet</td><td>Ahmet</td><td>Ahmet</td><td>Noun</td><td>Prop</td><td>A3sg|Pnon|Nom</td><td>6</td><td>SUBJECT</td><td>(50)</td></tr>
<tr><td>2</td><td>bugün</td><td>today</td><td>bugün</td><td>Noun</td><td>Noun</td><td>A3sg|Pnon|Nom</td><td>6</td><td>MODIFIER</td><td></td></tr>
<tr><td>3</td><td>yeni</td><td>new</td><td>yeni</td><td>Adj</td><td>Adj</td><td>_</td><td>4</td><td>MODIFIER</td><td>(17</td></tr>
<tr><td>4</td><td>okulunda</td><td>at his school</td><td>okul</td><td>Noun</td><td>Noun</td><td>A3sg|P3sg|Loc</td><td>6</td><td>MODIFIER</td><td>(50{P3sg}) | 17)</td></tr>
<tr><td>5</td><td>öğretmenliğe</td><td>teaching</td><td>öğretmenlik</td><td>Noun</td><td>Noun</td><td>A3sg|Pnon|Dat</td><td>6</td><td>MODIFIER</td><td></td></tr>
<tr><td>6</td><td>başladı</td><td>started</td><td>başla</td><td>Verb</td><td>Verb</td><td>Pos|Past|A3sg</td><td>0</td><td>PREDICATE</td><td>(50{A3sg})</td></tr>
<tr><td>7</td><td>.</td><td></td><td>.</td><td>Punc</td><td>Punc</td><td>_</td><td>6</td><td>PUNCTUATION</td><td></td></tr>
<tr><td colspan="10">#sntNo: 00002213_103</td></tr>
<tr><td>1</td><td>Okulunu</td><td>his school</td><td>okul</td><td>Noun</td><td>Noun</td><td>A3sg|P3sg|Acc</td><td>3</td><td>OBJECT</td><td>(50{P3sg}) | (17)</td></tr>
<tr><td>2</td><td>çok</td><td>very much</td><td>çok</td><td>Adverb</td><td>Adverb</td><td>_</td><td>3</td><td>DETERMINER</td><td></td></tr>
<tr><td>3</td><td>sevmiş</td><td>liked</td><td>sev</td><td>Verb</td><td>Verb</td><td>Pos|Narr|A3sg</td><td>0</td><td>PREDICATE</td><td>(50{A3sg})</td></tr>
<tr><td>4</td><td>.</td><td></td><td>.</td><td>Punc</td><td>Punc</td><td>_</td><td>3</td><td>PUNCTUATION</td><td></td></tr>
</table>

Figure 1: Annotated CoNLL dataset sample

a possessive marker, `P3sg`. This suffix shows that a third singular person possessor, 'onun' (*his*), modifies the word. The pronoun is not explicitly defined in the context; that is a dropped pronoun. Therefore, the coreferential relation of the dropped possessive pronoun is annotated on an existing token, `okulunda`. The predicates of both sentences, 'başladı' (*start*) and 'sevmiş' (*like*) are coreferential mentions due to the personal markers deducible from their morphological analyses. These personal markers refer to the same person, 'Ahmet'. In the first sentence, the person who started teaching can be directly obtained from the syntactic analysis of the sentence. However, the second sentence does not contain an overt-subject. The predicate, 'sevmiş' (*like'*), carries a personal marker in its morphological analysis, `A3sg`. This suffix shows that a third singular person, 'o' (*he*), is the subject of this verb. The coreferential relations between the person and his personal markers are annotated on existing verbal tokens. Additionally, the word 'okulunda' (*at his school*) has two coreferential mentions: the possessive marker ('-u' holds for the pronoun 'onun' (*his*)) and the word 'okulunda', which is a mention itself. According to the proposed scheme, verbs are considered potential coreferential mentions due to the pronoun markers in their morphological analyses[7]; and possessive markers in nouns are also regarded as coreferential mentions besides the noun itself.

Figure 1 shows how coreferential relations are represented on top of the base CoNLL format for a Turkish sample. In the base CoNLL format, coreference annotations are given in the last column. Each sentence is labeled by a unique identifier containing the document and sentence number (#sntNo). Coreferential mentions are annotated by their numerical cluster identifiers, and this number is encapsulated by an opened and a closed parenthesis symbol to specify the initial and final words of a mention span. Mentions referring to the same real-world entity are labeled with the same cluster number. In Figure 1, 'Ahmet' is a coreferential mention parenthesized by the cluster number 50. Another mention 'yeni okulunda' is a bi-token mention with a cluster id 17. While the parenthesis is opened with cluster 17 for the first token, it is closed with the same number for the last token to mark the mention's border. As may be seen from the figure, relations are inter-sentential. For example, the mention 'yeni okulunda' in the first sentence has a coreference annotation with the cluster 17, and its referent, 'Okulunu', which is in the second sentence, is also annotated with the same cluster number.

The base CoNLL format assumes and describes one coreference annotation per token; however, as described in previous sections, a nominal token may contain multiple coreference relations. Therefore, in the proposed scheme, additional coreferential relations coming from dropped pronouns are annotated with the help of curly brackets including pronominal markers' information. In this way, pronominal markers existing in nominal and verbal tokens are annotated as a coreferential mention rather than adding a new token for each dropped pronoun. With this representation, the dependency tree of the actual sentence is not affected as in the newly inserted token approach.

In Figure 1, the predicate 'başladı' in the first sentence contains the third singular personal marker, `A3sg`, in its morphological analysis. This marker is annotated as a mention with cluster number 50. The marker and the person 'Ahmet' are coreferential within the same cluster. Similarly, in the second sentence, the possessive marker of the first

[7]On the contrary for null-subjects, it is not a tradition to produce morphological markers for the null-object cases (Nivre et al., 2016, 2017). However, the proposed scheme is also applicable to null-objects when needed.

token, 'Okulunu', {P3sg}, also exists in the same cluster, 50. Moreover, the first token of the second sentence contains multiple annotations separated by the pipe symbol. The first annotation stands for the coreferential relation of its possessive marker, whereas the second annotation with cluster number 17 shows the relation of the word itself.

4.2 Adaptation of Evaluators

Although in practice, the widely-used CoNLL coreference scorer accepts multiple coreference annotations per token in its input, it is reported[5] that this situation is only limitedly supported. Table 1 exemplifies this situation on some randomly selected documents having a diverse number of multiple annotations; the number of tokens having multiple coreference annotations is reported in the last column of the table. The table provides the drop in evaluation scores on gold-standard data where the key and the predicted inputs are exactly the same; in other words, we expect 100% F-Scores on all metrics. However, as it can be seen from the table, the performances are dropped as far as the number of tokens with multiple annotations increases; e.g. 9.20 percentage point drop in MUC score for the last document having 98 tokens with multiple annotations.

	MUC	B-Cubed	CEAF$_e$	#Tokens w MultAnn.
D#1	↓0.82	↓0.79	↓0.47	4
D#2	↓1.25	↓1.34	↓0.79	8
D#3	↓3.09	↓3.31	↓1.07	16
D#4	↓3.56	↓3.20	↓1.83	20
D#5	↓6.62	↓7.99	↓3.03	42
D#6	↓9.20	↓14.51	↓6.08	98

Table 1: Performance drops reported by the CoNLL scorer on documents having multiple mentions per token.

A solution to the above-described problem is to automatically create temporary tokens for dropped pronouns on the backstage, to use the scorer, and finally to remove these temporary tokens. In this manner, the scorer will not encounter problems evaluating the relations of dropped pronouns. That is, the need of artificial tokens introduced in Section 3 for dropped pronouns are handled at the software level rather than the human-annotation level, which eliminates the deficiencies listed in the same section. The proposed pre-processor[4] copies a token having multiple annotations, as many as the number of its annotations caused by pronominal markers. Then, these duplicated tokens are concatenated to the end of the sentence. After preprocessing, each copy token carries only one annotation related to a pronominal marker, whereas these relations are removed from the original token. We use the syntactic head identifier field (the seventh column in the CoNLL format in Figure 1) to keep the links between the original and temporary tokens, and use this information to aggregate everything during the post-processor stage.

4.3 Validation

We validated our proposed scheme on the Turkish language which is a strong representative of PD-MRLs. As the first step, using the proposed dataset representation, we reannotated a Turkish CR dataset (MTCC[8]) to include the dropped pronouns which were not available in the original annotations.

	MTCC	ITCC
# Documents	24	24
# Paragraphs	1564	1562
# Sentences	4744	4732
# Tokens	60788	60772
# Overt Mentions	3696	10031
# Dropped Pronouns	n/a	11584
# Total Mentions	3696	21615
# Mention Clusters	691	4065
# Multiple Annotations/doc	n/a	$21.3_{\pm 23.5}$

Table 2: Dataset statistics.

Table 2 provides statistics about the original MTCC and its extended version (referred as ITCC[4] from now on). Sentences containing only punctuations are removed from ITCC. As seen from the table, the number of dropped pronouns annotated in ITCC is 11584, which resulted in the need for the annotation of 6335 additional overt mentions and the creation of 3374 new mention clusters. An example to this may be as the following: when we annotate the dropped pronoun 'onun' (*its*) on the word 'rengi' (*its color*), we also need to annotate its referent overt mention (e.g., the cat) within the text although it had not been annotated initially due to some decisions about neglecting singletons[9]. ITCC includes 21615 mentions in total collected

[8]MTCC from Pamay and Eryiğit (2018) comes with automatically produced morphological and syntactic analyses in the CoNLL format.

[9]Singleton in CR is the situation where there appears only a single mention within a mention cluster; i.e., a mention with no coreferential antecedent.

under 4065 clusters and contains $21.3_{\pm 23.5}$ multiple coreference annotations on average with a high standard deviation. While 11 documents have less than 10 multiple annotations, this number goes up to 98 among the remaining 13 documents. Table 3 shows the distribution of referential pronominal markers in ITCC. The personal marker 'A3sg' (the third singular person, 'o' *(s/he/it)*) is the most frequent one. Similarly, possessive marker 'P3sg' (the third singular possessor, 'onun' *(his/her/its)*) has the highest distribution percentage among all types of possessive markers. One should note that there is no gender in Turkish morphology; thus, s/he/it pronouns all appear under the same surface form, which yields higher complexity in their coreference resolution.

Personal Marker					
A1sg	A2sg	A3sg	A1pl	A2pl	A3pl
815	262	3846	313	207	303
Possessive Marker					
P1sg	P2sg	P3sg	P1pl	P2pl	P3pl
499	124	4595	214	80	326

Table 3: Distribution of referential pronominal markers.

As the second step, we validate that the introduced evaluation components eliminate the errors coming from multiple annotations. The stand-alone CoNLL scorer reports the following performances on the gold-standard ITCC (as introduced in Section 4.2): MUC=96.99%, B-Cubed=96.85%, and $CEAF_e$=97.84% F-scores on average. After the introduced pre and post-processors are used together with the CoNLL scorer, the expected 100% F-Scores on all metrics are successfully obtained on the gold-standard key and predicted inputs.

5 Experiments & Results

This section introduces the first neural Turkish coreference resolution results which provides a strong baseline for future studies in the field.

5.1 Experimental setup

The neural Turkish CR performances are reported using a neural coreference resolution architecture (Klemen and Žitnik, 2021) which was introduced for Slovene, another PD-MRL. The model uses a mention-ranking approach and resolves coreferential relations on gold-standard mentions. The replicated model consists of three sequential, fully connected layers with ReLU as an activation function. The model takes a mention-pair (mention$_1$ (i.e., a head mention) and mention$_2$ (i.e., an antecedent of the head mention) as input and produces a score about how well these mentions are coreferential. Mentions and their antecedents are paired to create positive (coreferential) or negative (non-coreferential) samples. The order of mentions' occurrence in a document is also considered during pairing. A mention is paired with its antecedents that are at most 50 mention-away[10]. During inference, the model generates a score for each antecedent and the most probable one is selected as the model's prediction.

The model may utilize either word embeddings (word2vec[11] and fastText[12]) or contextual neural language models (ELMo[11] and BERT[13]). In addition to dense representations, we also extended the replicated model by including hand-crafted features used in previous Turkish studies (Schüller et al., 2017; Pamay and Eryiğit, 2018) to analyze their representation power for morphological richness. A mention is considered as a sequence of tokens so that its embedding is created from its words' embeddings. A mention embedding contains three parts: the initial token's embedding, the final token's embedding, and the weighted average of all its tokens' embeddings. The averaging step allows the model to learn the most essential token in the mention (i.e., the head token in the mention) with an intermediate fully connected layer, which may be assumed as an attention mechanism. As a result, the produced mention embedding comprises information about the head token in the mention and its right and left contexts. This paper replicates the neural CR model with the default hyper-parameters from Klemen and Žitnik (2021). Documents are split into train/validation/test parts by considering their genres. Documents having common genres are used in validation and test datasets separately. While the development set has 2 documents from news and novel, the test set contains 3 documents from news, novel, and story genres. The rest 19 documents are selected as the training dataset. The model is evaluated on four coreference metrics: MUC (Vilain et al., 1995), B-Cubed (Bagga and Baldwin, 1998), entity-based CEAF (Luo, 2005) and average CoNLL. The enhanced coreference

[10]The average mention-distance between referential mentions in a chain is 50,3 in ITCC

[11]http:/vectors.nlpl.eu/repository/

[12]http:/fasttext.cc/docs/en/crawl-vectors.html

[13]http:/huggingface.co/dbmdz/bert-base-turkish-cased

	MUC			B-Cubed			$CEAF_e$			CoNLL		
	P	R	F	P	R	F	P	R	F	P	R	F
word2vec	45.26	16.34	23.91	**80.03**	18.76	30.17	11.22	51.62	18.29	45.50	28.91	24.12
fastText	52.66	37.62	43.86	56.75	26.17	35.70	18.60	48.73	26.77	42.67	37.51	35.44
ELMo	54.19	30.76	39.02	70.29	22.50	33.84	16.31	56.06	25.08	46.93	36.44	32.71
BERT	**64.77**	**53.10**	**58.34**	56.88	**31.00**	**39.89**	**28.26**	**56.70**	**37.62**	**49.97**	**46.93**	**45.28**

Table 4: The neural CR results on ITCC with different neural language models.

		MUC	B-Cubed	$CEAF_e$	CoNLL
word2vec	None	23,91	30,17	18,29	24,12
	+feats	57,14	41,18	36,33	44,88
	Diff	↑ 33,23	↑ 11,01	↑ 18,04	↑20,76
fastText	None	43,86	35,70	26,77	35,44
	+feats	**63,80**	**45,12**	**41,15**	**50,02**
	Diff	↑ 19,94	↑ 9,42	↑ 14,38	↑ 14,58
ELMo	None	39,20	33,84	25,08	32,71
	+feats	46,80	34,56	29,37	36,91
	Diff	↑ 7,60	↑ 0,72	↑ 4,29	↑ 4,20
BERT	None	58,34	39,89	37,62	45,28
	+feats	58,22	40,06	38,56	45,61
	Diff	↓ 0,12	↑ 0,17	↑ 0,94	↑ 0,33

Table 5: The impact of the hand-crafted features on the CR models with various word embeddings.

scorer (The CoNLL-2012 Scorer[5] + our pre-post processors[4]) is used to evaluate the model.

5.2 Experimental results

The preliminary results with different word embeddings and language models are given in Table 4. We observed that the gap between precision and recall values decrease with the use of contextual models (i.e. ELMo and BERT). fastText performs better than word2vec which is expected for an MRL. The highest F-scores on all metrics are obtained with the pre-trained BERT language model. The base Turkish CR model provides a 45.28% average CoNLL F-score with BERT.

The Turkish CR model is also enhanced with hand-crafted morpho-syntactic and lexical features, and the results are presented in Table 5 in terms of F-scores for all metrics. External linguistic features predicted by Turkish NLP Pipeline[14] are integrated as a one-hot vector to mentions' representations. The table's 'Diff' raw indicates whether the external features positively or negatively impact each model. 'None' indicates that no external features are utilized, whereas the '+feats' setting benefits from features as in Pamay and Eryiğit (2018). The results show that although incorporating hand-crafted linguistic features into the CR neural model improves performances on all scenarios; its impact is higher with less-powerful word embeddings. Using the external linguistic information increases the CoNLL F-score by 20.76, 14.58, 4.2, and 0.33 percentage points for word2vec, fastText, ELMo, and BERT, respectively.

The Turkish CR model performance is increased to 50.2% average CoNLL F-score with fastText by incorporating hand-crafted linguistic features. This model performs the best over all others and provides a 5 percentage points improvement over BERT. Adding external linguistic features does not improve the performance considerably for BERT. A similar conclusion was also obtained by adding morphological information into BERT- and LSTM-based downstream tasks on several languages: Named Entity Recognition (NER) and Dependency Parsing (DP). As introduced in Klemen et al. (2022), the features help the LSTM-based models perform better on the NER and DP tasks. However, for BERT-based models, the additional morphological features only positively impact DP performance when they are gold-standard but not when they are predicted.

6 Conclusion

The paper proposed a language-independent representation and evaluation scheme to incorporate dropped pronouns into coreference resolution for pro-drop and morphologically rich languages. Pre and post-processors to enhance available CR evaluators to cover dropped pronouns (i.e., multiple annotations over a single word) are developed. The scheme was validated on the Turkish language. The study revealed the first Turkish CR dataset including the annotations for dropped pronouns and the first neural CR results for this language as a strong baseline for future studies. The impact of interaction between different text encodings and linguistic features were investigated on this task. The best performance was achieved by using fastText embeddings together with hand-crafted linguistic features with 50.2% CoNLL F-Score, which provides a 5 percentage points improvement over a BERT baseline.

[14] http://tools.nlp.itu.edu.tr/

Limitations

The main limitation of the study is that the proposed representation scheme was validated on Turkish for now. This limitation may affect the reliability of the proposed scheme. However, it is foreseen that theoretically, the proposed representation scheme can be applied to other PD-MRLs. The proposed dataset is built on top of the widely used CoNLL format to which most datasets can be converted smoothly, and all necessary morpho-syntactic information for the conversion is already available in the CoNLL format.

A neural CR model (originally developed for Slovene) was chosen to validate the proposed scheme in Turkish due to the similar pro-dropping structure of these PD-MRLs. However, the Turkish dataset contains more complex mention spans: 1) wider types of dropped pronouns (null-subjects and also elided possessive pronouns), and 2) longer coreferential spans due to the chain of noun phrases and adjectival clauses. Even if our study introduced a strong baseline, we did not examine whether another neural, more powerful CR architecture would provide higher performance on Turkish.

Beyond the listed limitations, this paper analyzed and compared available representation schemes of dropped pronouns in the literature and introduced an easily applicable one by solving their deficiencies. The Turkish, a highly complex PD-MRL, was chosen for the validation to emphasize the importance of incorporating dropped pronouns into CR systems. Despite the increasing popularity and power of neural networks for NLP from scratch, this paper showed that employing hand-crafted linguistic features in a neural model still provides improvement for morphologically rich languages. As future work, we plan to expand the neural CR architecture with a mention prediction stage to resolve coreferential relations of automatically predicted mentions and explore the ways of improving the success on the resolution of dropped pronouns. The other future directions would be applying the proposed scheme to other pro-drop and morphologically rich languages and examining how the representation scheme affects the neural CR performance.

Ethics Statement

ITCC contains 24 documents from METU Turkish Corpus (Say et al., 2002). All necessary permissions have been obtained to use and distribute these documents.

Acknowledgements

This study was supported by İTÜ-Scientific Research Projects Coordination Unit with under project number #MDK-2022-43607#. Computing resources used in this work were provided by İTÜ Artificial Intelligence and Data Science Application and Research Center. The authors thank Prof. Deniz Zeyrek Bozşahin for allowing us to use and share subset of documents of METU Turkish Corpus (Say et al., 2002).

References

Amit Bagga and Breck Baldwin. 1998. Algorithms for scoring coreference chains. In *Proceedings of the 1st International Conference on Language Resources and Evaluation Workshop on Linguistics Coreference*, volume 1, pages 563–566. Granada, Spain.

Anders Björkelund and Jonas Kuhn. 2014. Learning structured perceptrons for coreference resolution with latent antecedents and non-local features. In *Proceedings of the 52nd Annual Meeting of the Association for Computational Linguistics (Volume 1: Long Papers)*, pages 47–57, Baltimore, Maryland. Association for Computational Linguistics.

Chen Chen and Vincent Ng. 2013. Chinese zero pronoun resolution: Some recent advances. In *Proceedings of the 2013 conference on empirical methods in natural language processing*, pages 1360–1365.

Chen Chen and Vincent Ng. 2016. Chinese zero pronoun resolution with deep neural networks. In *Proceedings of the 54th Annual Meeting of the Association for Computational Linguistics (Volume 1: Long Papers)*, pages 778–788.

Nancy Chinchor. 2001. Message understanding conference (muc) 7. LDC2001T02.

Nancy Chinchor and Beth Sundheim. 2003. Message understanding conference (muc) 6. LDC2003T13.

Kevin Clark, Minh-Thang Luong, Quoc V Le, and Christopher D Manning. 2020. Electra: Pre-training text encoders as discriminators rather than generators. *arXiv preprint arXiv:2003.10555*.

Kevin Clark and Christopher D. Manning. 2015. Entity-centric coreference resolution with model stacking. In *Proceedings of the 53rd Annual Meeting of the Association for Computational Linguistics and the 7th International Joint Conference on Natural Language Processing (Volume 1: Long Papers)*, pages 1405–1415, Beijing, China. Association for Computational Linguistics.

Aron Culotta, Michael L Wick, and Andrew McCallum. 2007. First-order probabilistic models for coreference resolution. In *Human Language Technologies: The Annual Conference of the North American Chapter of the Association for Computational Linguistics (HLT-NAACL)*, pages 81–88.

Pascal Denis and Jason Baldridge. 2007a. Joint determination of anaphoricity and coreference resolution using integer programming. In *Human Language Technologies 2007: The Conference of the North American Chapter of the Association for Computational Linguistics; Proceedings of the Main Conference*, pages 236–243.

Pascal Denis and Jason Baldridge. 2007b. A ranking approach to pronoun resolution. In *Proceedings of the 20th International Joint Conference on Artificial Intelligence (IJCAI)*, pages 1588–1593.

Pascal Denis and Jason Baldridge. 2009. Global joint models for coreference resolution and named entity classification. *Procesamiento del lenguaje natural*, 42.

Jacob Devlin, Ming-Wei Chang, Kenton Lee, and Kristina Toutanova. 2018. Bert: Pre-training of deep bidirectional transformers for language understanding. *arXiv preprint arXiv:1810.04805*.

George R Doddington, Alexis Mitchell, Mark A Przybocki, Lance A Ramshaw, Stephanie M Strassel, and Ralph M Weischedel. 2004. The automatic content extraction (ace) program-tasks, data, and evaluation. In *Lrec*, volume 2, pages 837–840. Lisbon.

Greg Durrett and Dan Klein. 2013. Easy victories and uphill battles in coreference resolution. In *Proceedings of the 2013 Conference on Empirical Methods in Natural Language Processing*, pages 1971–1982, Seattle, Washington, USA. Association for Computational Linguistics.

Gülşen Eryiğit. 2014. ITU Turkish NLP web service. In *Proceedings of the Demonstrations at the 14th Conference of the European Chapter of the Association for Computational Linguistics (EACL)*, Gothenburg, Sweden. Association for Computational Linguistics.

Eraldo Fernandes, Cícero dos Santos, and Ruy Milidiú. 2012. Latent structure perceptron with feature induction for unrestricted coreference resolution. In *Joint Conference on EMNLP and CoNLL - Shared Task*, pages 41–48, Jeju Island, Korea. Association for Computational Linguistics.

Edouard Grave, Piotr Bojanowski, Prakhar Gupta, Armand Joulin, and Tomas Mikolov. 2018. Learning word vectors for 157 languages. In *Proceedings of the International Conference on Language Resources and Evaluation (LREC 2018)*.

Raffaele Guarasci, Aniello Minutolo, Emanuele Damiano, Giuseppe De Pietro, Hamido Fujita, and Massimo Esposito. 2021. Electra for neural coreference resolution in italian. *IEEE Access*, 9:115643–115654.

Iryna Haponchyk and Alessandro Moschitti. 2017. A practical perspective on latent structured prediction for coreference resolution. In *Proceedings of the 15th Conference of the European Chapter of the Association for Computational Linguistics(EACL)*, pages 143–149, Valencia, Spain,.

Lynette Hirschman and Nancy Chinchor. 1998. Appendix F: MUC-7 coreference task definition (version 3.0). In *Seventh Message Understanding Conference (MUC-7): Proceedings of a Conference Held in Fairfax, Virginia, April 29 - May 1, 1998*.

Ryu Iida and Massimo Poesio. 2011. A cross-lingual ilp solution to zero anaphora resolution. In *Proceedings of the 49th Annual Meeting of the Association for Computational Linguistics: Human Language Technologies*, pages 804–813.

Heng Ji, David Westbrook, and Ralph Grishman. 2005. Using semantic relations to refine coreference decisions. In *Proceedings of the conference on Human Language Technology and Empirical Methods in Natural Language Processing*, pages 17–24. Association for Computational Linguistics.

Mandar Joshi, Danqi Chen, Yinhan Liu, Daniel S. Weld, Luke Zettlemoyer, and Omer Levy. 2020. SpanBERT: Improving pre-training by representing and predicting spans. *Transactions of the Association for Computational Linguistics*, 8:64–77.

Mandar Joshi, Omer Levy, Luke Zettlemoyer, and Daniel Weld. 2019. BERT for coreference resolution: Baselines and analysis. In *Proceedings of the 2019 Conference on Empirical Methods in Natural Language Processing and the 9th International Joint Conference on Natural Language Processing (EMNLP-IJCNLP)*, pages 5803–5808, Hong Kong, China. Association for Computational Linguistics.

Yılmaz Kılıçaslan, Edip Serdar Güner, and Savaş Yıldırım. 2009. Learning-based pronoun resolution for Turkish with a comparative evaluation. *Computer Speech & Language*, 23(3):311–331.

Matej Klemen, Luka Krsnik, and Marko Robnik-Šikonja. 2022. Enhancing deep neural networks with morphological information. *Natural Language Engineering*, page 1–26.

Matej Klemen and Slavko Žitnik. 2021. Neural coreference resolution for slovene language. *Computer Science and Information Systems*, (00):60–60.

Fang Kong and Hwee Tou Ng. 2013. Exploiting zero pronouns to improve chinese coreference resolution. In *Proceedings of the 2013 conference on empirical methods in natural language processing*, pages 278–288.

Dilek Küçük and Meltem Turhan Yöndem. 2015. A knowledge-poor pronoun resolution system for Turkish. *arXiv preprint arXiv:1504.04751*.

Kenton Lee, Luheng He, Mike Lewis, and Luke Zettlemoyer. 2017. End-to-end neural coreference resolution. In *Proceedings of the 2017 Conference on Empirical Methods in Natural Language Processing*, pages 188–197, Copenhagen, Denmark. Association for Computational Linguistics.

Kenton Lee, Luheng He, and Luke Zettlemoyer. 2018. Higher-order coreference resolution with coarse-to-fine inference. In *Proceedings of the 2018 Conference of the North American Chapter of the Association for Computational Linguistics: Human Language Technologies, Volume 2 (Short Papers)*, pages 687–692, New Orleans, Louisiana. Association for Computational Linguistics.

Lu Liu, Zhenqiao Song, and Xiaoqing Zheng. 2020. Improving coreference resolution by leveraging entity-centric features with graph neural networks and second-order inference. *arXiv preprint arXiv:2009.04639*.

Xiaoqiang Luo. 2005. On coreference resolution performance metrics. In *Proceedings of Human Language Technology Conference and Conference on Empirical Methods in Natural Language Processing*, pages 25–32.

Sebastian Martschat and Michael Strube. 2015. Latent structures for coreference resolution. *Transactions of the Association for Computational Linguistics*, 3:405–418.

Andrew McCallum and Ben Wellner. 2005. Conditional models of identity uncertainty with application to noun coreference. In *Advances in Neural Information Processing Systems*, pages 905–912.

Tomas Mikolov, Kai Chen, Greg Corrado, and Jeffrey Dean. 2013a. Efficient estimation of word representations in vector space. *arXiv preprint arXiv:1301.3781*.

Tomas Mikolov, Ilya Sutskever, Kai Chen, Greg S Corrado, and Jeff Dean. 2013b. Distributed representations of words and phrases and their compositionality. *Advances in neural information processing systems*, 26.

Anna Nedoluzhko, Michal Novák, Martin Popel, Zdenek Žabokrtský, Amir Zeldes, and Daniel Zeman. 2022. Corefud 1.0: Coreference meets universal dependencies. In *Proceedings of LREC*.

Vincent Ng. 2005. Machine learning for coreference resolution: From local classification to global ranking. In *Proceedings of the 43rd Annual Meeting on Association for Computational Linguistics*, pages 157–164. Association for Computational Linguistics.

Vincent Ng and Claire Cardie. 2002. Improving machine learning approaches to coreference resolution. In *Proceedings of the 40th Annual Meeting on association for computational linguistics*, pages 104–111. Association for Computational Linguistics.

Cristina Nicolae and Gabriel Nicolae. 2006. Bestcut: A graph algorithm for coreference resolution. In *Proceedings of the 2006 conference on empirical methods in natural language processing*, pages 275–283. Association for Computational Linguistics.

Joakim Nivre, Željko Agić, Lars Ahrenberg, Lene Antonsen, Maria Jesus Aranzabe, Masayuki Asahara, Luma Ateyah, Mohammed Attia, Aitziber Atutxa, Liesbeth Augustinus, et al. 2017. Universal dependencies 2.1.

Joakim Nivre, Marie-Catherine De Marneffe, Filip Ginter, Yoav Goldberg, Jan Hajic, Christopher D Manning, Ryan McDonald, Slav Petrov, Sampo Pyysalo, Natalia Silveira, et al. 2016. Universal dependencies v1: A multilingual treebank collection. In *Proceedings of the Tenth International Conference on Language Resources and Evaluation (LREC'16)*, pages 1659–1666.

Tuğba Pamay and Gülşen Eryiğit. 2018. Turkish coreference resolution. In *2018 Innovations in Intelligent Systems and Applications (INISTA)*, pages 1–7. IEEE.

Cheoneum Park, Jamin Shin, Sungjoon Park, Joonho Lim, and Changki Lee. 2020. Fast end-to-end coreference resolution for korean. In *Proceedings of the 2020 Conference on Empirical Methods in Natural Language Processing: Findings*, pages 2610–2624.

Matthew E. Peters, Mark Neumann, Mohit Iyyer, Matt Gardner, Christopher Clark, Kenton Lee, and Luke Zettlemoyer. 2018. Deep contextualized word representations. In *Proceedings of the 2018 Conference of the North American Chapter of the Association for Computational Linguistics: Human Language Technologies, Volume 1 (Long Papers)*, pages 2227–2237, New Orleans, Louisiana. Association for Computational Linguistics.

Sameer Pradhan, Xiaoqiang Luo, Marta Recasens, Eduard Hovy, Vincent Ng, and Michael Strube. 2014. Scoring coreference partitions of predicted mentions: A reference implementation. In *Proceedings of the 52nd Annual Meeting of the Association for Computational Linguistics (Volume 2: Short Papers)*, pages 30–35, Baltimore, Maryland. Association for Computational Linguistics.

Sameer Pradhan, Alessandro Moschitti, Nianwen Xue, Olga Uryupina, and Yuchen Zhang. 2012a. CoNLL-2012 shared task: Modeling multilingual unrestricted coreference in OntoNotes. In *Joint Conference on EMNLP and CoNLL - Shared Task*, pages 1–40, Jeju Island, Korea. Association for Computational Linguistics.

Sameer Pradhan, Alessandro Moschitti, Nianwen Xue, Olga Uryupina, and Yuchen Zhang. 2012b. CoNLL-2012 shared task: Modeling multilingual unrestricted coreference in OntoNotes. In *Joint Conference on EMNLP and CoNLL - Shared Task*, pages 1–40, Jeju Island, Korea. Association for Computational Linguistics.

Sameer S Pradhan, Eduard Hovy, Mitch Marcus, Martha Palmer, Lance Ramshaw, and Ralph Weischedel. 2007. Ontonotes: A unified relational semantic representation. In *International Conference on Semantic Computing (ICSC 2007)*, pages 517–526. IEEE.

Altaf Rahman and Vincent Ng. 2009. Supervised models for coreference resolution. In *Proceedings of the 14th Conference on Empirical Methods in Natural Language Processing*, pages 968–977.

Altaf Rahman and Vincent Ng. 2011. Ensemble based coreference resolution. In *Proceedings of the 24th International Joint Conference on Artificial Intelligence (IJCAI)*, pages 1884–1889.

Marta Recasens and Eduard Hovy. 2011. Blanc: Implementing the rand index for coreference evaluation. *Natural Language Engineering*, 17(4):485–510.

Marta Recasens, Lluís Màrquez, Emili Sapena, M Antònia Martí, Mariona Taulé, Véronique Hoste, Massimo Poesio, and Yannick Versley. 2010. Semeval-2010 task 1: Coreference resolution in multiple languages. In *Proceedings of the 5th International Workshop on Semantic Evaluation*, pages 1–8.

Marta Recasens and M Antònia Martí. 2010. Ancora-co: Coreferentially annotated corpora for spanish and catalan. *Language resources and evaluation*, 44(4):315–345.

Kepa Joseba Rodrıguez, Francesca Delogu, Yannick Versley, Egon W Stemle, and Massimo Poesio. 2010. Anaphoric annotation of wikipedia and blogs in the live memories corpus. In *Proceedings of LREC*, pages 157–163.

Bilge Say, Deniz Zeyrek, Kemal Oflazer, and Umut Özge. 2002. Development of a corpus and a treebank for present-day written turkish. In *Proceedings of the 11th International Conference of Turkish Linguistics*, pages 183–192, Northern Cyprus.

Peter Schüller, Kübra Cıngıllı, Ferit Tunçer, Barış Gün Sürmeli, Ayşegül Pekel, Ayşe Hande Karatay, and Hacer Ezgi Karakaş. 2017. Marmara Turkish coreference corpus and coreference resolution baseline. *arXiv preprint arXiv:1706.01863*.

Stefan Schweter. 2020. Berturk - bert models for turkish.

Rhea Sukthanker, Soujanya Poria, Erik Cambria, and Ramkumar Thirunavukarasu. 2020. Anaphora and coreference resolution: A review. *Information Fusion*, 59:139–162.

Marc Vilain, John Burger, John Aberdeen, Dennis Connolly, and Lynette Hirschman. 1995. A model-theoretic coreference scoring scheme. In *Proceedings of the 6th Conference on Message Understanding*, pages 45–52. Association for Computational Linguistics.

Sam Wiseman, Alexander M Rush, and Stuart M Shieber. 2016. Learning global features for coreference resolution. *arXiv preprint arXiv:1604.03035*.

Sam Joshua Wiseman, Alexander Matthew Rush, Stuart Merrill Shieber, and Jason Weston. 2015. Learning anaphoricity and antecedent ranking features for coreference resolution. In *Proceedings of the 53rd Annual Meeting of the Association for Computational Linguistics*, pages 1416–1426.

Liyan Xu and Jinho D Choi. 2020. Revealing the myth of higher-order inference in coreference resolution. *arXiv preprint arXiv:2009.12013*.

Xiaofeng Yang, Jian Su, and Chew Lim Tan. 2006. Kernel-based pronoun resolution with structured syntactic knowledge. In *Proceedings of the 21st International Conference on Computational Linguistics and the 44th Annual Meeting of the Association for Computational Linguistics*, pages 41–48. Association for Computational Linguistics.

Savaş Yıldırım and Yılmaz Kılıçaslan. 2007. A machine learning approach to personal pronoun resolution in Turkish. In *Proceedings of the American Association for Artificial Intelligence*, pages 269–270.

Savaş Yıldırım, Yılmaz Kılıçaslan, and Tuğba Yıldız. 2007. Pronoun resolution in Turkish using decision tree and rule-based learning algorithms. In *Language and Technology Conference*, pages 270–278. Springer.

Qingyu Yin, Weinan Zhang, Yu Zhang, and Ting Liu. 2016. A deep neural network for chinese zero pronoun resolution. *arXiv preprint arXiv:1604.05800*.

Shanheng Zhao and Hwee Tou Ng. 2007. Identification and resolution of chinese zero pronouns: A machine learning approach. In *Proceedings of the 2007 joint conference on empirical methods in natural language processing and computational natural language learning (EMNLP-CoNLL)*, pages 541–550.

Towards Generation and Recognition of Humorous Texts in Portuguese

Marcio Lima Inácio and **Hugo Gonçalo Oliveira**
CISUC - Centre for Informatics and Systems of the University of Coimbra
Department of Informatics Engineerings
Polo II, Pinhal de Marrocos, 3030-290
Coimbra, Portugal
{mlinacio, hroliv}@dei.uc.pt

Abstract

Dealing with humor is an important step to develop Natural Language Processing tools capable of handling sophisticated semantic and pragmatic knowledge. In this context, this PhD thesis focuses on the automatic generation and recognition of verbal punning humor in Portuguese, which is still an underdeveloped language when compared to English. One of the main goals of this research is to conciliate Natural Language Generation computational models with existing theories of humor from the Humanities while avoiding mere generation by including contextual information into the generation process. Another point that is of utmost importance is the inclusion of the listener as an active part in the process of understanding and creating humor; we hope to achieve this by using concepts from Recommender Systems in our methods. Ultimately, we want to not only advance the current state-of-the-art in humor generation and recognition, but also to help the general Portuguese-speaking research community with methods, tools and resources that may aid in the development of further techniques for this language. We also expect our systems to provide insightful ideas about how humor is created and perceived by both humans and machines.

1 Introduction

Natural Language Processing (NLP) research tends toward even more complex types of linguistic phenomena, requiring systems that are capable to deal with sophisticated semantic and pragmatic information (Cambria and White, 2014). To achieve such goals, it is essential to handle figurative and creative language (Reyes et al., 2012), which humor is a part of. Additionally, introducing the ability to recognize and create humor benefits general natural language-based systems, e.g. virtual agents, which can exploit such knowledge to make interaction with the user more pleasant and human-like, or news aggregators capable of dealing with satirical and comical articles.

This PhD thesis is also related to Computational Creativity (CC), a multidisciplinary field of research that is concerned with replicating, understanding and enhancing human creativity through computational tools (Veale and Pérez y Pérez, 2020).[1] In language, this has to deal with artifacts such as poetry, literature, and, especially for us, verbal humor. We refer to this intersection between NLP and CC with a focus on humor as Computational Humor Processing.

Although research on Computational Humor Processing dates back to the 1990s (Binsted and Ritchie, 1994; Ritchie, 1999), there is still much to advance on this area due to the complexity of the tasks involved. As mentioned by Amin and Burghardt (2020), the most successful systems for humor generation are based on predefined templates and rules, which is limiting in terms of linguistic realization. Furthermore, Clemêncio (2019) mention that humor recognition can be improved by exploiting new features and models, as well as through the creation of larger corpora with humorous texts, especially for the Portuguese language, the main focus of this proposal.

Within this context, this thesis proposes to tackle two main tasks related to computational humor processing: automatic recognition and generation of verbal humor, with a special focus on Portuguese, which still receives less attention than other more researched languages, such as English or Mandarin Chinese (Bender, 2019).

As verbal humor is a largely diverse phenomenon conveyed through many different ways, we decided to concentrate this research on a specific kind of humorous format: puns. This individ-

[1] For a more complete definition of Computational Creativity, we recommend the Association for Computational Creativity website: http://computationalcreativity.net/home/about/computational-creativity/. Accessed on: 28 nov. 2022.

Proceedings of the 17th Conference of the European Chapter of the Association for Computational Linguistics: Student Research Workshop, pages 26–36
May 2-4, 2023 ©2023 Association for Computational Linguistics

ual type of wordplay has had a special attention of the community as it is considered to be a simpler instance of linguistic artifact capable of expressing funniness exploiting word ambiguity (Kao et al., 2016). Nonetheless, this joke format still requires dealing with complex language information (e.g. common knowledge, semantic relations, linguistic realization, and surprise) which could be useful not only in Humor Processing, for instance systems that handle sarcasm, but also in other areas of NLP, such as Natural Language Understanding or Sentiment Analysis.

To this extent, our main research objectives are (i) to conciliate explicit theories from the Humanities with sophisticated computational models to exploit their different advantages to the tasks in matter, (ii) to avoid mere generation by incorporating contextual information to the creation of humorous puns, and (iii) to include the role of the user into the generation and understanding of humor by modelling their sense of humor and creating a personalized experience. As expected, the developed methods will be evaluated in comparison to existing techniques from the literature, which will be adapted to the Portuguese language if needed.

After this introduction, the remainder of the paper is organized as follows: in section 2 we present in more detail the concepts, motivations, and general background for this project, followed by a discussion about punning humor in section 3. The research proposal alongside the intended methodologies are mentioned in section 4. Finally, we include considerations about the limitations of the project and some ethical concerns that may rise from this research.

2 Background

This project has two main fronts, humor recognition and humor generation, which are discussed in more detail below.

2.1 Humor generation

Works on the computational processing of humor date back to 1994, with two prominent systems named LIBJOG (Raskin and Attardo, 1994) and JAPE (Binsted and Ritchie, 1994) created specifically for the creation of jokes based on explicit templates to be filled according to a predefined set of rules; this kind of rule-based approach has been the most used for the task (Ritchie et al., 2006; Stock and Strapparava, 2003; Winters et al., 2018). Later, Hong and Ong (2009) created T-PEG, a system capable of learning templates and rule sets automatically from given punning riddles.

Another approach explored for humor generation is through lexical replacement on input texts, for instance the methods by Valitutti et al. (2016) and He et al. (2019). Lastly the most recent systems use some modern Natural Language Generation (NLG) techniques to create punning jokes, for example via Neural Networks (Yu et al., 2018).

In their recent survey about humor generation methods, Amin and Burghardt (2020) point out that neural-based systems are considered by users to create texts with a higher degree of linguistic complexity, using a larger variety of textual devices to convey the intended message; however, they also state that such techniques are still far from achieving a decent level of humorousness when compared to the usual template-based approaches. These observations reveal that both techniques have their strengths and their shortcomings, opening some path for future research on the matter.

Some authors also advocate that typical NLG methods are not suitable for creating creative texts, as they are built to approximate the general patterns of language which is usually the opposite goal of linguistic creativity (He et al., 2019). Hempelmann (2008) even mentioned that the only way to capture complex irregular phenomena of language is through explicit linguistic theories besides Machine Learning (ML) algorithms. However, even though they might not be completely fit for complex semantic reasoning (Bender and Koller, 2020) or creative tasks, modern techniques, such as Large Language Models (LLMs), still show impressive results producing human-like texts (Stevenson et al., 2022), justifying some research on integrating both points of view for the proposed task.

Investigation about automatic humor generation can also be done toward the personalization of the content being produced. As mentioned by Siekiera et al. (2022), "the success of a joke is strongly cultural-based", which raises questions about the role of the listener in the process of creating and perceiving humor (Veale, 2004); from this point of view, the authors indicate that future work can take into account the cultural background — and we might also include personal preferences — of the user in computational tools for humor processing. This perspective is also shared by Winters et al. (2018), who mention that creating adaptive systems capable of generating jokes based on the user's personal preferences is prone to outperform other methods that do not have such ability.

A further argument for the insertion of the user's preferences into humor generation process lies in the evaluation of such approaches. It is not unusual that authors mention that their proposed scores do not correlate with human ratings of funniness (Kao et al., 2016; He et al., 2019; Gonçalo Oliveira and Rodrigues, 2018). This may be due to the fact that human evaluation is usually done without taking into account the evaluators' personal preferences, resulting in a general neutral sentiment; for example, even for human-made jokes, He et al. (2019) report that the average rating obtained was 3 in a scale from 1 to 5. These observations show that including the reader actively in the process may be fruitful not only for the development of better methods, but also for the formulation of more robust evaluation methodologies for such systems.

2.2 Humor recognition

The recognition of humorous texts has been traditionally tackled as a binary classification problem dating back to the early 2000s (Yokogawa, 2002; Taylor and Mazlack, 2004; Mihalcea and Strapparava, 2005). Usually, such systems differ on their choices concerning the feature set used, as the ML algorithms are frequently the same: Naïve Bayes, Support Vector Machines (SVM), Decision Trees, and Random Forest. For example, Mihalcea and Strapparava (2005) features were primarily stylistic ones (alliteration, adult slangs, and antonymy) while Mihalcea and Pulman (2007) focus on semantic characteristics such as negations, negative human trains, and words related to professional communities. In their turn, Sjöbergh and Araki (2007) aim at using shallow textual features without any intent to capture meaning, identifying some relevant traits as frequent words, text similarity with known jokes, and idiomatic expressions.

Despite being the most common approach, some authors do not use ML for the task. An example is the work by Tinholt and Nijholt (2007) who create a rule-based system that recognizes humor potential in non-humorous texts by identifying ambiguous anaphora cases through a semantic graph. Alternately, Kao et al. (2016) developed probabilistic metrics for ambiguity and distinctiveness to recognize humor in homophonic and paronymic puns; their results were promising as the scores were successful in differentiating puns from non-puns, but determining the level of funniness of a joke is still a challenging task.

Another interesting observation by Kao et al. (2016) was that their measures gave hints about which words in the text were mostly related to the humorous effect, opening a new path of research toward not only identifying humor but also explaining why a certain text might be considered funny. This kind of task has also been approached by Yang et al. (2015), which use a funniness model to determine humor-inducing words.

As mentioned in subsection 2.1, humor processing systems usually do not take into account the user's specific preferences when creating jokes. For humor recognition, the same concepts may also be applied, it might be an interesting approach to not only identify whether an artifact is funny, but also to whom (or to which groups of people) it may have the intended humorous effect, in a manner similar to demographic filtering present in Recommender Systems (Bobadilla et al., 2013).

2.3 Computational humor processing in Portuguese

The majority of works in Computational Humor are focused on the English language, requiring large robust lexical resources — e.g. WordNet (Fellbaum, 1998) and ConceptNet (Speer et al., 2017) — and annotated corpora, which are not always available or fully developed for other languages such as Portuguese. Although there are initiatives to create the needed resources, they are still limited when compared to their English counterparts, which is a natural consequence of the smaller number of researchers interested in the Portuguese language.

For such reasons, Computational Humor systems for Portuguese are clearly in an early stage, with most generation approaches based on handcrafted templates and rules (Gonçalo Oliveira et al., 2016; Gonçalo Oliveira and Rodrigues, 2018). Alternately, Mendes and Gonçalo Oliveira (2020) propose a method to create humor by editing an input text. Humor recognition, in its turn, has been tackled through traditional ML with stylistic and semantic features (Clemêncio, 2019; Gonçalo Oliveira et al., 2020), similar to the previous works for the English language.

Data availability is also a concern, as there are few annotated corpora with humorous texts in Portuguese. For example, Gonçalo Oliveira et al.

(2020) introduced a collection of one-liners (short jokes) and riddles with a binary annotation created automatically according to their source. On a more broad relation to this project, some other corpora deal with other types of figurative language: Wick-Pedro et al. (2020) provide a corpus of tweets related to satirical news with a manual annotation on the intents of the users, as well as their sentiment toward the subject; furthermore, some authors also provide collections of user-generated content with annotations and linguistic descriptions about irony in such texts (Carvalho et al., 2009; de Freitas et al., 2014; Wick-Pedro et al., 2020).

In sum, working with a language as Portuguese is challenging due to the lack of large corpora, robust resources, and more modern methods to start with. Therefore, we believe that this thesis will be of great value, not only to research on Computational Humor Processing or Computational Creativity, but also to the general Portuguese-speaking NLP community.

3 Punning Humor

As mentioned by Kao et al. (2016), puns are a simpler instance of verbal humor based on phrase and word ambiguity, which makes them an ideal starting point for research on the area. This thought is shared by Aleksandrova (2022), who also mentions that puns are relevant due to their frequency in everyday live.

Even though they may be simpler and shorter, Hempelmann (2008) argues that punning jokes still require sophisticated models for doing meaningful research, as they contain all necessary elements to create a humorous effect, a sufficiently complex phenomenon by itself. Therefore, research on this kind of humor can produce knowledge that might be generalizable to other types of humor or serve as a basis for investigating other humor-related phenomena.

For those reasons, this project focuses exclusively on puns and punning jokes. Our working definition for this kind of verbal humor is as follows:

> *A pun is a form of wordplay in which one sign (e.g., a word or phrase) suggests two or more meanings by exploiting polysemy, homonymy, or phonological similarity to another sign, for an intended humorous or rhetorical effect.*
>
> Miller et al. (2017)

From the definition, punning humor is created through a relation between form (spoken or written) and meaning, requiring that a sign must evoke multiple meanings in the given context. Some examples of puns from Miller and Gurevych (2015) with different characteristics are presented below; the punning word is highlighted in bold and the specific relation is between parentheses.

1. A lumberjack's world revolves on its **axes**. (homography)
2. She fell through the window but felt no **pane**. (homophony)
3. A political prisoner is one who stands behind her **convictions**. (homonymy)
4. The sign at the nudist camp read, "**Clothed** until April." (paronymy)

It is important to stress that the pun relates to not only words but linguistic signs in general: word segments, phrases, acronyms, graphemes, onomatopoeias, and others, as illustrated by some of the examples provided by Aleksandrova (2022).

1. In English, we '**drive** cars on parkways' and 'park cars on **drive**ways'. (word segments)
2. What four letters frighten a thief? **O.I.C.U.** (phrase and graphemes)
3. How much space will Brexit free up in the European Union? 1 **GB**. (acronym)

For the reasons mentioned, in this thesis, we will focus on puns and punning humor. With this, we hope to advance the current research on the computational processing of verbal humor in Portuguese, as we will elaborate further in the next sections.

4 Research Proposal

The main objective of this thesis is to **develop methods and resources for the computational recognition, analysis, and generation of verbal punning humor in Portuguese**. To this extent, we defined some specific goals to be reached throughout the development of the research work.

- Develop, evaluate and, if needed, adapt to the Portuguese language existing methods for the automatic recognition and generation of puns;

- Create a corpus of short punning jokes in Portuguese with user ratings on their funniness alongside annotations of humor-inducing words;
- Create new methods for pun generation and recognition by determining and adapting linguistic and psycholinguistic theories of humor, surprise, or creativity to a computational scenario, combining them with different approaches for NLG and ML, especially LLMs;
- Avoid mere generation by including contextual information — automatically generated or not — to novel or existing methods for computational humor generation systems;
- Include specificities of the target audience in the process of generation, evaluation, and ranking of punning humor through concepts of Recommender Systems filtering;
- Evaluate the proposed techniques, comparing them against each other, existing methods, and baseline systems.

To come to each objective, we defined some methodologies to be followed during the research, which will be discussed as follows.

4.1 Adaptation of the literature methods

Since most of the techniques for computational humor processing are based on rules or large robust resources, they tend to be limited to a single language, usually English. To provide a fair comparison with our novel methods, and also to stimulate research on rules and resources for the Portuguese language, our first objective is to select, implement and adapt systems from the literature to our working language.

For pun recognition, as mentioned in subsection 2.3, most of this work for the ML-based methods has been done by Gonçalo Oliveira et al. (2020); however, we might still implement other methods, such as the ones by Yang et al. (2015) and Kao et al. (2016), which also incorporate to some extent the tasks of automatically determining levels of funniness and identifying humor triggering words in the input text.

For the creation of puns, there is still much work to be done. The first method that seems interesting to be adapted is the one by Hong and Ong (2009), which automatically learns templates and rules from pre-existing puns. This system is especially challenging, as it relies on some specific resources for phonological, lexical, and semantic analyses that should have their counterparts in Portuguese. Other techniques are the ones by Yu et al. (2018), a recurrent neural network to create homographic puns, and He et al. (2019), which is based on probabilistic models of surprise to edit input texts to create punning humor.

Implementing such systems for a language other than English will help to start advancing the current studies on the matter and also bring attention to specificities of the Portuguese language and its resources that need to be taken into account when developing further methods.

4.2 Corpus Creation

A key point of this thesis will be the creation of a corpus of short punning jokes in Portuguese, which will enable not only our research on automatic pun identification and generation, but also linguistic studies on this format of verbal humor. We intend to make the corpus publicly available, alongside every annotation that results from this project.

The corpus will be gathered manually from websites, social media, and YouTube videos, following some guidelines regarding the definition of punning humor by Miller et al. (2017) (section 3) and the textual format aimed for: short texts capable of being written in a single line, this means that dialogues or narrative arcs will not be included in this first version of the corpus. We will also provide a classification following the taxonomy defined by Hempelmann and Miller (2017), explicitly marking homophony and homography, which, despite not being our main focus, might help other researchers to better filter the data for their analyses.

During the data gathering, there will surely be some hard cases, i.e. texts in which the gatherer has some doubt about the nature of the humorous effect or if the instance should be included into the corpus, needing to refer back to the guidelines document. Such cases will be highlighted to enable a deeper discussion about what is punning humor, how it occurs in general, and how we created our corpus. As this is an ongoing work, we have already found some interesting examples, presented below in Table 1, that will need to be further analyzed to be discussed in deeper detail.

Table 1: Example of hard cases from the ongoing corpus collection, including onomatopoeias, neologisms, foreign languages, and others.

Original joke in Portuguese	English translation	Comments
Qual é a consola de jogos preferida dos polícias? Wii U! Wii U! Wii U! Wii U!	*What is the policemen favorite video game console? Wii U! Wii U! Wii U! Wii U!*	This joke uses an onomatopoeia, as the sound of "Wii U" resembles the sound of the sirens used in police cars.
Que nome se dá a uma freira no casino? Católica apostólica.	*How does one call a nun in a casino? Catholic Apostolic.*	This joke turns an existing word, "apostólica" (*apostolic*), into a neologism that relates to the concepts of "aposta" (*bet*) and "alcoólica" (*alcoholic*), creating a new word that describes a person addicted to gambling.
Como é que se diz "fim" em japonês? Sakabô.	*How does one say "end" in Japanese? Sakabô.*	This pun creates the word "sakabô", whose sounds resemble a foreign language (Japanese) and approximate the pronunciation of "se acabou" (*it is over*).
O que diz um castor excitado? Suck my dique!	*What does a horny beaver say? Suck my dam.*	This text uses a mix of languages, Portuguese and English, taking advantage of the similairy in pronunciation of the words "dique" (*dam*) in Portuguese and *dick* in English.
Sonhei que pesava menos de uma milésima de grama. E fiquei tipo "0mg".	*I had a dream that I wheighted less than one milligram. And I was like "0mg".*	This joke uses the written resemblance of not entire words, but the graphical symbols themselves: 0 (*zero*) and O (the letter *O*), to create a pun between "0mg" (*zero milligrams*) and "omg" (acronym for *oh my god*).

4.3 Use of explicit theories

In this project, we share the points of view by Hempelmann (2008) and Amin and Burghardt (2020) that explicit linguistic theories have much to offer when dealing with tasks that handle complex irregular phenomena of the language, such as creativity and humor. Nonetheless, as noted by Stevenson et al. (2022), the power of LLMs to create human-like linguistically complex text is too strong even for creative tasks, but with clear limitations on how creative or funny their outputs are. This indicates that it might be fruitful to use such explicit theories to overcome these limitations, for example by including richer knowledge in prompts or by using Augmented Language Model (ALM) techniques (Mialon et al., 2023).

For humor detection, Kao et al. (2016) show that linguistic-inspired scores can be a promising path for research, capable not only of differentiating puns from non-puns, but also to give hints about which are the words in the text mostly related to the proposed humorous effect. Such results can be combined with features from the literature known to be effective in the task — such as ambiguity and taboo language — as well as with novel latent semantic and language models that have been achieving impressive results in various NLP tasks (Bender and Koller, 2020).

Accordingly, for our second objective, we decided to create new methods for the computational processing of puns by exploiting concepts and findings of explicit theories from the Humanities (Linguitics, Psycholinguistics, Cognitive Linguistics, Psychology, and others) to help overcome the limitations of existing computational models for the processing of language.

Some examples of theories that can be studied and exploited in our research are: Script-based Semantic Theory of Humor (SSTH; Raskin, 1984), General Theory of Verbal Humor (GTVH; Attardo and Raskin, 1991), Optimal Innovation Hypothesis (Giora et al., 2004), models for surprise (Macedo and Cardoso, 2001; Tobin, 2018; Chieppe et al., 2022), and theories on sense of humor (Martin, 2003).

4.4 Avoiding mere generation

The majority of systems that generate humorous texts do not take into account some contextual information to constrain the creation process, a phenomenon that we call "mere generation" (Ventura, 2016). For example, the method developed by Winters and Delobelle (2021) uses Language Models and Genetic Algorithms to edit news headlines to make them sound funnier, however there is no effort to use the actual text of the article to ensure that the title will match to its content, which is a desirable characteristic in a real-life scenario.

Another instance, for the Portuguese language, is the SECO system (Gonçalo Oliveira and Rodrigues, 2018) that creates funny riddles from a list of compound words through pre-defined templates and rules. The tool exhaustively tries to create a joke for every entry in the list and each template, regardless of any input about the content or topic of the intended output. This process generates a large amount of riddles that are not necessarily funny nor suitable for any unrestricted context.

To make our methods more fit to final applications, one of the objectives of this thesis is to avoid mere generation by including contextual information to constrain the generation process. This can be achieved through keywords, topics, conversation utterances, narrative texts, news articles, and so on.

4.5 Include the user in the process

As mentioned by Winters et al. (2018), "*an integrated humor generator that is capable of generating jokes adapted to the user might [...] outperform a generator that does not possess this capability.*" This quote explicits the necessity of considering the sense of humor of the listener — the user — in Computational Humor Processing systems. Something along these lines was also discussed by Veale (2004) when the author mentions that an essentialist view of humor, i.e. an interpretation of humor simply as a result of language-related characteristics, is insufficient to deal with the complexity of this phenomenon.

In this context, one of the main objectives of this thesis is to create methods for both pun recognition and pun generation that take into account the user's personal sense of humor to create a more personalized experience. As the two tasks are distinct, we give more details on them separately.

Pun recognition Few jokes are considered universally funny, as their humorous effect is dependent not only on their textual characteristics, but also on the cultural and personal background of the listener; therefore, systems that categorically determine if some artifact is funny or not might be flawed (or at least limited). To deal with this, we might create systems that, besides predicting if a text is funny, also detect which users or demographic groups might perceive them as so.

Pun generation For our second task, some model of the user's interests should constrain, prime, or guide the generation process to create puns with a higher chance of producing a funny outcome for that specific person.

In both cases, we need to capture the user's preferences into a model to be used by the systems in their specific tasks. For this modelling, Recommender Systems (RS) seem to be an interesting field of research that has much to offer in terms of concepts, techniques, and scores (Bobadilla et al., 2013).

As in this research we deal with an indefinite set of artifacts, using content filtering is essential; this is a category of methods for RS that focus on recommending items according to similarities between their content (text, image, sound, etc.) and the user's profile created from their previous choices (purchases, likes, shares, and others). Additionally, demographic filtering can also be valuable to identify social groups prone to find some artifact funny by analyzing personal characteristics of individuals, such as age, gender, country, and the like.

There exist other filtering techniques — e.g. collaborative and social filtering — however, we believe that the ones mentioned above are a satisfying starting point to include into our methods for Computational Humor Processing so that the user has a more active role in such processes.

More details about how these techniques are to be used depend on the amount of human resources we will have available, as datasets on RS usually deal with thousands of users. For example, Jester (Goldberg et al., 2001), a well-known data set for joke recommendation, has 100 jokes evaluated by 73,421 users in their original version.

Another possibility to achieve this goal is to use Reinforcement Learning techniques, in which the model is fine-tuned according to a user feedback (ranking, scoring, or classification) to result in a modified system that takes into account their personal tastes.

4.6 Evaluation

The evaluation of humor processing systems is extremely complex, the whole phenomenon alike; therefore, automatic scores are scarce, especially for generation. As our two main tasks require different evaluation process, we detail them separately below.

Pun recognition As humor recognition is usually interpreted as a classification or regression task, all available automatic evaluation methods can be used, such as precision, recall, accuracy, Mean Square Error (MSE), Mean Absolute Error (MAE), R Square (R^2), and so on. However, when including the user as an active part of the process (according to our intentions stated in subsection 4.5), the evaluation becomes more complex and needs to be further thought of carefully.

Pun generation As reported by Amin and Burghardt (2020), the evaluation of humor generation systems does not count with any satisfying widely-adopted automatic scoring method; therefore, this process is in general performed manually. A possibility is to evaluate the generated texts according to the five criteria used by Gonçalo Oliveira and Rodrigues (2018): interpretation, surprise, novelty, and humor. It is also possible to analyze the linguistic complexity of the outputs, as previously done by Amin and Burghardt (2020). Since the evaluation will be made mainly by hand, the quality of our user-focused pun generation methods will naturally take into account their personal point of view and interests, meaning that this evaluation procedure seems suitable to every system we might create for this task. On the other hand, we may study the possibility of using the developed Pun Recognition systems to evaluate the generation results automatically.

In sum, in this research project, we will focus on already established evaluation methods used by the scientific community. However, there are cases in which we might need to develop custom methodologies to better attain valuable and fair evaluations of the proposed methods.

4.7 Expected results

As main results, we expect to develop computational methods for automatically generating, identifying, analyzing, and, possibly, evaluating punning humor in Portuguese. Such techniques can be incorporated into general applications to aid the final user in their needs to create and recognize humorous texts. Additionally, we believe that our systems may also help other researchers to better understand how verbal humor is created and perceived by both machines and humans.

Another goal we would like to achieve is to bring awareness to the Academia about the importance of multidisciplinarity in NLP and how research on Humanities may help to overcome the limitations of usual computational methods. Besides the already mentioned expectations, we ultimately hope that the resources and tools created during this research project help the community on a wide range of NLP problems, especially for the Portuguese language.

Limitations

As every research, this thesis has challenges and limitations regarding its execution and methodological decisions, which are discussed below.

The first limitation we point out is that this research focuses mainly on a very specific kind of verbal humor: puns; in addition, we aim only at short punning jokes. Therefore, we might not deal directly with a large amount of other phenomena, such as metaphors, narratives, dialogues, and so on. Nonetheless, as argued in section 3, this is a good starting point to advance the research on Computational Humor Processing for Portuguese.

Finally, the last limitation to which we call attention concerns the usage of concepts from Recommender Systems in the developed methods. There are some issues with RS, which our techniques will probably be subject to, especially the cold-start problem, which occurs when it is not possible to provide reliable recommendations for new items or new users, due to a lack of initial ratings.

Ethics Statement

Despite having positive effects, such as promoting solidarity, bringing people together, and creating social acceptance and approval, humor can also be harmful, as it can be used as a form of social control, a correction for deviant behaviors, or as a way to legitimize social prejudice and stereotypes against marginalized groups (Crawford, 2003; Kuipers, 2008; Bemiller and Schneider, 2010).

Additionally, there are jokes which are not suitable for specific vulnerable groups, such as children, due to their possibly problematic content, e.g. sexual relations, pedophilia, harassment, xenophobic stereotypes, etc.

Therefore, it is important to bear these aspects of humor in mind throughout the whole research, including the data collection and the development of our methods. This will help to bring awareness and raise questions about how these systems, corpora, and resources might affect society not only in a positive light but also from a critical point of view.

Acknowledgments

This work is funded by national funds through the FCT – Foundation for Science and Technology, I.P. (grant number UI/BD/153496/2022), within the scope of the project CISUC (UID/CEC/00326/2020) and by the European Social Fund, through the Regional Operational Program Centro 2020.

References

Elena Aleksandrova. 2022. Pun-based jokes and linguistic creativity: Designing 3R-module. *The European Journal of Humour Research*, 10(1):88–107.

Miriam Amin and Manuel Burghardt. 2020. A survey on approaches to computational humor generation. In *Proceedings of the the 4th Joint SIGHUM Workshop on Computational Linguistics for Cultural Heritage, Social Sciences, Humanities and Literature*, pages 29–41, Online. International Committee on Computational Linguistics.

Salvatore Attardo and Victor Raskin. 1991. Script theory revis(it)ed: Joke similarity and joke representation model. *Humor - International Journal of Humor Research*, 4(3-4).

Michelle L. Bemiller and Rachel Zimmer Schneider. 2010. IT'S NOT JUST A JOKE. *Sociological Spectrum*, 30(4):459–479.

Emily M. Bender. 2019. The #BenderRule: On Naming the Languages We Study and Why It Matters. The Gradient.

Emily M. Bender and Alexander Koller. 2020. Climbing towards NLU: On Meaning, Form, and Understanding in the Age of Data. In *Proceedings of the 58th Annual Meeting of the Association for Computational Linguistics*, pages 5185–5198, Online. Association for Computational Linguistics.

Kim Binsted and Graeme Ritchie. 1994. An implemented model of punning riddles. In *Proceedings of the 12th National Conference on Artificial Intelligence*, volume 1, pages 633–638, Seattle. AAAI Press / The MIT Press.

J. Bobadilla, F. Ortega, A. Hernando, and A. Gutiérrez. 2013. Recommender systems survey. *Knowledge-Based Systems*, 46:109–132.

Erik Cambria and Bebo White. 2014. Jumping NLP Curves: A Review of Natural Language Processing Research. *IEEE Computational Intelligence Magazine*, 9(2):48–57.

Paula Carvalho, Luís Sarmento, Mário J. Silva, and Eugénio de Oliveira. 2009. Clues for detecting irony in user-generated contents: Oh...!! it's "so easy" ;-). In *Proceeding of the 1st International CIKM Workshop on Topic-sentiment Analysis for Mass Opinion - TSA '09*, page 53, Hong Kong, China. ACM Press.

Patrick Chieppe, Penny Sweetser, and Eryn Newman. 2022. Bayesian Modelling of the Well-Made Surprise. In *International Conference on Computational Creativity*, Bolzano-Bozen. Association for Computational Creativity (ACC).

André Clemêncio. 2019. *Reconhecimento Automático de Humor Verbal*. MSc, Universidade de Coimbra, Coimbra.

Mary Crawford. 2003. Gender and humor in social context. *Journal of Pragmatics*, 35(9):1413–1430.

Larissa A. de Freitas, Aline A. Vanin, Denise N. Hogetop, Marco N. Bochernitsan, and Renata Vieira. 2014. Pathways for irony detection in tweets. In *Proceedings of the 29th Annual ACM Symposium on Applied Computing*, pages 628–633, Gyeongju Republic of Korea. ACM.

Christiane Fellbaum, editor. 1998. *WordNet: An Electronic Lexical Database*. Language, Speech, and Communication. MIT Press, Cambridge, Mass.

Rachel Giora, Ofer Fein, Ann Kronrod, Idit Elnatan, Noa Shuval, and Adi Zur. 2004. Weapons of Mass Distraction: Optimal Innovation and Pleasure Ratings. *Metaphor and Symbol*, 19(2):115–141.

Ken Goldberg, Theresa Roeder, Dhruv Gupta, and Chris Perkins. 2001. Eigentaste: A Constant Time Collaborative Filtering Algorithm. *Information Retrieval*, 4(2):133–151.

Hugo Gonçalo Oliveira, André Clemêncio, and Ana Alves. 2020. Corpora and baselines for humour recognition in Portuguese. In *Proceedings of the 12th Language Resources and Evaluation Conference*, pages 1278–1285, Marseille, France. European Language Resources Association.

Hugo Gonçalo Oliveira, Diogo Costa, and Alexandre Miguel Pinto. 2016. One does not simply produce funny memes! - Explorations on the Automatic Generation of Internet humor. In *Proceedings of the Seventh International Conference on Computational Creativity*, pages 238–245, Paris. Sony CSL Paris, France.

Hugo Gonçalo Oliveira and Ricardo Rodrigues. 2018. Explorando a Geração Automática de Adivinhas em Português. *Linguamática*, 10(1):3–18.

He He, Nanyun Peng, and Percy Liang. 2019. Pun Generation with Surprise. In *Proceedings of the 2019 Conference of the North American Chapter of the Association for Computational Linguistics: Human Language Technologies*, volume 1, pages 1734–1744, Minneapolis. Association for Computational Linguistics.

Christian F. Hempelmann. 2008. Computational humor: Beyond the pun? In *The Primer of Humor Research*, number 8 in Humor Research, pages 333–360. Victor Raskin, Berlin, New York.

Christian F. Hempelmann and Tristan Miller. 2017. Puns: Taxonomy and Phonology. In *The Routledge Handbook of Language and Humor*, first edition, Routledge Handbooks in Linguistics, pages 95–108. Routledge.

Bryan Anthony Hong and Ethel Ong. 2009. Automatically extracting word relationships as templates for pun generation. In *Proceedings of the Workshop on Computational Approaches to Linguistic Creativity*, pages 24–31, Boulder, Colorado. Association for Computational Linguistics.

Justine T. Kao, Roger Levy, and Noah D. Goodman. 2016. A Computational Model of Linguistic Humor in Puns. *Cognitive Science*, 40(5):1270–1285.

Giselinde Kuipers. 2008. The Sociology of Humor. In *The Primer of Humor Research*, number 8 in Humor Research, pages 361–398. Victor Raskin, Berlin, New York.

Luís Macedo and Amílcar Cardoso. 2001. Modeling Forms of Surprise in an Artificial Agent. In *Proceedings of the Annual Meeting of the Cognitive Science Society*, volume 23.

Rod Martin. 2003. Sense of humor. In Shane J. Lopez and C. R. Snyder, editors, *Positive Psychological Assessment: A Handbook of Models and Measures.*, pages 313–326. American Psychological Association, Washington.

Rui Mendes and Hugo Gonçalo Oliveira. 2020. TECo: Exploring word embeddings for text adaptation to a given context. In *Proceedings of the Eleventh International Conference on Computational Creativity*, pages 185–188, Coimbra. Association for Computational Creativity (ACC).

Grégoire Mialon, Roberto Dessì, Maria Lomeli, Christoforos Nalmpantis, Ram Pasunuru, Roberta Raileanu, Baptiste Rozière, Timo Schick, Jane Dwivedi-Yu, Asli Celikyilmaz, Edouard Grave, Yann LeCun, and Thomas Scialom. 2023. Augmented Language Models: A Survey. *arXiv*.

Rada Mihalcea and Stephen Pulman. 2007. Characterizing Humour: An Exploration of Features in Humorous Texts. In Alexander Gelbukh, editor, *Computational Linguistics and Intelligent Text Processing*, volume 4394, pages 337–347. Springer Berlin Heidelberg, Berlin, Heidelberg.

Rada Mihalcea and Carlo Strapparava. 2005. Making computers laugh: Investigations in automatic humor recognition. In *Proceedings of Human Language Technology Conference and Conference on Empirical Methods in Natural Language Processing*, pages 531–538, Vancouver, British Columbia, Canada. Association for Computational Linguistics.

Tristan Miller and Iryna Gurevych. 2015. Automatic disambiguation of English puns. In *Proceedings of the 53rd Annual Meeting of the Association for Computational Linguistics and the 7th International Joint Conference on Natural Language Processing (Volume 1: Long Papers)*, pages 719–729, Beijing, China. Association for Computational Linguistics.

Tristan Miller, Christian Hempelmann, and Iryna Gurevych. 2017. SemEval-2017 Task 7: Detection and Interpretation of English Puns. In *Proceedings of the 11th International Workshop on Semantic Evaluation (SemEval-2017)*, pages 58–68, Vancouver, Canada. Association for Computational Linguistics.

Jonathan D. Raskin and Salvatore Attardo. 1994. Non-literalness and non-bona-fide in language: An approach to formal and computational treatments of humor. *Pragmatics & Cognition*, 2(1):31–69.

Victor Raskin. 1984. *Semantic Mechanisms of Humor*. Springer Netherlands, Dordrecht.

Antonio Reyes, Paolo Rosso, and Davide Buscaldi. 2012. From humor recognition to irony detection: The figurative language of social media. *Data & Knowledge Engineering*, 74:1–12.

Graeme Ritchie. 1999. Developing the Incongruity-Resolution Theory. Technical Report EDI-INF-RR-0007, Division of Informatics, University of Edinburgh, Edinburgh.

Graeme D Ritchie, Ruli Manurung, Helen Pain, Annalu Waller, and Dave O'Mara. 2006. The STANDUP interactive riddle builder. *IEEE Intelligent Systems*, 21(2):67–69.

Julia Siekiera, Marius Köppel, Edwin Simpson, Kevin Stowe, Iryna Gurevych, and Stefan Kramer. 2022. Ranking Creative Language Characteristics in Small Data Scenarios. In *International Conference on Computational Creativity*, Bolzano-Bozen. Association for Computational Creativity (ACC).

Jonas Sjöbergh and Kenji Araki. 2007. Recognizing Humor Without Recognizing Meaning. In Francesco Masulli, Sushmita Mitra, and Gabriella Pasi, editors, *Applications of Fuzzy Sets Theory*, volume 4578, pages 469–476. Springer Berlin Heidelberg, Berlin, Heidelberg.

Robyn Speer, Joshua Chin, and Catherine Havasi. 2017. ConceptNet 5.5: An open multilingual graph of general knowledge. In *Proceedings of the 31st AAAI Conference on Artificial Intelligence and the Twenty-ninth Innovative Applications of Artificial Intelligence Conference*, 4444-4451.

Claire Stevenson, Iris Smal, Raoul Grasman, Matthijs Baas, and Han Van Der Maas. 2022. Putting GPT-3's Creativity to the (Alternative Uses) Test. In *International Conference on Computational Creativity*, Bolzano-Bozen. Association for Computational Creativity (ACC).

Oliviero Stock and Carlo Strapparava. 2003. HAHAcronym: Humorous Agents for Humorous Acronyms. *Humor - International Journal of Humor Research*, 16(3).

J.M. Taylor and L.J. Mazlack. 2004. Humorous wordplay recognition. In *2004 IEEE International Conference on Systems, Man and Cybernetics (IEEE Cat. No.04CH37583)*, pages 3306–3311, The Hague, Netherlands. IEEE.

Hans Wim Tinholt and Anton Nijholt. 2007. Computational Humour: Utilizing Cross-Reference Ambiguity for Conversational Jokes. In Francesco Masulli, Sushmita Mitra, and Gabriella Pasi, editors, *Applications of Fuzzy Sets Theory*, volume 4578, pages 477–483. Springer Berlin Heidelberg, Berlin, Heidelberg.

Vera Tobin. 2018. *Elements of Surprise: Our Mental Limits and the Satisfactions of Plot*. Harvard University Press, Cambridge, Massachusetts.

Alessandro Valitutti, Antoine Doucet, Jukka M. Toivanen, and Hannu Toivonen. 2016. Computational generation and dissection of lexical replacement humor. *Natural Language Engineering*, 22(5):727–749.

Tony Veale. 2004. Incongruity in humor: Root cause or epiphenomenon? *Humor - International Journal of Humor Research*, 17(4).

Tony Veale and Rafael Pérez y Pérez. 2020. Leaps and Bounds: An Introduction to the Field of Computational Creativity. *New Generation Computing*, 38(4):551–563.

Dan Ventura. 2016. Mere generation: Essential barometer or dated concept. In *Proceedings of the Seventh International Conference on Computational Creativity*, pages 17–24. Sony CSL, Paris.

Gabriela Wick-Pedro, Roney L. S. Santos, Oto A. Vale, Thiago A. S. Pardo, Kalina Bontcheva, and Carolina Scarton. 2020. Linguistic Analysis Model for Monitoring User Reaction on Satirical News for Brazilian Portuguese. In Paulo Quaresma, Renata Vieira, Sandra Aluísio, Helena Moniz, Fernando Batista, and Teresa Gonçalves, editors, *Computational Processing of the Portuguese Language*, volume 12037, pages 313–320. Springer International Publishing, Cham.

Thomas Winters and Pieter Delobelle. 2021. Survival of the Wittiest: Evolving Satire with Language Models. In *Proceedings of the Twelfth International Conference on Computational Creativity*, pages 82–86, Mexico City, Mexico. Association for Computational Creativity (ACC).

Thomas Winters, Vincent Nys, and Daniel De Schreye. 2018. Automatic Joke Generation: Learning Humor from Examples. In Norbert Streitz and Shin'ichi Konomi, editors, *Distributed, Ambient and Pervasive Interactions: Technologies and Contexts*, volume 10922, pages 360–377. Springer International Publishing, Cham.

Diyi Yang, Alon Lavie, Chris Dyer, and Eduard Hovy. 2015. Humor Recognition and Humor Anchor Extraction. In *Proceedings of the 2015 Conference on Empirical Methods in Natural Language Processing*, pages 2367–2376, Lisbon, Portugal. Association for Computational Linguistics.

T. Yokogawa. 2002. Japanese pun analyzer using articulation similarities. In *2002 IEEE World Congress on Computational Intelligence. 2002 IEEE International Conference on Fuzzy Systems. FUZZ-IEEE'02. Proceedings (Cat. No.02CH37291)*, volume 2, pages 1114–1119, Honolulu, HI, USA. IEEE.

Zhiwei Yu, Jiwei Tan, and Xiaojun Wan. 2018. A Neural Approach to Pun Generation. In *Proceedings of the 56th Annual Meeting of the Association for Computational Linguistics (Volume 1: Long Papers)*, pages 1650–1660, Melbourne, Australia. Association for Computational Linguistics.

GAP-Gen: Guided Automatic Python Code Generation

Junchen Zhao * junchez3@uci.edu
Yurun Song * yuruns@uci.edu
Junlin Wang junliw1@uci.edu
Ian G. Harris harris@ics.uci.edu
University of California, Irvine

Abstract

Automatic code generation from natural language descriptions can be highly beneficial during the process of software development. In this work, we propose GAP-Gen, a **G**uided **A**utomatic **P**ython **C**ode **G**eneration method based on Python syntactic constraints and semantic constraints. We first introduce Python syntactic constraints in the form of **Syntax-Flow**, which is a simplified version of Abstract Syntax Tree (AST) reducing the size and high complexity of real python AST but maintaining crucial syntactic information of Python code. In addition to Syntax-Flow, we introduce **Variable-Flow** which abstracts variable and function names consistently throughout the code. In our work, rather than pre-training, we focus on modifying the fine-tuning process which reduces computational requirements but retains high generation performance on automatic Python code generation task. GAP-Gen fine-tunes the transformer-based language models T5 and CodeT5 using the Code-to-Docstring datasets CodeSearchNet, CodeSearchNet AdvTest and Code-Docstring-Corpus from EdinburghNLP. Our experiments show that GAP-Gen achieves better results on automatic Python code generation task than previous works. Our implementation is available on the github[1].

1 Introduction

With billions of people relying on software for their everyday work and life, developers face an ongoing challenge to create programs efficiently. One potential solution to this challenge is to use human descriptions to generate the corresponding source code. By using this approach, developers can write software specifications in natural language, which are then translated into code through code generation mechanism. Early attempts to tackle this problem were rule-based, identifying syntactic patterns in text and using handcrafted rules to map the patterns to code. Methods used to recognize syntactic structure include regular patterns (Gulwani and Marron, 2014; Kate et al., 2005; Le et al., 2013) and parse trees produced using context-free grammars (Kate et al., 2005; Le et al., 2013; Ballard and Biermann, 1979; Price et al., 2000). Several previous approaches convert a sentence into a formal statement by mapping verbs to functions in the formal language, and mapping the objects of the verb in the sentence to function arguments in the formal language (Ballard and Biermann, 1979; Price et al., 2000; Little and Miller, 2006). For example, the sentence, "Add r1 to r2" might be mapped to add(r1, r2) in a procedural language. The problem of finding the objects of the verb to use as function arguments is simple if the sentence structure is strictly limited. Several approaches use regular expressions (Le et al., 2013) or context-free grammars (Kate et al., 2005) to identify the objects in the sentence.

More recent approaches are data-driven and leverage machine learning methods, e.g., (Desai et al., 2016) uses a Naive Bayesian Classifier to map English words to a domain-specific language, and (Quirk et al., 2015) learns production rules for a semantic parser. (Rahit et al., 2019) uses a Long-Short Term Memory (LSTM) Recurrent Neural Network (RNN) architecture to implement their neural machine translation approach . Work presented in (Ling et al., 2016) introduces the Latent Predictor Network (LPN) architecture which treats code generation as a sequence-to-sequence modeling problem. (Yin and Neubig, 2017) builds upon this approach by leveraging the grammar model of the target language as prior knowledge.

Research presented in (Clement et al., 2020; Feng et al., 2020; Lu et al., 2021) introduced transformer-based language model pre-training methods to map the natural language semantic with

* Equally contributed

[1] https://github.com/Rain9876/Auto-Code-Generator

Proceedings of the 17th Conference of the European Chapter of the Association for Computational Linguistics: Student Research Workshop, pages 37–51
May 2-4, 2023 ©2023 Association for Computational Linguistics

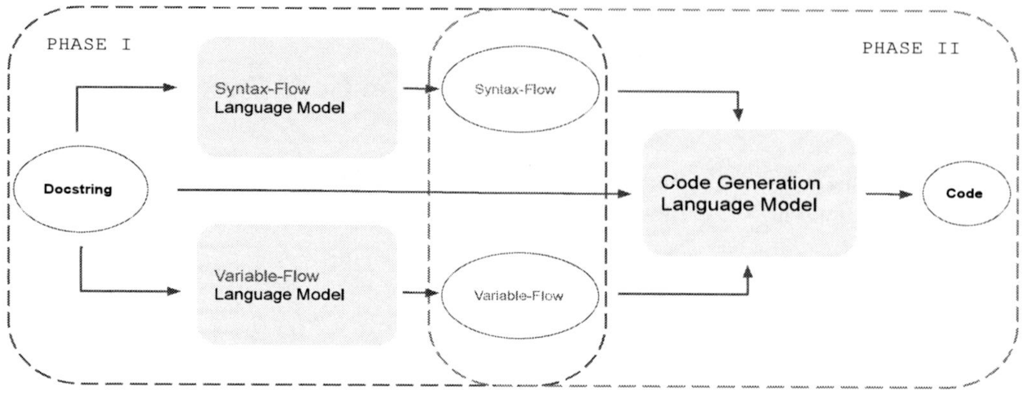

Figure 1: **An overview of the proposed approach** Phase I has two language models generating Syntax-Flow and Variable-Flow. In Phase II, another language model encodes these two types of information as well as the docstring to generate code.

the code. Although these works have relatively good performance on source code generation task, they require high computational resources, which are difficult to acquire. They also usually consider the code as a sequence of tokens (Feng et al., 2020; Kanade et al., 2020; Lu et al., 2021) and ignore either the source code's syntactic-level or semantic-level information, which could improve the language models' code understanding capability, during their pre-training process.

In this work, we present GAP-Gen, a method to improve automatic Python source code generation from natural language description. Our GAP-Gen is fine-tuning of the pre-trained T5-English (Raffel et al., 2020a) and CodeT5 (Wang et al., 2021) language models that employ Syntax-Flow and Variable-Flow as guidance and has shown on being able to understand the relationship between natural language description and Python code from syntactic and semantic level of the Python code.

Our GAP-Gen training pipeline is composed of two phases. As shown in Figure 1, **Phase I**, fine-tunes our pre-trained language model for the purpose of generating Python code's syntactic constraints and semantic-level structure, the Syntax-Flow and the Variable-Flow. **Phase II**, fine-tunes a separate language model by encoding natural language description of the code, the generated code syntactic constrains (Syntax-Flow) and abstracted variable names (Variable-Flow) from Phase I to generate Python code. By doing so, language models fine-tuned with GAP-Gen training pipeline are able to surpass many previous works' performances, which rely on the pre-training process of language models without considering code's syntactic and semantic information.

Our **main contributions** are:

- We introduce Syntax-Flow and demonstrate the importance of the source code's syntactic information in the automatic Python code generation task.
- We show that abstracting variable and function names through Variable-Flow is effective in maintaining the naming semantics of the code.
- We achieve high performance on automatic Python source code generation task without language model pre-training.

2 Related Works

Language Models for Programming Languages. Transformer-based language models that utilize attention mechanisms have been dominating NLP benchmarks (Vaswani et al., 2017; Wang et al., 2018). The novel attention-based message passing techniques plus multi-task pre-training (Devlin et al., 2019) have been through extensive studies. This leads to a deeper understanding of the representational power of transformer-based models (Ethayarajh, 2019; Kovaleva et al., 2019; Jain and Wallace, 2019).

At the same time, transformer-based auto-regressive language models consisting of encoder/decoder demonstrate stellar performances on many NLP generative tasks (Radford et al., 2019; Lewis et al., 2020; Raffel et al., 2020b). These tasks include but not limited to story generation (See et al., 2019), dialogue (Budzianowski and Vulic, 2019), summarization (Lewis et al., 2020), Entity

Retrieval (Cao et al., 2021), Question Answering (Guu et al., 2020), and so on. Similar advances have also been made in Programming Language relevant tasks.

Programming language generation tasks, although not considered as natural language generation tasks, have been demonstrated to have great results when they are modeled similarly as natural language generation tasks. (Feng et al., 2020) pre-trains on Mask Language Modeling (MLM) and replaced-token detection for code understanding tas. In (Liu et al., 2020), the authors develop a code completion transformer-based model by jointly predicting the probability and type of the next token. For the task of code summarization, transformer-based models outperform the other neural approaches (Yu et al., 2020; Ahmad et al., 2020); Svyatkovskiy et al., 2020; Liu et al., 2020) use GPT and UniLM respectively for code completion. More related to our work, (Husain et al., 2019; Clement et al., 2020) explore pre-training methodologies for learning better structural and syntactical information for automatic code generation. Moreover, (Wang et al., 2021; Guo et al., 2021) incorporates Variable-Flows and identifier information into their pre-training process for better code generation performance.

Guided Text Generative Models. Generative modeling is powerful but often falls short in many conditions. The behavior of auto-regressive language models cannot be explicitly controlled, and was shown to be very easy to degenerate (Holtzman et al., 2020; Welleck et al., 2020; Meister et al., 2020). This is also the case for code generation. This prompts researchers to combat this issue by looking at either the training time or the decoding time. Work in (Fan et al., 2018) constrains the sample space to top-k tokens in the softmax logistics to avoid introducing highly unlikely tokens. (Holtzman et al., 2020) instead restricts the sampling space to the smallest set of space above some probability mass. Using simple decoding variants is lightweight to implement, but does not change the predicted likelihood of each token. (Welleck et al., 2020) argues that the likelihood objectives is at fault, and proposes unlikelihood training objective, which forces lower probabilities on unlikely generations.

Furthermore, practitioners have also injected priors or structural information into the language model for better generation. (Zhang et al., 2020; Lagutin et al., 2021) utilizes policy learning to control model behaviors. However, this approach suffers from high variance (Choshen et al., 2020). Recently work in story generation (Yao et al., 2019; Rashkin et al., 2020; Goldfarb-Tarrant et al., 2020) uses a plotline/storyline as an intermediate state for generation. This alleviates the language modeling tasks and sets up the model to better learn the structure of the stories. Being motivated by story generation, our work injects syntactic and semantic structural information in a setup that is similar to this line of works. For the code generation task, we utilize our proposed Syntax-Flow and Variable-Flow as the intermediate state to help language model better understand code's syntactic and semantic structure information and improve its performance.

3 Method

In this section, we describe our method by introducing Syntax-Flow and Variable-Flow. Then we present the generation process of Syntax-Flow and Variable-Flow. Finally, we present the Python code generation process guided by Syntax-Flow and Variable-Flow.

3.1 Syntax-Flow

Unlike other methods that generate code directly from source input with pre-training, our approach works in a pipeline by generating the structure of the code as an intermediate state first and then generating the detailed code using the code structure.

Procedural structure can be expressed formally as an Abstract Syntax Tree (AST). An AST contains two major components: **STMT (Statement)** and **Expr (Expression)**. STMT describes the general structure of code including the high-level Python code syntactic constraints. Expr is the detailed content of the code, mainly including the function variables and operations. Additionally, there are some special components in an AST such as the exceptional handler, import alias, arguments, etc.

Due to the AST's formality and rich expressiveness regarding the syntactic information of code, there are works that generate an AST first and then use it to aid code generation, such as (Yin and Neubig, 2017; Ling et al., 2016), but these works usually require composite model architecture changes. Also, the AST is too complex for models to directly generate information. The length of ASTs typically

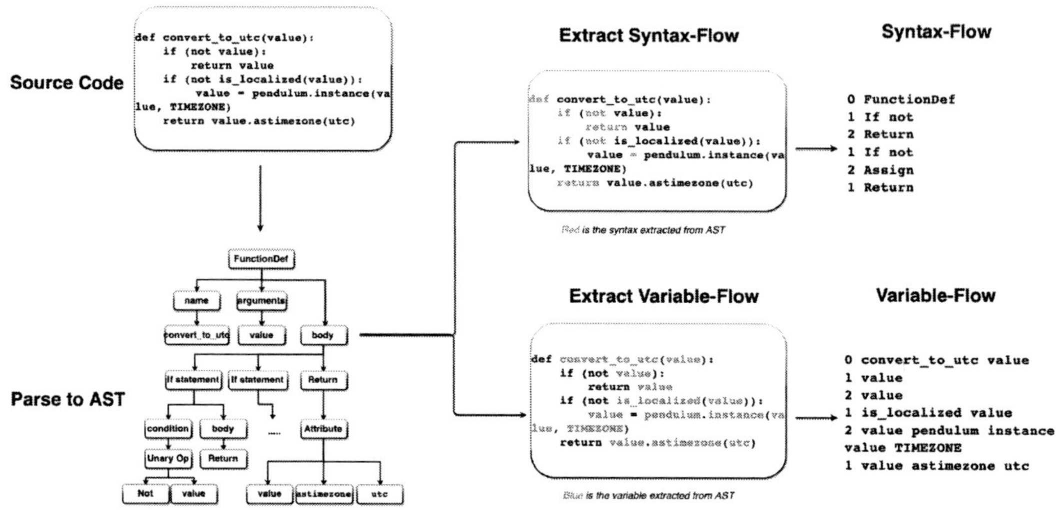

Figure 2: **An overview of the Syntax-Flow and Variable-Flow Generation** . The numbers refer to the number of indentations (4 spaces) required at the beginning of the command line. For Syntax-Flow, statements (STMTs) immediately follow the required indentation and are then followed by several built-in expressions (Exprs). In contrast, Variable Flow follows the function and variable names.

makes it impractical to directly input them into transformer-based language models due to their input sequence length limitation. As a result, we propose a simplified version of an AST, namely Syntax-Flow.

Instead of using the entire tree structure of the AST, we only extract crucial information including Indentation, STMT, and some parts of Expr. By doing so, we reduce the complexity of AST but retain its crucial syntactic structure of Python code, and is small enough to be compatible with transformer-based language models.

In our proposed Syntax-Flow, there are three critical components: **Indentation**, **STMT** and **Default Functions**. These three components are viewed as invariants which means that these components are kept unchanged for maintaining code's correct functionality.

3.2 Variable-Flow

Variable-Flow is another indispensable component in automatic code generation task. It can be effectively applied to maintain the naming semantics of the code during the code generation process. (Wang et al., 2021; Guo et al., 2021) use Variable-Flow during their pre-training process and achieve good performances on programming language-relevant tasks. In their works, they extract function variables names as Variable-Flow which is integrated into their pre-training process for improving language models' capability on understanding the code semantic structure.

In our work, rather than extract variable names only as Variable-Flow, our Variable-Flow contains **Indentation**, **variable names**, and **function names**. Variable names and function names are uniformly free to change. In other words, Python code's functionality remains correct regardless of the changes in these two Variable-Flow components. Therefore, compared with Syntax-Flow, our Variable-Flow contains variant components and is more dynamic.

3.3 Phase I - Generation of Syntax-Flow and Variable-Flow

3.3.1 Generation of Syntax-Flow

Figure 2 shows the Syntax-Flow and Variable-Flow generation pipeline. With regard to Syntax-Flow, the numbers represent the number of indentations (4 spaces) required at the beginning of the command line. Then, a statement is immediately next to the Indentation, followed by several built-in expressions. This feature is extracted from Python code through AST syntax visitor method, a method to go through every detail of the AST nodes recursively and extracts all necessary nodes for use, such as FunctionDef, STMT, exception handler etc, with the count of indentation at the same time.

The simplified generation process of Syntax-Flow is shown in Algorithm 1 Appendix B.4. For each line of source code, we generate one line of Syntax-Flow as you can see in Figure 2. Formally we denote the source code to be $y = (y_1, y_2, ..., y_n)$, and let $E = [e_1, e_2, ..., e_L]$ be the list of indexes of the newline character. Hence, y_{e_1} is the first line break, and $Y_1 = (y_1, ..., y_{e_1})$ is the first line of the source code, $Y_2 = (y_{e_1+1}, ..., y_{e_2})$ the second and so on. Then for each such line of the code, we generate a pair $a = (t, c)$. t is the indentation of the current line of code or number of tabs, and c is the code logic which includes control flow or function definitions. In other words, we are looking for,

$$p(t_i, c_i|Y_i) = p(a_i|Y_i) \tag{1}$$

where i denotes the ith line. Both properties are derived from an AST, which is generated by a standard toolkit. For more detailed steps, refer to Algorithm 1 in Appendix B.4.

3.3.2 Syntax-Flow Language Model

To better learn and utilize the syntactical information of the source code, we use the Syntax-Flow language model to first encode docstrings and then generate Syntax-Flow. Here we use a pre-trained auto-regressive language model. We do not do any additional pre-training, so computing resource is restricted to a manageable amount. As shown in Algorithm 2 in Appendix B.4, to fine-tune the language model, we first generate AST from the ground golden source code $|\boldsymbol{y} = (\boldsymbol{y_1}, \boldsymbol{y_2}, \ldots, \boldsymbol{y_n})$. Then we transform the AST of the source code to Syntax-Flow in a deterministic process,

$$a = \text{SYNPARSE}(\text{AST-PARSE}(y)) \tag{2}$$

where SYNPARSE stands for Syntax-Flow Parse. Both SYNPARSE and ASTPARSE are deterministic functions that generate the Syntax-Flow a. We take this as our true reference and model the process as a standard generative task $P_{LM_S}(\hat{a}_i|x, \hat{a}_1...\hat{a}_{i-1})$, namely,

$$\hat{a} = LM_S(x) \tag{3}$$

where x is the input (docstring for code generation). During inference, given a docstring, this language model is able to generate Syntax-Flow directly for the latter use.

3.3.3 Generation of Variable-Flow

We define the format of Variable-Flow in our work similar to that of Syntax-Flow as shown in Figure 2. For each line of code, it has an indentation t followed by $V = [v_1, ..., v_j]$. V is the list of Variable-Flow which can be either variable names or function names. Multiple variable names can exist in the same line. Its sequential nature alleviates language models like T5 during the generation process. Similar to the setup of Syntax-Flow, we are looking for

$$p(t_i, V_i|Y_i) = p(b_i|Y_i) \tag{4}$$

where Y_i is the ith line of source code and $b_i = (t_i, V_i)$.

3.3.4 Variable-Flow Language Model

We generate Variable-Flow from source code $\boldsymbol{y} = (\boldsymbol{y_1}, \boldsymbol{y_2}, \ldots, \boldsymbol{y_n})$. Then we can safely extract Variable-Flow determinedly from AST:

$$b = \text{VARPARSE}(\text{ASTPARSE}(y)) \tag{5}$$

where VARPARSE stands for Variable-Flow Parse. We take this as our true reference and fine-tune the Variable-Flow Language Model on the source code and Variable-Flow pairs. Specifically, we are modeling $P_{LM_V}(\hat{b}_i|x, \hat{b}_1...\hat{b}_{i-1})$. Hence,

$$\hat{b} = LM_V(x) \tag{6}$$

for the ith line. At inference time, the model is expected to generate Variable-Flow for the latter models to encode.

3.4 Phase II – Generation of Code

Code generation is built on the same language model as Syntax-Flow and Variable-Flow language model. However, unlike the generation of Syntax-Flow or Variable-Flow, an issue in the code generation task is that the length of code description is usually much shorter than the length of generated code. For example, in the CodeSearchNet dataset, many function code data length is over 128 tokens while the description only has an average length is about 50 tokens per sequence. This means that the input information is limited and not enough to generate plausible code unless the language model is available to have more prepared features during the code generation process. For this reason, we use the information generated from Phase I as intermediate features to guide the language model generating Python code in Phase II.

3.4.1 Guided Code Generation Language Model

Our Code Generation Language Model depends on the docstring and the corresponding Syntax-Flow and the Variable-Flow. The language model is obtained from a pre-trained auto-regressive language model T5. In our work, we use the T5-based language model as our guided Code Generation Language Model LM_G.

$$\hat{y} = LM_G(x, LM_S(x), LM_V(x)) \quad (7)$$

The Guided Code Generation Language Model takes in the input docstrings x as well as the outputs of the Syntax-Flow Language Model and Variable-Flow Language Model.

4 Experiment

In this section, we present our experiment in detail. First, we introduce the datasets we use and our data processing approach in our experiment. Then, we present our experimental setup. Finally, we introduce our evaluation metrics in the last subsections.

4.1 Datasets

Code Search Net (CSN)[2] (Husain et al., 2019) is collected from publicly available open-source non-forked GitHub repositories. Only projects that are referenced by at least one other project are included. The original paper filters around 500k code-documentation pairs for Python. They removed pairs where either the documents are less than 3 words or methods less than 3 lines. They also removed duplicate code, constructor and extension methods. After processing, there are 412k training data, 22k validation data and 22k test data.

Edinburgh Code-to-Docstring dataset (CDC)[3] (Barone and Sennrich, 2017) is a parallel Python function-to-docstring corpus collected and processed from Github. The Edinburgh Code-to-Docstring dataset contains 150,370 triples of function declarations, docstrings and bodies in the main parallel corpus. This parallel corpus is partitioned into training/ validation/ testing data, in which the training data contains 109,108 training data, 2,000 validation data and 2000 testing data.

CodeSearchNet AdvTest (Adv)[4] (Lu et al., 2021) is a Python dataset derived from the CodeSearchNet (CSN) corpus. The individual example in CodeSearchNet AdvTest is designed for the code search task. (Lu et al., 2021) took the first paragraph of the docstring as the query for the corresponding Python function. The function names and variables are replaced by special tokens, which we recover back with the original variables name. The CodeSearchNet Advtest dataset contains 251,820 training data, 9,640 validation data, and 19,210 testing data.

4.2 Data Processing

In our experiment, we process our data in 3 steps. **(1)** Clean up Raw Code: All Python 2 code is converted to Python 3 using package 2to3[5], and all Python code styles remain consistent with package pep8[6]. Similar with the step of (Clement et al., 2020). We also remove all invalid code samples that cannot be parsed to AST. After cleaning up the raw code, 99.92% code data is remaining. **(2)** Remove comments and docstrings: Comments and docstrings are removed from the code, since these will not be predicted. **(3)** Replace indentation and newline: Indentation and newline is critical for generation a structured Python code. In our work, we replace them with special symbol § for Indentation and δ for newline.

4.3 Experimental Set Up

In both Phases, we use T5-based models. For Phase I and II, the code description is the main source inputs for the encoder.

Encoding Setup. We use the AdamW optimizer for all the T5 models and assign learning rate 1e-4 for Phase I and Phase II. The training step for Phase I is kept at 75K and batch size at 32. The training step for Phase II is kept at 100K and batch size at 32.The learning scheduler is inverse root square and has warm-up step of 5000 for phase I and 10000 for Phase II.

Decoding Setup. Both Phase I and Phase II take length 512 as input and have output length of 128 for phase I and 256 for Phase II. The beam size is 5 for all Phases fine-tuning. We add repetition penalty of 2 for Syntax-Flow and Variable-Flow generation considering the case that repeated statements occur frequently. All the tasks are run on the two Nvidia GeForce A6000 with 48GB GPU memory each.

Evaluation. For our experimental evaluation, we use the metrics BLEU (Papineni et al., 2002),

[2]https://github.com/github/CodeSearchNet

[3]https://github.com/EdinburghNLP/code-docstring-corpus

[4]https://github.com/microsoft/CodeXGLUE

[5]https://pypi.org/project/2to3/

[6]https://pypi.org/project/autopep8/

	Rouge1-F1	Rouge2-F1	RougeL-F1	BLEU
CSN Syntax-Flow	49.1	35.8	47.7	12.7
CSN Variable-Flow	36.7	15.7	33.7	11.4
CDC Syntax-Flow	51.8	41.4	50.4	15.2
CDC Variable-Flow	37.4	18.9	34.8	11.9
Adv Syntax-Flow	50.4	36.9	48.9	13.6
Adv Variable-Flow	37.3	15.6	34.0	11.1

Table 1: The results of Syntax-Flow and Variable-Flow generation for all three datasets in Phase I with T5. The performance is evaluated through Rouge and BLUE.

	Rouge1-F1	Rouge2-F1	RougeL-F1	BLEU	CodeBLEU
CSN	31.1	12.1	27.9	21.2	22.1
CDC	**32.3**	**15.7**	**29.3**	**22.6**	**22.4**
Adv	29.8	11.0	26.7	20.7	20.9

Table 2: The results of Python code generation for CSN, CDC and Adv in Phase II using GAP-Gen pipeline with T5. The performance is evaluated through Rouge, BLUE and CodeBLEU.

ROUGE (Lin, 2004) and CodeBLUE (Ren et al., 2020). BLUE and Rouge are the most common metrics to evaluate generated text. CodeBLUE is a metric specifically designed for the evaluation of generated programming languages. Apart from the similarity of the tokens, it also considers the syntax of commands and logic.

5 Results and Analysis

In this section, we first present our Phase I experimental results, which contain the performance of Syntax-Flow and Variable-Flow generation on the CSN, CDC, and Adv Test datasets. Then, we present our Phase II experimental results on CSN, CDC, and Adv Test datasets. We train our models on each dataset's training data, and run evaluations on the corresponding testing data. Finally, we compare our approach's performance on automatic Python code generation task with previous works.

5.1 Results of Phase I

Syntax-Flow Results. We first show our results on generating Syntax-Flow using T5 language model. We evaluate the generated Syntax-Flow with Rouge and BLEU metrics, as shown in Table 1. The Syntax-Flow performance of CSN, CDC, and Adv is around 50% in Rouge-F1 and Rouge-F2, and over 35% in Rouge-F2. These results are good considering the real vocabulary size used in Syntax-Flow is relatively smaller and syntax tokens are generally similar. When we make a comparison among the three corpora, results from CDC are slightly better than that of Adv and CSN for all the metrics consistently. CDC is a well-organized dataset that's specifically designed for Python automatic code generation task. Considering Adv is derived from CSN and thus more organized, there is only 1.3% in Rouge score and 1% in BLEU improvement.

Variable-Flow Results. We evaluate our generated Variable-Flow results from code docstrings using the Rouge and BLEU metrics. Our evaluation results regarding the generated Variable-Flow are shown in Table 1. Similar to the results in Syntax-Flow, the performance of Variable-Flow in CDC is slightly better than the other two datasets for all the metrics scores. The average results of the Variable-Flow are not as good as those of Syntax-Flow because the generation of Variable-Flow variant components is much more difficult than the Syntax-Flow invariant components. Moreover, over 95% of Syntax-Flow samples' lengths are shorter than 125 tokens. The Rouge F1 is over 35% and Rouge F2 is over 15% on average.

5.2 Results of Phase II

From Table 2, we observe the performance of final Python code generation with Rouge, BLEU and CodeBLEU. The result of CDC is the best among the three corpora because of its cleaner data as well as the effect of better Phase I performance (Syntax-Flow and Variable-Flow). CSN's results were slightly better than Adv's since CSN had about twice as much training data as Adv. As we can see from Table 3, the performance of GAP-Gen slightly outperforms the T5 model that's directly

	Rouge1-F1	Rouge2-F1	RougeL-F1	BLEU	CodeBLEU
GPT2 (Clement et al., 2020)	20.9	7.6	21.9	2.8	–
PyMT5 (Clement et al., 2020)	28.4	13.5	24.8	8.6	–
T5	30.4	11.7	27.4	20.7	21.7
GAP-Gen T5	**31.1**	**12.1**	**27.9**	**21.2**	**22.1**
CodeT5 (Wang et al., 2021)	34.6	14.6	30.2	21.6	23.4
GAP-Gen CodeT5	**35.1**	**14.9**	**30.6**	**22.3**	**24.1**

Table 3: The results of GAP-Gen with other models fine-tuning on CSN datasets for Python code generation task. We report the Rouge, BLUE and CodeBLEU score for all different models, where GAP-Gen T5 and GAP-Gen CodeT5 are the models built on the T5 and CodeT5 model separately using GAP-Gen pipeline.

trained to generate Python code for both Rouge and BLEU metrics. It indicates that our pipeline approach is effective in improving Python code generation. Similar conclusion can be proved by fine-tuning the CodeT5 language model with our GAP-Gen training pipeline. We apply our training pipeline with CodeT5 in Phase II and show that GAP-Gen CodeT5 achieves the best Rouge, BLEU and CodeBLEU scores compared with other models on the same fine-tuning task.

There is a large gap between GAP-Gen and PyMT5 on BLEU and CodeBLEU, which is because PyMT5 generates sequence with max tokens 1024. We limit the maximum target length to 256, which covers about 75% of code lengths. Based on our comparison between T5 and GAP-Gen, the results of GAP-Gen have improved due to the prerequisite of Syntax-Flow and Variable-Flow generation.

5.3 Discussion

Unlike other works focused on pre-training, we design a pipeline approach to achieve a better fine-tuning result. Given the same training configuration, our results prove that there is an improvement derived from using docstring, Syntax-Flow and Variable-Flow together, as compared to using the docstring only. Code generation is a translation task but has its own difficulties. First, our docstring inputs are usually very short, while code outputs are long. For example, there is about 85% of the input sequences in CSN, CDC, and Adv are less than 128 tokens while over half of codes that are longer than 128 tokens. Moreover, code has stricter syntax and less ambivalent semantics. Our pipeline, by dividing the load of generating syntax and semantic information to multiple language models, bypasses the above difficulties and achieves better generation results.

The data leaking issue exists in many previous works using the pre-training technique on the automatic code generation task. For example, in previous work (Clement et al., 2020), the dataset CodeSearchNet used for fine-tuning overlaps with their data used for pre-training. Both of them are collected from the public github repositories. Data leaking will tend to result in high performance on the fine-tuning task but usually is dubious in practice because model should generalize on the unseen data. In our work, we fine-tune our model using T5 which is not pre-trained on existing Code-to-Docstring datasets. Hence, T5 does not have the data leaking problem. However, CodeT5 is pre-trained on the CSN dataset, which may lead to the data leaking problem in code generation task. This can be the reason that CodeT5 alone without using our training pipeline can achieve very good results. However, after we fine-tune CodeT5 using our training pipeline, CodeT5 shows better performance on the Python code generation task, as you can see in Table 2.

At the same time, due to the computational resources limitation, the maximum batch size we can use is 32. Although we are limited by computational resources, we still achieve result improvements in the code generation task. In the future, better computational resources would probably increase the performance further.

6 Conclusions

In this work, we demonstrate the effectiveness of injecting Python syntactic and semantic information into the code generation tasks. We design and implement two different types of information components: Syntax-Flow and Variable-Flow. To incorporate this information, we encode them using separate language models and then feed them along with the docstring input into the final language model. Pre-trained language models fine-tuned with our proposed pipeline show better performances over state-of-the-art code generation models. For future directions, new strategies for incorporating that information can be explored.

References

Wasi Uddin Ahmad, Saikat Chakraborty, Baishakhi Ray, and Kai-Wei Chang. 2020. A transformer-based approach for source code summarization. *ArXiv*, abs/2005.00653.

Bruce W. Ballard and Alan W. Biermann. 1979. Programming in natural language: "nlc" as a prototype. In *ACM '79*.

Antonio Valerio Miceli Barone and Rico Sennrich. 2017. A parallel corpus of python functions and documentation strings for automated code documentation and code generation. In *IJCNLP*.

Paweł Budzianowski and Ivan Vulic. 2019. Hello, it's gpt-2 - how can i help you? towards the use of pre-trained language models for task-oriented dialogue systems. In *EMNLP*.

Nicola De Cao, Gautier Izacard, Sebastian Riedel, and Fabio Petroni. 2021. Autoregressive entity retrieval. *ArXiv*, abs/2010.00904.

Leshem Choshen, Lior Fox, Zohar Aizenbud, and Omri Abend. 2020. On the weaknesses of reinforcement learning for neural machine translation. *ArXiv*, abs/1907.01752.

Colin B. Clement, Dawn Drain, Jonathan Timcheck, Alexey Svyatkovskiy, and Neel Sundaresan. 2020. Pymt5: Multi-mode translation of natural language and python code with transformers. *ArXiv*, abs/2010.03150.

Aditya Desai, Sumit Gulwani, Vineeta Lokhande Hingorani, Nidhi Jain, Amey Karkare, Mark Marron, R Sailesh, and Subhajit Roy. 2016. Program synthesis using natural language. *2016 IEEE/ACM 38th International Conference on Software Engineering (ICSE)*, pages 345–356.

Jacob Devlin, Ming-Wei Chang, Kenton Lee, and Kristina Toutanova. 2019. Bert: Pre-training of deep bidirectional transformers for language understanding. In *NAACL*.

Kawin Ethayarajh. 2019. How contextual are contextualized word representations? comparing the geometry of bert, elmo, and gpt-2 embeddings. In *EMNLP*.

Angela Fan, Mike Lewis, and Yann Dauphin. 2018. Hierarchical neural story generation. In *ACL*.

Zhangyin Feng, Daya Guo, Duyu Tang, Nan Duan, Xiaocheng Feng, Ming Gong, Linjun Shou, Bing Qin, Ting Liu, Daxin Jiang, and Ming Zhou. 2020. Codebert: A pre-trained model for programming and natural languages. *ArXiv*, abs/2002.08155.

Seraphina Goldfarb-Tarrant, Tuhin Chakrabarty, Ralph M. Weischedel, and Nanyun Peng. 2020. Content planning for neural story generation with aristotelian rescoring. In *EMNLP*.

Sumit Gulwani and Mark Marron. 2014. Nlyze: interactive programming by natural language for spreadsheet data analysis and manipulation. In *SIGMOD Conference*, pages 803–814. ACM.

Daya Guo, Shuo Ren, Shuai Lu, Zhangyin Feng, Duyu Tang, Shujie Liu, Long Zhou, Nan Duan, Alexey Svyatkovskiy, Shengyu Fu, Michele Tufano, Shao Kun Deng, Colin Clement, Dawn Drain, Neel Sundaresan, Jian Yin, Daxin Jiang, and Ming Zhou. 2021. Graphcodebert: Pre-training code representations with data flow.

Kelvin Guu, Kenton Lee, Zora Tung, Panupong Pasupat, and Ming-Wei Chang. 2020. Realm: Retrieval-augmented language model pre-training. *ArXiv*, abs/2002.08909.

Ari Holtzman, Jan Buys, Maxwell Forbes, and Yejin Choi. 2020. The curious case of neural text degeneration. *ArXiv*, abs/1904.09751.

Hamel Husain, Hongqi Wu, Tiferet Gazit, Miltiadis Allamanis, and Marc Brockschmidt. 2019. Codesearchnet challenge: Evaluating the state of semantic code search. *ArXiv*, abs/1909.09436.

Sarthak Jain and Byron C. Wallace. 2019. Attention is not explanation. In *NAACL*.

Aditya Kanade, Petros Maniatis, Gogul Balakrishnan, and Kensen Shi. 2020. Learning and evaluating contextual embedding of source code.

Rohit J. Kate, Yuk Wah Wong, and Raymond J. Mooney. 2005. Learning to transform natural to formal languages. In *AAAI*, pages 1062–1068. AAAI Press / The MIT Press.

Olga Kovaleva, Alexey Romanov, Anna Rogers, and Anna Rumshisky. 2019. Revealing the dark secrets of bert. *ArXiv*, abs/1908.08593.

Evgeny Lagutin, Daniil Gavrilov, and Pavel Kalaidin. 2021. Implicit unlikelihood training: Improving neural text generation with reinforcement learning. *ArXiv*, abs/2101.04229.

Vu Le, Sumit Gulwani, and Zhendong Su. 2013. Smartsynth: synthesizing smartphone automation scripts from natural language. In *MobiSys '13*.

Mike Lewis, Yinhan Liu, Naman Goyal, Marjan Ghazvininejad, Abdelrahman Mohamed, Omer Levy, Veselin Stoyanov, and Luke Zettlemoyer. 2020. Bart: Denoising sequence-to-sequence pre-training for natural language generation, translation, and comprehension. *ArXiv*, abs/1910.13461.

Chin-Yew Lin. 2004. Rouge: A package for automatic evaluation of summaries. In *ACL 2004*.

Wang Ling, Phil Blunsom, Edward Grefenstette, Karl Moritz Hermann, Tomás Kociský, Fumin Wang, and Andrew W. Senior. 2016. Latent predictor networks for code generation. *ArXiv*, abs/1603.06744.

Greg Little and Rob Miller. 2006. Translating keyword commands into executable code. In *UIST*.

F. Liu, Ge Li, Yunfei Zhao, and Zhi Jin. 2020. Multi-task learning based pre-trained language model for code completion. *2020 35th IEEE/ACM International Conference on Automated Software Engineering (ASE)*, pages 473–485.

Shuai Lu, Daya Guo, Shuo Ren, Junjie Huang, Alexey Svyatkovskiy, Ambrosio Blanco, Colin Clement, Dawn Drain, Daxin Jiang, Duyu Tang, Ge Li, Lidong Zhou, Linjun Shou, Long Zhou, Michele Tufano, Ming Gong, Ming Zhou, Nan Duan, Neel Sundaresan, Shao Kun Deng, Shengyu Fu, and Shujie Liu. 2021. Codexglue: A machine learning benchmark dataset for code understanding and generation. *ArXiv*, abs/2102.04664.

Clara Meister, Tim Vieira, and Ryan Cotterell. 2020. If beam search is the answer, what was the question? *ArXiv*, abs/2010.02650.

Kishore Papineni, Salim Roukos, Todd Ward, and Wei-Jing Zhu. 2002. Bleu: a method for automatic evaluation of machine translation. In *Proceedings of the 40th Annual Meeting of the Association for Computational Linguistics*, pages 311–318, Philadelphia, Pennsylvania, USA. Association for Computational Linguistics.

David Price, Ellen Riloff, Joseph L. Zachary, and Brandon Harvey. 2000. Naturaljava: a natural language interface for programming in java. In *IUI '00*.

Chris Quirk, Raymond J. Mooney, and Michel Galley. 2015. Language to code: Learning semantic parsers for if-this-then-that recipes. In *ACL*.

Alec Radford, Jeff Wu, Rewon Child, David Luan, Dario Amodei, and Ilya Sutskever. 2019. Language models are unsupervised multitask learners.

Colin Raffel, Noam Shazeer, Adam Roberts, Katherine Lee, Sharan Narang, Michael Matena, Yanqi Zhou, Wei Li, and Peter J. Liu. 2020a. Exploring the limits of transfer learning with a unified text-to-text transformer.

Colin Raffel, Noam M. Shazeer, Adam Roberts, Katherine Lee, Sharan Narang, Michael Matena, Yanqi Zhou, Wei Li, and Peter J. Liu. 2020b. Exploring the limits of transfer learning with a unified text-to-text transformer. *ArXiv*, abs/1910.10683.

K. M. Tahsin Hassan Rahit, Rashidul Hasan Nabil, and Md Hasibul Huq. 2019. Machine translation from natural language to code using long-short term memory. *ArXiv*, abs/1910.11471.

Hannah Rashkin, Asli Çelikyilmaz, Yejin Choi, and Jianfeng Gao. 2020. Plotmachines: Outline-conditioned generation with dynamic plot state tracking. In *EMNLP*.

Shuo Ren, Daya Guo, Shuai Lu, Long Zhou, Shujie Liu, Duyu Tang, M. Zhou, Ambrosio Blanco, and Shuai Ma. 2020. Codebleu: a method for automatic evaluation of code synthesis. *ArXiv*, abs/2009.10297.

A. See, Aneesh S. Pappu, Rohun Saxena, Akhila Yerukola, and Christopher D. Manning. 2019. Do massively pretrained language models make better storytellers? *ArXiv*, abs/1909.10705.

Alexey Svyatkovskiy, Shao Kun Deng, Shengyu Fu, and Neel Sundaresan. 2020. Intellicode compose: Code generation using transformer. In *Proceedings of the 28th ACM Joint Meeting on European Software Engineering Conference and Symposium on the Foundations of Software Engineering*, ESEC/FSE 2020, page 1433–1443, New York, NY, USA. Association for Computing Machinery.

Ashish Vaswani, Noam M. Shazeer, Niki Parmar, Jakob Uszkoreit, Llion Jones, Aidan N. Gomez, Lukasz Kaiser, and Illia Polosukhin. 2017. Attention is all you need. *ArXiv*, abs/1706.03762.

Alex Wang, Amanpreet Singh, Julian Michael, Felix Hill, Omer Levy, and Samuel R. Bowman. 2018. Glue: A multi-task benchmark and analysis platform for natural language understanding. *ArXiv*, abs/1804.07461.

Yue Wang, Weishi Wang, Shafiq Joty, and Steven C. H. Hoi. 2021. Codet5: Identifier-aware unified pre-trained encoder-decoder models for code understanding and generation.

Sean Welleck, Ilia Kulikov, Stephen Roller, Emily Dinan, Kyunghyun Cho, and Jason Weston. 2020. Neural text generation with unlikelihood training. *ArXiv*, abs/1908.04319.

Lili Yao, Nanyun Peng, Ralph M. Weischedel, Kevin Knight, Dongyan Zhao, and Rui Yan. 2019. Plan-and-write: Towards better automatic storytelling. *ArXiv*, abs/1811.05701.

Pengcheng Yin and Graham Neubig. 2017. A syntactic neural model for general-purpose code generation. In *ACL*.

Xiaohan Yu, Quzhe Huang, Zongge Wang, Yansong Feng, and Dongyan Zhao. 2020. Towards context-aware code comment generation. In *FINDINGS*.

Yuhao Zhang, Derek Merck, Emily B Tsai, Christopher D. Manning, and C. Langlotz. 2020. Optimizing the factual correctness of a summary: A study of summarizing radiology reports. In *ACL*.

A Appendix

B Ablation Study

B.1 Effectiveness of Syntax-Flow

In order to show the effectiveness of Syntax-Flow on improving the language model's capability for the Python code generation task, we make comparisons between the results of T5 fine-tuned with docstrings only and T5 fine-tuned with docstrings and Syntax-Flow shown in Table 4. Based on the comparisons of the results, we can observe that T5$__{Syntax-Flow}$ has outperformed the performance of T5 on the majority of evaluation metric scores. Since code has a tree structure and needs to be compiled based on the corresponding AST, it is particularly important to make sure that the syntactic structure included in the generated code is correct. In T5$__{Syntax-Flow}$, we inject the syntactic structure of code, the Syntax-Flow, into the fine-tuning process of the T5 model so that the T5 can learn how the syntactic structure of code should be incorporated to generate higher quality code, a fact which we believe is the reason that T5$__{Syntax-Flow}$ has better code generation performance.

B.2 Effectiveness of Variable-Flow

We also make experiments to show the effectiveness of Variable-Flow for the Python code generation task. Similarly, we make comparisons between the results of T5 fine-tuned with docstrings only and T5 fine-tuned with docstrings and Variable-Flow shown in Table 4. As we can observe from the result comparison, T5$__{Variable-Flow}$ only does not achieve significant improvements regarding the evaluation metric scores and we believe that there are two potential reasons causing this to happen. First, comparing the evaluation score of the generated Syntax-Flow with that of Variable-Flow shown in Table 1, we can see that the generated Variable-Flow's evaluation scores are worse than that of the Syntax-Flow. It happens because the length of generated Variable-Flow is much longer than that of Syntax-Flow due to the characteristics of Variable-Flow that it supposes to contain general semantic information of code. Second, due to the longer length of the generated Variable-Flow, the inputs to T5$__{Variable-Flow}$ are much longer than that of T5$__{Syntax-Flow}$, and T5$__{Variable-Flow}$ does not know which line of generated code the variable should be assigned to because of the lack of syntac-

	Rouge1-F1	Rouge2-F1	RougeL-F1	BLEU	CodeBLEU
T5	30.4	11.7	27.4	20.7	21.7
T5-Syntax-Flow	30.9	12.1	27.7	20.7	21.9
T5-Variable-Flow	30.5	11.8	27.4	20.6	21.7
GAP-Gen-T5	**31.1**	**12.1**	**27.9**	**21.2**	**22.1**

Table 4: Results Comparisons of GAP-Gen-T5 components on CSN datasets for Python code generation task.

Docstrings:
Method used to retrieve the contents of a log file into a list.
Parameters ---------- path
Returns ---------- list or None
Contents of the provided file, each line as a list entry

Reference code:

```
def _retrieve_log(path):
  if (not os.path.exists(path)):
    return None
  with open(path) as fh:
    return fh.readlines()
```

T5 Generated Code:

```
def _read_log_file(self, path):
  with open(path, 'r') as f:
    lines = f.readlines()
  return lines
```

GAP-Gen T5 Generated Code:

```
def read_log_file(self, path):
  with open(path, 'r') as f:
    lines = f.readlines()
  if (not lines):
    return None
  return lines
```

Figure 3: Sample code generated from the docstring in CSN datasets. **The most left code** is the golden standard reference code. **The middle code** is generated directly from T5 fine-tuned with docstring. **The most right code** is generated using our GAP-Gen fine-tuning pipeline.

Docstrings:
Find out what items are documented in source/*.rst.
See `find_autosummary_in_lines`.

Reference Code:

```
def find_autosummary_in_files(filenames):
  documented = []
  for filename in filenames:
    f = open(filename, 'r')
    lines = f.read().splitlines()
    documented.extend(
          find_autosummary_in_lines
          (lines, filename=filename))
    f.close()
  return documented
```

T5 Generated Code:

```
def find_docs(source):
  docs = []
  for line in find_autosummary_in_lines
        (source):
    docs.append(line)
  return docs
```

GAP_Gen T5 Generated Code:

```
def find_docstrings_in_source_files(source_files):
  docstrings = []
  for source_file in source_files:
    with open(source_file) as f:
      docstrings.extend(
          find_autosummary_in_lines(f))
  return docstrings
```

Figure 4: Sample code generated from the docstring in CSN datasets.

tic structure information, then much longer code is likely to be generated. However, the effectiveness of Variable-Flow can also be reflected from the loss of T5 with Variable-Flow only from Figure 6. A lower perplexity can be obtained, and the generated code is more fluent on average.

B.3 Samples Analysis

To illustrate the usefulness of our proposed Syntax-Flow and Variable-Flow components, we have attached the generated Python code samples using Syntax-Flow and Variable-Flow with the corresponding docstrings in the CSN dataset. We have also provided sample analysis of them in the following paragraphs.

As we have demonstrated in our paper, in order to generate well-working Python code, the language model should not only understand the text semantic information from a given docstring but also should be capable of considering the code syntactic information and the code variable semantic information.

Based on the given sample codes shown in Figure 3, it is clear that the code, which is generated directly from T5 without having Syntax-Flow and Variable-Flow injected, cannot properly handle both the code syntactic information and the code variable semantic information. For example, the docstring specifies that the code should return a list or None variable, suggesting that there are 2 different return values that should be generated under different conditions. As a result, the fine-tuned model should consider both the code syntax logic, the boolean operation, and the variable semantic, the generated variables, during the code generation process. However, due to the lack of Syntax-Flow and Variable-Flow components, the T5 model fine-tuned with docstring only is unable to learn the code syntactic information and the code variable semantic information, resulting in the fine-tuned model generates code that is not able to determine where the boolean operation should be generated to handle multiple return values. Similar trends happen in the sample codes shown in Figure 4 as well.

In contrast, in our work GAP-Gen, we consider the Syntax-Flow and Variable-Flow during the code generation process. Due to the support of these two components, we can successfully generate a higher-quality code with the boolean operation and different return values.

B.4 Training Algorithms

In this subsection, we include the training algorithms for **1.** generating the Syntax-Flow and Variable-Flow, and **2.** fine-tuning the pre-trained Language Model with Syntax-Flow and Variable-Flow.

Algorithm 1 Generate Syntax-Flow & Variable-Flow

Require:
$x = (x_1, x_2, ..., x_n) \in X$: input docstring
LM_S: Language Model being used for Syntax-Flow
LM_V: Language Model being used for Variable-Flow
Ensure:
$A = (a_1, a_2, ..., a_n)$: Syntax-Flow
$B = (b_1, b_2, ..., b_k)$: k Variable-Flow
Initialize A, B to be empty arrays
for each docstring:$x \in X$ **do**
    $a \leftarrow LM_S(x)$
    $b \leftarrow LM_V(x)$
    Append(A,a)
    Append(A,a)
end for
return A,B

B.5 Code Generation Loss Analysis

We further analyze the loss trend for generating the Python code using T5 and our GAP-Gen training pipeline. In our analysis, we show three loss trend comparisons:

Algorithm 2 Fine-tuning Language Model with Syntax-Flow

Require:
$x = (x_1, x_2, ..., x_n) \in X$: input docstring
LM_S: Pre-trained Language Model being used for Syntax-Flow
Ensure:
LM_S: Language Model fine-tuned for generating Syntax-Flow
Initialize D to be empty array
for each docstring:$x \in X$ **do**
    $p \leftarrow$ ASTPARSE(X) AST parsed by standard Python AST parser
    $d \leftarrow$ SYNPARSE(p)
    Append(D,d)
end for
for i = 1 to |X| **do**
    $a' \leftarrow LM_S(X[i])$
    $l = loss(D[i], a')$
    $LM_S.backwards(l)$
end for
return LM_S

- T5 vs GAP-Gen with Syntax-Flow only in Figure 5,
- T5 vs GAP-Gen with Variable-Flow only in Figure 6,
- T5 vs GAP-Gen with both Syntax-Flow and Variable-Flow in Figure 8.

Based on our observations, we find the global loss trends between T5 and GAP-Gen are similar. However, when we zoom into the last 10k steps, the training and validation loss of GAP-Gen are consistently lower than those of T5 on the Python code generation task from all three scenarios.

By comparing with the loss trend between T5 and GAP-Gen with Syntax-Flow only and GAP-Gen with Variable-Flow only, we find both scenarios have lower training and validation loss in the last 10k steps than those of T5. This fact shows that both of Syntax-Flow and Variable-Flow are contributing to the Language Model fine-tuning process. At the same time, we find GAP-Gen with both the Variable-Flow and Syntax-Flow results in the lowest training and validation loss compared with those of the other two scenarios. This finding further illustrates that our method GAP-Gen does have improvement on the Python code generation task.

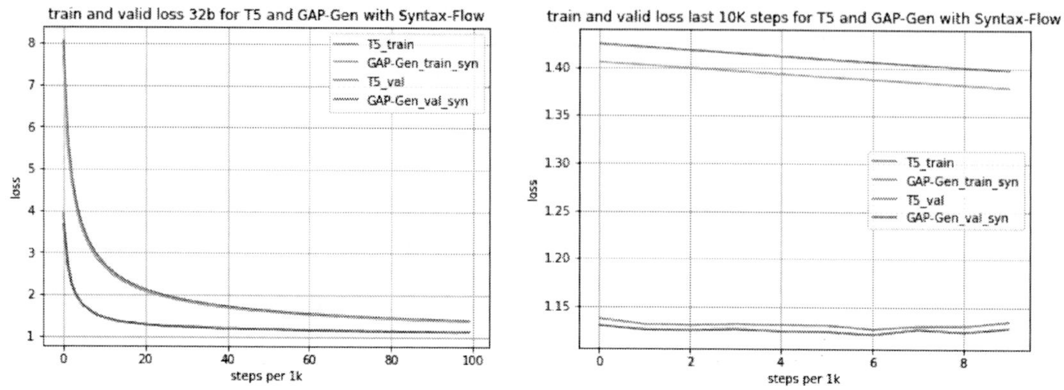

Figure 5: Loss comparison visualization between T5 and GAP-Gen using Syntax-Flow only.

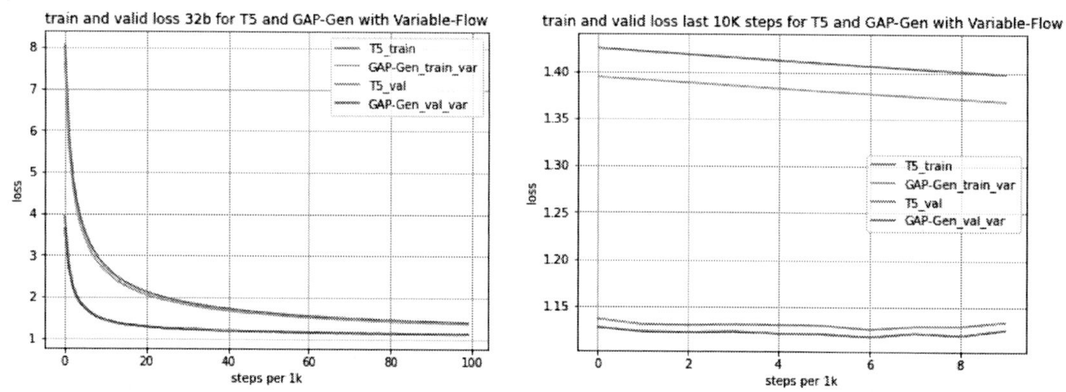

Figure 6: Loss comparison visualization between T5 and GAP-Gen using Variable-Flow only.

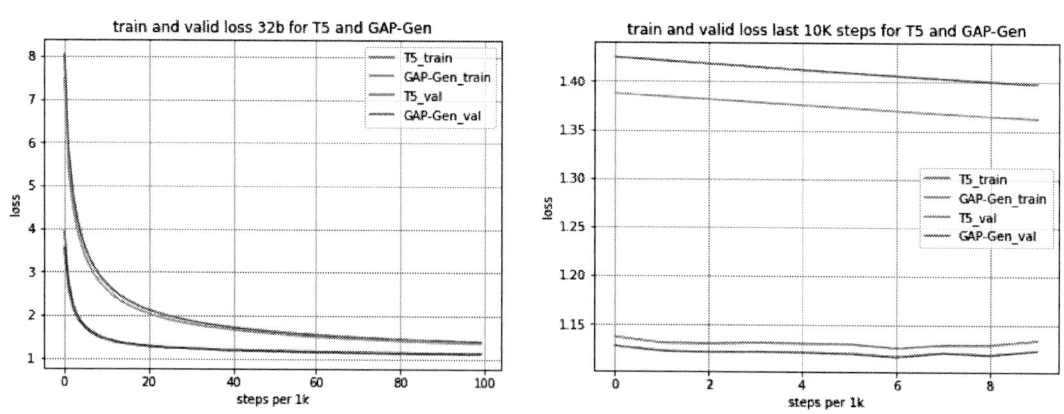

Figure 7: Loss comparison visualization between T5 and GAP-Gen.

Docstrings:
Lists all of the reports currently available.

Reference Code:
```
def reports_list(request):
    reports = []
    for report in get_all_reports():
        reports.append({'name': report.__name__, 'url':
            reverse(report), 'description': report.__doc__})
    reports.sort(key=(lambda report: report['name']))
    ctx = {'reports': reports}
    return render(request,'registrasion/reports_list.html', ctx)
```

T5 Generated Code:
```
def list_reports(self):
    if (self._reports is None):
        self._reports = []
        for report in self.get_reports():
            self._reports.append(report)
```

GAP_Gen T5 Generated Code:
```
def list_reports(self):
    report_list = []
    for report in self.reports:
        report_list.append(report)
    return sorted(report_list, key=(lambda x: x[0]))
```

Docstrings:
Build a file path from *paths* and return the contents

Reference Code:
```
def read(*paths):
    with open(os.path.join(*paths), 'r')
        as file_handler:
    return file_handler.read()
```

T5 Generated Code:
```
def read(*paths):
    for path in paths:
        path = os.path.expanduser(path)
        if os.path.exists(path):
            with open(path, 'r') as f:
                return f.read()
    return ''
```

GAP_Gen T5 Generated Code:
```
def read(*paths):
    with open(os.path.join(*paths), 'r') as f:
     return f.read()
```

Docstrings:
Validate that all required type methods are implemented.
    At minimum a type must have:
    - a convert() or convert_binary() function
    - a default_formatter() function
    Raises an ArgumentError if the type is not valid

Reference Code:
```
def _validate_type(cls, typeobj):
    if (not (hasattr(typeobj, 'convert') or hasattr(typeobj, 'convert_binary'))):
        raise ArgumentError('type is invalid, does not have convert or convert_binary function',
            type=typeobj, methods=dir(typeobj))
    if (not hasattr(typeobj, 'default_formatter')):
        raise ArgumentError('type is invalid, does not have default_formatter function',
            type=typeobj, methods=dir(typeobj))
```

T5 Generated Code:
```
def validate_type_methods(self):
    for method_name in dir(self):
        method = getattr(self, method_name)
        if (not hasattr(method, 'convert')):
            raise ArgumentError(('Method %s must have a convert() or convert_binary() function'
                % method_name))
        if (not hasattr(method, 'default_formatter')):
            raise ArgumentError(('Method %s must have a default_formatter function' % method_name))
```

T5-GAP-Gen Generated Code:
```
def _validate_type(self, type):
    if (not hasattr(type, 'convert')):
        raise ArgumentError('Type must have a convert() or convert_binary() function')
    if (not hasattr(type, 'default_formatter')):
        raise ArgumentError('Type must have a default_formatter function')
```

Figure 8: Additional generated sample codes from our experiments.

Development of pre-trained language models for clinical NLP in Spanish

Claudio Aracena[1,2] **and Jocelyn Dunstan**[2,3,4,5]
[1]Faculty of Physical and Mathematical Sciences, University of Chile
[2]Millennium Institute Foundational Research on Data, Chile
[3]Department of Computer Science, Pontifical Catholic University of Chile
[4]Institute for Computational Mathematics, Pontifical Catholic University of Chile
[5]Center for Mathematical Modeling, University of Chile
claudio.aracena@uchile.cl, jdunstan@uc.cl

Abstract

Clinical natural language processing aims to tackle language and prediction tasks using text from medical practice, such as clinical notes, prescriptions, and discharge summaries. Several approaches have been tried to deal with these tasks. Since 2017, pre-trained language models (PLMs) have achieved state-of-the-art performance in many tasks. However, most works have been developed in English. This PhD research proposal addresses the development of PLMs for clinical NLP in Spanish. To carry out this study, we will build a clinical corpus big enough to implement a functional PLM. We will test several PLM architectures and evaluate them with language and prediction tasks. The novelty of this work lies in the use of only clinical text, while previous clinical PLMs have used a mix of general, biomedical, and clinical text.

1 Introduction

Clinical text is one of the richest forms of information in electronic health records. Therefore, developing tools to extract useful information from clinical text has become relevant in clinical natural language processing (NLP). However, processing unstructured text is challenging due to the complexity of human languages. Moreover, the clinical text has its own complexities, including non-standard abbreviations, misspellings, specific vocabulary, and jargon (Dalianis, 2018).

Clinical NLP aims to address several tasks in this complex scenario. These tasks can range from language tasks such as extracting entities, text classification, and relation extraction, among others, to prediction tasks such as predicting patient mortality, length of hospital stay, unplanned readmissions, etc. Several works have been carried out to tackle these tasks generating specific models.

However, since 2017, the NLP field has worked towards the creation of pre-trained language models (PLMs) that can be fine-tuned for any specific downstream task. These language models are built for a much simpler task, such as next-word or masked-word prediction in a huge amount of text. This process, known as pre-training, allows the language model to acquire language understanding that can be used for any text-related task (Tunstall et al., 2022).

As soon as the NLP field started to work in PLMs, clinical NLP introduced this type of model into its set of techniques to improve performance in its own tasks. Some examples of clinical PLMs are two different versions of ClinicalBERT (Alsentzer et al., 2019; Huang et al., 2020). These models show a significant improvement in language tasks and a moderate improvement in prediction tasks.

Most of the research in clinical NLP has been done for text written in English, but not so much for other languages (Névéol et al., 2018). In Spanish, some publicly available PLMs relevant to clinical NLP are bsc-bio-ehr-es (Carrino et al., 2022) and Spanish Clinical Flair (Rojas et al., 2022). These PLMs were pre-trained heavily in general and biomedical text with some additions of clinical text. Despite this drawback, they outperform general and biomedical PLMs in language tasks.

There are two approaches to evaluate PLMs, intrinsic and extrinsic. An intrinsic approach measures the model quality independently of an application in any specific task. Examples of intrinsic metrics are perplexity and word similarity. Meanwhile, an extrinsic approach evaluates the model performance in downstream tasks, such as text classification or named entity recognition (NER). Extrinsic evaluations are more expensive and time-consuming than intrinsic evaluations (Jurafsky and Martin, 2021).

In Biomedical NLP, some relevant benchmarks have been developed for extrinsic evaluations, such as BLUE (Peng et al., 2019) and BLURB (Gu et al., 2021). Given their close relation to the clinical context, they are also used to evaluate clinical PLMs.

Proceedings of the 17th Conference of the European Chapter of the Association for Computational Linguistics: Student Research Workshop, pages 52–60
May 2-4, 2023

However, these benchmarks are built with tasks in English. There are no such benchmarks in Spanish, thus the research community evaluates their models in downstream tasks for biomedical and clinical corpora. Most of these downstream tasks are language tasks, and few works focus on prediction tasks.

In this research proposal, we aim to develop clinical PLMs in Spanish using mostly clinical text and evaluate them with intrinsic and extrinsic approaches. The expected results are as follows:

- The development of a PLM in Spanish with a large clinical corpus, instead of general or biomedical text, will improve performance in intrinsic and extrinsic clinical evaluations.
- The clinical PLM will perform similarly in language tasks compared to existing PLMs, but it will outperform them for prediction tasks. This work focuses on prediction tasks due to their applicability to real problems. Thus, the expected results aim for better performance in prediction tasks.

This research proposal shows a literature review of PLMs architectures for general, biomedical, and clinical domains. Then, it states the research questions and their implications. Later, it describes the methodology to carry out this research and details the expected results.

2 Literature review

Since the creation of transformers (Vaswani et al., 2017) and ULMFiT (Howard and Ruder, 2018), we have witnessed the development of several PLMs that have become state-of-the-art on different tasks. Starting with GPT (Radford et al., 2018) and BERT (Devlin et al., 2019), continuing with RoBERTa (Liu et al., 2019), and DeBERTa (He et al., 2021b,a), among others, the research community has focused on finding new architectures that can beat current benchmarks and apply them in many areas as possible.

One of the areas where it is possible to find several PLMs is health. Just a few months after the publication of BERT, PLMs using clinical text were released (Alsentzer et al., 2019; Huang et al., 2020). Moreover, even though PLMs are built mostly for English text, it is still possible to find clinical and biomedical PLMs for Spanish (Carrino et al., 2022; Rojas et al., 2022).

This section introduces PLMs in the clinical and biomedical fields and describes significant clinical and biomedical PLMs in English and Spanish. Also, it shows some evaluation benchmarks and tasks for biomedical and clinical NLP in English and Spanish.

2.1 Biomedical and Clinical PLMs for English

Biomedical PLMs refer to models pre-trained in medical text from academic sources, such as scientific publications. Meanwhile, clinical PLMs refer to models pre-trained in medical text from the medical practice, such as clinical notes and prescriptions.

2.1.1 BioBERT

Following BERT's success, other fields created their own versions of this model. BioBERT was the first BERT-based PLM pre-trained in a biomedical corpus (Lee et al., 2020). Using BERT architecture, BioBERT was pre-trained with the English Wikipedia, BookCorpus (Zhu et al., 2015), PubMed abstracts, and PubMedCentral (PMC) full-text articles, totaling 21 billion words. BioBERT was fine-tuned on a series of biomedical NLP tasks, such as NER, relation extraction (RE), and QA. BioBERT achieved state-of-the-art in most of the tasks under study and significantly outperforms BERT, showing that pre-training in specific domain data is a key step for downstream tasks' performance.

2.1.2 ClinicalBERT (2019)

One of the first BERT-based clinical PLMs was ClinicalBERT (Alsentzer et al., 2019). Unlike BioBERT, ClinicalBERT used clinical text such as physician notes and discharge summaries, both extracted from MIMIC-III database (Johnson et al., 2016). Several versions of ClinicalBERT were implemented using a technique currently known as continual pre-training. Continual pre-training means starting from an existing PLM to continue the pre-training process on additional data. In the case of ClinicalBERT, BERT and BioBERT were used as starting points, and clinical notes and discharge summaries as additional data to continue pre-training. One task of NLI and four NER tasks were used for the fine-tuning process. In just two tasks, Bio+ClinicalBERT (ClinicalBERT starting from BioBERT) outperforms BioBERT, showing that adding additional clinical text in continual pre-training can help performance, but not in all cases.in all cases.

2.1.3 ClinicalBERT (2020)

Concurrently with the previous work, another ClinicalBERT was being developed (Huang et al., 2020). In this case, a continual pre-training process was implemented using BERT as starting point and clinical notes from MIMIC-III as additional data, similar to ClinicalBERT (2019). However, a readmission task was used for the fine-tuning process. This task aims to predict if a patient will be readmitted in the next 30 days after discharge, a clinical-specific task. For readmission prediction, the ClinicalBERT (2020) output for the classification token [CLS] is passed to a classification layer with a sigmoid function. ClinicalBERT (2020) outperforms BERT and the other two methods by more than 2% in AUC.

2.1.4 PubMedBERT

One of the latest and state-of-the-art biomedical PLMs is PubMedBERT (Gu et al., 2021). The assumption that general domain text can help pre-training to introduce general language knowledge into PLMs is challenged by this work. In mixed-domain pre-training, the vocabulary and the pre-training corpus come from general-domain text. Some models, like BioBERT, add text from biomedical sources to the pre-training corpus, and others, like ClinicalBERT, do continual pre-training over clinical text. On the other hand, domain-specific pre-training from scratch generates both the vocabulary and the pre-training corpus from specific-domain text. PubMedBERT implements the latter approach.

The domain-specific pre-training approach requires a large amount of text, which in the field of biomedicine can be found in PubMed. PubMedBERT pre-training corpus consists of 14 million abstracts, and 3.2 billion words, totaling 21 GB of uncompressed text. Out of 13 tasks, including NER, RE, QA, sentence similarity (SS), and document classification, PubMedBERT outperforms 11, showing that domain-specific pre-training is a better option for downstream tasks' performance.

2.2 General-domain, Biomedical, and Clinical PLMs for Spanish

2.2.1 BETO

The first implementation of BERT for Spanish is called BETO (Cañete et al., 2020). BETO used the same architecture that the original BERT model, but for the pre-training process it used some changes introduced by RoBERTa such as dynamic masking. Spanish Wikipedia and the Spanish parts of the OPUS Project (Tiedemann, 2012) were used as a pre-training corpus, totaling 3 billion words. A benchmark of tasks, GLUES (Cañete et al., 2020), was built to compare BETO to a multilingual implementation of BERT, mBERT (Wu and Dredze, 2019). BETO outperforms most of the mBERT results, excluding some QA tasks. These results show that pre-training with Spanish text improves performance for most downstream tasks compared with multilingual PLM.

2.2.2 RoBERTa-bne

MarIA is a family of PLMs for Spanish (Gutiérrez-Fandiño et al., 2022). One PLM of interest in MarIA is the implementation of RoBERTa with Spanish text, RoBERTa-bne. RoBERTa-bne was pre-trained with text extracted from The National Library of Spain (Biblioteca Nacional de España or BNE). The pre-trained corpus consists of more than 200 million documents, and 135 billion tokens, totaling 570GB of uncompressed text. Two versions of RoBERTa-bne. Out of nine tasks, RoBERTa-bne outperforms eight compared to BETO and mBERT.

2.2.3 Bsc-bio-es and bsc-bio-ehr-es

The previous PLMs for Spanish were pre-trained in general-domain text. bsc-bio-es and bsc-bio-ehr-es are the first PLMs trained with exclusively biomedical and clinical text in Spanish (Carrino et al., 2022). Two corpora were built for this purpose, biomedical and clinical. The biomedical corpus consists of 2.5 million documents and 1.1 billion tokens, and the clinical corpus consists of 514k documents and 95 million tokens. Bsc-bio-es was pre-trained only with the biomedical corpus and bsc-bio-ehr-es with the biomedical and clinical corpora. The reason behind this design decision is two-fold; the clinical corpus is too small to create a functional PLM by itself, and to assess if adding a small clinical corpus to a large biomedical corpus has a positive impact on clinical NLP tasks.

Three tasks were used to benchmark the PLMs against others such as BETO-Galén, mBERT, mBERT-Galén, RoBERTa-bne, among others. BETO-Galén and mBERT-Galén are BETO and mBERT versions with continual pre-training in the Galén Oncology corpus (López-García et al., 2021), respectively. bsc-bio-ehr-es outperforms all other PLMs, including bsc-bio-es, in two tasks, and bsc-bio-es came in second place. For the remaining task, another PLM, XLM-R-Galén (a continual pre-training version of XML-R (Conneau et al., 2020), a multilingual version of RoBERTa) outperforms all the other PLMs, but bsc-bio-es and bsc-bio-ehr-es came in second and third place, respectively.

These results show that using only biomedical and clinical corpora for the pre-training process improves performance compared to general-domain text in Spanish. This result is congruent with PubMedBERT findings for English. The results remain true even when the comparison is made with RoBERTa-bne, a model pre-trained with 100 times more text than bsc-bio-es and bsc-bio-ehr-es. Interestingly, XLM-R-Galén, trained in more than 2TB of general-domain data in 100 languages, has the best results for one task, but bsc-bio-es and bsc-bio-ehr-es are around 0.1% of F-score away.

2.2.4 Clinical Flair

Every PLM shown until this point has its architecture built upon transformers (Vaswani et al., 2017). However, there are PLM based on other architectures, such as Flair. Flair is a character-level language model, representing words as sequences of characters contextualized by close words. Flair uses the internal states of a bidirectional character-level LSTM to obtain contextualized word representations (Akbik et al., 2018).

Clinical Flair for Spanish (Rojas et al., 2022) is a continual pre-training version of a Flair implementation in Spanish (Akbik et al., 2019), which was trained over the Spanish Wikipedia. As additional data for pre-training, the Chilean Waiting List corpus was used (Báez et al., 2020; Báez et al., 2022). The corpus consists of 5 million diagnostic suspicions and 68 million words. Four NER tasks were used to evaluate the Clinical Flair. As Flair generates contextualized embeddings, an algorithm has to be used to solve NER tasks. The LSTM-CRF technique was used (Lample et al., 2016). Clinical Flair outperforms other Spanish Flair models in three tasks. For the remaining task, SciELO Flair (Akhtyamova et al., 2020), a biomedical Flair PLM, had the best results. These results also show the importance of domain-specific data, even when using continual pre-training.

2.3 Biomedical and Clinical PLMs evaluation

As mentioned in section 1, there are two approaches to evaluate PLMs, intrinsic and extrinsic. The intrinsic approach measures PLM representation's quality independently of any downstream task. Meanwhile, the extrinsic approach evaluates the PLM quality using downstream tasks.

2.3.1 Intrinsic evaluation

One of the most used intrinsic metrics is perplexity, which is the inverse probability of a word sequence normalized by the number of words (Jurafsky and Martin, 2021). Intuitively, the perplexity measures how well a language model predicts a sequence of words. Another metric is a medical graph-based intrinsic test, specifically built for biomedical and clinical PLMs. This intrinsic test proposes that using semantic distances between medical concepts extracted from a medical knowledge graph can help to measure the quality of representations made by the PLMs (Aracena et al., 2022). Both metrics can be applied to English and Spanish languages.

2.3.2 Extrinsic evaluation

In terms of extrinsic metrics, there are several benchmarks, such as the biomedical language understanding evaluation benchmark (BLUE) (Peng et al., 2019) and the biomedical language understanding reasoning benchmark (BLURB) (Gu et al., 2021). However, these benchmarks are based on datasets in English. In addition to the mentioned benchmarks, BigBio (Fries et al., 2022), a framework that gathers 126+ biomedical NLP datasets, covering 13 task categories and 10+ languages, can be used for extrinsic evaluation.

Unlike previous benchmarks, no biomedical nor clinical benchmark has been built with Spanish texts. However, there are NER tasks commonly used to evaluate PLMs built with Spanish corpora. Following is a list of tasks of interest for this proposal, and in Table 1, their details.:

CANTEMIST-NER[1] (Miranda-Escalada et al., 2020): annotated corpus with tumor morphology mentions in 1,301 oncological clinical case reports.

PharmaCoNER[2] (Gonzalez-Agirre et al., 2019): annotated corpus with entities such as chemical compounds and drugs in 1,000 clinical case studies.

CT-EBM-SP[3] (Campillos-Llanos et al., 2021): annotated corpus with UMLS entities in 1,200 texts about clinical trials studies and announcements.

The Chilean Waiting List Corpus[4] (Báez et al., 2020; Báez et al., 2022): annotated corpus with

[1] https://zenodo.org/record/3978041

[2] https://zenodo.org/record/4270158

[3] http://www.lllf.uam.es/ESP/nlpmedterm$_e n$

[4] https://zenodo.org/record/5591011

	CANTEMIST-NER			PharmaCoNER			CT-EBM-SP		
	Train	Test	Dev	Train	Test	Dev	Train	Test	Dev
Tokens	442,097	240,326	396,457	210,778	104,201	100,147	208,188	68,994	69,319
Sentences	19,397	11,168	18,165	8,177	3,976	3,790	12,555	4,506	4,550
Avg sentence length	22.8	21.5	21.8	25.8	26.2	26.4	16.6	15.3	15.3
Entities	6,347	3,596	5,948	3,821	1,876	1,926	24,224	7,717	8,258
Avg entity length	2.4	2.3	2.3	1.4	1.4	1.4	2.0	2.0	2.0

	Chilean Waiting List			NUBes		
	Train	Test	Dev	Train	Test	Dev
Tokens	291,561	36,963	34,987	255,897	51,233	35,416
Sentences	15,290	1,912	1,911	13,802	2,762	1,840
Avg sentence length	19.07	19.33	18.31	18.5	18.6	19,2
Entities	69,847	8,837	8,340	17,122	3,548	2,293
Avg entity length	2.7	2.7	2.7	2.6	2.6	2.6

Table 1: Statistics of the NER tasks.

clinical entities such as findings, procedures, medications, etc. in 10,000 anonymized referrals for specialty consultations from the waiting list in Chilean public hospitals.

NUBes[5] (Lima Lopez et al., 2020): annotated corpus with negation and uncertainty entities in anonymized health records.

3 Research questions

From the literature review, it is possible to identify some research opportunities. These opportunities are mostly related to which data we can use to pre-train PLMs and which architecture best fits a specific task. Also, the evaluation process should be clear and easy for comparison, which in the case of clinical NLP in Spanish, there are still missing parts. Additionally, there is an opportunity to advance clinical NLP in Spanish by adopting strategies used in English and joining current efforts in the field.

From the identified opportunities, we can state the research questions as follows:

1. Will it be better to pre-train a PLM exclusively with clinical data compared to combinations of clinical and biomedical data for solving downstream clinical tasks in Spanish?
2. Is there a specific PLM architecture that outperforms others for solving downstream clinical tasks in Spanish?

To answer question one, we have to build a clinical corpus in Spanish big enough to implement a functional PLM. However, building a clinical corpus is a difficult task since there are privacy and confidentiality issues that may arise. The PLM trained over this corpus will be compared to biomedical and clinical PLMs for Spanish described in the literature review.

To answer question two, we have to test several PLMs architectures over the generated corpus. The literature review shows some interesting architecture to try in this research. However, as PLM architectures are being developed periodically, there is always the risk of becoming obsolete.

For both questions, we have to create an evaluation process that can include clinical intrinsic and extrinsic downstream tasks, as well as, language and prediction tasks. This evaluation process will allow us to clarify the research questions, but probably the answers will depend on the several tasks that we will include.

Hopefully, answering these research questions will contribute to the current efforts made by other laboratories working in clinical NLP in Spanish and languages other than English.

4 Methods

The methodology for this research proposal consists of three parts: build a clinical corpus for pretraining PLMs in Spanish, test different PLM architectures, and evaluate the implemented PLMs. This section will explain in detail every part.

4.1 Build a clinical corpus in Spanish

The literature review shows several corpora that can be used to pre-train PLMs. However, clinical corpora are hard to find, and some publications do

[5]https://github.com/Vicomtech/NUBes-negation-uncertainty-biomedical-corpus

not release them given privacy and confidentiality issues. For example, the clinical corpus of bsc-bio-ehr-es is not publicly available, even though the biomedical corpora are available to download.

For this research proposal, an agreement with two medical institutions is in place. The agreement allows us to access clinical notes from both institutions. As a safety measure, we cannot use the data outside each institution to avoid unexpected privacy issues. We expect to use both sources to build two clinical corpora, one for each institution. Depending on the data quality of each source we will have to adjust the pre-processing steps to build each corpus. According to the authors of bsc-bio-ehr-es, the clinical corpus was left in its original form. Therefore, no pre-processing will be used in the first version of a PLM. Nevertheless, it is foreseeable that quality issues can appear, thus a cleaning process will be carried out for the second version.

Preliminary analysis of the data of the clinical institution shows that clinical notes consist of nearly one billion words. This situation shows that functional PLMs could be built from scratch.

4.2 Test different PLM architectures

As seen in the literature review, transformer-based architectures, such as BERT and RoBERTa, are the most common in building biomedical and clinical PLMs. In this proposal, we will test BERT and RoBERTa architectures as baselines. Apart from those two, DeBERTa is a relevant architecture to test, since it introduces important changes to the BERT architecture and it outperforms BERT and RoBERTa for general-domain downstream tasks. Additionally, we will test a non-transformer-based architecture, Flair, as it has not been previously pre-trained in clinical data exclusively, which can improve performance in downstream tasks. After this part, eight clinical PLMs will be implemented. Those PLMs will be BERT, RoBERTa, DeBERTa, and Flair versions for each clinical corpus.

4.3 Evaluate implemented PLMs

The evaluation process of the implemented PLMs has to consider intrinsic and extrinsic tasks as well as language and prediction tasks. Intrinsic tasks allow us to measure the internal quality of PLM independently of downstream tasks, so it is a good way to compare transformer-based architectures with others. Extrinsic tasks allow measuring performance in relevant downstream tasks for clinical NLP. Some of these tasks can be language tasks such as NER, QA, and document classification, among others, which are important to build tools to extract information from clinical text. Other tasks are prediction tasks such as prediction of unplanned readmissions, treatment length, diagnostic, etc., which support the decision-making of medical personnel.

For intrinsic tasks, we will use perplexity and the medical graph-based intrinsic test. The medical graph-based intrinsic test will be used to compare PLM where it is expected to have better results for clinical and biomedical PLM compared to general ones. For extrinsic tasks, we will use NER tasks such as CANTEMIST-NER, PharmaCoNER, CT-EBM-SP, NUBes, and the Chilean Waiting List. Additionally, we will use prediction tasks such as predicting unplanned readmissions and treatment length.

The implemented PLMs will be compared with existing and available general, biomedical and clinical PLMs using the evaluation process. Those PLMs will be BETO, mBERT, RoBERTa-bne, XLM-R, bsc-bio-es, bsc-bio-ehr-es, and clinical Flair.

5 Expected results

The expected results for this proposal are as follows:

- The implemented clinical PLM, mentioned in subsection 4.2, will outperform existing general, biomedical, and clinical PLM, mentioned in subsection 4.3. This result is expected given that evaluation tasks are mostly clinical-related and the new corpora are clinical.

- The implemented clinical PLM will have similar performance in language tasks compared to existing biomedical and clinical PLM, but it will outperform them for prediction tasks. This result is expected given that language tasks measure the quality of PLM in linguistic tasks related to the clinical context, and most existing biomedical and clinical PLM were pre-trained in corpora with some clinical context. However, prediction tasks measure how well PLM can extract information to predict a clinical outcome, and it is reasonable to believe that a PLM pre-trained only with a clinical corpus will outperform PLM pre-trained with a combination of biomedical and clinical text.

- The implemented PLM with DeBERTa architecture will outperform the RoBERTa version, and the latter PLM will outperform the BERT version. Given the previous performance for general, biomedical, and clinical PLM for English and Spanish, these results are expected. There is not enough evidence to draw a similar conclusion for the implemented PLM with Flair architecture.

- As an indirect result, if an implemented PLM considerably improves the evaluation in the task of prediction of treatment length, it could be integrated into the current institutions' systems to replace the already-in-use machine learning models.

6 Conclusions

This work presents a PhD research proposal for developing clinical PLMs in Spanish that can outperform general-domain, biomedical, and current clinical PLMs. As a result, it is expected to answer the research questions regarding whether using only clinical text to create a PLM can outperform current approaches and if a particular PLM architecture is better for clinical purposes.

We expect this work can help to understand how PLMs work in the clinical domain and in languages other than English.

Limitations

Limitations of this work can be listed as follows:

- This work will not test larger PLM architectures, such as large versions of BERT, RoBERTa, and DeBERTa, given the availability of computational resources and data.

- This paper focuses on encoder-only PLM architectures. This type of architecture has been heavily studied for biomedical and clinical PLMs and we continue with that line of research. However, decoder or encoder-decoder architectures can be tried to solve the same tasks.

- The clinical corpora to be built can introduce non-standard abbreviations and jargon unique to the clinical institutions providing the data. This can lower the performance of language tasks in other contexts.

- The clinical text will not be released given confidentiality issues which increment the gap between advances in general-domain and clinical NLP research.

Ethics Statement

We state that this work complies with the ACL Code of Ethics. We believe this work could help the research community with new information about clinical and biomedical PLM. The data for this work will not be released and will be used according to the ethical and confidentiality standards provided by the clinical institutions.

Acknowledgements

This work was funded by ANID Chile: Basal Funds for Center of Excellence FB210005 (CMM); Millennium Science Initiative Program ICN17_002 (IMFD) and ICN2021_004 (iHealth), Fondecyt grant 11201250, and National Doctoral Scholarships 21211659 (Claudio Aracena).

References

Alan Akbik, Tanja Bergmann, Duncan Blythe, Kashif Rasul, Stefan Schweter, and Roland Vollgraf. 2019. FLAIR: An Easy-to-Use Framework for State-of-the-Art NLP. In *Proceedings of the 2019 Conference of the North American Chapter of the Association for Computational Linguistics (Demonstrations)*, pages 54–59, Minneapolis, Minnesota. Association for Computational Linguistics.

Alan Akbik, Duncan Blythe, and Roland Vollgraf. 2018. Contextual String Embeddings for Sequence Labeling. In *Proceedings of the 27th International Conference on Computational Linguistics*, pages 1638–1649, Santa Fe, New Mexico, USA. Association for Computational Linguistics.

Liliya Akhtyamova, Paloma Martínez, Karin Verspoor, and John Cardiff. 2020. Testing Contextualized Word Embeddings to Improve NER in Spanish Clinical Case Narratives. *IEEE Access*, 8:164717–164726. Conference Name: IEEE Access.

Emily Alsentzer, John Murphy, William Boag, Wei-Hung Weng, Di Jindi, Tristan Naumann, and Matthew McDermott. 2019. Publicly Available Clinical BERT Embeddings. In *Proceedings of the 2nd Clinical Natural Language Processing Workshop*, pages 72–78, Minneapolis, Minnesota, USA. Association for Computational Linguistics.

Claudio Aracena, Fabián Villena, Matías Rojas, and Jocelyn Dunstan. 2022. A knowledge-graph-based intrinsic test for benchmarking medical concept embeddings and pretrained language models. In *Proceedings of the 13th International Workshop on Health Text Mining and Information Analysis*, Abu Dhabi, UAE. Association for Computational Linguistics.

Pablo Báez, Felipe Bravo-Marquez, Jocelyn Dunstan, Matías Rojas, and Fabián Villena. 2022. Automatic extraction of nested entities in clinical referrals in spanish. *ACM Transactions on Computing for Healthcare (HEALTH)*, 3(3):1–22.

Pablo Báez, Fabián Villena, Matías Rojas, Manuel Durán, and Jocelyn Dunstan. 2020. The Chilean Waiting List Corpus: a new resource for clinical Named Entity Recognition in Spanish. In *Proceedings of the 3rd Clinical Natural Language Processing Workshop*, pages 291–300, Online. Association for Computational Linguistics.

Leonardo Campillos-Llanos, Ana Valverde-Mateos, Adrián Capllonch-Carrión, and Antonio Moreno-Sandoval. 2021. A clinical trials corpus annotated with UMLS entities to enhance the access to evidence-based medicine. *BMC Medical Informatics and Decision Making*, 21(1):69.

Casimiro Pio Carrino, Joan Llop, Marc Pàmies, Asier Gutiérrez-Fandiño, Jordi Armengol-Estapé, Joaquín Silveira-Ocampo, Alfonso Valencia, Aitor Gonzalez-Agirre, and Marta Villegas. 2022. Pretrained Biomedical Language Models for Clinical NLP in Spanish. In *Proceedings of the 21st Workshop on Biomedical Language Processing*, pages 193–199, Dublin, Ireland. Association for Computational Linguistics.

José Cañete, Gabriel Chaperon, Rodrigo Fuentes, Ho Jou-Hui, Kang Hojin, and Jorge Pérez. 2020. Spanish pre-trained BERT model and evaluation data. In *Practical ML for Developing Countries Workshop @ ICLR 2020*.

Alexis Conneau, Kartikay Khandelwal, Naman Goyal, Vishrav Chaudhary, Guillaume Wenzek, Francisco Guzmán, Edouard Grave, Myle Ott, Luke Zettlemoyer, and Veselin Stoyanov. 2020. Unsupervised Cross-lingual Representation Learning at Scale. In *Proceedings of the 58th Annual Meeting of the Association for Computational Linguistics*, pages 8440–8451, Online. Association for Computational Linguistics.

Hercules Dalianis. 2018. *Clinical Text Mining: Secondary Use of Electronic Patient Records*. Springer International Publishing.

Jacob Devlin, Ming-Wei Chang, Kenton Lee, and Kristina Toutanova. 2019. BERT: Pre-training of Deep Bidirectional Transformers for Language Understanding. In *Proceedings of the 2019 Conference of the North American Chapter of the Association for Computational Linguistics: Human Language Technologies, Volume 1 (Long and Short Papers)*, pages 4171–4186, Minneapolis, Minnesota. Association for Computational Linguistics.

Jason Alan Fries, Leon Weber, Natasha Seelam, Gabriel Altay, Debajyoti Datta, Samuele Garda, Myungsun Kang, Ruisi Su, Wojciech Kusa, Samuel Cahyawijaya, Fabio Barth, Simon Ott, Matthias Samwald, Stephen Bach, Stella Biderman, Mario Sänger, Bo Wang, Alison Callahan, Daniel León Periñán, Théo Gigant, Patrick Haller, Jenny Chim, Jose David Posada, John Michael Giorgi, Karthik Rangasai Sivaraman, Marc Pàmies, Marianna Nezhurina, Robert Martin, Michael Cullan, Moritz Freidank, Nathan Dahlberg, Shubhanshu Mishra, Shamik Bose, Nicholas Michio Broad, Yanis Labrak, Shlok S Deshmukh, Sid Kiblawi, Ayush Singh, Minh Chien Vu, Trishala Neeraj, Jonas Golde, Albert Villanova del Moral, and Benjamin Beilharz. 2022. BigBio: A framework for data-centric biomedical natural language processing. In *Thirty-sixth Conference on Neural Information Processing Systems Datasets and Benchmarks Track*.

Aitor Gonzalez-Agirre, Montserrat Marimon, Ander Intxaurrondo, Obdulia Rabal, Marta Villegas, and Martin Krallinger. 2019. PharmaCoNER: Pharmacological Substances, Compounds and proteins Named Entity Recognition track. In *Proceedings of the 5th Workshop on BioNLP Open Shared Tasks*, pages 1–10, Hong Kong, China. Association for Computational Linguistics.

Yu Gu, Robert Tinn, Hao Cheng, Michael Lucas, Naoto Usuyama, Xiaodong Liu, Tristan Naumann, Jianfeng Gao, and Hoifung Poon. 2021. Domain-Specific Language Model Pretraining for Biomedical Natural Language Processing. *ACM Transactions on Computing for Healthcare*, 3(1):2:1–2:23.

Asier Gutiérrez-Fandiño, Jordi Armengol-Estapé, Marc Pàmies, Joan Llop-Palao, Joaquin Silveira-Ocampo, Casimiro Pio Carrino, Carme Armentano-Oller, Carlos Rodriguez-Penagos, Aitor Gonzalez-Agirre, and Marta Villegas. 2022. MarIA: Spanish Language Models. *Procesamiento del Lenguaje Natural*, 68(0):39–60. Number: 0.

Pengcheng He, Jianfeng Gao, and Weizhu Chen. 2021a. DeBERTaV3: Improving DeBERTa using ELECTRA-style pre-training with gradient-disentangled embedding sharing. arXiv.

Pengcheng He, Xiaodong Liu, Jianfeng Gao, and Weizhu Chen. 2021b. Deberta: Decoding-enhanced BERT with disentangled attention. In *International Conference on Learning Representations*.

Jeremy Howard and Sebastian Ruder. 2018. Universal Language Model Fine-tuning for Text Classification. In *Proceedings of the 56th Annual Meeting of the Association for Computational Linguistics (Volume 1: Long Papers)*, pages 328–339, Melbourne, Australia. Association for Computational Linguistics.

Kexin Huang, Jaan Altosaar, and Rajesh Ranganath. 2020. ClinicalBERT: Modeling Clinical Notes and Predicting Hospital Readmission.

Alistair E. W. Johnson, Tom J. Pollard, Lu Shen, Li-wei H. Lehman, Mengling Feng, Mohammad Ghassemi, Benjamin Moody, Peter Szolovits, Leo Anthony Celi, and Roger G. Mark. 2016. MIMIC-III, a freely accessible critical care database. *Scientific Data*, 3(1):160035. Number: 1 Publisher: Nature Publishing Group.

Daniel Jurafsky and James H. Martin. 2021. *Speech and Language Processing*.

Guillaume Lample, Miguel Ballesteros, Sandeep Subramanian, Kazuya Kawakami, and Chris Dyer. 2016. Neural Architectures for Named Entity Recognition. In *Proceedings of the 2016 Conference of the North American Chapter of the Association for Computational Linguistics: Human Language Technologies*, pages 260–270, San Diego, California. Association for Computational Linguistics.

Jinhyuk Lee, Wonjin Yoon, Sungdong Kim, Donghyeon Kim, Sunkyu Kim, Chan Ho So, and Jaewoo Kang. 2020. BioBERT: a pre-trained biomedical language representation model for biomedical text mining. *Bioinformatics*, 36(4):1234–1240.

Salvador Lima Lopez, Naiara Perez, Montse Cuadros, and German Rigau. 2020. NUBes: A Corpus of Negation and Uncertainty in Spanish Clinical Texts. In *Proceedings of the Twelfth Language Resources and Evaluation Conference*, pages 5772–5781, Marseille, France. European Language Resources Association.

Yinhan Liu, Myle Ott, Naman Goyal, Jingfei Du, Mandar Joshi, Danqi Chen, Omer Levy, Mike Lewis, Luke Zettlemoyer, and Veselin Stoyanov. 2019. RoBERTa: A robustly optimized BERT pretraining approach. *arXiv preprint arXiv:1907.11692*.

Guillermo López-García, José M. Jerez, Nuria Ribelles, Emilio Alba, and Francisco J. Veredas. 2021. Transformers for Clinical Coding in Spanish. *IEEE Access*, 9:72387–72397. Conference Name: IEEE Access.

Antonio Miranda-Escalada, Eulàlia Farré, and Martin Krallinger. 2020. Cantemist corpus: gold standard of oncology clinical cases annotated with CIE-O 3 terminology. Version Number: 1.6 Type: dataset.

Aurélie Névéol, Hercules Dalianis, Sumithra Velupillai, Guergana Savova, and Pierre Zweigenbaum. 2018. Clinical Natural Language Processing in languages other than English: opportunities and challenges. *Journal of Biomedical Semantics*, 9(1):12.

Yifan Peng, Shankai Yan, and Zhiyong Lu. 2019. Transfer Learning in Biomedical Natural Language Processing: An Evaluation of BERT and ELMo on Ten Benchmarking Datasets. In *Proceedings of the 18th BioNLP Workshop and Shared Task*, pages 58–65, Florence, Italy. Association for Computational Linguistics.

Alec Radford, Karthik Narasimhan, Tim Salimans, and Ilya Sutskever. 2018. Improving Language Understanding by Generative Pre-Training.

Matías Rojas, Jocelyn Dunstan, and Fabián Villena. 2022. Clinical Flair: A Pre-Trained Language Model for Spanish Clinical Natural Language Processing. In *Proceedings of the 4th Clinical Natural Language Processing Workshop*, pages 87–92, Seattle, WA. Association for Computational Linguistics.

Jörg Tiedemann. 2012. Parallel Data, Tools and Interfaces in OPUS. In *Proceedings of the Eighth International Conference on Language Resources and Evaluation (LREC'12)*, pages 2214–2218, Istanbul, Turkey. European Language Resources Association (ELRA).

Lewis Tunstall, Leandro von Werra, and Thomas Wolf. 2022. *Natural Language Processing with Transformers*. O'Reilly Media, Inc.

Ashish Vaswani, Noam Shazeer, Niki Parmar, Jakob Uszkoreit, Llion Jones, Aidan N Gomez, Łukasz Kaiser, and Illia Polosukhin. 2017. Attention is All you Need. In *Advances in Neural Information Processing Systems*, volume 30. Curran Associates, Inc.

Shijie Wu and Mark Dredze. 2019. Beto, Bentz, Becas: The Surprising Cross-Lingual Effectiveness of BERT. In *Proceedings of the 2019 Conference on Empirical Methods in Natural Language Processing and the 9th International Joint Conference on Natural Language Processing (EMNLP-IJCNLP)*, pages 833–844, Hong Kong, China. Association for Computational Linguistics.

Yukun Zhu, Ryan Kiros, Rich Zemel, Ruslan Salakhutdinov, Raquel Urtasun, Antonio Torralba, and Sanja Fidler. 2015. Aligning Books and Movies: Towards Story-Like Visual Explanations by Watching Movies and Reading Books. pages 19–27.

Which One Are You Referring To? Multimodal Object Identification in Situated Dialogue

Holy Lovenia*, **Samuel Cahyawijaya***, **Pascale Fung**
Center for Artificial Intelligence Research (CAiRE),
The Hong Kong University of Science and Technology
{hlovenia, scahyawijaya}@connect.ust.hk

Abstract

The demand for multimodal dialogue systems has been rising in various domains, emphasizing the importance of interpreting multimodal inputs from conversational and situational contexts. One main challenge in multimodal dialogue understanding is multimodal object identification, which constitutes the ability to identify objects relevant to a multimodal user-system conversation. We explore three methods to tackle this problem and evaluate them on the largest situated dialogue dataset, SIMMC 2.1. Our best method, scene-dialogue alignment, improves the performance by ~20% F1-score compared to the SIMMC 2.1 baselines. We provide analysis and discussion regarding the limitation of our methods and the potential directions for future works. Our code is publicly available at https://github.com/holylovenia/multimodal-object-identification.

1 Introduction

Recent advancements in multimodal dialogue systems have gained more traction in various domains such as retail, travel, fashion, interior design, and many others. A real-world application of multimodal dialogue systems is situated dialogue, where a dialogue agent shares a co-observed vision or physical space with the user, and is responsible for handling user requests based on the situational context, which are often about the objects in their surroundings. This makes multimodal object identification from a dialogue (i.e., identifying objects that fit a dialogue context) an indispensable skill in multimodal dialogue understanding, built on cross-modal understanding to comprehend the relations between linguistic expressions and visual cues.

Various methods have been proposed to perform multimodal object identification through different paradigms (Yu et al., 2016; Hu et al., 2016; Ilinykh et al., 2019; Kamath et al., 2021; Kuo and Kira, 2022). These efforts have established remarkable progress in solving this problem. However, aside from an observed gap between the performance of the existing works and human-level performance in multimodal object identification, prior works also rely on a presumption that the information given by the textual context will only lead to specific (i.e., unambiguous) objects, which does not conform to real-world multimodal conversations where ambiguity exists.

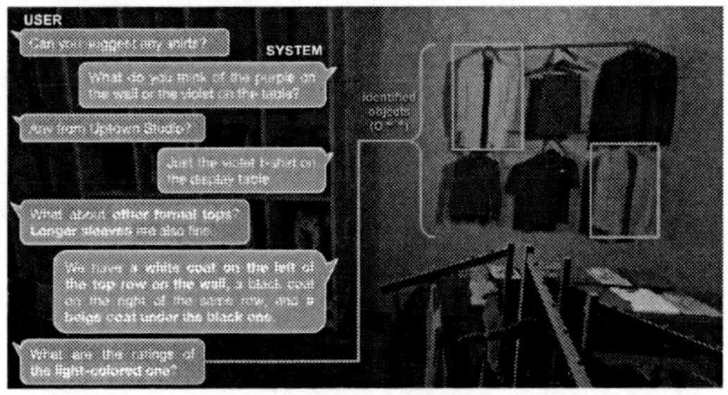

Figure 1: Multimodal object identification is the fundamental step required to enable multimodal dialogue systems to understand the object referred to by the user. Image is adapted from (Kottur et al., 2021).

Therefore, in this work, we explore three different solutions to enable multimodal object identification in the situated dialogue system, i.e., dialogue-contextualized object detection, object-dialogue alignment, and scene-dialogue alignment, without adopting the unambiguity assumption. Dialogue-contextualized object detection utilizes the spatial and object understanding capability of a pre-trained object detection model, to generate semantic representation containing both visual cues and the spatial understanding of the object. Object-dialogue alignment incorporates the image-text alignment capability of CLIP (Radford et al., 2021), which has been pre-trained on large image-text corpora to perform multimodal object identification from the given dialogue context. Scene-object alignment

*Equal contribution.

Proceedings of the 17th Conference of the European Chapter of the Association for Computational Linguistics: Student Research Workshop, pages 61–72
May 2-4, 2023

combines the spatial and object understanding capability of a pre-trained object detection model and a pre-trained textual understanding model to produce better semantic vision-language alignment.

Our contributions are three-fold:

- We introduce three different methods for handling multimodal object identification in situated dialogue, i.e., dialogue-contextualized object detection, object-dialogue alignment, and scene-dialogue alignment;
- We show the dialogue-contextualized object detection method fails to outperform even the heuristic baselines despite having an acceptable performance on the object detection task;
- We show the effectiveness of the other two methods which significantly outperform the SIMMC 2.1 baselines by $\sim$5% F1-score for object-dialogue alignment and $\sim$20% F1-score for scene-dialogue alignment;

2 Related Work

Multimodal Dialogue System Multiple studies have attempted to enable the skills required for multimodal dialogue system, e.g., understanding visual (Antol et al., 2015; Das et al., 2017; Kottur et al., 2019) or visual-temporal (Alamri et al., 2019) content to answer user's questions, grounding conversations to images (Mostafazadeh et al., 2017; Shuster et al., 2020), interpreting multimodal inputs and responding with multimodal output to assist users with their goal (Saha et al., 2018) or as a means to converse (Sun et al., 2022), and perceiving the shared environment to grasp situational context to enable proper navigation, adaptation, and communication (Lukin et al., 2018; Brawer et al., 2018; Kottur et al., 2021).

At the core of these efforts, the ability to understand language and vision, as well as integrate both representations to align the linguistic expressions in the dialogue with the relevant visual concepts or perceived objects, is the key to multimodal dialogue understanding (Landragin, 2006; Loáiciga et al., 2021b,a; Kottur et al., 2018; Utescher and Zarrieß, 2021; Sundar and Heck, 2022; Dai et al., 2021).

Multimodal Object Identification Identifying objects or visual concepts related to a linguistic expression is an incremental exploration in vision-language research. It starts with identifying simple objects in a sanitized environment (Mitchell et al., 2010) based on image descriptions or captions. Then, multimodal object identification has been gradually increasing in complexity and realism by involving visual contexts with cluttered and diverse scenes (Kazemzadeh et al., 2014; Gkatzia et al., 2015; Yu et al., 2016; Mao et al., 2016; Hu et al., 2016; Ilinykh et al., 2019; Kamath et al., 2021; Kuo and Kira, 2022).

While these works base their multimodal object identification on single-turn text contexts, another line of works explores the usage of multi-turn sequences as a textual context to enable identifying objects based on implicit constraints deduced through multi-round reasoning (Seo et al., 2017; Johnson et al., 2017; Liu et al., 2019; Moon et al., 2020). However, they focus on identifying only the specific (i.e., unambiguous) objects, in which only a certain object in the scene fits the corresponding linguistic context. This is quite dissimilar from real-world multimodal object identification, where multiple objects could fit a given textual context and induce ambiguity into the conversation (Kottur et al., 2021). For this reason, existing works are not equipped with the ability to identify all objects that *plausibly* fit those constraints although this skill is required to perform multimodal object identification in situated dialogue.

Multimodal and Cross-Modal Learning Past works have studied multimodal and cross-modal alignment, grounding, and generation to solve various vision-language tasks, e.g., image captioning (Hossain et al., 2019; Sharma et al., 2018), generating stories from image (Min et al., 2021; Lovenia et al., 2022), as well as multimodal object identification (Li et al., 2019; Wang et al., 2022). These attempts become more substantial and extensive after the rise of pre-trained vision-language models such as CLIP (Radford et al., 2021), ALIGN (Jia et al., 2021), and FLAVA (Singh et al., 2022), which allows transfer knowledge obtained from the large-scale pre-training to downstream tasks.

3 Methodology

In this section, we describe the preliminaries of our work (§3.1) and extensively elaborate on each of our approaches, i.e., dialogue-contextualized object detection (§3.2), object-dialogue alignment (§3.3), and scene-dialogue alignment (§3.4).

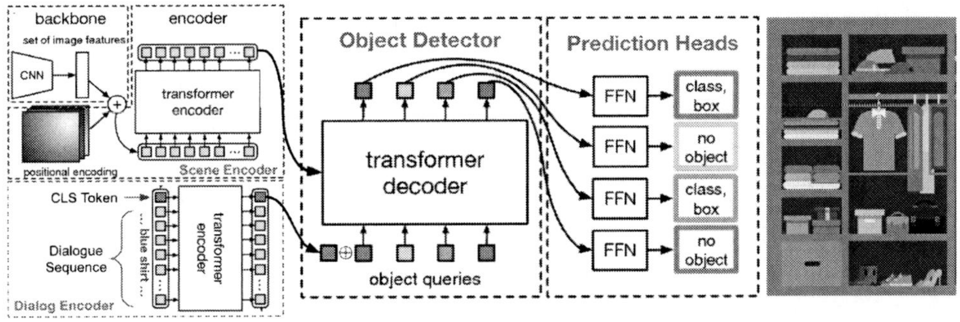

Figure 2: The architecture of SitCoM-DETR. SitCoM-DETR consists of a scene encoder and a dialogue encoder to extract multimodal content, respectively. The dialogue representation is used to guide the object detector module to judiciously filter out unrelated scene objects.

3.1 Preliminaries

The goal of multimodal object identification in situated dialogue is to identify objects from a given scene image that fulfill the user's request gathered from the user-system interactions. To identify the object(s) that could satisfy a user's request in a dialogue, it is crucial to match the objects and the implicit constraints interwoven in the dialogue, e.g., S: "*I do! Take a look at these. I have a brown coat towards the far end on the left wall, another brown coat on the left side of the front floor rack, and a black coat on the front of the same rack.*", U: "*Awesome! Tell me the cost and label on that one.*". Thus, it is essential for the system to understand the relation between the visual perception of the objects in the scenes and the natural language used to verbalize these constraints, which describe the target object(s) by visual attributes (e.g., color, object category or type, etc.), location (i.e., absolute or relative position), or the combination of both.

We define a dialogue between a user and a system as $D = \{u_1, s_1, u_2, s_2, \ldots, u_n, s_n\}$, a scene consisting of images corresponding to multiple viewpoints of the scene as $\{I_1^{scene}, I_2^{scene}, \ldots, I_n^{scene}\}$, and a set of objects in the scene as $O^{scene} = \{(b_1, c_1), (b_2, c_2), \ldots, (b_n, c_n)\}$, where u_i and s_i respectively denote the user utterance and the system utterance, and c_i and b_i denote the bounding box and the class category of an object. Given a user dialogue turn $D_i^{user} = \{u_1, s_1, u_2, s_2, \ldots, u_i\}$, $i \leq n$, and a scene image I_i^{scene}, the goal of the task is to select a subset of scene objects $O^{match} \subseteq O^{scene}$ that could satisfy the referred criteria in D_i^{user}.

3.2 Approach 1: Dialogue-Contextualized Object Detection

For dialogue-contextualized object detection, we frame the task of multimodal object identification as the contextualized object detection task. In object detection, given a scene image I^{scene}, we aim to detect all objects O^{scene} in the scene by predicting their bounding box and class category. While in contextualized object detection, the aim is instead to select only a set of scene objects O^{match} that satisfy a given context.

Our approach for dialogue-contextualized object detection extends a state-of-the-art object detection model, namely DETR (Carion et al., 2020), by injecting dialogue information as the context to guide the detection model to filter out unidentified objects. A similar solution has been proposed by Modulated DETR (MDETR) (Kamath et al., 2021). Despite its strong performance on text-contextualized object detection, MDETR requires an aligned annotation between the text phrase and the visual object for training. Such annotation is not available on SIMMC 2.1, hence we develop a new text-contextualized object detection model namely Situational Context for Multimodal DETR (**SitCoM-DETR**). Unlike MDETR which concatenates the textual representation along with the visual representation before feeding them into the transformer encoder of DETR (shown in Appendix A), **SitCoM-DETR** injects a dialogue-level semantic representation vector into the input query of the transformer decoder of DETR in order to guide the model to select objects that match the dialogue context. We incorporate the same loss functions as the original DETR model. The depiction of our **SitCoM-DETR** model is shown in Figure 2.

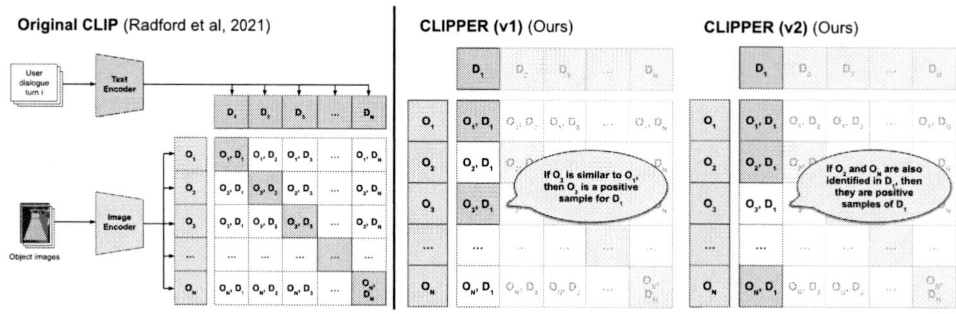

Figure 3: Learning objectives of the original CLIP (Radford et al., 2021), CLIPPER (v1), and CLIPPER (v2) for the object-dialogue alignment approach. The similarities of the positive pairs (blue) are maximized while the similarities of the negative pairs (white) are minimized.

3.3 Approach 2: Object-Dialogue Alignment

For object-dialogue alignment, we frame the task of multimodal object identification as the alignment between a target object O_i^{match} and a user dialogue turn D_i^{user} pair. Given a user dialogue turn D_i^{user} and its corresponding scene image I_i^{scene}, we first preprocess I_i^{scene} to extract the object images of O^{match}. Each of the object images is paired with D_i^{user} as the positive pairs. We obtain the visual embeddings from the image by feeding it to an image encoder, and the textual embeddings from the dialogue turn by feeding it to a text encoder. After these embeddings pass through a linear projection, we calculate the similarity using the dot product between the two resulting vectors. Utilizing the contrastive learning objective, on a batch of object-dialogue pairs, this cross-modal alignment architecture learns by maximizing the similarity of the positive pairs and minimizing the similarity of the negative pairs (Figure 3).

Object-Dialogue Similarity Learning Strategy The original contrastive learning approaches the object-dialogue alignment task as a one-to-one function, where the positive sample of D_i is only O_i in Figure 3. This is different from the actual nature of multimodal object identification, where more than one object could be relevant to a dialogue turn. For this reason, in addition to the original contrastive learning, we explore two modifications of the learning objective, where: 1) the positive samples of D_i include O_i (image pair) and similar objects[1] to O_i; and 2) the positive samples of D_i include O_i and other supposedly identified objects in D_i. For simplicity, we refer to these methods as **CLIPPER (v1)** and **CLIPPER (v2)**.

[1]We define similar objects to O_i as any other objects in the corresponding scene that use the same prefabricated design as O_i in the SIMMC 2.1 dataset.

3.4 Approach 3: Scene-Dialogue Alignment

For scene-dialogue alignment, we aim to combine the spatial understanding learned from object detection training with the image-text matching for multimodal similarity learning to solve multimodal object identification. For this approach, we utilize a pre-trained object detection model, i.e., DETR, and two pre-trained language models, i.e., BERT and GPT2. The resulting models are referred to as **DETR-BERT** and **DETR-GPT2**, respectively. We illustrate the overview of this approach in Figure 4.

In this approach, we first frame our dataset as an object detection task, where a data instance consists of a scene image I_i^{scene} and its object annotations $O^{scene} = \{(b_1, c_1), (b_2, c_2), ..., (b_m, c_m)\}$, and train an object detection model (DETR) on it. The resulting model is then used to extract the visual representations of all objects in the scene image I^{scene} by matching the object queries with O^{scene} using Hungarian matching (Stewart et al., 2016).

For the next step, we frame our dataset as a binary classification task, where a data instance consists of a user dialogue turn D_i^{user}, an object O_j^{scene} in a corresponding scene I_i^{scene}, and a binary label (i.e., whether the object is identified by the user dialogue turn or not). We utilize a dialogue encoder to extract textual representation from a user dialogue turn D_i^{user}. The textual representation of D_i^{user} and the visual representation of O_j^{scene} are projected into a latent space. We compute the dot product of the two and use the resulting vector as the prediction logits for training and inference.

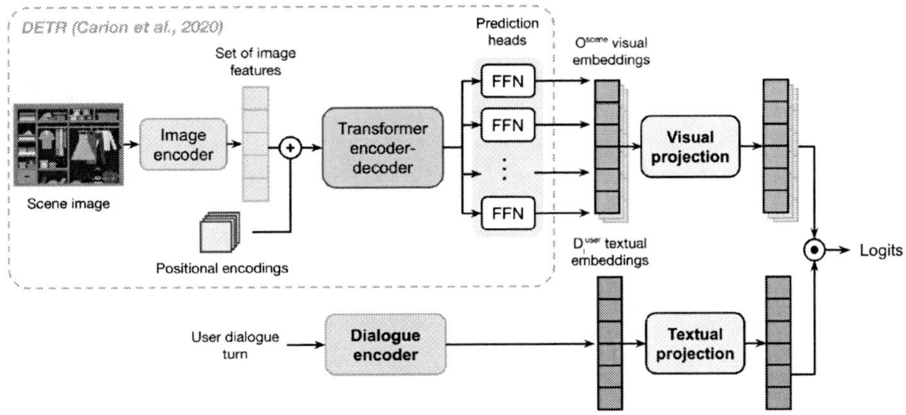

Figure 4: Scene-dialogue alignment. We pre-extract the visual embeddings from an object detection model trained on our dataset. The visual embeddings are used together with dialogue embeddings in the next training to perform multimodal object detection as a binary classification task.

4 Experiment

4.1 Dataset

For all of our experiments, we utilize the ambiguous candidate identification task from the SIMMC 2.1 dataset (Kottur et al., 2021). The dataset studies conversational scenarios where the system shares a co-observed vision (i.e., the same scene) with the user. The dataset focuses on improving the shopping experience in two domains: fashion and furniture. In the setting of SIMMC 2.1, the system is able to access the ground truth meta information of all objects (e.g., object price, size, material, brand, etc.) in the scene O^{scene}, while the user observes objects only through the scene viewpoints $\{I_1^{scene}, I_2^{scene}, \ldots, I_n^{scene}\}$ to describe a request.

Each dialogue in the dataset can utilize different scene viewpoints at different dialogue turns throughout the session. This represents scenarios where the user navigates the scene during the interaction in a real physical store. Therefore, the multimodal dialogue system needs to understand user requests using both the dialogue history and the scene image as a unified multimodal context. The statistics of the ambiguous candidate identification of SIMMC 2.1 dataset is presented in Table 1.[2]

Split	# Sample	# Dialogue	$\frac{O^{match}}{O^{scene}}$
Train	4239	3983	28.74%
Validation	414	371	24.72%
Test	940	905	30.78%

Table 1: Statistics of the ambiguous candidates identification of the SIMMC 2.1 dataset.

4.2 Baselines

We incorporate various baselines including simple heuristics and deep learning based multimodal matching methods from SIMMC 2.1.[3] For the heuristic methods, we incorporate uniform random prediction (**Random**), empty prediction (**No object**), and all objects prediction (**All objects**) as our baselines. For the deep learning approaches (**ResNet50-BERT** and **ResNet50-GPT2**), we apply cosine similarity between the feature extracted from ResNet-50 (He et al., 2016)[4] and two widely-used pre-trained LMs, i.e., BERT (Devlin et al., 2019)[5] and GPT2 (Radford et al., 2019)[6].

In addition to these baselines, we incorporate several additional baselines: 1) pre-trained CLIP (Radford et al., 2021)[7], which serves as a baseline for the object-dialogue alignment approach and 2) pre-trained MDETR (Kamath et al., 2021)[8], which represents a text-conditioned object detection baseline trained with an explicit align-

[2]We use the devtest split of SIMMC 2.1 dataset as the test set in our experiment.

[3]SIMMC 2.1 repository: https://github.com/facebookresearch/simmc2.

[4]We use the pre-extracted visual feature provided in the SIMMC 2.1 repository.

[5] https://huggingface.co/bert-base-uncased.

[6] https://huggingface.co/gpt2.

[7]We use the checkpoint from https://huggingface.co/openai/clip-vit-base-patch32.

[8]We use the EfficientNet B5 (ENB5) backbone checkpoint from https://github.com/ashkamath/mdetr.

ment between phrases and objects. For CLIP, we report both zero-shot (**CLIP (zero-shot)**) and direct fine-tuning (**CLIP**) performances, while for MDETR, we only use the zero-shot performance (**MDETR (zero-shot)**) due to the unavailability of the explicit alignment between objects and dialogues in the dataset.

4.3 Models

We propose three different approaches to solve the multimodal object identification task §3. For the dialogue-contextualized object detection approach, we incorporate one model, namely **SitCoM-DETR** which will be compared to the MDETR baseline. For the object-dialogue alignment approach, we incorporate two model variants, i.e., **CLIPPER (v1)** and **CLIPPER (v2)**. For the scene-object alignment approach, we incorporate two model variants, i.e., **DETR-BERT** and **DETR-GPT2**.

4.4 Evaluation

Given a label set L and a prediction set P, we define the number of true positive $N^{correct}$ as the objects that appear in both the prediction and the label sets. Using this definition, we evaluate the models' performance on the multimodal object identification task using three evaluation metrics, i.e., recall, precision, and F1-score. The definition of each metric is defined as:

$$Recall = \frac{N^{correct}}{\|L\|} \quad (1)$$

$$Precision = \frac{N^{correct}}{\|P\|} \quad (2)$$

$$F1 = \frac{2 * Precision * Recall}{Precision + Recall} \quad (3)$$

4.5 Implementation Details

Dialogue Preprocessing In all of our experiments, following prior works in end-to-end task-oriented dialogue system, we encode the last three utterances from the dialogue into a single text. For example a user dialogue turn $D_i^{user} = \{u_1, s_1, u_2, s_2, \ldots, u_i\}$ is encoded into a text "U: <u_{i-1}> S: <s_{i-1}> U: <u_i>" to be further processed by the dialogue encoder.

Inference strategy for object-dialogue alignment For the proposed CLIPPER model in the object-dialogue alignment approach, we simply apply sigmoid to the logits and use a threshold value of 0.5 (denoted as *Sigmoid*), since it has a built-in capability to perform multi-label classification. While for the CLIP model, which serves as a baseline, does not have the same capability, hence we use the mean value of the logits as the threshold (denoted as *Mean*). Additionally, we also evaluate the performance of the model if the top-k objects with the highest logits are considered valid predictions, where k denotes the correct amount of objects in the ground-truth label (denoted as *Oracle*).

Inference strategy for dialogue-contextualized object detection For the dialogue-contextualized object detection, since the model is originally for the object detection task, we develop our own inference strategy to allow it to perform multi-label classification for object identification. This is done through several steps: 1) we perform Hungarian matching using all objects, 2) we compute intersection over union (IoU) of all pairs of matched prediction and ground-truth bounding boxes[9], and 3) we take all objects having IoU score $\geq 10\%$[10].

Hyperparameter Details For the dialogue-contextualized object detection, we fine-tune the SitCoM-DETR model for a maximum of 200 epochs with AdamW optimizer using a linear learning rate decay, a learning rate between [1e-4..1e-5], and an early stopping of 10 epochs. For the object-dialogue alignment, we fine-tune the CLIP and CLIPPER models for a maximum of 200 epochs with AdamW optimizer using a linear learning rate decay, a learning rate between [1e-4..1e-5], and an early stopping of 10 epochs. For the scene-dialogue alignment, we fine-tune the DETR-BERT and DETR-GPT2 models for a maximum of 200 epochs with AdamW optimizer using a linear learning rate decay, a learning rate between [1e-4..1e-5], and an early stopping of 10 epochs.

5 Result and Analysis

5.1 Result Overview

The results of our experiments are shown in Table 2. The best baseline performance is achieved by **CLIP (fine-tuned)** with 45.09% F1-score outperforming the baselines provided by the SIMMC 2.1 (i.e., **ResNet50-GPT2** and **ResNet50-BERT**), showing the superiority of image-text alignment pre-training over separate unimodal pre-trainings for multimodal object identification. For the

[9]We do not consider the class label in the scoring to have a fairer comparison with the zero-shot MDETR approach.

[10]We align this with MDETR's class probability setting during inference.

Method Type	Approach	Recall	Precision	F1-score
	Baselines			
	No object	0.00%	0.00%	0.00%
Heuristic	Random	49.90%	22.43%	30.95%
	All objects	**100.00%**	22.34%	36.52%
SIMMC 2.1	ResNet50-GPT2	36.40%	42.26%	39.11%
	ResNet50-BERT	36.70%	**43.39%**	39.76%
Dialogue-Contextualized Object Detection	MDETR (zero-shot)	16.33%	29.70%	21.07%
Object-Dialogue Alignment	CLIP (zero-shot)	55.70%	26.39%	35.81%
	CLIP (fine-tuned)	73.00%	32.62%	**45.09%**
	Proposed Methods			
Dialogue-Contextualized Object Detection	SitCoM-DETR (aug)	47.82%	25.69%	33.42%
	SitCoM-DETR (no aug)	49.51%	25.81%	33.93%
Object-Dialogue Alignment	CLIPPER (v1)	**73.41%**	33.00%	45.53%
	CLIPPER (v2)	59.95%	25.60%	35.88%
Scene-Dialogue Alignment	DETR-BERT	65.47%	51.48%	57.64%
	DETR-GPT2	63.81%	**56.79%**	**60.10%**

Table 2: Experimental results of multimodal object identification on the SIMMC 2.1 dataset (Kottur et al., 2021). **Bold** denotes the best performances of baselines and proposed methods. Underline denotes the best performances within a method type.

dialogue-contextualized object detection methods, the proposed **SitCoM-DETR** outperforms **MDETR (zero-shot)**. Nevertheless, its performance for multimodal object identification is low despite having an acceptable object detection quality. We conjecture that a better method for adapting an object detection model for multimodal object identification is required, which is also shown by our *scene-dialogue alignment* approach in §3.4.

For the object-dialogue alignment, our **CLIPPER (v1)** marginally outperforms the **CLIP (fine-tuned)** baseline. This shows the effectiveness of modifying the CLIP objective which is explained in more detail in §5.3. For the scene-dialogue alignment (i.e., **DETR-BERT** and **DETR-GPT2**), where we combine the object detection and the image-text contrastive objective, we show a significant improvement over **CLIP (fine-tuned)**, which is the highest-performing baseline, by ~10-15% F1-score. This suggests the importance of combining object detection representation and image-text contrastive learning to fulfill the need for both visual and spatial matching to solve multimodal object identification.

5.2 Pitfalls of the Best Performing Models

We manually analyze the incorrect predictions made by our scene-dialogue alignment approaches, i.e., **DETR-BERT** and **DETR-GPT2**. Based on our analysis in Table 5, our models encounter two main issues. First, our models have difficulties in identifying objects when faced with a sudden object shift in the dialogue, e.g., the sudden shift from beds to a chair in this user dialogue turn U: "*I need a new bed too. Any suggestions?*", S: "*Both of these grey beds are in stock.*", U: "*What's the rating on that chair?*".

The second issue is the ineffectiveness of handling textual coreferences. For instance, in the user dialogue turn U: "*How about a hat, but cheap and in a small?*", S: "*I have the black hat third from the front, the white hat at the front, and the black hat between them.*", U: "*What's the brand and reviews for the black hat?*", the models fail to recognize that "the black hat" in the user utterance is anaphoric to either "the black hat third from the front" or "the black hat between them" in the system utterance, which leads to the system's failure to identify both black hats as O^{match}. This shortcoming also be-

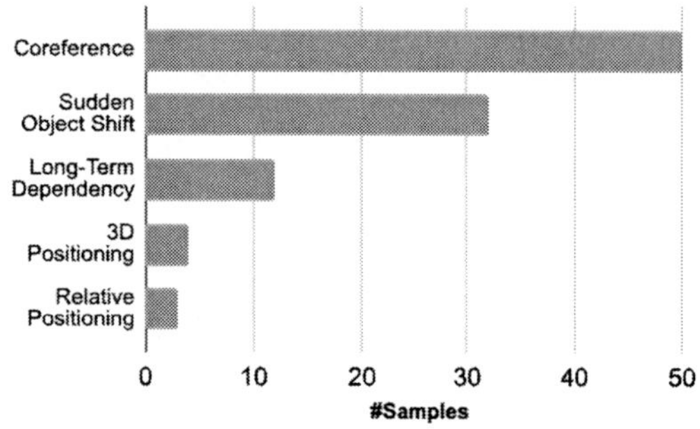

Figure 5: Frequency of error types of 100 misclassified samples from **DETR-BERT** and **DETR-GPT2**.

comes more pronounced if the coreference chains are longer.

These issues show the limitation of pre-trained LMs for discourse understanding and analysis, especially in terms of coreference and entity linking (Jurafsky and Martin, 2019; Pandia et al., 2021; Koto et al., 2021). Additionally, some other cases require the model to process long-term dialogue history dependency which existing LMs are not able to handle because of the quadratic cost bottleneck of the attention mechanism of the transformer architecture (Vaswani et al., 2017). Adapting an efficient attention mechanism with linear complexity might be beneficial to mitigate this problem.

5.3 Impact of Changing CLIP Objective

As shown in Table 3, the CLIPPER models with binary cross-entropy objective have a built-in capability for multi-label classification with **Sigmoid** which consistently performs better compared to the **Mean** thresholding. In addition, **CLIPPER (v1)** outperforms the original CLIP model which is trained with the cross-entropy loss. These facts suggest that changing the CLIP objective is beneficial for performing multi-label classification tasks such as multimodal object identification.

When using **Oracle**, we can observe a significant improvement in F1-score score, which mainly comes from the improvement in the precision with only a minor degradation on recall. This suggests that there is a very sensitive range of logits which consists of many negative samples with a few positive samples. To better segregate these few positive samples from the negative ones, hard negative mining techniques such as focal loss (Lin et al., 2020) might be beneficial to alleviate this problem.

Approach	**Rec.**	**Prec.**	**F1**
CLIP — Cross-Entropy			
Mean	73.00%	32.62%	<u>45.09%</u>
Oracle	74.99%	74.96%	**74.98%**
CLIPPER (v1) — Binary Cross-Entropy			
Sigmoid	73.41%	33.00%	<u>45.53%</u>
Mean	73.08%	31.97%	44.48%
Oracle	73.37%	73.34%	**73.36%**
CLIPPER (v2) — Binary Cross-Entropy			
Sigmoid	59.95%	25.60%	<u>35.88%</u>
Mean	53.90%	23.42%	32.65%
Oracle	54.92%	54.89%	**54.91%**

Table 3: Results for object-dialogue alignment models with different thresholding strategies.

6 Discussion

Based on the results and analysis, we show that the *scene-object alignment* approach is the best performing approach, achieving ~55-60% F1-score in the multimodal object identification task of SIMMC 2.1. We analyze the behavior of the model and conjecture that existing LMs have a limitation on understanding discourse. Additionally, we show the potential benefit of modeling the long-term dependency of dialogue history to further improve the quality of multimodal object identification task (§5.2). Lastly, we analyze the limitation of the existing image-text contrastive approaches for multimodal object identification and propose an alternative objective to alleviate this limitation (§5.3).

For future work, we aim to focus on the scene-dialogue alignment methods to further improve the model performance on the multimodal object identification capability. We note five potential points of improvement that can be further explored to improve the model performance in multimodal object identification: 1) the incorporation of cross-object attention in the modality fusion phase to enable a better relative position understanding between objects, 2) the incorporation of linear attention mechanism to handle the long-term dependency of dialogue history, 3) the exploration on better contrastive objectives for multimodal object identification, 4) the exploration on improving discourse understanding for LMs to better handle coreference and sudden object shift, and 5) the synthetic scene-dialogue data augmentation through the utilization of other publicly available object detection datasets to handle the in-domain data scarcity problem.

7 Conclusion

In this paper, we explore three methods to tackle multimodal object identification and evaluate them on SIMMC 2.1. Our best method, scene-dialogue alignment, improves the performance by $\sim$20% F1-score compared to the SIMMC 2.1 baselines. We provide an analysis of incorrect predictions by our best approach and the impact of changing the CLIP learning objective. We further provide discussion regarding the limitation of our methods and the potential directions for future works.

Acknowledgement

We appreciate the guidance that Prof. Dan Xu has provided for this research. This work has been supported by the School of Engineering PhD Fellowship Award, the Hong Kong University of Science and Technology and PF20-43679 Hong Kong PhD Fellowship Scheme, Research Grant Council, Hong Kong.

References

Huda Alamri, Vincent Cartillier, Abhishek Das, Jue Wang, Anoop Cherian, Irfan Essa, Dhruv Batra, Tim K Marks, Chiori Hori, Peter Anderson, et al. 2019. Audio visual scene-aware dialog. In *Proceedings of the IEEE/CVF Conference on Computer Vision and Pattern Recognition*, pages 7558–7567.

Stanislaw Antol, Aishwarya Agrawal, Jiasen Lu, Margaret Mitchell, Dhruv Batra, C Lawrence Zitnick, and Devi Parikh. 2015. Vqa: Visual question answering. In *Proceedings of the IEEE international conference on computer vision*, pages 2425–2433.

Jake Brawer, Olivier Mangin, Alessandro Roncone, Sarah Widder, and Brian Scassellati. 2018. Situated human–robot collaboration: predicting intent from grounded natural language. In *2018 IEEE/RSJ International Conference on Intelligent Robots and Systems (IROS)*, pages 827–833. IEEE.

Nicolas Carion, Francisco Massa, Gabriel Synnaeve, Nicolas Usunier, Alexander Kirillov, and Sergey Zagoruyko. 2020. End-to-end object detection with transformers. In *Computer Vision – ECCV 2020*, pages 213–229, Cham. Springer International Publishing.

Wenliang Dai, Samuel Cahyawijaya, Zihan Liu, and Pascale Fung. 2021. Multimodal end-to-end sparse model for emotion recognition. In *Proceedings of the 2021 Conference of the North American Chapter of the Association for Computational Linguistics: Human Language Technologies*, pages 5305–5316, Online. Association for Computational Linguistics.

Abhishek Das, Satwik Kottur, Khushi Gupta, Avi Singh, Deshraj Yadav, José MF Moura, Devi Parikh, and Dhruv Batra. 2017. Visual dialog. In *Proceedings of the IEEE conference on computer vision and pattern recognition*, pages 326–335.

Jacob Devlin, Ming-Wei Chang, Kenton Lee, and Kristina Toutanova. 2019. BERT: Pre-training of deep bidirectional transformers for language understanding. In *Proceedings of the 2019 Conference of the North American Chapter of the Association for Computational Linguistics: Human Language Technologies, Volume 1 (Long and Short Papers)*, pages 4171–4186, Minneapolis, Minnesota. Association for Computational Linguistics.

Dimitra Gkatzia, Verena Rieser, Phil Bartie, and William Mackaness. 2015. From the virtual to the RealWorld: Referring to objects in real-world spatial scenes. In *Proceedings of the 2015 Conference on Empirical Methods in Natural Language Processing*, pages 1936–1942, Lisbon, Portugal. Association for Computational Linguistics.

Kaiming He, Xiangyu Zhang, Shaoqing Ren, and Jian Sun. 2016. Deep residual learning for image recognition. In *2016 IEEE Conference on Computer Vision and Pattern Recognition (CVPR)*, pages 770–778.

MD Zakir Hossain, Ferdous Sohel, Mohd Fairuz Shiratuddin, and Hamid Laga. 2019. A comprehensive survey of deep learning for image captioning. *ACM Computing Surveys (CsUR)*, 51(6):1–36.

Ronghang Hu, Huazhe Xu, Marcus Rohrbach, Jiashi Feng, Kate Saenko, and Trevor Darrell. 2016. Natural language object retrieval. In *Proceedings of the IEEE conference on computer vision and pattern recognition*, pages 4555–4564.

Nikolai Ilinykh, Sina Zarrieß, and David Schlangen. 2019. Tell me more: A dataset of visual scene description sequences. In *Proceedings of the 12th International Conference on Natural Language Generation*, pages 152–157, Tokyo, Japan. Association for Computational Linguistics.

Chao Jia, Yinfei Yang, Ye Xia, Yi-Ting Chen, Zarana Parekh, Hieu Pham, Quoc Le, Yun-Hsuan Sung, Zhen Li, and Tom Duerig. 2021. Scaling up visual and vision-language representation learning with noisy text supervision. In *International Conference on Machine Learning*, pages 4904–4916. PMLR.

Justin Johnson, Bharath Hariharan, Laurens Van Der Maaten, Li Fei-Fei, C Lawrence Zitnick, and Ross Girshick. 2017. Clevr: A diagnostic dataset for compositional language and elementary visual reasoning. In *Proceedings of the IEEE conference on computer vision and pattern recognition*, pages 2901–2910.

Dan Jurafsky and James H Martin. 2019. *Speech and Language Processing: An Introduction to Natural Language Processing, Computational Linguistics, and Speech Recognition (3rd draft ed.).* Stanford Univ.

Aishwarya Kamath, Mannat Singh, Yann LeCun, Gabriel Synnaeve, Ishan Misra, and Nicolas Carion. 2021. MDETR - modulated detection for end-to-end multi-modal understanding. In *2021 IEEE/CVF International Conference on Computer Vision (ICCV)*. IEEE.

Sahar Kazemzadeh, Vicente Ordonez, Mark Matten, and Tamara Berg. 2014. ReferItGame: Referring to objects in photographs of natural scenes. In *Proceedings of the 2014 Conference on Empirical Methods in Natural Language Processing (EMNLP)*, pages 787–798, Doha, Qatar. Association for Computational Linguistics.

Fajri Koto, Jey Han Lau, and Timothy Baldwin. 2021. Discourse probing of pretrained language models. In *Proceedings of the 2021 Conference of the North American Chapter of the Association for Computational Linguistics: Human Language Technologies*, pages 3849–3864, Online. Association for Computational Linguistics.

Satwik Kottur, Seungwhan Moon, Alborz Geramifard, and Babak Damavandi. 2021. SIMMC 2.0: A task-oriented dialog dataset for immersive multimodal conversations. In *Proceedings of the 2021 Conference on Empirical Methods in Natural Language Processing*, pages 4903–4912, Online and Punta Cana, Dominican Republic. Association for Computational Linguistics.

Satwik Kottur, José M. F. Moura, Devi Parikh, Dhruv Batra, and Marcus Rohrbach. 2019. CLEVR-dialog: A diagnostic dataset for multi-round reasoning in visual dialog. In *Proceedings of the 2019 Conference of the North American Chapter of the Association for Computational Linguistics: Human Language Technologies, Volume 1 (Long and Short Papers)*, pages 582–595, Minneapolis, Minnesota. Association for Computational Linguistics.

Satwik Kottur, José MF Moura, Devi Parikh, Dhruv Batra, and Marcus Rohrbach. 2018. Visual coreference resolution in visual dialog using neural module networks. In *Proceedings of the European Conference on Computer Vision (ECCV)*, pages 153–169.

Chia-Wen Kuo and Zsolt Kira. 2022. Beyond a pre-trained object detector: Cross-modal textual and visual context for image captioning. In *Proceedings of the IEEE/CVF Conference on Computer Vision and Pattern Recognition*, pages 17969–17979.

Frédéric Landragin. 2006. Visual perception, language and gesture: A model for their understanding in multimodal dialogue systems. *Signal Processing*, 86(12):3578–3595.

Zhihui Li, Lina Yao, Xiaoqin Zhang, Xianzhi Wang, Salil Kanhere, and Huaxiang Zhang. 2019. Zero-shot object detection with textual descriptions. In *Proceedings of the AAAI Conference on Artificial Intelligence*, volume 33, pages 8690–8697.

Tsung-Yi Lin, Priya Goyal, Ross Girshick, Kaiming He, and Piotr Dollár. 2020. Focal loss for dense object detection. *IEEE Transactions on Pattern Analysis and Machine Intelligence*, 42(2):318–327.

Runtao Liu, Chenxi Liu, Yutong Bai, and Alan L Yuille. 2019. Clevr-ref+: Diagnosing visual reasoning with referring expressions. In *Proceedings of the IEEE/CVF Conference on Computer Vision and Pattern Recognition*, pages 4185–4194.

Sharid Loáiciga, Simon Dobnik, and David Schlangen. 2021a. Annotating anaphoric phenomena in situated dialogue. In *Proceedings of the 1st Workshop on Multimodal Semantic Representations (MMSR)*, pages 78–88, Groningen, Netherlands (Online). Association for Computational Linguistics.

Sharid Loáiciga, Simon Dobnik, and David Schlangen. 2021b. Reference and coreference in situated dialogue. In *Proceedings of the Second Workshop on Advances in Language and Vision Research*, pages 39–44, Online. Association for Computational Linguistics.

Holy Lovenia, Bryan Wilie, Romain Barraud, Samuel Cahyawijaya, Willy Chung, and Pascale Fung. 2022. Every picture tells a story: Image-grounded controllable stylistic story generation. In *Proceedings of the 6th Joint SIGHUM Workshop on Computational Linguistics for Cultural Heritage, Social Sciences, Humanities and Literature*, pages 40–52, Gyeongju, Republic of Korea. International Conference on Computational Linguistics.

Stephanie M. Lukin, Felix Gervits, Cory J. Hayes, Pooja Moolchandani, Anton Leuski, John G. Rogers III, Carlos Sanchez Amaro, Matthew Marge, Clare R. Voss, and David Traum. 2018. ScoutBot: A dialogue system for collaborative navigation. In *Proceedings of ACL 2018, System Demonstrations*, pages 93–98, Melbourne, Australia. Association for Computational Linguistics.

Junhua Mao, Jonathan Huang, Alexander Toshev, Oana Camburu, Alan L Yuille, and Kevin Murphy. 2016. Generation and comprehension of unambiguous object descriptions. In *Proceedings of the IEEE conference on computer vision and pattern recognition*, pages 11–20.

Kyungbok Min, Minh Dang, and Hyeonjoon Moon. 2021. Deep learning-based short story generation for an image using the encoder-decoder structure. *IEEE Access*, 9:113550–113557.

Margaret Mitchell, Kees van Deemter, and Ehud Reiter. 2010. Natural reference to objects in a visual domain. In *Proceedings of the 6th international natural language generation conference*.

Seungwhan Moon, Satwik Kottur, Paul Crook, Ankita De, Shivani Poddar, Theodore Levin, David Whitney, Daniel Difranco, Ahmad Beirami, Eunjoon Cho, Rajen Subba, and Alborz Geramifard. 2020. Situated and interactive multimodal conversations. In *Proceedings of the 28th International Conference on Computational Linguistics*, pages 1103–1121, Barcelona, Spain (Online). International Committee on Computational Linguistics.

Nasrin Mostafazadeh, Chris Brockett, Bill Dolan, Michel Galley, Jianfeng Gao, Georgios Spithourakis, and Lucy Vanderwende. 2017. Image-grounded conversations: Multimodal context for natural question and response generation. In *Proceedings of the Eighth International Joint Conference on Natural Language Processing (Volume 1: Long Papers)*, pages 462–472, Taipei, Taiwan. Asian Federation of Natural Language Processing.

Lalchand Pandia, Yan Cong, and Allyson Ettinger. 2021. Pragmatic competence of pre-trained language models through the lens of discourse connectives. In *Proceedings of the 25th Conference on Computational Natural Language Learning*, pages 367–379, Online. Association for Computational Linguistics.

Alec Radford, Jong Wook Kim, Chris Hallacy, Aditya Ramesh, Gabriel Goh, Sandhini Agarwal, Girish Sastry, Amanda Askell, Pamela Mishkin, Jack Clark, Gretchen Krueger, and Ilya Sutskever. 2021. Learning transferable visual models from natural language supervision. In *Proceedings of the 38th International Conference on Machine Learning*, volume 139 of *Proceedings of Machine Learning Research*, pages 8748–8763. PMLR.

Alec Radford, Jeff Wu, Rewon Child, David Luan, Dario Amodei, and Ilya Sutskever. 2019. Language models are unsupervised multitask learners.

Amrita Saha, Mitesh Khapra, and Karthik Sankaranarayanan. 2018. Towards building large scale multimodal domain-aware conversation systems. In *Proceedings of the AAAI Conference on Artificial Intelligence*, volume 32.

Paul Hongsuck Seo, Andreas Lehrmann, Bohyung Han, and Leonid Sigal. 2017. Visual reference resolution using attention memory for visual dialog. *Advances in neural information processing systems*, 30.

Piyush Sharma, Nan Ding, Sebastian Goodman, and Radu Soricut. 2018. Conceptual captions: A cleaned, hypernymed, image alt-text dataset for automatic image captioning. In *Proceedings of the 56th Annual Meeting of the Association for Computational Linguistics (Volume 1: Long Papers)*, pages 2556–2565.

Kurt Shuster, Samuel Humeau, Antoine Bordes, and Jason Weston. 2020. Image-chat: Engaging grounded conversations. In *Proceedings of the 58th Annual Meeting of the Association for Computational Linguistics*, pages 2414–2429, Online. Association for Computational Linguistics.

Amanpreet Singh, Ronghang Hu, Vedanuj Goswami, Guillaume Couairon, Wojciech Galuba, Marcus Rohrbach, and Douwe Kiela. 2022. Flava: A foundational language and vision alignment model. In *Proceedings of the IEEE/CVF Conference on Computer Vision and Pattern Recognition*, pages 15638–15650.

Russell Stewart, Mykhaylo Andriluka, and Andrew Y. Ng. 2016. End-to-end people detection in crowded scenes. In *2016 IEEE Conference on Computer Vision and Pattern Recognition (CVPR)*, pages 2325–2333.

Qingfeng Sun, Yujing Wang, Can Xu, Kai Zheng, Yaming Yang, Huang Hu, Fei Xu, Jessica Zhang, Xiubo Geng, and Daxin Jiang. 2022. Multimodal dialogue response generation. In *Proceedings of the 60th Annual Meeting of the Association for Computational Linguistics (Volume 1: Long Papers)*, pages 2854–2866, Dublin, Ireland. Association for Computational Linguistics.

Anirudh Sundar and Larry Heck. 2022. Multimodal conversational AI: A survey of datasets and approaches. In *Proceedings of the 4th Workshop on NLP for Conversational AI*, pages 131–147, Dublin, Ireland. Association for Computational Linguistics.

Ronja Utescher and Sina Zarrieß. 2021. What did this castle look like before? exploring referential relations in naturally occurring multimodal texts. In *Proceedings of the Third Workshop on Beyond Vision and LANguage: inTEgrating Real-world kNowledge (LANTERN)*, pages 53–60.

Ashish Vaswani, Noam Shazeer, Niki Parmar, Jakob Uszkoreit, Llion Jones, Aidan N Gomez, Łukasz Kaiser, and Illia Polosukhin. 2017. Attention is all you need. *Advances in neural information processing systems*, 30.

Zhaoqing Wang, Yu Lu, Qiang Li, Xunqiang Tao, Yandong Guo, Mingming Gong, and Tongliang Liu. 2022. Cris: Clip-driven referring image segmentation. In *Proceedings of the IEEE/CVF Conference on Computer Vision and Pattern Recognition*, pages 11686–11695.

Licheng Yu, Patrick Poirson, Shan Yang, Alexander C Berg, and Tamara L Berg. 2016. Modeling context in referring expressions. In *European Conference on Computer Vision*, pages 69–85. Springer.

A MDETR Architecture

We provide Figure 6 for illustrative comparison with our proposed SitCoM-DETR in §3.2.

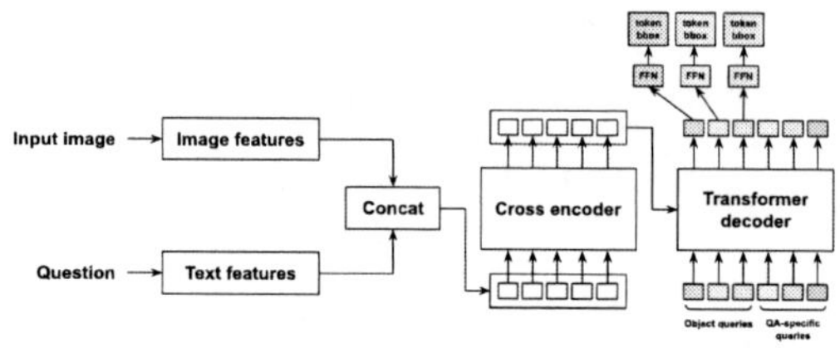

Figure 6: MDETR architecture.

A Unified Framework for Emotion Identification and Generation in Dialogues

Avinash Madasu[*†] **Mauajama Firdaus**[*] **Asif Ekbal**
Indian Institute of Technology Patna, India
avinashmadasu17@gmail.com; {mauajama.pcs16,asif}@iitp.ac.in

Abstract

Social chatbots have gained immense popularity, and their appeal lies not just in their capacity to respond to the diverse requests from users, but also in the ability to develop an emotional connection with users. To further develop and promote social chatbots, we need to concentrate on increasing user interaction and take into account both the intellectual and emotional quotient in the conversational agents. In this paper, we propose a multi-task framework that jointly identifies the emotion of a given dialogue and generates response in accordance to the identified emotion. We employ a BERT based network for creating an empathetic system and use a mixed objective function that trains the end-to-end network with both the classification and generation loss. Experimental results show that our proposed framework outperforms current state-of-the-art models.

1 Introduction

One of the significant challenges of artificial intelligence (AI) is to endow the machine with the ability to interact in natural language with humans. The personal assistants in our mobile devices invariably assist in our day-to-day lives by answering a wide range of queries. Such assistants act as social agents that take care of the various activities of their users. Besides reacting passively to user requests, they also proactively anticipate user needs and provide in-time assistance, such as reminding of an upcoming event or suggesting a useful service without receiving explicit user requests (Sarikaya, 2017). The daunting task for these agents is that they have to work well in open domain scenarios as people learn to rely on them to effectively maintain their works and lives efficiently.

Building social chatbots to tackle the emotional needs is indeed of great benefit to our society. The primary objective of these chatbots is not inherently to answer all the users' questions, but rather to be a virtual companion of the users. Therefore, it is essential to empower the conversational agents with the ability to perceive and express emotions to make them capable of interacting with the user at the human level. These agents help enhance user satisfaction (Prendinger et al., 2005), while reducing the breakdowns in conversations (Martinovski and Traum, 2003) and providing user retention. Hence, dialogue systems capable of generating replies while considering the user's emotional state is the most desirable advancement in Artificial Intelligence (AI). Previously, researchers have focused upon classifying user emotions (Poria et al., 2019; Chauhan et al., 2019) in conversations. For building an intelligent agent, sheer understanding of emotions is insufficient; hence several works (Song et al., 2019; Colombo et al., 2019) have concentrated in inducing emotions into the dialogue system. Most of these existing research have focused on generating emotionally aware (Rashkin et al., 2019; Lin et al., 2019) or emotionally controlled responses (Zhou et al., 2018; Huang et al., 2018).

In our current work, we focus on creating an end-to-end emotional response generation system that is capable of identifying the emotions and use the emotional information simultaneously for generating empathetic and emotionally coherent responses. The key contributions of our current work are three-fold: (i) We propose a joint model that is able to simultaneously identify the emotions from the utterances and incorporate the emotional information for generation; (ii) We design a multi-task hierarchical framework with a mixed objective function that jointly optimize the classification and generation loss; (iii) Experimental analysis shows that the proposed multi-task framework is better in generating empathetic responses as opposed to single task emotion generation networks.

[*]Both authors contributed equally to this research.
[†]Work done as an intern at IIT Patna.

Proceedings of the 17th Conference of the European Chapter of the Association for Computational Linguistics: Student Research Workshop, pages 73–78
May 2-4, 2023 ©2023 Association for Computational Linguistics

2 Related Work

In (Welivita et al., 2020), the authors proposed a novel large-scale emotional dialogue dataset, consisting of 1M dialogues and annotated with 32 emotions and 9 empathetic response intents using a BERT-based fine-grained dialogue emotion classifier. Most of the early research on emotion classification was performed upon textual datasets mostly taken from twitter (Colneriĉ and Demsar, 2018; Ghosal et al., 2018). The authors in (Chen et al., 2018), propose a multi-party conversational dataset for emotions. Lately, emotional text generation has gained immense popularity (Huang et al., 2018; Li and Sun, 2018; Lin et al., 2019; Li et al., 2017; Ghosh et al., 2017; Rashkin et al., 2019). In (Zhou et al., 2018), an emotional chatting machine (ECM) was built based on seq2seq framework for generating emotional responses. Recently, a lexicon-based attention framework was employed to generate responses with a specific emotion (Song et al., 2019). Emotional embedding, affective sampling and regularizer were employed to generate the affect driven dialogues in (Colombo et al., 2019). The authors employed curriculum dual learning (Shen and Feng, 2020) for emotion controllable response generation. In (Asghar et al., 2018; Lubis et al., 2018; Zhong et al., 2019; Li et al., 2020), the authors proposed an end-to-end neural framework that captures the emotional state of the user for generating empathetic responses. Our present research differs from these as we propose and address a novel task of generating responses and simultaneously identifying the emotions in a multi-task framework.

3 Problem Definition

In this paper, we address the problem of identifying emotion from a user utterance and generate empathetic responses accordingly. In this setting, emotion remains the same throughout the conversation. Let $U_p = u_{p,1}, u_{p,2}, ..., u_{p,j}$ be the set of utterances in a conversation and E_p denotes the emotion for the conversation. We aim to identify E_p through our emotion classification sub-network and use this emotion information to generate responses to the user utterances U_p. Understanding emotion initially is very crucial to empathetic response generation and cannot be treated independently. Hence, we aim to propose an end-to-end model capable to identifying emotions and utilizes this emotion information for generation.

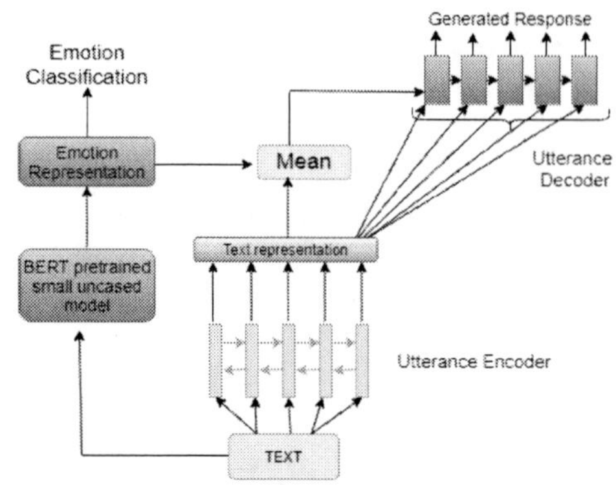

Figure 1: Architecture of the proposed model

4 Proposed Model

In this section, we present the proposed model. It has two sub-networks: Emotion classification sub-network and Generation sub-network.

4.1 Emotion classification sub-network

The input to this sub-network is a user utterance and the output is predicted emotion for this utterance. We employed a pre-trained BERT (Devlin et al., 2019) small uncased model. Instead of taking $[CLS]$ token from just the final layer, we learn a weighted representation on $[CLS]$ tokens from all the layers.

$$\begin{aligned} h^l_{cls} &= \text{BERT}(U_p) l \in \{1, \dots, 12\} \\ C_E &= \sum_{i=1}^{l} \alpha_{t,i} h^l_{cls} \\ \alpha_{t,i} &= softmax({h^l_{cls}}^T W_g h_{cls,t}) \\ P(\tilde{y_{em}} \mid y_{em}) &= softmax(W_E C_E), \end{aligned} \tag{1}$$

y_{em} is the true emotion labels and $\tilde{y_{em}}$ is the predicted emotion label. The emotion classifier is trained by minimizing the negative log-likelihood

$$\mathcal{L}_{Emo} = - \sum_{em=1}^{N} y_{em} \log \tilde{y_{em}} \tag{2}$$

4.2 Generation sub-network

Utterance Encoder For a given utterance U_p, we employ a bidirectional Gated Recurrent Units (Bi-GRU) (Cho et al., 2014) to encode each word $u_{p,j}$, where $j \in (1, 2, 3, ...n)$ having d-dimensional embedding vectors into the hidden representation $h_{U_k,i}$. We concatenate the last hidden representation from both the unidirectional GRUs to form the final hidden representation of a given utterance as follows:

$$h^{en}_{U_p,i} = [GRU(u_{p,j}, \overrightarrow{h_{U_p,i-1}}), GRU(u_{p,j}, \overleftarrow{h_{U_p,i-1}})] \quad (3)$$

Utterance Decoder For decoding the response to a given user utterance, we build a GRU which takes encoder last hidden state as the initial hidden state and words generated previously. To integrate emotion information, we compute the mean of emotion representation obtained using C_E and the encoder's last hidden state to initialize as decoder's initial state. We use the input feeding decoding along with the attention (Luong et al., 2015) mechanism for enhancing the performance of the model. Using the decoder state $h^{dec}_{d,t}$ as the query vector, we apply self-attention on the hidden representation of the utterance encoder. The decoder state and the encoder vector are concatenated and used to calculate a final distribution of the probability over the output tokens.

$$\begin{aligned} h_{d,t-1} &= Mean(C_E, h^{en}_{c,t}) \\ h^{dec}_{d,t} &= GRU_d(y_{k,t-1}, h_{d,t-1}) \\ c_t &= \sum_{i=1}^{k} \alpha_{t,i} h^{ctx}_{c,p}, \\ \alpha_{t,i} &= softmax({h^{en}_{c,p}}^T W_f h_{d,t}) \\ \tilde{h}_t &= tanh(W_{\tilde{h}}[h_{d,t}; c_t]) \\ P(\tilde{y}_t \mid y^*_t) &= softmax(W_V \tilde{h}_t) \end{aligned} \quad (4)$$

where, W_f, W_V and $W_{\tilde{h}}$ are the trainable weight matrices. y^*_t, $\tilde{y}_t$ are the ground truth and generated words at each time-step respectively. We employ the teacher forcing (Williams and Zipser, 1989) algorithm at every decoding step to minimize the negative log-likelihood on the model distribution.

$$\mathcal{L}_{Gen} = -\sum_{t=1}^{m} \log p(y^*_t | y^*_1, \ldots, y^*_{t-1}) \quad (5)$$

4.3 Joint Training (JT)

To train an end-to-end model, we jointly optimize the emotion classification loss and the generation loss. The final loss of the entire model is:

$$\mathcal{L}_{JT} = \mathcal{L}_{Emo} + \mathcal{L}_{Gen} \quad (6)$$

5 Dataset and Experimentation

Dataset We conduct our experiment on the EmpatheticDialogues (Rashkin et al., 2019) dataset which consist of 25k open-domain conversations grounded in emotional situations and provides 32 emotion classes. We used the train, test splits provided by the authors.

Implementation Details The hidden size of utterance encoder Bi-GRU is 768 and the hidden size of utterance decoder GRU is 768. A dropout of 0.3 is applied on both the utterance encoder and decoder layers. A dropout of 0.1 is applied on the weighted emotion representation obtained from 1 just before the final softmax layer. All the models are trained with a batch size of 32 for 10 epochs. AdamW is used as the optimizer with a learning rate of 0.0001. The maximum sentence length used is 80.

6 Baseline Methods and Metrics

We compare our model to the below SoTA models.

Pretrained:
It is a transformer model trained on 1.7 billion REDDIT conversations (Lin et al., 2019).

Fine-Tuned:
The above pre-trained model is fine-tuned on Emotion Dialogue Dataset (Lin et al., 2019).

MULTITASK:
It is an emotion classifier trained using a linear layer on the top of a transformer (Lin et al., 2019).

EmoPrepend-1:
A top-1 predicted emotion is appended to the beginning of input sentence (Lin et al., 2019).

ENSEM-DM:
The representations obtained from transformer encoder and pre-trained emotion classifier are concatenated and then fed to transformer decoder (Lin et al., 2019).

CAiRE:
It is the current State-of-the-art model. In this model, a large language model is jointly trained for multiple objectives response language modeling, response prediction, and dialogue emotion detection. It is then fine-tuned on EmphatheticDialogues dataset (Lin et al., 2019).

Bi-LSTM-Attn (JT):
To signify the importance of a BERT pre-trained model, we replace BERT with Bi-LSTM layer with attention applied on the top of it.

Metrics:
We use AVG BLEU, the average of BLEU-1, BLEU-2, BLEU-3, BLEU-4 (Papineni et al., 2002) and emotion F1 for comparison. As the dataset is unbalanced, we didn't use emotion accuracy for models' comparison. We used balanced emotion

labels during manual evaluation and hence we included emotion accuracy.

Table 1: Automatic evaluation results of emotion identification and generation. Here: JT-joint training

Models	AVG BLEU	EMO F1
Pretrained (Lin et al., 2019)	5.01	-
Fine-Tuned (Lin et al., 2019)	6.27	-
MULTITASK (Lin et al., 2019)	5.42	-
EmoPrepend-1 (Lin et al., 2019)	4.36	-
ENSEM-DM (Lin et al., 2019)	6.83	-
CAiRE (Lin et al., 2019)	7.03	-
Bi-LSTM (JT)	6.84	8.22
Bi-LSTM + Attn (JT)	6.13	19.89
BERT (JT)	**7.71**	**25.2**

7 Result and Analysis

In this section, we present the results of our proposed framework. We compute average BLEU scores for the model response, comparing against the gold label (the actual response). From the Table 1, it is evident that our proposed framework performs significantly better in comparison to the existing baselines[1]. As compared to CAiRE, we see an improvement of 0.68 in average BLEU score. Emotion identification is crucial for relevant empathetic responses and the generated responses should be in accordance to sentiment expressed by the user. Joint training helps in learning better emotion representations thereby generating contextually coherent, interactive, engaging and empathetic responses. The emotion classification results reported in Table 1, demonstrates effectiveness of joint training. From table 1, it is visible that the F1-score of BERT based classifier is better in comparison to the joint training Bi-LSTM and Bi-LSTM + Attn with a gain in performance of 17% and 6% respectively.

We recruit six annotators (in a similar manner as (Shang et al., 2015; Tian et al., 2019)) from a third party company, having high-level language skills. In Table 2 we present the results of human evaluation. We sampled 250 responses per model for evaluation with the utterance and the conversational history provided for generation. First, we evaluate the quality of the response on two conventional criteria: *Fluency* and *Consistency*. These are rated

[1]all the results are statistically significant. We perform statistical significance t-test (Welch, 1947), and it is conducted at 5% (0.05) significance level

Table 2: Human evaluation results of emotion identification and generation. Here: Flu-Fluency; Cons-Consistency; EmoAcc-Emotion Accuracy

Model	Flu	Cons	EmoAcc
Bi-LSTM (JT)	3.82	3.73	48%
Bi-LSTM + Attn (JT)	3.93	3.82	55%
BERT (JT)	**4.11**	**3.96**	**69%**

on a five-scale, where 1, 3, 5 indicate unacceptable, moderate, and excellent performance, respectively, while 2 and 4 are used for unsure. Secondly, we evaluate the emotion quotient of a response in terms of *Emotion Accuracy* metric that measures whether the emotion induced in the response is in accordance with the predicted emotion information and the dialogue history. Here, 0 indicates irrelevant or contradictory, and 1 indicates consistent with the predicted emotion and dialogue context. We compute Fleiss' kappa (Fleiss, 1971) to measure inter-rater consistency. The Fleiss' kappa for Fluency and Consistency is 0.53 and 0.49, indicating moderate agreement. For Emotion Accuracy, we get 0.65 as the kappa scores indicating substantial agreement. From the table, it is evident that our proposed framework performs better for all the human evaluation metrics. The responses generated are fluent, consistent to the dialogue history and the emotion quotient of the generated response is higher in comparison to the baselines. Also, the joint training mechanism proves to be efficient for simultaneously identifying the emotions and using the emotional information for generation.

8 Conclusion and Future Work

In our current work, we propose the task of jointly identifying the emotions in dialogues and use the emotional information for generating empathetic responses. For our proposed task, we design a BERT-based multi-task framework, that simultaneously identifies the emotion of the speaker and generate the response in accordance to the situation, conversational history and the predicted emotions. Experimental analysis on the EmpatheticDialogues dataset shows that the proposed framework achieved State-of-the-art results. In future, we look forward to designing sophisticated joint mechanisms to enhance empathetic response generation.

References

Nabiha Asghar, Pascal Poupart, Jesse Hoey, Xin Jiang, and Lili Mou. 2018. Affective neural response generation. In *Advances in Information Retrieval - 40th European Conference on IR Research, ECIR 2018, Grenoble, France, March 26-29, 2018, Proceedings*, pages 154–166. Springer.

Dushyant Singh Chauhan, Md Shad Akhtar, Asif Ekbal, and Pushpak Bhattacharyya. 2019. Context-aware interactive attention for multi-modal sentiment and emotion analysis. In *Proceedings of the 2019 Conference on Empirical Methods in Natural Language Processing and the 9th International Joint Conference on Natural Language Processing (EMNLP-IJCNLP)*, pages 5651–5661.

Sheng-Yeh Chen, Chao-Chun Hsu, Chuan-Chun Kuo, Lun-Wei Ku, et al. 2018. Emotionlines: An emotion corpus of multi-party conversations. *arXiv preprint arXiv:1802.08379*.

Kyunghyun Cho, Bart Van Merriënboer, Caglar Gulcehre, Dzmitry Bahdanau, Fethi Bougares, Holger Schwenk, and Yoshua Bengio. 2014. Learning phrase representations using rnn encoder-decoder for statistical machine translation. *arXiv preprint arXiv:1406.1078*.

Niko Colneriĉ and Janez Demsar. 2018. Emotion recognition on twitter: Comparative study and training a unison model. *IEEE Transactions on Affective Computing*, 11(3):433–446.

Pierre Colombo, Wojciech Witon, Ashutosh Modi, James Kennedy, and Mubbasir Kapadia. 2019. Affect-driven dialog generation. *Proceedings of the 2019 Conference of the North American Chapter of the Association for Computational Linguistics: Human Language Technologies, NAACL-HLT 2019, Minneapolis, MN, USA, June 2-7, 2019, Volume 1 (Long and Short Papers)*, pages 3734–3743.

Jacob Devlin, Ming-Wei Chang, Kenton Lee, and Kristina Toutanova. 2019. BERT: Pre-training of deep bidirectional transformers for language understanding. In *Proceedings of the 2019 Conference of the North American Chapter of the Association for Computational Linguistics: Human Language Technologies, Volume 1 (Long and Short Papers)*, pages 4171–4186, Minneapolis, Minnesota. Association for Computational Linguistics.

Joseph L Fleiss. 1971. Measuring nominal scale agreement among many raters. *Psychological bulletin*, 76(5):378.

Deepanway Ghosal, Md Shad Akhtar, Dushyant Chauhan, Soujanya Poria, Asif Ekbal, and Pushpak Bhattacharyya. 2018. Contextual inter-modal attention for multi-modal sentiment analysis. In *Proceedings of the 2018 Conference on Empirical Methods in Natural Language Processing, Brussels, Belgium, October 31 - November 4, 2018*, pages 3454–3466.

Sayan Ghosh, Mathieu Chollet, Eugene Laksana, Louis-Philippe Morency, and Stefan Scherer. 2017. Affect-lm: A neural language model for customizable affective text generation. *Proceedings of the 55th Annual Meeting of the Association for Computational Linguistics, ACL 2017, Vancouver, Canada, July 30 - August 4, Volume 1: Long Papers*, pages 634–642.

Chenyang Huang, Osmar R Zaiane, Amine Trabelsi, and Nouha Dziri. 2018. Automatic dialogue generation with expressed emotions. In *Proceedings of the 2018 Conference of the North American Chapter of the Association for Computational Linguistics: Human Language Technologies, NAACL-HLT, New Orleans, Louisiana, USA, June 1-6, 2018, Volume 2 (Short Papers)*, pages 49–54.

Jingyuan Li and Xiao Sun. 2018. A syntactically constrained bidirectional-asynchronous approach for emotional conversation generation. *Proceedings of the 2018 Conference on Empirical Methods in Natural Language Processing, Brussels, Belgium, October 31 - November 4, 2018*, pages 678–683.

Qintong Li, Hongshen Chen, Zhaochun Ren, Zhumin Chen, Zhaopeng Tu, and Jun Ma. 2020. Empgan: Multi-resolution interactive empathetic dialogue generation. *AAAI*.

Yanran Li, Hui Su, Xiaoyu Shen, Wenjie Li, Ziqiang Cao, and Shuzi Niu. 2017. Dailydialog: A manually labelled multi-turn dialogue dataset. *Proceedings of the Eighth International Joint Conference on Natural Language Processing, IJCNLP 2017, Taipei, Taiwan, November 27 - December 1, 2017 - Volume 1: Long Papers*, pages 986–995.

Zhaojiang Lin, Peng Xu, Genta Indra Winata, Zihan Liu, and Pascale Fung. 2019. Caire: An end-to-end empathetic chatbot. *arXiv preprint arXiv:1907.12108*.

Nurul Lubis, Sakriani Sakti, Koichiro Yoshino, and Satoshi Nakamura. 2018. Eliciting positive emotion through affect-sensitive dialogue response generation: A neural network approach. In *Proceedings of the Thirty-Second AAAI Conference on Artificial Intelligence, (AAAI-18), New Orleans, Louisiana, USA, February 2-7, 2018*, pages 5293–5300.

Minh-Thang Luong, Hieu Pham, and Christopher D Manning. 2015. Effective approaches to attention-based neural machine translation. *arXiv preprint arXiv:1508.04025*.

Bilyana Martinovski and David Traum. 2003. Breakdown in human-machine interaction: The error is the clue. In *Proceedings of the ISCA tutorial and research workshop on Error handling in dialogue systems*, pages 11–16.

Kishore Papineni, Salim Roukos, Todd Ward, and Wei-Jing Zhu. 2002. Bleu: a method for automatic evaluation of machine translation. In *Proceedings of the 40th Annual Meeting of the Association for Computational Linguistics, July 6-12, 2002, Philadelphia, PA,*

USA, pages 311–318. Association for Computational Linguistics.

Soujanya Poria, Devamanyu Hazarika, Navonil Majumder, Gautam Naik, Erik Cambria, and Rada Mihalcea. 2019. MELD: A multimodal multi-party dataset for emotion recognition in conversations. *Proceedings of the 57th Conference of the Association for Computational Linguistics, ACL 2019, Florence, Italy, July 28- August 2, 2019, Volume 1: Long Papers*, pages 527–536.

Helmut Prendinger, Junichiro Mori, and Mitsuru Ishizuka. 2005. Using human physiology to evaluate subtle expressivity of a virtual quizmaster in a mathematical game. *International journal of human-computer studies*, 62(2):231–245.

Hannah Rashkin, Eric Michael Smith, Margaret Li, and Y-Lan Boureau. 2019. Towards empathetic open-domain conversation models: A new benchmark and dataset. In *Proceedings of the 57th Conference of the Association for Computational Linguistics, ACL 2019, Florence, Italy, July 28- August 2, 2019, Volume 1: Long Papers*, pages 5370–5381.

Ruhi Sarikaya. 2017. The technology behind personal digital assistants: An overview of the system architecture and key components. *IEEE Signal Processing Magazine*, 34(1):67–81.

Lifeng Shang, Zhengdong Lu, and Hang Li. 2015. Neural responding machine for short-text conversation. In *Proceedings of the 53rd Annual Meeting of the Association for Computational Linguistics and the 7th International Joint Conference on Natural Language Processing (Volume 1: Long Papers)*, volume 1, pages 1577–1586.

Lei Shen and Yang Feng. 2020. Cdl: Curriculum dual learning for emotion-controllable response generation. *arXiv preprint arXiv:2005.00329*.

Zhenqiao Song, Xiaoqing Zheng, Lu Liu, Mu Xu, and Xuan-Jing Huang. 2019. Generating responses with a specific emotion in dialog. In *Proceedings of the 57th Conference of the Association for Computational Linguistics, ACL 2019, Florence, Italy, July 28- August 2, 2019, Volume 1: Long Papers*, pages 3685–3695.

Zhiliang Tian, Wei Bi, Xiaopeng Li, and Nevin L Zhang. 2019. Learning to abstract for memory-augmented conversational response generation. In *Proceedings of the 57th Conference of the Association for Computational Linguistics, ACL 2019, Florence, Italy, July 28- August 2, 2019, Volume 1: Long Papers*, pages 3816–3825.

Bernard L Welch. 1947. The generalization of student's' problem when several different population variances are involved. *Biometrika*, 34(1/2):28–35.

Anuradha Welivita, Yubo Xie, and Pearl Pu. 2020. Fine-grained emotion and intent learning in movie dialogues. *arXiv preprint arXiv:2012.13624*.

Ronald J Williams and David Zipser. 1989. A learning algorithm for continually running fully recurrent neural networks. *Neural computation*, 1(2):270–280.

Peixiang Zhong, Di Wang, and Chunyan Miao. 2019. An affect-rich neural conversational model with biased attention and weighted cross-entropy loss. In *The Thirty-Third AAAI Conference on Artificial Intelligence, AAAI 2019, The Thirty-First Innovative Applications of Artificial Intelligence Conference, Honolulu, Hawaii, USA, January 27 - February 1, 2019*, pages 7492–7500.

Hao Zhou, Minlie Huang, Tianyang Zhang, Xiaoyan Zhu, and Bing Liu. 2018. Emotional chatting machine: Emotional conversation generation with internal and external memory. In *Proceedings of the Thirty-Second AAAI Conference on Artificial Intelligence, (AAAI-18), New Orleans, Louisiana, USA, February 2-7, 2018*, pages 730–739.

A Example Appendix

This is a section in the appendix.

Improving and Simplifying Template-Based Named Entity Recognition

Murali Kondragunta **Olatz Perez-de-Viñaspre** **Maite Oronoz**
HiTZ Center - IXA research group,
University of the Basque Country
{mkondraguntaOO1}@ikasle.ehu.eus
{olatz.perezdevinaspre, maite.oronoz}@ehu.eus

Abstract

With the rise in larger language models, researchers started exploiting them by pivoting the downstream tasks as language modeling tasks using prompts. In this work, we convert the Named Entity Recognition task into a seq2seq task by generating the synthetic sentences using templates. Our main contribution is the conversion framework which provides faster inference. In addition, we test our method's performance in resource-rich, low resource and domain transfer settings. Results show that our method achieves comparable results in the resource-rich setting and outperforms the current seq2seq paradigm state-of-the-art approach in few-shot settings. Through the experiments, we observed that the negative examples play an important role in model's performance. We applied our approach over BART and T5-base models, and we notice that the T5 architecture aligns better with our task. The work is performed on the datasets in English language.

1 Introduction

Named Entity Recognition (NER) is traditionally approached as a sequence labeling task where a tag is predicted for each token. For a sentence with l tokens, the output would be l tags, usually, in the Inside–outside–beginning (IOB) tagging format (Ramshaw and Marcus, 1995).

Traditionally in probabilistic classification, Language Models (LMs) "compute the probability of a label, conditioned on the text" (Eisenstein, 2018), that is, they quantify the likelihood of a sentence to pertain to a language. Contextualized word representations are used nowadays as pre-trained language models that have shown to be effective in natural language processing tasks as co-reference resolution, gender resolution, etc.

Current language modeling approaches can be broadly divided into two types:

1. Auto-Regressive: Models that generate predictions, in our case pieces of text, using previous predictions. Architectures like Generative Pretrained Transformers (i.e GPT3) (Brown et al., 2020) follow this approach predicting the next word given a sequence of prior words.

2. Sentence-Reconstruction: In this approach, the input sentence is corrupted by either randomly dropping words (Devlin et al., 2018), spans (Joshi et al., 2019) or permutating the word order (Lewis et al., 2019) and the model is trained to reconstruct the original sentence. Architectures like Bidirectional Encoder Representations from Transformers or BERT models (Devlin et al., 2018) and T5 (Raffel et al., 2020) follow this approach.

Mou et al. (2016) and Dai and Le (2015) suggested transferring the knowledge learned during pre-training to downstream tasks but with limited success. However, with the advances in neural networks, (Howard and Ruder, 2018) proved that it is possible by successfully fine-tuning a pretrained LSTM (Hochreiter and Schmidhuber, 1997) language model on a downstream task. After pretraining, the model's last layer, which is used to predict the next word, is replaced with a new layer for a downstream task. This way, information from the remaining layers can help the model learn new tasks better.

Instead of introducing a new layer at the end of pre-trained models, Schick and Schütze (2020) converted the downstream task examples into a cloze-question format to leverage the knowledge acquired during the pre-training. Later, the pretrained model is further fine-tuned in a method called Pattern Exploitative Training (PET). Downstream tasks like sentiment analysis would be much simpler to adapt since one can just append a template at the end of the review and expect the model to predict words related to the corresponding label.

Proceedings of the 17th Conference of the European Chapter of the Association for Computational Linguistics: Student Research Workshop, pages 79–86
May 2-4, 2023 ©2023 Association for Computational Linguistics

For instance, if we are predicting the polarity of a movie review, we append a template to the review as follows *Overall, the movie is* $< mask >$ and fine-tune the language model to predict $< mask >$ with the words corresponding to the sentiment. However, PET cannot be directly applied to Named Entity Recognition (NER) since the outputs must be constrained to phrases within the sentence. *It is difficult (if not impossible) to provide a single task description which allows the language model to assign a label to each token in the input text* (Gatta et al., 2021). Gatta et al. (2021) handled this issue by appending a template, filled by each word and entity type, to the sentence where the model must predict if the word in the template is either beginning, inside or outside an entity type. The template is generated for all combinations of words in the sentence and entity types.

Cui et al. (2021) approached the problem by converting the NER identification task into a seq2seq task by generating synthetic target sentences. Figure 1 illustrates their data creation process. N-grams generated from the sentence are substituted in the template to generate positive and negative examples. The authors fine-tune BART language model (Lewis et al., 2019) to train a seq2seq model, which inputs the natural source sentence (sentence before the "$\rightarrow$" symbol in Figure 1) and outputs the synthetic target sentence (sentence after the "$\rightarrow$" symbol). At inference, the fine-tuned model is used to score the synthetic sentences generated from all the N-grams. A major limitation of this approach is the N-grams part because, during inference, for a given sentence, all the synthetic target sentences generated from all the N-grams ranging from $n = 1$ to 8 must be checked against all the entity types. This situation exacerbates with a larger sentence and more number of entity types in a task. Avoiding the problem of generating all possible N-grams, (Yan et al., 2021) proposed a pointer-based seq2seq (BARTNER) framework, which converts NER sub-tasks to a unified sequence generation task and predicts entities from the input sentences and the corresponding type indexes. LightNER (Chen et al., 2021) introduced prompt-tuning to the attention mechanism of BARTNER and achieved promising improvement in low-resource scenarios.

Our **contribution** is to avoid the usage of N-grams by pivoting our task from a sequence labeling task into a seq2seq task that aligns with the pre-training objective of certain generative models like T5, BART, etc. Specifically, we leverage templates to convert the target entities into sentences. Figure 2 illustrates the conversion process. Our approach performs better in low-resource settings and is comparable to existing works in resource-rich setting. In comparison to the recent works, our approach is faster than TemplateBART (Cui et al., 2021) in terms of real-time inference. Although BARTNER does inference in a single step, we observed that our approach yields better results at the cost of linear inference speed, proportional to the number of entity types. At the same time, our approach is simpler than LightNER.

We test our method's performance in resource-rich, low resource and domain transfer settings to prove its robustness. We approximate low resource setting by considering few-shot scenarios of the datasets. Results show that our method achieves comparable results in the resource-rich setting and outperforms the current seq2seq paradigm state-of-the-art approach in few-shot settings.

2 Related Work

To adapt the fine-tuning approach to the NER task, the standard norm has been to use architectures like LSTMs (Hochreiter and Schmidhuber, 1997), CNNs (LeCun et al., 1989), and Transformers (Vaswani et al., 2017) to extract token-level features which are later passed on for classification into the corresponding entity classes. In the final layer, the softmax function (Strubell et al., 2017; Chiu and Nichols, 2015; Cui and Zhang, 2019) or the Conditional Random Fields algorithm (CRF) (Lample et al., 2016; Ma and Hovy, 2016; Luo et al., 2019) are used for classification.

With the rise of powerful LMs, there has been a lot of interest in exploiting them for downstream tasks. ULMFit (Howard and Ruder, 2018) was the first approach to successfully fine-tune a pre-trained LSTM language model to a downstream task. However, this approach does not completely exploit the information LMs have learned during pre-training. Schick and Schütze (2020) converted the downstream tasks into cloze questions to probe LMs and leverage the knowledge learned during pre-training. Simultaneously, Brown et al. (2020) showed that, with large LMs (170 Billion parameters large), it is possible to probe information in a few-shot approach without having to train the full model. These methods gave rise to a new research field called Pattern Engineering (Liu et al., 2021).

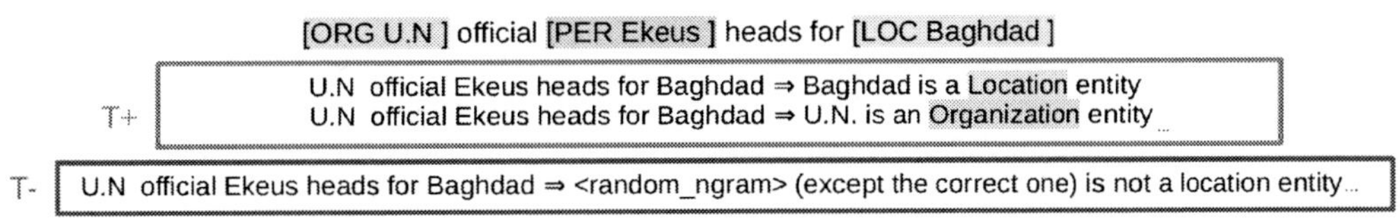

Figure 1: Template based NER approach by Cui et al. (2021)

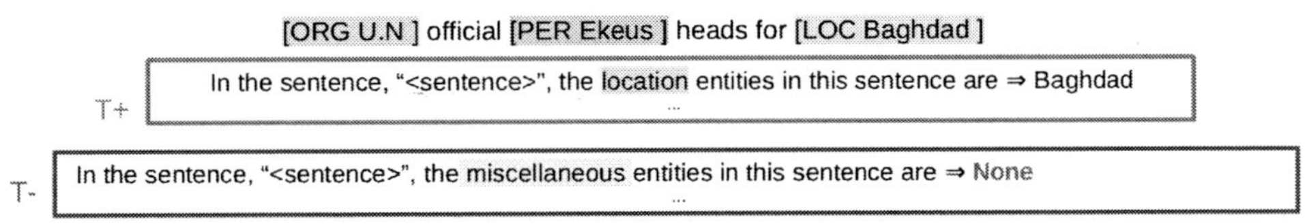

Figure 2: Our approach.

However, until recently, most prompt-based approaches were not designed for Named Entity Recognition. Cui et al. (2021) were the first to adopt the template-based approach for Sequence Labeling. They convert the task into a seq2seq task and use language models as a scoring function for each span. As mentioned before, Sainz et al. (2022) filter the n-grams by labels provided by a linguistic analyzer in a textual entailment task.

3 Methodology

We consider NER as a language model generation task where the input is a text written in natural language, appended by synthetic sentence generated by a template and the output is also a synthetic sentence but mentioning the corresponding entities. (see Section 3.1). We start this section by introducing the template creation process in Section 3.1, and then explain the training and inference processes in Sections 3.3 and 3.2, respectively. In later sections, we speak about the different assumptions made for different resource settings.

3.1 Template creation

Let us consider a dataset with n entity types. For each training instance, n synthetic sentences (corresponding to each entity type) are appended to the source sequence i.e. input text and the corresponding entities are provided as target sequences. In case of multiple entities for an entity type, they are separated by a delimiter in the output. Figure 2 explains our approach. The input template is as follows,

In the sentence, $< sentence >$*, the* $< entity-type >$ *entities are*

In this template $< sentence >$ is substituted by a sentence from the training set and $< entitytype >$ by an entity type. The training instance shown in the figure has three entity types, namely, ORG (organization), PER (person), and LOC (location). So, we will have 3 positive examples, one for each entity type. One such positive example is shown as T^+. Since MISC (miscellaneous) type entities are not present, we consider it as a negative example (T^-) and the output is made as "None" denoting that there are no entities for the entity type mentioned in the input.

3.2 Inference

During inference, for a given sentence, templates generated for each entity type are passed through the model for extracting entities. This approach invokes the model only n times whereas Cui et al. (2021)'s approach invokes the model $n \times k$ times, where k is the number of N-grams.

3.3 Training

As we are leveraging pre-trained language models as the base models, we fine-tune them on the downstream seq2seq task. During fine-tuning, the model is trained to predict the correct named entities word-by-word. In case of negative samples, the model must only output the word `None`. In the example in Figure 2, the system has generated the named entity "Baghdad" for the location (LOC) entity type and the label "None" for the "miscellaneous" type, or negative example. It is possible that the generative models may output partial entities or arbitrary text. In such cases, we consider the output as no match at all.

Considering the success of contrastive learning (Chen et al., 2020), we believe that the negative examples help the models in understanding the task better, especially when the training instances are less. Therefore, we consider all the n sequences (including positives and negatives) generated per each training instance for training. In later sections (Section 4.1), we evaluate our hypothesis by comparing the impact of negative examples against model performance. Experiments have been performed on different datasets with different entity classes (see Section 4).

3.4 Experimental settings

As mentioned earlier, we test our approach in three different scenarios. The following sub-sections explain the experimental settings of each scenario.

3.4.1 Resource-Rich setting

In this setting, we evaluate if it is worth adopting this approach when there is access to abundance of data.

3.4.2 Low Resource setting

In this setting, we measure the impact of the amount of examples against model's performance. We follow Cui et al. (2021)'s evaluation settings for better comparison. Specifically, we check the model's performance on different input data sizes $m = \{10, 20, 50, 100, 200, 500\}$, where m stands for number of instances per each entity type.

3.4.3 Domain Transfer

Since the input template and target sequences look like natural sentences, the model trained on one dataset should be able to adapt to another dataset with different entity types. The above hypothesis is made under the hypothesis that, with the first dataset, model understands the task format better.

We evaluate this hypothesis by training a model on a resource-rich dataset and later fune-tuning it on a low-resource dataset. In our case, it would mean, fine-tuning a pretrained model on a resource-rich dataset and further fine-tuning it on a low-resource dataset.

3.5 Adding special tokens

One-way of pre-training is to reconstruct the corrupted sentence by predicting the dropped spans (Joshi et al., 2019; Raffel et al., 2020). For instance, given a sentence, *I'm looking <X> to the party this <Y>*, the model is trained to predict the following text, *<X> forward <Y> weekend.*

In order to make our downstream task closer to the pre-training task of de-noising corrupted sentences, we append a special token to the source sentence and prepend the same token on the target side to mimic the pre-training style. In the results, we call this method as "Ours+ (T5 pretraining-style)".

Ours: *In the sentence,* $< sentence >$*, the* $< entity - type >$ *entities are*

Ours + (T5 pretraining-style): *In the sentence,* $< sentence >$*, the* $< entity - type >$ *entities are* $< X >$

4 Results

For benchmarking, we use CoNLL03 dataset for resource-rich setting and MIT restaurant (Liu et al., 2013), MIT movie (Liu et al., 2013) and ATIS (Hakkani-Tur et al., 2016) datasets are used for low-resource and domain transfer settings. See Table 4 in Appendix for more details. ATIS dataset contains highly imbalanced entity types with one entity type containing around 3705 instances while another type occurring only once. All the scores reported in this section are an average of 5 runs.

We conjecture that our hypothesis aligns better with T5 considering the closeness to its pre-training task. In order to evaluate this, we train T5-base and BART-large (Lewis et al., 2019) on CoNLL03 (Tjong Kim Sang and De Meulder, 2003) and check the performance. Table 2 shows that T5-base performs better than BART-large. It is interesting to note that T5-base, with 3x fewer parameters, performs better.

From here on, we will be using T5-base model for the experiments. **The improvements reported can be attributed to T5 but the inference speed is due to our approach.** For instance, when tested on `Titan XP` GPU with the same pre-trained model, T5, our approach takes 2 minutes to complete the inference whereas `TemplateBART` (Cui et al., 2021) approach takes 68 minutes.[1].

Resource-rich setting: Table 2 shows that, when tested in a resource-rich setting, (CoNLL03),

[1]We use a batch size of 32 and TemplateBART use a dynamic batch size varying between 5 to 40 with an average batch size of 31

Source	Method	MIT Movies						MIT Restaurant						ATIS		
		10	20	50	100	200	500	10	20	50	100	200	500	10	20	50
None	TemplateBART	37.3	48.5	52.2	56.3	62.0	74.9	46	57.1	58.7	60.1	62.8	65	71.7	79.4	92.6
	LightNER	41.7	57.8	73.1	78.0	80.6	84.8	48.5	58.0	62.0	70.8	75.5	80.2	76.3	85.3	92.8
	BARTNER*	41.1	54.0	67.7	NA	NA	NA	44.0	56.0	64.0	NA	NA	NA	77.7	86.1	93.4
	Ours	**53.29**	**61.89**	**75.75**	**79.99**	**81.61**	**83.08**	47.09	60.25	**67.02**	72.7	74.15	75.69	**91.9**	**93.8**	**94.58**
	Ours2	52.1	60.43	75.23	78.3	81.07	82.47	**51.34**	**61.97**	65.86	**73.64**	**76.31**	**77.24**	**92.75**	**93.57**	**94.66**
CoNLL03	TemplateBART	42.4	54.2	59.6	65.3	69.6	80.3	53.1	60.3	64.1	67.3	72.2	75.7	77.3	88.9	93.5
	LightNER	62.9	75.6	78.8	82.2	84.5	85.7	58.1	67.4	69.5	73.7	78.4	81.1	86.9	89.4	93.9
	Ours	62.27	72.24	76.67	78.98	81.72	82.89	56.55	64.73	69.84	73.39	75.46	74.41	**93.34**	**94.25**	**95**
	Ours2	62.07	70.52	75.64	78.84	81.09	82.56	59.03	64.06	67.72	74.21	75.47	75.94	92.9	93.83	94.68

Table 1: Few-shot results (including domain-transfer settings) on various input sizes. The first column "Source" refers to the domain-transfer setting where we first train on CoNLL03 dataset or from scratch (None) and later fine-tune on the current dataset. The scores reported are an average of 5 runs with a standard deviation around 2-3. "Ours" and "Ours2" refer to the two training styles followed in section 3.5. BARTNER* scores are taken from the publication. Hence, couldn't get its scores on size=100, 200 and 500.

Models	P	R	F
LightNER	92.39	93.48	92.93
TemplateBART	90.51	93.34	91.90
Ours (T5-base)	91	89	90
Ours (BART-large)	90	80	85

Table 2: CoNLL03 results: Comparing our approach with TemplateBART and LightNER

`TemplateBART` and `LightNER` perform better than our approach. We conclude that our approach is not a value addition when there is access to enough labeled data.

Low Resource setting: In the few shot setting, we check the model's performance on different input data sizes $m = \{10, 20, 50, 100, 200, 500\}$, where m stands for number of instances per each entity type. Table 1 shows that our approaches perform comparatively better.

Domain Transfer: Initially, we fine-tune the T5 model on the full CoNLL03 dataset and later fine-tune it on the few-shot scenarios of MIT restaurant, MIT movie and ATIS datasets. Table 1 shows that our approaches indeed leverage the knowledge gained from one task to learn another. However, it only performs comparably to LightNER.

4.1 Ratio of negative samples

In case of resource-rich setting (Table 2), we can observe that the precision of the system is comparable to other baselines. We believe that this is due to the large number of negative examples we are considering while training. As a result, model is producing less false positives.

In order to check the hypothesis that more negative examples can be helpful, we experimented with different negative-positive ratio sentences per each training instance. Table 3 shows that the negative samples are extremely important in few-shot scenarios, especially when m (number of instances per entity type) is small. We can also observe that learning is saturated quickly when m is bigger. For instance, for m=200 & 500, there is no considerable improvement despite the increase in negative samples.

-ve to +ve ratio	10	20	50	100	200	500
1:1	18.32	42.97	57.58	67.06	71.83	75.43
2:1	26.25	53.95	62.88	70.55	75.13	77.24
3:1	34.32	55.91	64.68	71.1	75.37	77.2

Table 3: Effect of negative samples on model's performance. Scores reported on MIT restaurant. 10 indicates 10 instances for each entity types. The scores reported are an average of 5 runs with a standard deviation around 2-3.

5 Conclusions and Future Work

In this work, we project NER as a seq2seq task by generating synthetic sentences from templates and show that our approach is faster than the current state-of-the-art. We also show that our approach works better in few-shot and domain transfer scenarios especially when the input size is small, although the approach can be used in other scenarios. While performing the experiments, we found T5 to better align with our task and also observed the importance of negative examples.

Our system has been compared against seq2seq systems (TemplateNER, LightNER and BARTNER). But Instruction-NER (Wang et al., 2022) leverages auxiliary training and obtains better results than our system. For instance, in MIT movies few shot scenario (n=10), our approach has 53 F1 score and instructionNER 65 F1 score. In future, it would be interesting to explore automatic template generation along with auxiliary training.

6 Acknowledgments

We would like to thank the members of IXA research group for the discussion and feedback. The first author is supported by the Erasmus Mundus Master's Programme "Language and Communication Technologies".

References

Tom B. Brown, Benjamin Mann, Nick Ryder, Melanie Subbiah, Jared Kaplan, Prafulla Dhariwal, Arvind Neelakantan, Pranav Shyam, Girish Sastry, Amanda Askell, Sandhini Agarwal, Ariel Herbert-Voss, Gretchen Krueger, Tom Henighan, Rewon Child, Aditya Ramesh, Daniel M. Ziegler, Jeffrey Wu, Clemens Winter, Christopher Hesse, Mark Chen, Eric Sigler, Mateusz Litwin, Scott Gray, Benjamin Chess, Jack Clark, Christopher Berner, Sam McCandlish, Alec Radford, Ilya Sutskever, and Dario Amodei. 2020. Language models are few-shot learners. CoRR, abs/2005.14165.

Ting Chen, Simon Kornblith, Mohammad Norouzi, and Geoffrey E. Hinton. 2020. A simple framework for contrastive learning of visual representations.

Xiang Chen, Lei Li, Shumin Deng, Chuanqi Tan, Changliang Xu, Fei Huang, Luo Si, Huajun Chen, and Ningyu Zhang. 2021. Lightner: A lightweight tuning paradigm for low-resource NER via pluggable prompting. CoRR, abs/2109.00720.

Jason P. C. Chiu and Eric Nichols. 2015. Named entity recognition with bidirectional lstm-cnns. CoRR, abs/1511.08308.

Leyang Cui, Yu Wu, Jian Liu, Sen Yang, and Yue Zhang. 2021. Template-based named entity recognition using BART. CoRR, abs/2106.01760.

Leyang Cui and Yue Zhang. 2019. Hierarchically-refined label attention network for sequence labeling. CoRR, abs/1908.08676.

Andrew M. Dai and Quoc V. Le. 2015. Semi-supervised sequence learning. CoRR, abs/1511.01432.

Jacob Devlin, Ming-Wei Chang, Kenton Lee, and Kristina Toutanova. 2018. BERT: pre-training of deep bidirectional transformers for language understanding. CoRR, abs/1810.04805.

Jacob Eisenstein. 2018. Natural language processing.

Valerio La Gatta, Vincenzo Moscato, Marco Postiglione, and Giancarlo Sperlì. 2021. Few-shot named entity recognition with cloze questions. CoRR, abs/2111.12421.

Dilek Hakkani-Tur, Gokhan Tur, Celikyilmaz Asli, Yun-Nung Chen, Jianfeng Gao, li Deng, and Ye-Yi Wang. 2016. Multi-domain joint semantic frame parsing using bi-directional rnn-lstm.

Sepp Hochreiter and Jürgen Schmidhuber. 1997. Long short-term memory. Neural computation, 9(8):1735–1780.

Jeremy Howard and Sebastian Ruder. 2018. Fine-tuned language models for text classification. CoRR, abs/1801.06146.

Mandar Joshi, Danqi Chen, Yinhan Liu, Daniel S. Weld, Luke Zettlemoyer, and Omer Levy. 2019. Spanbert: Improving pre-training by representing and predicting spans. CoRR, abs/1907.10529.

Guillaume Lample, Miguel Ballesteros, Sandeep Subramanian, Kazuya Kawakami, and Chris Dyer. 2016. Neural architectures for named entity recognition. CoRR, abs/1603.01360.

Y. LeCun, B. Boser, J. S. Denker, D. Henderson, R. E. Howard, W. Hubbard, and L. D. Jackel. 1989. Backpropagation applied to handwritten zip code recognition. Neural Computation, 1(4):541–551.

Mike Lewis, Yinhan Liu, Naman Goyal, Marjan Ghazvininejad, Abdelrahman Mohamed, Omer Levy, Veselin Stoyanov, and Luke Zettlemoyer. 2019. BART: denoising sequence-to-sequence pre-training for natural language generation, translation, and comprehension. CoRR, abs/1910.13461.

Jingjing Liu, Panupong Pasupat, Scott Cyphers, and Jim Glass. 2013. Asgard: A portable architecture for multilingual dialogue systems. In 2013 IEEE International Conference on Acoustics, Speech and Signal Processing, pages 8386–8390.

Pengfei Liu, Weizhe Yuan, Jinlan Fu, Zhengbao Jiang, Hiroaki Hayashi, and Graham Neubig. 2021. Pre-train, prompt, and predict: A systematic survey of prompting methods in natural language processing. CoRR, abs/2107.13586.

Ying Luo, Fengshun Xiao, and Hai Zhao. 2019. Hierarchical contextualized representation for named entity recognition. CoRR, abs/1911.02257.

Xuezhe Ma and Eduard H. Hovy. 2016. End-to-end sequence labeling via bi-directional lstm-cnns-crf. CoRR, abs/1603.01354.

Lili Mou, Zhao Meng, Rui Yan, Ge Li, Yan Xu, Lu Zhang, and Zhi Jin. 2016. How transferable are neural networks in NLP applications? CoRR, abs/1603.06111.

Colin Raffel, Noam Shazeer, Adam Roberts, Katherine Lee, Sharan Narang, Michael Matena, Yanqi Zhou, Wei Li, and Peter J. Liu. 2020. Exploring the limits of transfer learning with a unified text-to-text transformer. Journal of Machine Learning Research, 21(140):1–67.

Lance Ramshaw and Mitch Marcus. 1995. Text chunking using transformation-based learning. In Third Workshop on Very Large Corpora.

Oscar Sainz, Haoling Qiu, Oier Lopez de Lacalle, Eneko Agirre, and Bonan Min. 2022. Zs4ie: A toolkit for zero-shot information extraction with simple verbalizations.

Timo Schick and Hinrich Schütze. 2020. Exploiting cloze questions for few-shot text classification and natural language inference. CoRR, abs/2001.07676.

Emma Strubell, Patrick Verga, David Belanger, and Andrew McCallum. 2017. Fast and accurate sequence labeling with iterated dilated convolutions. CoRR, abs/1702.02098.

Erik F. Tjong Kim Sang and Fien De Meulder. 2003. Introduction to the CoNLL-2003 shared task: Language-independent named entity recognition. In Proceedings of the Seventh Conference on Natural Language Learning at HLT-NAACL 2003, pages 142–147.

Ashish Vaswani, Noam Shazeer, Niki Parmar, Jakob Uszkoreit, Llion Jones, Aidan N. Gomez, Lukasz Kaiser, and Illia Polosukhin. 2017. Attention is all you need. CoRR, abs/1706.03762.

Liwen Wang, Rumei Li, Yang Yan, Yuanmeng Yan, Sirui Wang, Wei Wu, and Weiran Xu. 2022. Instructionner: A multi-task instruction-based generative framework for few-shot ner.

Hang Yan, Tao Gui, Junqi Dai, Qipeng Guo, Zheng Zhang, and Xipeng Qiu. 2021. A unified generative framework for various NER subtasks. CoRR, abs/2106.01223.

7 Appendix

Dataset	Number of entity types	# Training	# Validation	# Testing	Max	Min
CoNLL	4	14041	3250	3453	7141	3451
MIT Restaurant	8	6128	1225	1522	3031	581
MIT Movie	12	7821	1564	2444	3510	92
ATIS	79	4233	634	894	3705	1

Table 4: Datasets: Number of sentences in train, validation and testing splits in each dataset. # refers to number of sentences. The "Max" and "Min" columns refer to the entity types with maximum and minimum occurrences.

Polite Chatbot: A Text Style Transfer Application

Sourabrata Mukherjee and **Vojtěch Hudeček** and **Ondřej Dušek**
Charles University, Faculty of Mathematics and Physics
Institute of Formal and Applied Linguistics
Prague, Czech Republic
{mukherjee,hudecek,odusek}@ufal.mff.cuni.cz

Abstract

Generating polite responses is essential to build intelligent and engaging dialogue systems. However, this task is far from well-explored due to the difficulties of rendering a particular style in coherent responses, especially when parallel datasets for regular-to-polite pairs are usually unavailable. This paper proposes a polite chatbot that can produce responses that are polite and coherent to the given context. In this study, a politeness transfer model is first used to generate polite synthetic dialogue pairs of contexts and polite utterances. Then, these synthetic pairs are employed to train a dialogue model. Automatic and human evaluations demonstrate that our method outperforms baselines in producing polite dialogue responses while staying competitive in terms of coherent to the given context.[1]

1 Introduction

Building a chatbot agent that produces stylized and coherent responses can yield more engaging conversations (Niederhoffer and Pennebaker, 2002). Generating stylized dialogue responses has been investigated in various studies, with a broad understanding of style covering emotion (Zhou et al., 2018), personality (Li et al., 2016) or politeness (Niu and Bansal, 2018). In most cases, the stylistic features we want to capture are embedded in unpaired texts that cannot be directly utilized by supervised models (Gao et al., 2019). This typically leads stylized chatbot models to employ complex, multi-step setups, potentially involving reinforcement learning (Niu and Bansal, 2018; Sun et al., 2022; Firdaus et al., 2022).

In this paper, we propose a straightforward polite chatbot training procedure that uses a politeness transfer model to create synthetic training instances and results in an end-to-end model. We build upon the work of Madaan et al. (2020), who use a *tagger* and *generator* pipeline to generate polite sentences. However, we make their process more straightforward by merging these two sub-modules into a single step: We finetune the BART model (Lewis et al., 2020) to transfer neutral sentences into polite ones. Using this model, we then prepare synthetic pairs of contexts and polite responses and train a dialogue model on this synthetic data. We evaluate our approach on The DailyDialog dataset (Li et al., 2017). Automatic and human evaluations show that our method outperforms competitive baselines in response politeness while staying competitive in terms of coherence to the given context.

[1] Our code and related details are available at https://github.com/souro/polite_chatbot.

2 Related Work

Politeness Transfer in Text Politeness Transfer is a sub-task of Text Style Transfer (TST) (Madaan et al., 2020). McDonald and Pustejovsky (1985) have defined *style* as a notion that refers to the manner in which semantics is expressed. The aim of TST is to change the style of the text while preserving style-independent content. Politeness is a text style attribute that is closely related to social interactions, which enables smooth communication in conversations (Coppock, 2005), such as emails or memos, and it can be decoupled from content (Kang and Hovy, 2019). The task of politeness transfer (Madaan et al., 2020) aims to control the politeness of a text while preserving the original content. Madaan et al. (2020) use a two-step architecture here: (1) a tagger tags appropriate insertion points, and (2) a generator generates polite phrases to insert instead of the tags.

Polite Chatbot Response Generation Stylized dialogue generation attracted a lot of attention in recent years (Gao et al., 2019; Zheng et al., 2021; Zeng and Nie, 2021). Previous works focus on personalized (Li et al., 2016; Luan et al., 2017; Su et al., 2019), polite Niu and Bansal (2018) or

Proceedings of the 17th Conference of the European Chapter of the Association for Computational Linguistics: Student Research Workshop, pages 87–93
May 2-4, 2023 ©2023 Association for Computational Linguistics

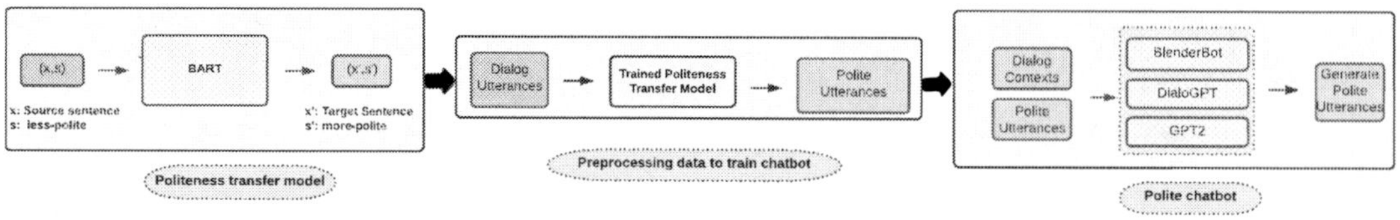

Figure 1: Our method: We (1) train the politeness transfer model; (2) generate synthetic training data by applying the transfer model to neutral utterances; (3) train the dialogue models using the synthetic data.

emotional (Zhou et al., 2018) dialogues.

For politeness, traditionally, polite chatbot responses are accomplished by manual dialogue design, where predefined rules or templates are used to generate responses based on certain keywords or scenarios (André et al., 2004; Gupta et al., 2007; de Jong et al., 2008). This approach has some limitations such as requiring a lot of human effort, being domain-specific, and lacking flexibility or diversity (Firdaus et al., 2022). Alternatively, recent works have used neural language models to generate polite chatbot responses automatically. Niu and Bansal (2018) used a politeness classifier and a language model trained on polite utterances to generate polite dialog responses. Sun et al. (2022) post-process a baseline system response using a two-step phrase replacement trained by reinforcement learning. Firdaus et al. (2022) proposed a two-step decoding approach that first generates a rough response based on the input text and then infuses human-written polite phrases into the response using a separate politeness model.

Perhaps the closest to ours is the work of Silva et al. (2022), who also adapts Niu and Bansal's and Madaan et al.'s models, but their focus is domain transfer, not simplifying the overall architecture.

3 Method

Our method consists of three steps (Figure 1). First, we train a politeness transfer model. Our goal here is to train a model that takes as input a neutral sentence x and outputs a sentence $\hat{x}$ that retains the content while increasing politeness. Second, we apply this politeness transfer model to generate synthetic polite chat data. Finally, we use the corpus $\hat{\mathcal{D}}$ to train a dialogue model.

Politeness Transfer Model Although we do not have parallel corpora available for politeness transfer, our transfer model is trained in a supervised fashion on synthetic input-output pairs. These are obtained following Madaan et al. (2020): polite phrases (politeness markers) are identified using TF-IDF over polite and non-polite texts.[2] The markers are removed from polite texts on the input, and a sequence-to-sequence model is trained to increase sentence politeness by reconstructing the politeness markers on the output. Unlike Madaan et al. (2020), we do not use separate tagging and generation steps here and join the task into a single step. Specifically, we finetune a pre-trained language model for this task using standard cross-entropy loss (see Section 4.2).

Models	PS	BLEU	CS
Madaan et al. (2020)	7.01	60.16	87.86
Ours	**8.68**	**71.65**	**93.25**

Table 1: Evaluation results of politeness transfer on the test set of Madaan et al. (2020)'s data. We measure the Polite Score (PS), BLEU Score, and Content Similarity (CS). Model outputs are predicted based on synthetic sentences where politeness markers have been removed. BLEU and CS compare against original human-written polite sentences.

Creating Synthetic Polite Data We apply our politeness transfer model to a dataset consisting of N dialogues $\mathcal{D} = \{C_1^{k_1}, ..., C_N^{k_N}\}$, where dialogue $C_i^{k_i}$ consists of k_i utterances $\{u_i^1, ..., u_i^{k_i}\}$. We create a corpus of context-utterance pairs $\hat{\mathcal{D}} = \{\langle C_1^1, \hat{u}_1^2\rangle, \langle C_1^2, \hat{u}_1^3\rangle, ..., \langle C_N^{K_N-1}, \hat{u}_N^{K_N}\rangle\}$ where C_1^1 is the first utterance of the first dialogue, C_1^2 are the first two utterances of the first dialogue, etc. In other words, for every partial context, we add a polite version of the next utterance.

Dialogue Model We use a standard dialogue response generation model that produces a dialogue utterance u_i based on context $\mathbf{C} = \{u_1, ..., u_{i-1}\}$, trained using cross-entropy loss. We experiment with multiple pre-trained language models here

[2]In principle, a much higher mean TF-IDF value over polite than non-polite texts means that a phrase is likely to be a politeness marker.

	BlenderBot				DialoGPT				GPT-2			
Finetuned on	PS	BLEU-1,2		CS	PS	BLEU-1,2		CS	PS	BLEU-1,2		CS
Vanilla (no FT)	7.06	9.80	2.58	20.31	6.31	9.38	1.98	19.33	4.91	0.15	0.09	8.31
DailyDialog (DD)	7.11	17.21	7.25	45.80	6.14	11.72	2.60	38.44	5.08	7.82	2.13	29.72
DD + Madaan et al. (2020)	6.75	17.16	6.73	45.17	6.17	11.47	2.19	35.08	5.99	7.32	1.49	27.42
DD + Ours	**7.65**	17.03	6.85	41.80	**7.75**	11.44	2.57	35.03	**7.20**	5.65	1.03	26.80

Table 2: Evaluation results of polite dialog models. We indicate what version of the DailyDialog dataset (DD) was used for Finetuning (FT) if any. We measure the Polite Score (PS), BLEU score, and Content Similarity (CS). BLEU Score (of n-gram = 1,2) and CS are computed between predicted polite utterances and the original utterances.

Models	PS	BLEU	CS
DailyDialog (DD)	5.41	–	–
DD + Madaan et al. (2020)	6.37	73.34	90.29
DD + Ours	**7.95**	70.21	89.07

Table 3: Evaluation of synthetic data generated using DailyDialogue (DD) to train polite dialog models. We measure the Polite Score (PS), BLEU Score, and Content Similarity (CS) The BLEU and CS are measured between original utterances and polite-transferred utterances.

BlenderBot finetuned on	Pol	CC	Flu
Vanilla (no FT)	3.46	1.16	4.64
DailyDialog (DD)	3.90	3.74	4.54
DD + Madaan et al. (2020)	3.50	3.06	3.98
DD + Ours	**4.26**	2.94	4.30

Table 4: Human Evaluation on BlenderBot outputs. We measured politeness (Pol), coherent to context (CC), and fluency (Flu).

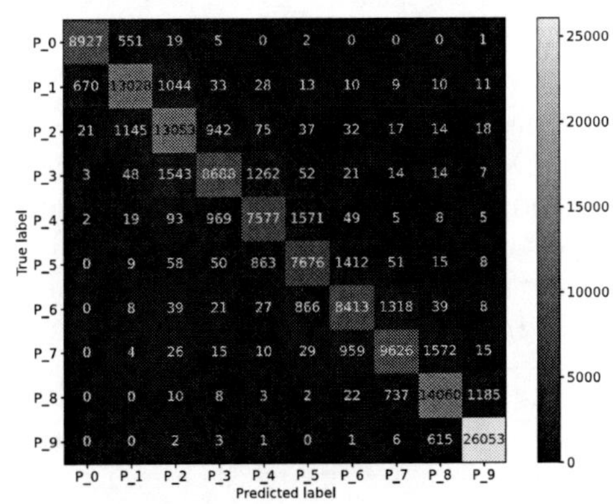

Figure 2: Confusion Matrix of multi-class politeness classification. We can see that the model confuses mainly neighboring buckets and the vast majority is classified correctly.

(see Section 4.2). To achieve politeness in responses, we use the synthetic polite dialogue corpus $\hat{\mathcal{D}}$ obtained using our politeness transfer model.

4 Experiment

4.1 Datasets

Politeness Transfer We use the dataset of Madaan et al. (2020), i.e. preprocessed and filtered sentences from the Enron e-mail dataset (Shetty and Adibi, 2004) into ten buckets (P_0-P_9) based on the score of a politeness classifier by Niu and Bansal (2018). We use Madaan et al. (2020)'s TF-IDF-based approach to remove politeness markers (see Section 3) from the sentences in the most polite P_9 bucket to prepare synthetic parallel data for training our politeness transfer models.

Dialogue To train our response generation models, we use DailyDialog (Li et al., 2017), an open-domain dataset of 13,118 human-human dialogues. DailyDialogue was collected to represent natural day-by-day conversations between human participants. It is constructed mainly from English learner websites and represents rather formal written conversations. Each conversation is focused on certain topics, but the domain is not restricted in general. The average length is 7.9 turns per dialogue. The dataset is split into a training set with 11,118 dialogues and validation and test sets with 1,000 dialogues each.

4.2 Settings

We use BART (Lewis et al., 2020) for politeness transfer. For dialogue modeling, we use multiple pre-trained models: (1) GPT-2 (Radford et al., 2019), which is a Transformer decoder trained for general language modeling (including dialogues), (2) DialoGPT (Zhang et al., 2020), which shares GPT-2's architecture but was pre-trained specifically on dialogue data, (3) BlenderBot (Roller et al., 2021), which is an encoder-decoder Transformer

Context : Nani Book Store. How can I help you? Do you have the 'The man and the Sea' by Ernest Hemingway?	
Ground Truth	**Yes, we have one copy left.**
Vanilla (no FT)	I would love to try it, but I don't think I'll be able to afford it.
DailyDialog (DD)	Yes, it ' s on that shelf. I ' ll get it for you right away.
DD + Madaan et al. (2020)	We do. Would you like a look at it?
DD + Ours	Yes, we do. Would you like to have a look at it? please let me know.

Table 5: A sample output using BlenderBot. Vanilla BlenderBot produces polite but irrelevant responses, and models finetuned on all DailyDialog data versions produce relevant responses, but ours is arguably the most polite.

specifically trained to learn dialogue skills such as empathy or engagement.[3]

4.3 Baselines

Politeness Transfer We compare our system against Madaan et al. (2020). They used 4-layered transformers (Vaswani et al., 2017) to train both tagger and generator modules. Each transformer has 4 attention heads with a 512 dimensional embedding layer and hidden state size.

Dialogue Model We evaluate all dialogue models against three baselines: (1) vanilla version of the model, (2) model fine-tuned on unchanged DailyDialog data, (3) model finetuned on synthetic polite DailyDialog data generated in the same fashion as in our full model, but using Madaan et al. (2020)'s politeness transfer instead of ours.

5 Evaluation

5.1 Metrics

Following prior work (Madaan et al., 2020; Niu and Bansal, 2018), we use automatic metrics for the evaluation of the models along two major dimensions: (1) style transfer and (2) content preservation and relevance. To measure politeness transfer quality, we compute *Polite Score*, which is defined as the average score given to the generated sequences by our politeness classifier, which we created by finetuning BERT (Devlin et al., 2019) on Madaan et al. (2020)'s Enron data (see Section 4.1).[4] Following prior work (Jin et al., 2022; Hu et al., 2022), we evaluate the relevance and content preservation using embedding similarity (Rahutomo et al., 2012) and BLEU score (Papineni et al., 2002). For embedding similarity, we use a pre-trained Sentence-BERT model (Reimers and Gurevych, 2019) and cosine similarity. We use BLEU-1 and BLEU-2 to account for the expected different phrasing in polite outputs and the high output variance common to open-domain dialogue response generation. As automated metrics for language generation do not correlate well with human judgments (Novikova et al., 2017), we conduct a small-scale in-house human evaluation with expert annotators (computational linguistics graduate students). We randomly select 50 context-utterance pairs from the DailyDialog test set for all models based on the strongest BlenderBot language model. The annotators rate model outputs using a 5-point Likert scale for politeness, coherence to context, and fluency.

5.2 Results

Politeness classification The accuracy of our BERT-based politeness classification model is 83.27% on the politeness transfer data. More importantly, the confusion matrix in Figure 2 shows that the model confuses mostly adjacent classes; the average error is only 0.98.

Politeness Transfer We compare the politeness transfer models on content preservation and politeness improvement using a test portion of Madaan et al. (2020)'s data used for training, which consists of synthetic non-polite sentences and the corresponding original polite sentences. Models are tasked with producing polite sentences from synthetic non-polite ones; the result is then compared to the original human-written polite sentences. Table 1 shows the results. Our model achieves a higher politeness score than Madaan et al. (2020) while producing sentences more similar to the original human-written ones based on BLEU and sentence similarity scores.

We also evaluate the performance of the politeness transfer models with respect to content preservation and politeness improvement on the synthetic

[3]We use AdamW optimizer with a learning rate of 5e-4 in all cases. The politeness transfer model is trained for 5 epochs using batch size 8. All dialogue models are finetuned for 4 epochs using batch size 3.

[4]Although the scale of politeness classes is not necessarily linear, we believe that this is still a good indicator of the overall politeness of the data.

pairs of contexts and polite utterances from the DailyDialog dataset we prepared. The results are shown in Table 3. Note that unlike in the previous experiment, we measure content preservation against the original (source) utterances. We observe that our model increases politeness over the source data and outperforms Madaan et al. (2020). We can see a slight drop in content preservation metrics against the original utterances, but this is expected as these metrics also reflect changes in phrasing.

Dialogue modeling Results of automatic metrics for dialogue modeling are shown in Table 2. The performance differences between the pre-trained models used are expected given the models' properties and intended use cases. While GPT-2 scores low on politeness, the dialogue-specific models obtain better results. As expected, all models perform much better in terms of content preservation after finetuning. Both ours and Madaan et al.'s politeness transfer result in an increase in politeness, and we can observe that our method consistently outperforms Madaan et al.'s. Moreover, our method is the only one that improves the Polite Score over the vanilla BlenderBot model. Finally, although the application of politeness transfer causes a decrease in content similarity with reference responses from DailyDialog, the drop is marginal, not consistent with all metrics, and could be caused by different phrasing, same as in the case of politeness transfer (cf. Table 3).

Human Evaluation We have evaluated 50 model outputs for each variant of the BlenderBot model (see Table 5 for a sample). The results are presented in Table 4. The human evaluation results mostly agree with our automatic evaluation results: our data preparation method performs better than Madaan et al. (2020)'s transfer in terms of politeness and is able to improve the base BlenderBot model. Both politeness-increasing methods cause a slight degradation in context coherency of the generated utterances; ours performs slightly worse in this aspect. However, our full approach yields more fluent outputs than the model trained on Madaan et al. (2020)'s politeness transfer.

6 Conclusion

We propose an innovative way of increasing dialogue models' politeness. Our method is trained in two steps: the creation of synthetic training corpora with increased politeness and dialogue model training. The resulting dialogue response generation model is end-to-end and does not require postprocessing. Compared against multiple baselines for both politeness transfer and dialogue modeling, our politeness transfer model and dialogue response generation achieve increased politeness while still preserving important content. In future work, we aim to extend our method to other stylized response generation tasks.

Acknowledgments

This research was supported by Charles University projects GAUK 392221, GAUK 302120, and SVV 260575, and by the European Research Council (Grant agreement No. 101039303 NG-NLG). We would like to express our gratitude to our colleague Zdeněk Kasner for his insightful discussions and helpful feedback on this project.

References

Elisabeth André, Matthias Rehm, Wolfgang Minker, and Dirk Bühler. 2004. Endowing spoken language dialogue systems with emotional intelligence. In *Affective Dialogue Systems, Tutorial and Research Workshop, ADS 2004, Kloster Irsee, Germany, June 14-16, 2004, Proceedings*, volume 3068 of *Lecture Notes in Computer Science*, pages 178–187. Springer.

Liz Coppock. 2005. Politeness strategies in conversation closings. *Unpublished manuscript: Stanford University*.

Markus de Jong, Mariët Theune, and Dennis Hofs. 2008. Politeness and alignment in dialogues with a virtual guide. In *7th International Joint Conference on Autonomous Agents and Multiagent Systems (AAMAS 2008), Estoril, Portugal, May 12-16, 2008, Volume 1*, pages 207–214. IFAAMAS.

Jacob Devlin, Ming-Wei Chang, Kenton Lee, and Kristina Toutanova. 2019. BERT: pre-training of deep bidirectional transformers for language understanding. In *Proceedings of the 2019 Conference of the North American Chapter of the Association for Computational Linguistics: Human Language Technologies, NAACL-HLT 2019, Minneapolis, MN, USA, June 2-7, 2019, Volume 1 (Long and Short Papers)*, pages 4171–4186. Association for Computational Linguistics.

Mauajama Firdaus, Arunav Shandilya, Asif Ekbal, and Pushpak Bhattacharyya. 2022. Being polite: Modeling politeness variation in a personalized dialog agent. *IEEE Transactions on Computational Social Systems*.

Xiang Gao, Yizhe Zhang, Sungjin Lee, Michel Galley, Chris Brockett, Jianfeng Gao, and Bill Dolan. 2019. Structuring latent spaces for stylized response generation. In *Proceedings of the 2019 Conference on Empirical Methods in Natural Language Processing and the 9th International Joint Conference on Natural Language Processing, EMNLP-IJCNLP 2019, Hong Kong, China, November 3-7, 2019*, pages 1814–1823. Association for Computational Linguistics.

Swati Gupta, Marilyn A. Walker, and Daniela M. Romano. 2007. How rude are you?: Evaluating politeness and affect in interaction. In *Affective Computing and Intelligent Interaction, Second International Conference, ACII 2007, Lisbon, Portugal, September 12-14, 2007, Proceedings*, volume 4738 of *Lecture Notes in Computer Science*, pages 203–217. Springer.

Zhiqiang Hu, Roy Ka-Wei Lee, Charu C. Aggarwal, and Aston Zhang. 2022. Text style transfer: A review and experimental evaluation. *SIGKDD Explor.*, 24(1):14–45.

Di Jin, Zhijing Jin, Zhiting Hu, Olga Vechtomova, and Rada Mihalcea. 2022. Deep learning for text style transfer: A survey. *Comput. Linguistics*, 48(1):155–205.

Dongyeop Kang and Eduard Hovy. 2019. xSLUE: A benchmark and analysis platform for cross-style language understanding and evaluation.

Mike Lewis, Yinhan Liu, Naman Goyal, Marjan Ghazvininejad, Abdelrahman Mohamed, Omer Levy, Veselin Stoyanov, and Luke Zettlemoyer. 2020. BART: denoising sequence-to-sequence pre-training for natural language generation, translation, and comprehension. In *Proceedings of the 58th Annual Meeting of the Association for Computational Linguistics, ACL 2020, Online, July 5-10, 2020*, pages 7871–7880. Association for Computational Linguistics.

Jiwei Li, Michel Galley, Chris Brockett, Georgios Spithourakis, Jianfeng Gao, and Bill Dolan. 2016. A persona-based neural conversation model. In *Proceedings of the 54th Annual Meeting of the Association for Computational Linguistics (Volume 1: Long Papers)*, pages 994–1003, Berlin, Germany. Association for Computational Linguistics.

Yanran Li, Hui Su, Xiaoyu Shen, Wenjie Li, Ziqiang Cao, and Shuzi Niu. 2017. DailyDialog: A manually labelled multi-turn dialogue dataset. In *Proceedings of the Eighth International Joint Conference on Natural Language Processing (Volume 1: Long Papers)*, pages 986–995, Taipei, Taiwan. Asian Federation of Natural Language Processing.

Yi Luan, Chris Brockett, Bill Dolan, Jianfeng Gao, and Michel Galley. 2017. Multi-task learning for speaker-role adaptation in neural conversation models. In *Proceedings of the Eighth International Joint Conference on Natural Language Processing (Volume 1: Long Papers)*, pages 605–614, Taipei, Taiwan. Asian Federation of Natural Language Processing.

Aman Madaan, Amrith Setlur, Tanmay Parekh, Barnabás Póczos, Graham Neubig, Yiming Yang, Ruslan Salakhutdinov, Alan W. Black, and Shrimai Prabhumoye. 2020. Politeness transfer: A tag and generate approach. In *Proceedings of the 58th Annual Meeting of the Association for Computational Linguistics, ACL 2020, Online, July 5-10, 2020*, pages 1869–1881. Association for Computational Linguistics.

David D. McDonald and James Pustejovsky. 1985. A computational theory of prose style for natural language generation. In *EACL 1985, 2nd Conference of the European Chapter of the Association for Computational Linguistics, March 27-29, 1985, University of Geneva, Geneva, Switzerland*, pages 187–193. The Association for Computer Linguistics.

Kate G Niederhoffer and James W Pennebaker. 2002. Linguistic style matching in social interaction. *Journal of Language and Social Psychology*, 21(4):337–360.

Tong Niu and Mohit Bansal. 2018. Polite dialogue generation without parallel data. *Transactions of the Association for Computational Linguistics*, 6:373–389.

Jekaterina Novikova, Ondrej Dusek, Amanda Cercas Curry, and Verena Rieser. 2017. Why we need new evaluation metrics for NLG. In *Proceedings of the 2017 Conference on Empirical Methods in Natural Language Processing, EMNLP 2017, Copenhagen, Denmark, September 9-11, 2017*, pages 2241–2252. Association for Computational Linguistics.

Kishore Papineni, Salim Roukos, Todd Ward, and Wei-Jing Zhu. 2002. Bleu: a method for automatic evaluation of machine translation. In *Proceedings of the 40th Annual Meeting of the Association for Computational Linguistics*, pages 311–318, Philadelphia, Pennsylvania, USA. Association for Computational Linguistics.

Alec Radford, Jeffrey Wu, Rewon Child, David Luan, Dario Amodei, and Ilya Sutskever. 2019. Language models are unsupervised multitask learners. *OpenAI Blog*.

Faisal Rahutomo, Teruaki Kitasuka, and Masayoshi Aritsugi. 2012. Semantic cosine similarity. In *The 7th international student conference on advanced science and technology ICAST*, volume 4, page 1.

Nils Reimers and Iryna Gurevych. 2019. Sentence-BERT: Sentence embeddings using siamese BERT-Networks. In *Proceedings of the 2019 Conference on Empirical Methods in Natural Language Processing and the 9th International Joint Conference on Natural Language Processing, EMNLP-IJCNLP 2019, Hong Kong, China, November 3-7, 2019*, pages 3980–3990. Association for Computational Linguistics.

Stephen Roller, Emily Dinan, Naman Goyal, Da Ju, Mary Williamson, Yinhan Liu, Jing Xu, Myle Ott, Eric Michael Smith, Y-Lan Boureau, and Jason Weston. 2021. Recipes for building an open-domain chatbot. In *Proceedings of the 16th Conference of the European Chapter of the Association for Computational Linguistics: Main Volume*, pages 300–325, Online. Association for Computational Linguistics.

Jitesh Shetty and Jafar Adibi. 2004. The enron email dataset database schema and brief statistical report. *Information sciences institute technical report, University of Southern California*, 4(1):120–128.

Diogo Silva, David Semedo, and João Magalhães. 2022. Polite task-oriented dialog agents: To generate or to rewrite? In *Proceedings of the 12th Workshop on Computational Approaches to Subjectivity, Sentiment & Social Media Analysis*, pages 304–314, Dublin, Ireland. Association for Computational Linguistics.

Feng-Guang Su, Aliyah R. Hsu, Yi-Lin Tuan, and Hung-yi Lee. 2019. Personalized dialogue response generation learned from monologues. In *Interspeech 2019, 20th Annual Conference of the International Speech Communication Association, Graz, Austria, 15-19 September 2019*, pages 4160–4164. ISCA.

Qingfeng Sun, Can Xu, Huang Hu, Yujing Wang, Jian Miao, Xiubo Geng, Yining Chen, Fei Xu, and Daxin Jiang. 2022. Stylized knowledge-grounded dialogue generation via disentangled template rewriting. In *Proceedings of the 2022 Conference of the North American Chapter of the Association for Computational Linguistics: Human Language Technologies*, pages 3304–3318, Seattle, United States. Association for Computational Linguistics.

Ashish Vaswani, Noam Shazeer, Niki Parmar, Jakob Uszkoreit, Llion Jones, Aidan N. Gomez, Lukasz Kaiser, and Illia Polosukhin. 2017. Attention is all you need. In *Advances in Neural Information Processing Systems 30: Annual Conference on Neural Information Processing Systems 2017, December 4-9, 2017, Long Beach, CA, USA*, pages 5998–6008.

Yan Zeng and Jian-Yun Nie. 2021. A simple and efficient multi-task learning approach for conditioned dialogue generation. In *Proceedings of the 2021 Conference of the North American Chapter of the Association for Computational Linguistics: Human Language Technologies*, pages 4927–4939, Online. Association for Computational Linguistics.

Yizhe Zhang, Siqi Sun, Michel Galley, Yen-Chun Chen, Chris Brockett, Xiang Gao, Jianfeng Gao, Jingjing Liu, and Bill Dolan. 2020. DIALOGPT : Large-scale generative pre-training for conversational response generation. In *Proceedings of the 58th Annual Meeting of the Association for Computational Linguistics: System Demonstrations, ACL 2020, Online, July 5-10, 2020*, pages 270–278. Association for Computational Linguistics.

Yinhe Zheng, Zikai Chen, Rongsheng Zhang, Shilei Huang, Xiaoxi Mao, and Minlie Huang. 2021. Stylized dialogue response generation using stylized unpaired texts. In *Thirty-Fifth AAAI Conference on Artificial Intelligence, AAAI 2021, Thirty-Third Conference on Innovative Applications of Artificial Intelligence, IAAI 2021, The Eleventh Symposium on Educational Advances in Artificial Intelligence, EAAI 2021, Virtual Event, February 2-9, 2021*, pages 14558–14567. AAAI Press.

Hao Zhou, Minlie Huang, Tianyang Zhang, Xiaoyan Zhu, and Bing Liu. 2018. Emotional chatting machine: Emotional conversation generation with internal and external memory. In *Proceedings of the Thirty-Second AAAI Conference on Artificial Intelligence, (AAAI-18), the 30th innovative Applications of Artificial Intelligence (IAAI-18), and the 8th AAAI Symposium on Educational Advances in Artificial Intelligence (EAAI-18), New Orleans, Louisiana, USA, February 2-7, 2018*, pages 730–739. AAAI Press.

Template-guided Grammatical Error Feedback Comment Generation

Steven Coyne
Tohoku University, Japan
RIKEN, Japan
coyne.steven.charles.q2@dc.tohoku.ac.jp

Abstract

Writing is an important element of language learning, and an increasing amount of learner writing is taking place in online environments. Teachers can provide valuable feedback by commenting on learner text. However, providing relevant feedback for every issue for every student can be time-consuming. To address this, we turn to the NLP subfield of feedback comment generation, the task of automatically generating explanatory notes for learner text with the goal of enhancing learning outcomes. However, freely-generated comments may mix multiple topics seen in the training data or even give misleading advice. In this thesis proposal, we seek to address these issues by categorizing comments and constraining the outputs of noisy classes. We describe an annotation scheme for feedback comment corpora using comment topics with a broader scope than existing typologies focused on error correction. We outline plans for experiments in grouping and clustering, replacing particularly diverse categories with modular templates, and comparing the generation results of using different linguistic features and model architectures with the original dataset versus the newly annotated one. This paper presents the first two years (the master's component) of a research project for a five-year combined master's and Ph.D program.

1 Introduction

Written corrective feedback on learner text is widespread in language education, and an active area of research in the field of second language acquisition (Kang and Han, 2015). Research has shown that properly administered teacher feedback has a positive effect on language acquisition (Ferris and Roberts, 2001; Bitchener, 2008), including in electronic settings (Ene and Upton, 2014). With the rise of shared online writing environments and e-learning platforms, it has become possible for teachers to assess and comment on learner text

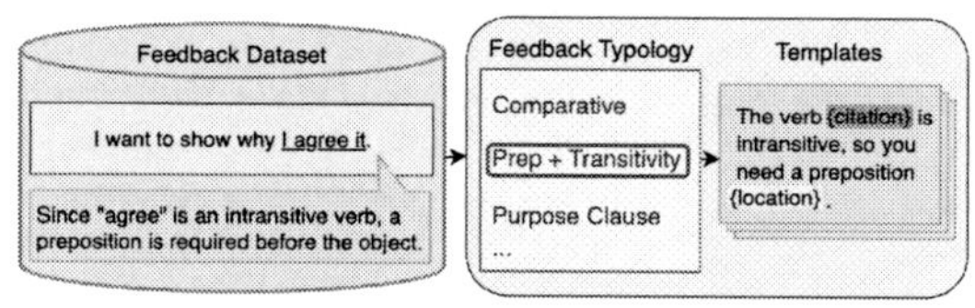

Figure 1: Visualization of the use of manually-labeled feedback comments to support the development of a template-based feedback comment generation system.

digitally. While these advancements in computer-assisted language learning (CALL) are helping revolutionize language education, it remains true that writing frequent and context-appropriate feedback comments on essays is a time-consuming task for teachers. It would be beneficial to provide instructors with automatically generated suggestions when writing comments, allowing them to accept or edit suitable feedback comments and reject unsuitable ones. Using similar technology, it is also possible to provide such feedback comments directly to learners in an intelligent tutoring setting as well. With such use cases in mind, we turn to the task of feedback comment generation.

In NLP, feedback comment generation is the task of generating hints or explanatory notes for language learners (Nagata, 2019). Data consists of learner sentences, associated feedback comments, and offsets or spans to highlight where the comments were attached to the sentence. An example, taken from the ICNALE Learner Essays with Feedback Comments dataset described in Nagata et al. (2020)[1] can be seen in Figure 2. This is one of a handful of corpora about this task, along with a translated subset used in GenChal 2022 (Nagata et al., 2021) and a separate corpus developed by Lee et al. (2015) and expanded upon in Pilan et al. (2020). The commented ICNALE corpus is fairly small, as seen in Table 1, and a lack of data is

[1]The dataset is available at https://www.gsk.or.jp/en/catalog/gsk2019-b

Proceedings of the 17th Conference of the European Chapter of the Association for Computational Linguistics: Student Research Workshop, pages 94–104

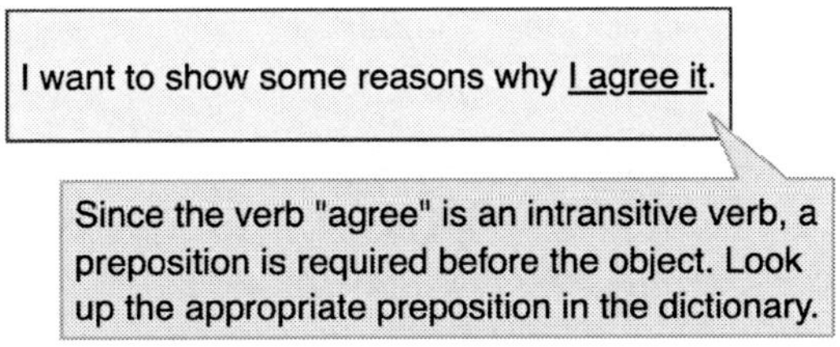

Figure 2: Example of an English learner's sentence with an annotator's feedback comment on a targeted span. Note that feedback comments in the source dataset are written in Japanese, but presented here in English.

one of the major challenges of feedback comment generation.

Additional challenges were revealed by Hanawa et al. (2021) and the participants of GenChal 2022. First, generation is confounded by a many-to-one issue in which multiple comments which ultimately concern the same topic may use different wording. Consider the following pair of sentences:

> **We reached to the station.*
>
> Because the verb "reach" is a transitive verb, the preposition "to" is not required.
>
> **I reached to New York.*
>
> "Reach" is a transitive verb. This verb does not require a preposition prior to the object.

The targeted error is the same, but the comments are superficially different. This diversity can result in mixed generations which are less clear, as shown in Hanawa et al. (2021).

Furthermore, there are a large number of very specific comments relating to particular words and their collocations. In relatively inflexible systems such as the neural retrieval model seen in Nagata (2019), these are rarely output, since the same words would have to occur with the same errors to produce a match. In more flexible generation systems, such comments show a great deal of diversity and contribute to the mixed output problem.

Finally, generation systems can produce inaccurate or misleading comments which can lead learners astray, as reported by Hanawa et al. (2021). It is important to constrain these false generations, which can have a negative learning effect or reduce confidence in the system.

This research seeks to improve the generation of educationally effective feedback comments by addressing the above challenges. We outline plans to group feedback comments with a set of annotations which focus on the "topic" of each comment, based on its communicative purpose and its connection to an issue in the sentence when applicable. We identify highly variable or noisy feedback comment categories and replace such categories with modular templates. We also describe experiments with textual features and generation architectures to be used in testing the effects of the above approaches. It is hoped that these contributions can enable additional research into feedback comment generation for language learning.

2 Related Work

Pedagogical feedback comments have long been studied in the field of education, including in the context of language learning. There is considerable debate about what kind of feedback works best and why, which includes dimensions such as directness (Ferris and Roberts, 2001), presence of metalinguistic terms (Bitchener, 2008), and hedging (Baker and Hansen Bricker, 2010). While there are some detractors (Truscott, 1996), written feedback has generally been found effective for language learning (Kang and Han, 2015).

Turning towards the online environment of our task, we must consider systems which already exist. There are various tools for grammatical error correction (GEC) and writing assistance, perhaps the most notable of which is Grammarly[2]. We define the purpose of these tools as *writing assistance*, in which the goal is to improve the content of the document. This overlaps with, but is distinct from, the purpose of this work, which we define as *learning assistance*. Our goal is to help learners notice and understand their errors, not just correct them. Defining and suggesting changes in sentences is a necessary step in the process, but it is done with an eye towards a long term learning effect. The generation goal is therefore different. In our case, it is acceptable if we do not produce a comment for every error in the sentence, since we prioritize precision to avoid misleading students, and because a large number of overlapping and uncoordinated feedback comments can overwhelm and demotivate students (Lee, 2013). On the other hand, a GEC or writing support system like Grammarly ideally has something to offer for all issues in a sentence. We also place more emphasis on explaining what is wrong and particularly why, rather than

[2]https://www.grammarly.com/

Dataset Information	General	Preposition	Combined
Sentences	43568	28829	72397
Feedback Comments	26592	5693	32285
Commented Sentences	19991	4931	24922
Comment/Sentence Ratio	0.459	0.171	0.344
Most Comments/Sentence	14	6	14

Table 1: Information about the "ICNALE Learner Essays with Feedback Comments" dataset. It is divided into two sub-corpora, one with comments on general topics, and the other focusing on preposition use.

what specific edits should be made, which the comments in this task often hint at rather than provide outright. This would quickly become frustrating in a writing support environment, but in the context of education, such comments have been found to be effective for long-term learning (Sheen, 2007; Bitchener and Knoch, 2010).

In the context of natural language processing, feedback generation was first formally defined in Nagata (2019), followed by the release of a dataset containing learner sentences and feedback comments, constructed from essays from The International Corpus Network of Asian Learners of English (ICNALE) (Ishikawa, 2013). The dataset contains triples consisting of English sentences written by learners, feedback comments added by professionals, and the offsets designating the target span of the comment. There were also developments by Lai and Chang (2019), who created a system which constructed feedback templates from word collocations, and Pilan et al. (2020), who added additional annotations to a corpus of textual revisions (Lee et al., 2015) and investigated the revision outcomes of various kinds of feedback comments.

Hanawa et al. (2021) performed experiments on the ICNALE feedback dataset, revealing challenges faced by models using neural retrieval, simple generation, and retrieve and edit (Hashimoto et al., 2018) architectures. Namely, the retrieval model can not generalize, the retrieve-and-edit model over-edited in an unconstrained manner, and the simple generation and retrieve-and edit models both produced mixed or misleading outputs. Following that, there was a shared task on feedback comment generation in GenChal 2022. Teams demonstrated various modeling and preprocessing techniques, particularly that it is possible to extract detailed linguistic features from the sentences and comments using existing NLP tools such as parsers and GEC systems and use them to enhance feedback comment output.[3] We discuss several such options in section 3.4.

3 Research Plan

Based on the above literature, we have identified two major challenges in this task:

1. Superficial diversity of comments. For a given error, there are any number of ways to describe or explain it, and any number of ways to phrase a suggestion. This manifests as superficial differences among multiple comments that are effectively the same in meaning, presenting a challenge when counting or classifying feedback comments. Such comments could be grouped into one category or "topic." Consider the examples below:

> **It should be a clean places for service everyone that comes to have in there.*
>
> The preposition "for" cannot be followed by the base form of a verb. Use a to-infinitive instead.

> **Sometimes students from the outside city will do this for earn some money.*
>
> The preposition "for" indicating the purpose of the sentence are followed by nouns including gerunds. You cannot put a verb in its original form after a preposition. Use to-infinitive to indicate the purpose.

The learner sentences have little in common beyond the presence of "for + base form of a verb," and the feedback comments are different in length and detail. The latter contains several words such as "gerunds" and "purpose" which the former lacks. There is also a difference in terminology: "base form" vs. "original form." It is possible that these differences may cause the two comments to be treated somewhat differently by models. It is ideal if they can be assigned to the same group.

[3]Participants' systems can be viewed on the GenChal 2022 website: https://fcg.sharedtask.org/links/

2. Unreliability of outputs. In the context of educational feedback comments, it is very important to provide accurate advice. Misleading outputs can confuse learners and lead them astray with false information. Furthermore, noticing inaccurate comments can erode trust in the system. The following example is taken from Hanawa et al. (2021):

> **I disagree* to *you.*
>
> Since the verb "disagree" is a transitive verb, the object does not require the preposition "to."

In this case, the comment is incorrect because "disagree" is in fact an intransitive verb. Furthermore, instead of removing "to," we should replace it with "with." The model may have found the correct word to change, but suggests both the wrong operation and the wrong reasoning. This example is also a case where the correction relies on a specific word's use and collocations. It would be beneficial to identify which kinds of comments are particularly likely to face these issues, and address them in a targeted manner. This would first necessitate some form of grouping the comments.

3.1 Feedback Topic Tagging

To address these points, we decided to manually tag all sentence-comment pairs in the dataset with a "topic." This is distinct from error typing, since it must include a broader scope to encapsulate what an instructor's comment is about. This can include comments on more abstract issues in learner text.

Currently, NLP tools can identify errors and predict an edit, but not necessarily describe the underlying rule. Just using the edit information to generate feedback might give us a comment that applies to the target text span in some way, but not necessarily match the advice we want to give, especially if we want to comment on something with a broader scope. Consider the following example:

> *If I will have chance, I must do part time job.*
>
> In the if clause "if... then", we do not use the auxiliary verb "will" to express the future. In the if clause, let's express the future with the present tense of the verb.

The correction is to change the verb's tense from future to present, but the reason is more complex, relying on a conditional clause. The topic of the comment could be thought of as "conditional." However, if we consider existing NLP frameworks for grammatical correction, we only find much more local categories. The most popular error typology in NLP is ERRANT (Bryant et al., 2017), which compares erroneous sentences and their corrections. ERRANT would characterize this as "U:VERB:TENSE," which does not take the broader picture of a conditional clause into consideration. GECToR (Omelianchuk et al., 2020), a sequence tagger which predicts grammatical corrections, tags this as "$DELETE," addressing only the edit operation of removing "will."

This is no indictment of these systems - indeed, the scale of the errors they consider is reasonable for the tasks they were designed for. Rather, we highlight the difference in scope between GEC and the present task, in which it is desirable to include broader structures in our analysis. Therefore, we seek to include information such as "conditional" in our labels. Furthermore, since many GEC tags can be returned automatically by present tools, it is prudent to include complementary information, and we thus use a set of categories which do not always focus on the same phenomena. These labels are based on the "topic" of the feedback, i.e. what the comment is about. In the very common case where a feedback comment targets an error, these topic labels will often overlap with error typologies, but they include broader-scoped perspectives of the errors which extend beyond the level of edit operations, perhaps focusing on the learner's attempted grammatical pattern (e.g. "conditional"). They also incorporate major types of teacher feedback which are not sufficiently covered by automatic systems, such as redundancy, parallelism, transitions, run-on sentences, fragments, tone, and idiom errors.

The current tags are presented in section 3.1.2. These were developed by first consulting previous typologies (see section 3.1.1), considering which categories are most likely to be used by English language teachers,[4] then checking them against the comments in the ICNALE feedback dataset, adapting to the data in the corpus. As a first step, we considered a subset consisting of of 250 sentences each from the General and Preposition sub-corpora, each with exactly one feedback comment. Comments extending across multiple sentences were excluded, since they exceed the sentence-level scope of this work. Sentences were then sampled with a particular random seed. The proposed tag set may

[4]The author worked in English education for five years, and drew on that experience in the process.

evolve further by the time all sentences in the data have been considered.

3.1.1 Existing Tag Systems

When designing the annotation system, consideration was given to existing tag sets from the fields of NLP, corpus linguistics, and second language acquisition (SLA).

The error typology used in the NUCLE dataset (Dahlmeier et al., 2013) contains 28 tags. Some examples work well for this task, such as redundancy, which may not be identified as a grammatical error per se, but which a critical teacher may certainly comment on. However, it has some categories which are too broad in some cases, such as Mec, which concerns spelling, punctuation, and capitalization, among others. These would have quite different feedback comments. There are also some very distinct subcategories of each topic, which may warrant more granular labels.

The system used in the Cambridge Learner Corpus (Nicholls, 2003) and seen in the First Certificate in English (FCE) dataset (Yannakoudakis et al., 2011) is more fine-grained, and contains detailed descriptions of various errors. It is also modular, with edit type (whether words are missing, unnecessary or should be replaced) as well as the relevant part of speech. It has 77 tags, making it quite expressive. Some of the tags are for quite rare or esoteric errors. Additionally, we find this system too linguistically oriented for this task, its original purpose being to describe a corpus of errors rather than the topic of teacher feedback.

ERRANT was created with both of the above in mind, and strikes a good balance between them, having quickly become the standard for GEC research. However, it too was created for the task of GEC specifically, and thus its error tags do not extend to the broader topics seen in the educational realm as ours do. This is understandable, because it is simply a tool for another (albeit related) field.

Meanwhile, educational researchers have also been considering learners and their errors, creating some typologies of their own. Error analysis studies such as Watcharapunyawong and Usaha (2013) and Darus and Subramaniam (2009) tend to use very broad categories, often with no section outlining their reasoning for them. These may be too broad to use for this task.

The most direct source of educational feedback topics may be the various sets of error code annotations used by English teachers. These tend to

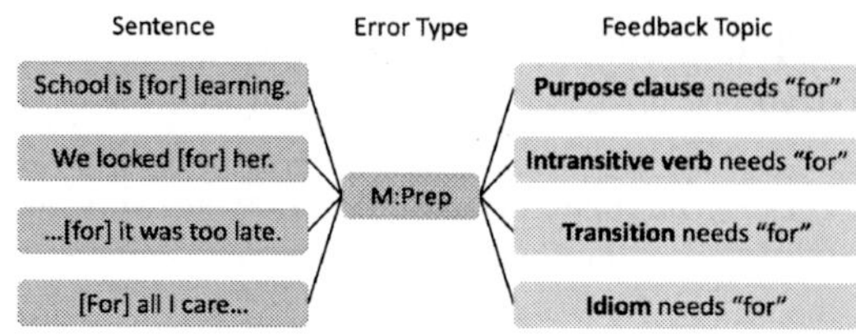

Figure 3: One grammatical error type (as identified by ERRANT) can be associated with several different underlying reasons, each with distinct comments.

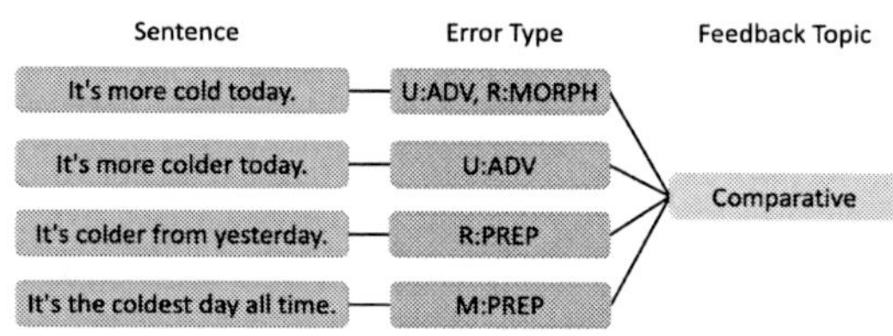

Figure 4: A variety of error types may be associated with a common attempted construction. "Grammatical Pattern" feedback topics seek to model this kind of broader phenomenon seen in learner errors.

include many of the more abstract categories we wish to address, such as redundancy, parallelism, and idiom. While there does not seem to be a well-accepted correction code standard in literature, there are a variety of systems shared online, many covering similar topics. One example is the system used for writing programs at the University of California, Irvine (UCI Writing Center, 2008).

3.1.2 Proposed Tag System

The proposed system is shown in Tables 2 and 3. The tags are divided into three levels of abstraction. The most concrete are "Operational" tags, which reflect direct changes to one or a few words in the text. These are expected to correlate very closely with existing error typologies. Examples include punctuation, spelling, and "missing noun." There are cases where this kind of straightforward word-level edit to the text is indeed the best summary of a feedback comment's content.

The next level of abstraction we call "Grammatical Patterns." These are essentially designed as a teacher's perspective of the violated "grammar point" that underlies the writer's error. They can thus serve to summarize a large portion of comments that target errors in an educational setting. If compared to GEC error types or the operational tags, these are expected to display complex mapping behaviors with many-to-one and one-to-many relationships, as demonstrated in Figures 3 and 4.

Tags at the highest level of abstraction are appropriately called "Abstract" tags, which may map to "any" or "none" of the theoretical errors in a sentence. An example is "unclear," which teachers apply to certain sentences which can display any of a vast variety of issues. Praise and complex rewrites are also in this category, as are comments pointing out language transfer. Specialized approaches may be necessary to best generate these comments, if a system's designers intend to include them at all.

3.2 Grouping Comments

Once comments have been classified by topic, it will be possible to run a variety of NLP tools on the dataset and explore the co-occurrence of their outputs with each of the tags. These include sequence taggers for parts of speech and dependencies as well as error correction systems. If it is discovered that some feedback comment types correlate very strongly with certain parse patterns or GEC error types, those system outputs may be useful as predictive features for the feedback comments.

Returning to the proposed use cases, it may be desirable in educational settings to focus feedback on a limited number of categories, or to adapt the system to the learner's level using a framework such as the Common European Framework of Reference for Languages (CEFR) (Council of Europe, 2001) or even specific curriculum goals laid out by a school board. This would also allow customization by users. Categorizing the comments is a useful first step towards realizing such options.

Additionally, it will be easier to explore automatic clustering once the comments have human-annotated categories. Nagata and Hanawa (2021) attempted to address the superficial diversity issue by clustering the comments with textual similarity, but the interpretability of the resulting categories is limited. It would be useful to compare such results to class labels added by a human.

In addition to surface similarity, we will experiment with clustering based on semantic similarity or with a topic-modeling approach as seen in Grootendorst (2022). Topic labels can be identified in the feedback comment text, and placed into hierarchical clusters. Given that there are many synonyms for grammatical terms in the feedback comments, we hypothesize that semantic or topic modeling will perform better than surface similarity. We will compare clusters to the manual tags, potentially revealing additional topic subtypes which can help improve the tagging logic.

Furthermore, it will be interesting to observe whether the clustering and classification strategies described above can generalize to other feedback comment data. If so, it may suggest that the strategies are sound. If not, useful observations may result which could suggest improvements to either the tagging logic or the application of these techniques. Any dataset with pairs of learner sentences and associated feedback comments made by humans can be a candidate. Presently, the only other suitable dataset we are aware of is the one described in Lee et al. (2015) and expanded in Pilan et al. (2020). We may additionally create our own dataset of feedback on learner sentences as part of future work on this topic, as noted in section 4.

3.3 Templates

To address the superficial diversity issue, we seek to replace the outputs of highly diverse comment categories with generalized templates. The manual tagging step will allow us to identify the feedback categories most in need of such attention. Tentatively, it seems that there are a large number of comments which contain content very specific to a single word, pair, or triple, often taking a form like the following:

> We do not use **«a»** with **«b»** to express "meaning of collocation." Think of an alternative **<(part of speech of a)>**.

Comments like these form a long tail of rare examples in the dataset, and the data may simplify significantly if they are unified into a limited number of semi-automatically generated templates with slot-filling. The slots can be filled with words from the sentence and information from open-source lexical resources. This can also help with the reliability challenge in this task, since we can more tightly control the output in these cases, and filter candidate comments if they do not contain certain words present in the original sentence.

The word designated **«b»** above is likely to prove hardest to handle. It is a non-erroneous word being combined erroneously in the original sentence. Lai and Chang (2019) call this is the "problem word," and Nagata and Hanawa (2020) call it the "attachment word." A collection of collocations or other lexical resources may be necessary to determine this word and its relationship to others in the sentence or its theoretical correction. It will also

Abstract Tags

Tag Name	Example
Fragment	**Obligation at home and at campus.**
Idiom	[**There's** → **That's**] the way it goes.
Language Transfer	I like riding [**jet** → **roller**] coasters.
Praise	(Various kinds of praise and encouragement)
Rewrite	(Used for explicit, complex revision suggestions)
Tone	It's maybe [**cause** → **because**] my work experience less than other people.
Unclear	**If home is not richness economically, everybody is only just doing it.**

Grammatical Pattern Tags

Tag Name	Example
Comparative	Maybe you will study [**more hard** → **harder**] in the class.
Causative	It will ruin our concentration and make everything [**getting**] worse.
Conditional	If I [**have** → **had**] a job, I could buy more things.
Dummy Subject	It is important [**that**] university students [**have**] a part time job.
Derivation	Due to the time, we lived in a [**peace** → **peaceful**] world.
Hyphenation	It is important for students to have a [**part time** → **part-time**] job.
Modal/Auxiliary	Students [**would better** → **should**] have part-time jobs.
Nominalization	[**Breathe** → **Breathing**] fresh air is important.
Noun Countability	Also, they can buy other [**stuffs** → **stuff**].
Parallel Structure	...hanging out with my best friend, [**buy** → **buying**] cosmetics, or shopping
Participle	In some restaurant, we can see students [**works** → **working**] as waiters.
Passive Voice	As a result, their performance in school may be [**get**] influenced.
Possessive	Studying is the main task [**to** → **of**] students.
Preposition + Transitivity	I completely agree [**with**] this opinion.
Purpose Clause	They should earn money [**for** → **to**] spend in the daily life by themselves.
Quantifier	Almost [**all**] non-smokers hate the cigarette smoke.
Question Formation	Why [**students must** → **must students**] do part time job[**.** → **?**]
Redundancy	I did part-time jobs last summer vacation to [**go travel**] to a foreign land.
Relative Clause	College students [**who**] jump in part-time job have a variety of reasons.
Run-on Sentence	In a word, I'll try[**,** → **.**] if I find a job fit me, I'll do that!
Subject-Verb Agreement	The [**students works**] part time job
Transitions	[**But** → **However,**] it costs a lot to go to the university.
Word Order	**What more serious is...** → **What is more serious...**

Table 2: Annotation System for Feedback Comment Topics, Abstract Tags and Grammatical Pattern Tags.

sometimes be necessary to refer to other words in the sentence which are not necessarily erroneous in order to explain the relative position of a suggested operation such as insertion. We will call such words "reference words."

Creating templates also allows us a chance to rewrite their contents to be more suitable to the task. For example, it may be ideal to limit the amount of direct citation which takes place, particularly for the meaning of collocations, which may be difficult to extract in a reliable manner. In addition to this, we find that many of the comments in the commented ICNALE dataset have fairly advanced grammatical explanations, which can be simplified to help learners understand them. An example of a modular feedback comment template with such revision can be seen in Figure 5.

3.4 Generation Experiments

After tagging, grouping, and template composition is complete, we move on to experiments with generation models. The experiments performed by teams in GenChal 2022 show that it is possible to enhance generation performance using a variety of supplemental features obtained from the data. Systems of interest include GECToR, which tags sequences with edit operations, as well as parsing trees which use recent strategies to specialize on erroneous text. These include the SynGEC system (Zhang et al., 2022), which can output special tags for words which are missing or which should be rewritten, as well as a parser trained on the Tenbusu Treebank (Morgado da Costa et al., 2022), which incorporates "mal-rules", specialized rules which match ungrammatical structures, allowing the parser to describe erroneous text.

There are additional systems to consider as well, with the caveat that they require corrected versions of the sentences. These include the aforementioned ERRANT as well as SERRANT (Choshen et al., 2021), a more recent addition which incorporates additional tags focused on syntax errors,

Operational Tags

Tag Name	Example
Capitalization	In [**korea** → **Korea**], it is common.
Incorrect/Double Negative	If smoking [**not be** → **is not**] banned, a lot of people will smoke.
Missing Adjective	Almost [**all**] restaurant in Japan have smoking seat.
Missing Adverb	And [**when**] they can get right answer, I feel very happy.
Missing Determiner	They will relax after having [**a**] meal.
Missing Noun	For students who don't have money, [**jobs**] are very necessary.
Missing Preposition	70% [**of**] men in this country is smoking
Missing Pronoun	Try to tell them what [**they**] should do, and what [**they**] should not to do.
Missing Verb	Some of them can not [**pay**] their education fees.
Noun Number	College students have a lot of [**times** → **time**].
Other	(Miscellaneous Topics)
Punctuation	They can learn the value of money[**,**] they use, too.
Replace Adjective	It 's [**interested** → **interesting**] to me .
Replace Adverb	I have [**ever** → **never**] been in this situation.
Replace Determiner	Second, they can know [**an** → **the**] importance of money.
Replace Noun	I will talk about my [**opinion** → **reason**] why.
Replace Preposition	I have three reasons [**about** → **for**] it.
Replace Pronoun	They need work for them or [**they** → **their**] family .
Replace Verb	It [**does** → **is**] important and helpful when taking a job.
Spacing	Customers [**may be** → **maybe**] don't want to go that restaurant again.
Spelling	[**The** → **They**] will make good use of the money.
Unnecessary Adjective	And it will be very [**important**] worthwhile in life.
Unnecessary Adverb	I feel bored every time [**when**] someone smokes near me.
Unnecessary Determiner	Nowadays it is [**a**] common for college students to have a part-time job.
Unnecessary Noun	Students have burden on a lot of assignments and expensive tuition [**fee**].
Unnecessary Preposition	Many students had a part-time job because they need [**to**] money.
Unnecessary Pronoun	I have acquaintances that [**he**] died from smoking.
Unnecessary Verb	Many of people [**are**] get a part time job for many reasons.
Verb Conjugation	Smoking [**are** → **is**] very popular these days.
Verb Form	How about [**give** → **giving**] sometime to think yourself.
Verb Tense	Most students [**are** → **were**] isolated from society before.

Table 3: Annotation System for Feedback Comment Topics, Operational Tags

outlined in Choshen et al. (2020). CEFR-J (Ishii and Tono, 2018), a framework for describing the features and proficiency level of learner text, offers a set of scripts to find grammatical items with regular expressions. Some of these are quite complex, and may be able to indicate broader grammatical structures in the dataset sentences. For example, CEFR-J scripts can recognize both "not as large" and "larger than" as part of a comparative group of tags starting with "COMP." These are promising as predictive features for a "comparative" topic tag.

We hypothesize that the tags output by these systems, especially those found to correlate with particular feedback topics, can provide useful information to language models when incorporated into input sequences. We can obtain these features by first creating a corrected version of the input sentence via an automatic tool such as GECToR or a generative model. We then apply SERRANT to the sentence-correction pair to obtain error annotations, and apply CEFR-J scripts to the corrected sentence to obtain grammatical item matches.

To assess whether the above strategies are effective for feedback comment generation, we will repeat the experiments from Hanawa et al. (2021), using simple generation, neural retrieval, and retrieve and edit models and assessing the differences associated with our changes. Given more time, we will move on to larger and more recent language models suited for generation tasks, such as GPT-2, T5, and BART to examine whether and how performance improves given the additional features.

4 Future Directions

This paper presents details about the first two years (the master's component) of a research project for a five-year combined master's and Ph.D program. There are many additional research directions and concepts which can be incorporated before the final thesis is complete.

For generation, given the mixed output issue observed in previous studies, and the overlapping nature of the tagging system, it may be prudent to separate generation models. Different models could be used for abstract comments versus the operational and grammatical pattern ones. If a more abstract comment is generated, the grammatical

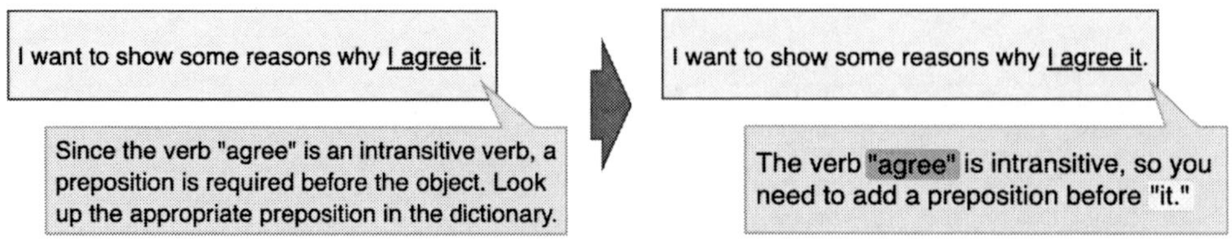

Figure 5: Example of a feedback comment rewritten as a template and simplified. This example template has two slots to fill with citations, a "problem word" whose mistaken combination caused the error ("agree"), and a "reference word" for indicating a position for a suggested operation ("it").

pattern and operational models can withhold suggestions. It may also be effective to separate the generators in a more horizontal manner, with some focusing on prepositions, others on verb errors, and so on, likely informed by the results of clustering analysis. A separate model would classify the errors and call the relevant generator.

There is also a general lack of corpora for the task of feedback comment generation. Given that each teacher has their own idiosyncrasies in correcting learner text, it is highly desirable to collect more data from a variety of writers. Furthermore, the ICNALE Learner Essays with Feedback Comments dataset contains only essays written by learners from China, India, Japan, Korea, Thailand, and Taiwan, and the number of comment writers is limited. The learner's CEFR levels range from A2 to B2, the ages range from 15 to 37, and all writing is in the context of a single-draft essay. Working with corpora with different learner first languages, age groups, or writing tasks may further affect the annotation sets and clusters discussed in this work, as well as provide valuable training data in the form of new and unique sentence-comment pairs, particularly for categories such as language transfer. We have preliminary plans to construct a new corpus of learner sentences, feedback comments, and comment topic labels, which will be informed by the insights gained during this research.

5 Summary

To assist in the task of feedback comment generation, we add manual labels to the feedback-enhanced ICNALE dataset which consider broad-scope errors, explore grouping comments using these manual labels as a reference, craft modular templates for highly diverse categories of feedback comments, and perform modeling experiments with a variety of architectures and using features obtained by parsers and GEC tools, reporting on the best combinations.

Limitations

Only sentence-level errors and comments are considered in this proposal. A separate body of work, automated essay scoring, addresses paragraph and document level writing issues. Extending feedback comment generation to that scope is left for future research. Both are useful for the intended settings of online essay grading and intelligent tutoring systems, so it would be ideal to see them connected.

The proposed tags are ultimately manual, so data from any new corpora must be tagged by hand as well if it is to align with this work.

There are some cases where the new tags offer little more than existing automatic tools, particularly for the operational annotations. Furthermore, some may question whether we need another tagging system for learner essays and their issues, especially after ERRANT was introduced to unify disparate systems such as the Cambridge Learner Corpus and NUCLE. Again, this is because this data, and thus the proposed tags, are focused on learner support, not grammatical error correction or writing support, and are meant to describe the topic of a comment and its link to an error rather than the local features of the error itself. Additionally, they are meant to complement existing error-focused systems such as ERRANT or GECToR, and therefore provide information from a slightly broader context which can be used to identify additional kinds of issues.

Acknowledgments

This work was supported by JSPS KAKENHI Grant Numbers JP22H00524 and JP21K21343. We thank Kentaro Inui, Diana Galvan, Keisuke Sakaguchi, Michael Zock, and Ryo Nagata, who shared their thoughts at various stages of this project. We also thank the reviewers of the 2023 EACL Student Research Workshop, whose insightful criticisms led to several improvements to this paper.

References

Wendy Baker and Rachel Hansen Bricker. 2010. The effects of direct and indirect speech acts on native english and esl speakers' perception of teacher written feedback. *System*, 38(1):75–84.

John Bitchener. 2008. Evidence in support of written corrective feedback. *Journal of Second Language Writing*, 17(2):102–118.

John Bitchener and Ute Knoch. 2010. Raising the linguistic accuracy level of advanced l2 writers with written corrective feedback. *Journal of Second Language Writing*, 19(4):207–217.

Christopher Bryant, Mariano Felice, and Ted Briscoe. 2017. Automatic annotation and evaluation of error types for grammatical error correction. In *Proceedings of the 55th Annual Meeting of the Association for Computational Linguistics (Volume 1: Long Papers)*, pages 793–805, Vancouver, Canada. Association for Computational Linguistics.

Leshem Choshen, Dmitry Nikolaev, Yevgeni Berzak, and Omri Abend. 2020. Classifying syntactic errors in learner language. In *Proceedings of the 24th Conference on Computational Natural Language Learning*, pages 97–107, Online. Association for Computational Linguistics.

Leshem Choshen, Matanel Oren, Dmitry Nikolaev, and Omri Abend. 2021. SERRANT: a syntactic classifier for english grammatical error types. *CoRR*, abs/2104.02310.

Council of Europe. 2001. *Common European Framework of Reference for Languages: Learning, Teaching, Assessment.* Cambridge: Cambridge University Press.

Daniel Dahlmeier, Hwee Tou Ng, and Siew Mei Wu. 2013. Building a large annotated corpus of learner English: The NUS corpus of learner English. In *Proceedings of the Eighth Workshop on Innovative Use of NLP for Building Educational Applications*, pages 22–31, Atlanta, Georgia. Association for Computational Linguistics.

Saadiyah Darus and Kaladevi Subramaniam. 2009. Error analysis of the written english essays of secondary school students in malaysia: A case study. *European Journal of Social Sciences*, 8:483–495.

Estela Ene and Thomas A. Upton. 2014. Learner uptake of teacher electronic feedback in esl composition. *System*, 46:80–95.

Dana Ferris and Barrie Roberts. 2001. Error feedback in l2 writing classes: How explicit does it need to be? *Journal of Second Language Writing*, 10(3):161–184.

Maarten Grootendorst. 2022. Bertopic: Neural topic modeling with a class-based tf-idf procedure. *arXiv preprint arXiv:2203.05794.*

Kazuaki Hanawa, Ryo Nagata, and Kentaro Inui. 2021. Exploring methods for generating feedback comments for writing learning. In *Proceedings of the 2021 Conference on Empirical Methods in Natural Language Processing*, pages 9719–9730, Online and Punta Cana, Dominican Republic. Association for Computational Linguistics.

Tatsunori B. Hashimoto, Kelvin Guu, Yonatan Oren, and Percy Liang. 2018. A retrieve-and-edit framework for predicting structured outputs. In *Neural Information Processing Systems.*

Yasutake Ishii and Yukio Tono. 2018. Investigating japanese efl learners' overuse/underuse of english grammar categories and their relevance to cefr levels. In *In Proceedings of Asia Pacific Corpus Linguistics Conference 2018*, pages 160–165.

Shin'ichiro Ishikawa. 2013. The icnale and sophisticated contrastive interlanguage analysis of asian learners of english. *Learner corpus studies in Asia and the world*, pages 91–118.

Eun Young Kang and ZhaoHong Han. 2015. The efficacy of written corrective feedback in improving l2 written accuracy: A meta-analysis. *The Modern Language Journal*, 99:1–18.

Yi-Huei Lai and Jason Chang. 2019. TellMeWhy: Learning to explain corrective feedback for second language learners. In *Proceedings of the 2019 Conference on Empirical Methods in Natural Language Processing and the 9th International Joint Conference on Natural Language Processing (EMNLP-IJCNLP): System Demonstrations*, pages 235–240, Hong Kong, China. Association for Computational Linguistics.

Icy Lee. 2013. Research into practice: Written corrective feedback. *Language Teaching*, 46(1):108–119.

John Sie Yuen Lee, Chak Yan Yeung, Amir Zeldes, Marc Reznicek, Anke Lüdeling, and Jonathan James Webster. 2015. Cityu corpus of essay drafts of english language learners: a corpus of textual revision in second language writing. *Language Resources and Evaluation*, 49:659–683.

Luís Morgado da Costa, Francis Bond, and Roger V. P. Winder. 2022. The tembusu treebank: An English learner treebank. In *Proceedings of the Thirteenth Language Resources and Evaluation Conference*, pages 4817–4826, Marseille, France. European Language Resources Association.

Ryo Nagata. 2019. Toward a task of feedback comment generation for writing learning. In *Proceedings of the 2019 Conference on Empirical Methods in Natural Language Processing and the 9th International Joint Conference on Natural Language Processing (EMNLP-IJCNLP)*, pages 3206–3215, Hong Kong, China. Association for Computational Linguistics.

Ryo Nagata, Masato Hagiwara, Kazuaki Hanawa, Masato Mita, Artem Chernodub, and Olena Nahorna. 2021. Shared task on feedback comment generation for language learners. In *Proceedings of the 14th International Conference on Natural Language Generation*, pages 320–324, Aberdeen, Scotland, UK. Association for Computational Linguistics.

Ryo Nagata and Kazuaki Hanawa. 2020. Bunpo ayamari kaisetsubun seisei to wa dono yona tasuku na no ka? [what kind of task is grammatical error commentary generation?]. In *Proceedings of the 26th Annual Conference of the Association for Natural Language Processing*, pages 513–516.

Ryo Nagata and Kazuaki Hanawa. 2021. Kasotekina ayamari taipu no wariate ni yoru kaisetsubun seisei no seino kojo [improving the performance of commentary generation by assigning virtual error types]. In *Proceedings of the 27th Annual Conference of the Association for Natural Language Processing*, pages 679–684.

Ryo Nagata, Kentaro Inui, and Shin'ichiro Ishikawa. 2020. Creating corpora for research in feedback comment generation. In *Proceedings of the 12th Language Resources and Evaluation Conference*, pages 340–345, Marseille, France. European Language Resources Association.

Diane Nicholls. 2003. The cambridge learner corpus: Error coding and analysis for lexicography and elt. *Proceedings of the Corpus Linguistics 2003 conference*, page 572–581.

Kostiantyn Omelianchuk, Vitaliy Atrasevych, Artem Chernodub, and Oleksandr Skurzhanskyi. 2020. GECToR – grammatical error correction: Tag, not rewrite. In *Proceedings of the Fifteenth Workshop on Innovative Use of NLP for Building Educational Applications*, pages 163–170, Seattle, WA, USA → Online. Association for Computational Linguistics.

Ildiko Pilan, John Lee, Chak Yan Yeung, and Jonathan Webster. 2020. A dataset for investigating the impact of feedback on student revision outcome. In *Proceedings of the 12th Language Resources and Evaluation Conference*, pages 332–339, Marseille, France. European Language Resources Association.

Younghee Sheen. 2007. The effect of focused written corrective feedback and language aptitude on esl learners' acquisition of articles. *TESOL Quarterly*, 41(2):255–283.

John Truscott. 1996. The case against grammar correction in l2 writing classes. *Language learning*, 46(2):327–369.

UCI Writing Center. Correction symbols for uci writing programs [online]. 2008.

Somchai Watcharapunyawong and Siriluck Usaha. 2013. Thai efl students' writing errors in different text types: The interference of the first language. *English Language Teaching*, 6:67–78.

Helen Yannakoudakis, Ted Briscoe, and Ben Medlock. 2011. A new dataset and method for automatically grading ESOL texts. In *Proceedings of the 49th Annual Meeting of the Association for Computational Linguistics: Human Language Technologies*, pages 180–189, Portland, Oregon, USA. Association for Computational Linguistics.

Yue Zhang, Bo Zhang, Zhenghua Li, Zuyi Bao, Chen Li, and Min Zhang. 2022. Syngec: Syntax-enhanced grammatical error correction with a tailored gec-oriented parser. In *Proceedings of EMNLP*.

Clinical Text Anonymization, its Influence on Downstream NLP Tasks and the Risk of Re-Identification

Iyadh Ben Cheikh Larbi and **Aljoscha Burchardt** and **Roland Roller**
German Research Center for Artificial Intelligence (DFKI)
Alt-Moabit 91c, Berlin, Germany
firstname.lastname@dfki.de

Abstract

While text-based medical applications have become increasingly prominent, access to clinical data remains a major concern. To resolve this issue, further de-identification and anonymization of the data are required. This might, however, alter the contextual information within the clinical texts and therefore influence the learning and performance of possible language models. This paper systematically analyses the potential effects of various anonymization techniques on the performance of state-of-the-art machine learning models based on several datasets corresponding to five different NLP tasks. On this basis, we derive insightful findings and recommendations concerning text anonymization with regard to the performance of machine learning models. In addition, we present a simple re-identification attack applied to the anonymized text data, which can break the anonymization.

1 Introduction

Although clinical text processing is gaining more and more attention, access to data remains a significant challenge as it typically contains sensitive, patient-related information. Thus, personal information needs to be removed by applying one of the many existing de-identification and anonymization techniques and controlling access to the data (see, e.g., Kittner et al. (2021), Henry et al. (2019))

Following the HIPAA Safe Harbor (HIPAA, 2022) method, we define de-identification as the removal of protected health information (PHI) that directly relates to an individual, such as name, address, birth date, etc. However, de-identification does not guarantee anonymity for data subjects. On the other hand, anonymization is defined as any irreversible procedure, which is applied to the data, such that no information can be linked to any specific individual anymore (Meystre et al., 2010), making the data subjects anonymous and no longer identifiable. De-identification might be sufficient to conceal sensitive patient data for many existing NLP tasks and datasets. Conversely, to train models on a broader patient record provided by healthcare practitioners, including text and structured information, to support more complex medical problems, anonymization must be considered to protect patients' privacy. Initiatives to make holistic patient data available for research are currently in planning (EHDS, 2022).

In this work, we only consider text data, which is one crucial aspect of a patient history. Each text anonymization technique has different characteristics and brings modifications to the source text which might affect the machine learning potential. Therefore, in this work, we explore the following questions: **RQ1**: What happens when ML models are trained on anonymized corpora and tested on non-anonymized data? **RQ2**: In which ways does this affect the learning procedure of NLP tasks and the final performance of the models? **RQ3**: To share data for a specific NLP task, which techniques would be best, based on their characteristics, anonymization strength, and effects on model performance? **RQ4**: How effective are these techniques against re-identification?"

To explore those questions, this work conducts a systematic analysis regarding the influence of text anonymization and their effects on the performance of (state-of-the-art) ML models. In course of this, we train and test context-sensitive language representation models using various datasets corresponding to different NLP tasks. The main contributions of this paper include a set of findings and recommendations regarding text anonymization for NLP tasks in the context of ML, as well as, a fictitious re-identification experiment investigating the (in)effectiveness of the different techniques.

2 Related Work

A range of different text anonymization approaches exist in the literature, which modify the text struc-

Proceedings of the 17th Conference of the European Chapter of the Association for Computational Linguistics: Student Research Workshop, pages 105–111
May 2-4, 2023

ture within a dataset, delete, replace, or introduce synthetic information, making it harder to identify or infer factual information about the patient. The following approaches have been explored and adapted for this work:

Suppression (Mamede et al., 2016) is a technique that either completely removes certain words or sentences or masks them with a neutral label denoting their suppression.

Perturbation (Zuo et al., 2021) modifies data through permutation or data swapping, in the case of text, similarly to data augmentation, by flipping characters or changing the order of words.

Substitution (Mamede et al., 2016) replaces certain information with other related or more general terms.

Aggregation (k-anonymity) (Samarati and Sweeney, 1998) groups individual data subjects together, e.g., by their attribute values, to make it more difficult to identify a single individual.

Only limited work has been done to describe the systematic influence of text anonymization on the performance of ML models. Berg et al. (2020), explore the effect of different PHI concealment strategies on named entity recognition (NER) tasks, Lange et al. (2020) explore the performance of concept extraction using de-identified data, as well as Vakili et al. (2022) explore the effects pseudonymizing/removing PHI data. The three papers mentioned above conclude that de-identification does not have a (strong) negative effect on the model performance regarding downstream NLP tasks. Finally, although not clinical text, Lampoltshammer et al. (2019) show that anonymization can cause significant negative changes in the sentiment analysis performance on Twitter data. This work, however, goes beyond existing related work, as we conduct the first analysis regarding the anonymization of clinical text and the effects thereof on ML models. In this regard, we report the results and findings obtained mainly through seven different techniques we tested, on six datasets, corresponding to five different NLP tasks.

3 Data and Methods

The experiments in this work are based on the following datasets and tasks:

- **2010 i2b2/VA** (Uzuner et al., 2011) (NER)
- **2018 n2c2** (Henry et al., 2019) (NER)
- **2006 Smoking Challenge** (Uzuner et al., 2008) (multi-class classification, MCC)
- **2008 Obesity Challenge** (Uzuner, 2009) (multi-label classification, MLC)
- **MedNLI** (Shivade, 2019) (natural language inference, NLI)
- **ClinSTS** (Wang et al., 2020) (semantic textual similarity, STS).

While the first four datasets include annotated discharge summaries, the last two datasets include pairs of sentences extracted from MIMIC-III (Johnson et al., 2016). Due to limited space, we refer the reader to the source papers.

Using those datasets, different text anonymization techniques are applied to the training split. The following techniques are implemented, based on Suppression, Perturbation, Substitution, and Aggregation, as described above:

De-identification (DeI) Although the documents already are pseudonymized, de-identification through masking might have an influence on the performance which we want to examine. In this case, using the tool Philter (Norgeot et al., 2020), all PHI data such as synthetic names and dates in the text are replaced by "XXXX".

Mask Numbers (Mask) All occurrences of numbers in a given text, both in numerical or alphabetical form, are replaced using "XX". In this case, any numerical data that can hint to the patient, such as drug dosages, types of diabetes, quantities, hours, etc. is masked.

Shuffle Sentences (Shuf) Sentences in a given text are shuffled.

Random Swap (Swap) A certain percentage of words are randomly chosen and swapped all over the document. The two previous procedures make it harder (to different degrees) to infer factual information about the data subject since the logical relationships between the sentences, such as temporality and causality, are broken (Sugawara et al., 2020).

Synonym Replacement (Syno) A certain percentage of the non-stop words in the document are replaced with WordNet synonyms.

Clinical Concept Synonym Replacement (Cnpt) All signs/symptoms, diseases/disorders, and medications are replaced by a random UMLS synonym, using cTAKES (Savova et al., 2010) for entity linking. In the two previous procedures, the original terms are replaced with new related concepts, which should keep the same context but also prevent finding a patient through specific keyword searches.

Text Aggregation (AgX) is done by merging a certain amount of shuffled documents (X) into one. This procedure conceals a patient among other patients.

Finally, in order to experiment and examine the effect of anonymization on the performance of state-of-the-art machine learning models, we rely on the pre-trained BERT models, which have achieved promising results on the different datasets in the recent past. More specifically, we rely on **BERT base (uncased)** (Devlin et al., 2019), **Bio+Clinical BERT** (Alsentzer et al., 2019), as well as **BERT long document classification** (Mulyar et al., 2019).

4 Experiments

For our experiments, we rely, if possible, on the original setup and configuration as described in the original publications. Given the clinical corpus, the data is split into training and test data. Next, anonymization is applied to the training data. For each anonymization technique, a model is trained and then evaluated on the original (not anonymized) text of the test split. The model is trained and evaluated five times to get reliable results in each experiment. If the anonymization technique is not deterministic and produces a different anonymized dataset each time, we repeat the text anonymization five times. This results in 25 runs. The results of each approach are averaged and compared to the base model's performance (without anonymization).

We test the models on the original data for two main reasons: First, it's closer to a real-world scenario, where the (publicly available) data is anonymized to train an ML model, and the test data consists of the non-anonymized local patient data at a health care facility. Second, this allows us to compare the effects of different techniques fairly.

All experiments are conducted with **BERT base** and **Bio+Clinical BERT**. The experiments corresponding to the classification tasks (Smoking and Obesity) are additionally conducted with **BERT long document classification**, as documents in those tasks are quite long. In the case of *Random Swap* and *Random Replacement*, we have tested these techniques with different degrees of difficulty, however, in the main article we only report the results in which the techniques are applied to 20% and 100% of the data.

Model	Smoking	Obesity	MedNLI	ClinSTS	2010	2018
BERT	77.89	67.58	76.9	83.88	82.62	87.84
BioC	75.48	70.73	**80.49**	**84.83**	**84.54**	**89.03**
LDoc	**87.69**	**82.51**	-	-	-	-
Eval	F1	F1	Acc.	Pearson	F1	F1

Table 1: Base results on all datasets in terms of average scores across all runs, using BERT base, Bio+Clinical BERT (BioC), and BERT long document classification.

Moreover, we do not apply the aggregation on the NER tasks (2010 i2b2 and 2018 n2c2) as NER is only carried out on the sentence level. Thus, the aggregation would not influence the execution of the task. Similarly, the *Shuffle Sentences* technique can only be applied to the Smoking and Obesity tasks.

4.1 Results

First, each model has been trained and tested on the original data, without applying the anonymization beforehand. Results are presented in Table 1.

Next, we apply the different text anonymization techniques to the training data, train the models and test them on the original data. The results of the different techniques, compared to the best-performing base system on that task, are presented in Table 2.

4.2 Analysis

The conducted suppression methods *de-identification* (DeI) and *mask number* (Mask), mask some information with a neutral label ('XXXX'). In most cases, the general effect is rather minimal. Particularly in the case of *DeI*, the table shows a slight performance improvement. A reason could be that, from a model perspective, the less relevant information has been discarded and it learned to rely on more significant information to make a prediction. However, the results are significantly better only in the case of **MedNLI**. *Mask* on the **2018** task causes a moderate performance loss due to entities related to numerical values, such as dosage or strength. Overall, the results align with the findings presented by Berg et al. (2020) and Lange et al. (2020).

	Suppression		Perturbation			Substitution			Aggregation		
Corpus	**Del**	**Mask**	**Shuf**	**Swap 20%**	**Swap 100%**	**Syno 20%**	**Syno 100%**	**Cnpt**	**Ag2**	**Ag3**	**Ag4**
Smoking	+1.43	+0.27	+1.05	-5.09*	-5.46*	-4.74	-8.31*	+0.22	-6.34*	-6.80*	-7.25*
Obesity	+0.80	-0.61	-2.55*	-1.94*	-5.09*	-2.99*	-8.96*	-1.31*	-12.48*	-22.59*	-36.97*
MedNLI	+1.55*	+0.14	-	-1.13	-1.93*	-2.52*	-8.42*	-0.73	-7.98*	-13.34*	-14.81*
ClinSTS	-1.21	-0.12	-	-1.36	-0.95	-1.92	-21.96*	-1.84*	-3.30*	-7.26*	-24.31*
2010	-0.32	-0.50*	-	-4.34*	-16.94*	-5.96*	-15.77*	-2.48*	-	-	-
2018	-0.83	-5.10*	-	-3.04*	-25.12*	-2.73*	-9.72*	-1.19*	-	-	-
mean	+0.368	-0.855	-0.355	-2.692	-3.353	-8.907	-12.232	-1.092	-7.342	-12.315	-20.655

Table 2: Anonymization Effects: Average performance drop/gain across all runs in percent compared to the best-performing system on the corresponding task, according to Table 1. Significant (p<0.05) results are marked with *.

	Del	**Mask**	**Shuf**	**Swap 20%**	**Swap 100%**	**Syno 20%**	**Syno 100%**	**Cnpt**	**Ag2**	**Ag3**	**Ag4**
found	1.0	1.0	1.0	1.0	1.0	1.0	1.0	1.0	0.9063	0.6351	0.2789
a/o sim	0.9529	0.8949	1.0	0.9986	0.9986	0.5486	0.2442	0.7512	0.5758	0.4261	0.3470
avg-sim	0.1502	0.1458	0.1524	0.1518	0.1518	0.1084	0.0589	0.1388	0.1646	0.1603	0.1531

Table 3: Re-identification of patients using different text anonymization techniques. *found* refers to the ratio of cases in which the most similar original document, i.e. highest ranked based on the Jaccard index, was the correct one, i.e. corresponds to the anonymized document; *a/o sim* describes the similarity between the anonymized document and its original version; *avg-sim* describes the average similarity between a given anonymized document all 3500 original documents.

In our experiment, perturbation changes the sentence order (*sentence shuffle*; *Shuf*) and the order of the words within the document (*random swap*; *Swap*). Unlike suppression, the technique shows a more substantial performance loss, particularly in the case of *Swap*. The more words swapped across the document, the stronger, in most cases the drop in performance (Swap 20% versus 100%). The technique has a particularly strong influence on NER tasks, in which the word order plays an important role. Conversely, using *sentence shuffle*, a significant negative effect can be observed on the obesity task. Generally, the negative influence of perturbation is expected, as the context and word order play an important role.

We can observe a similar behavior with the substitution techniques *synonym replacement* and *clinical concept synonym replacement*. Generally, both techniques lead to a drop in performance, which is stronger the more words affected by the technique (applying to 20% of the data versus 100%). The drop is notably stronger in the case of *synonym replacement*, as more words are affected and possibly also out-of-context synonyms might have been inserted. For *clinical concept synonym replacement*, the performance loss is notably smaller, as possibly fewer words are affected. Also, according to the frequency of UMLS mentions, in various cases, the preferred concept mention might have been chosen.

Finally, text aggregation, which merges documents according to different characteristics, has the strongest effect on the model performance. For all tasks, we can observe that the more files are aggregated, the stronger the drop in performance. We stopped with a maximum of 4 documents (Ag4), as the document length of the merged case reports was too long otherwise. For multi-class classification (Smoking) and NLI, documents with the same class have been merged, thus the effect might not be too strong. For STS, we average the similarity score of the merged texts. Here, increasing the number of texts makes it harder for the model to learn to predict the correct score. However, for multi-label classification (Obesity), the new aggregated documents are now not only larger but also contain more labels, leading to a heavy drop in performance.

4.3 Re-Identification Experiment

Now, we examine the robustness of each anonymization technique. To do so, we assume a fictitious secure data repository in which the complete patient data can be stored and accessed for research. Data could be, for instance, provided by healthcare physicians and includes the complete patient history. The data would be semi-structured and anonymized, but all information of one patient is linked to the same ID. In order to train a more complex machine learning model, it may be necessary to learn from clinical data over time.

We assume the following re-identification attack: An attacker a) has access to the secure data repository and b) has one single document of a known patient. In the following, we examine if the corresponding anonymized document can be found in the repository - and if so - it means that the complete patient history can be re-identified.

The small fictitious re-identification experiment is conducted using 3500 texts from MIMIC-III. The setup is as follows: First, we run the different anonymization techniques on the data. Then we start a similarity search by calculating the Jaccard Index on the word level between each anonymized document and all (original) 3500 MIMIC texts to find the original text in the data repository. Finding the exact original document means that, technically, the complete patient history can be re-identified. In a less severe scenario, the attacker would have some prior knowledge of a target patient and they would try to find the patient using a synthetic document containing the appropriate keywords and relying on the same similarity search approach.

As depicted in Table 3, the average similarity (avg-sim) from an anonymized document to the documents in the MIMIC dataset is mostly about *0.15*. Instead, the similarity to the correct document (a/o-sim) is always above this average score. However, while in the case of suppression and perturbation techniques, the a/o-sim score is about *0.9–1*, the similarity strongly decreases with substitution and aggregation, most notably with Syno 100% and Ag4. Conversely, only in case of aggregation, the highest ranked documents are not necessarily the corresponding original documents, thus providing some (minor) security against a possible re-identification in our scenario. Based on the outcomes, we define anonymization as 'stronger' the lower the values *a/o sim* and *found* are. This means the anonymized document should be as dissimilar as possible to the original document and therefore cannot be easily found.

5 Discussion

Based on the outcomes of the previous experiments, we draw the following insights regarding clinical text anonymization:

First, de-identification is an indispensable technique as it removes all direct identifiers. It provides the lowest level of anonymity and causes minimal performance loss but it must be combined with other anonymization techniques. Based on our results and analysis, we can deduce that some anonymization techniques affect the performance of the models on specific tasks more than others. Therefore, there is no single one-fits-all anonymization technique that can always be recommended. The optimal technique needs to be selected depending on the (security) requirements, the sensitivity of the data as well as the NLP task. Overall, the results indicate a correlation between the performance loss and the strength of the anonymization technique, but each technique comes with different costs that should be considered.

Text aggregation is the strongest of the presented techniques. It offers relatively good security against re-identification but leads to the most substantial performance loss. Moreover, the technique has various disadvantages: a) it leads to fewer training examples as data is merged, b) and longer text documents which might cause problems with standard BERT models, which can only process up to 512 input tokens. Finally, c) a patient data repository loses relevant information as data is mixed up with other patients.

Moreover, the simple fictitious re-identification experiment showed that patients could potentially be re-identified through a similarity search attack. Although the scenario is hypothetical, it highlights the importance of providing additional security mechanisms for future health data repositories. One of the problems of our attack was that although sensitive data was removed and text modified, most of the text (words) remained the same. To make anonymization more secure, coming up with more advanced techniques might be necessary, such as modifying the overall text without changing the main content and meaning (a re-formulation task). This could be possibly overcome by generating synthetic data from real examples.

6 Conclusion

This work presented a first structured analysis regarding text anonymization and its effects on the performance of state-of-the-art machine learning models. Extensive experiments have been conducted including seven different anonymization techniques on multiple datasets, which cover five different clinical NLP tasks. On the grounds of this experimentation, we can analyse the results and extract valuable insights regarding the effects of different types of anonymization on machine learning performance with respect to a given task. For short, we did not find a universal one-fits-all anonymization technique that would perform best in all tasks. Instead, the particular decision depends on several factors such as the type and strength of the anonymization technique, the underlying NLP task, desired level of anonymity, etc. In addition, we conducted a simple re-identification experiment to examine the robustness of each technique on a fictitious data repository. Our initial results show that depending on the setup, the tested anonymization may not be strong enough to prevent re-identification.

Acknowledgment

This research was supported by the German Federal Ministry of Education and Research (BMBF) through the project Medinym (16KISA007).

References

Emily Alsentzer, John Murphy, William Boag, Wei-Hung Weng, Di Jindi, Tristan Naumann, and Matthew McDermott. 2019. Publicly Available Clinical BERT Embeddings. In *Proceedings of the 2nd Clinical Natural Language Processing Workshop*, pages 72–78, Minneapolis, Minnesota, USA. Association for Computational Linguistics.

Hanna Berg, Aron Henriksson, and Hercules Dalianis. 2020. The Impact of De-identification on Downstream Named Entity Recognition in Clinical Text. In *Proceedings of the 11th International Workshop on Health Text Mining and Information Analysis*, pages 1–11.

Jacob Devlin, Ming-Wei Chang, Kenton Lee, and Kristina Toutanova. 2019. BERT: Pre-training of Deep Bidirectional Transformers for Language Understanding. *ArXiv*, abs/1810.04805.

EHDS. 2022. European Health Data Space, accessed: 2022-12-12.

Sam Henry, Kevin Buchan, Michele Filannino, Amber Stubbs, and Ozlem Uzuner. 2019. 2018 n2c2 shared task on adverse drug events and medication extraction in electronic health records. *Journal of the American Medical Informatics Association*, 27(1):3–12.

HIPAA. 2022. Guidance Regarding Methods for De-identification of Protected Health Information in Accordance with the Health Insurance Portability and Accountability Act (HIPAA) Privacy Rule, accessed: 2022-01-18.

Alistair EW Johnson, Tom J Pollard, Lu Shen, H Lehman Li-Wei, Mengling Feng, Mohammad Ghassemi, Benjamin Moody, Peter Szolovits, Leo Anthony Celi, and Roger G Mark. 2016. MIMIC-III, a freely accessible critical care database. *Scientific data*, 3(1):1–9.

Madeleine Kittner, Mario Lamping, Damian T Rieke, Julian Götze, Bariya Bajwa, Ivan Jelas, Gina Rüter, Hanjo Hautow, Mario Sänger, Maryam Habibi, et al. 2021. Annotation and initial evaluation of a large annotated German oncological corpus. *JAMIA open*, 4(2):ooab025.

Thomas J Lampoltshammer, Lőrinc Thurnay, Gregor Eibl, et al. 2019. Impact of Anonymization on Sentiment Analysis of Twitter Postings. In *Data Science–Analytics and Applications*, pages 41–48. Springer.

Lukas Lange, Heike Adel, and Jannik Strötgen. 2020. Closing the Gap: Joint De-Identification and Concept Extraction in the Clinical Domain. In *Proceedings of the 58th Annual Meeting of the Association for Computational Linguistics*, pages 6945–6952, Online. Association for Computational Linguistics.

Nuno Mamede, Jorge Baptista, and Francisco Dias. 2016. Automated anonymization of text documents. In *2016 IEEE congress on evolutionary computation (CEC)*, pages 1287–1294. IEEE.

Stephane M Meystre, F Jeffrey Friedlin, Brett R South, Shuying Shen, and Matthew H Samore. 2010. Automatic de-identification of textual documents in the electronic health record: a review of recent research. *BMC medical research methodology*, 10(1):1–16.

Andriy Mulyar, Elliot Schumacher, Masoud Rouhizadeh, and Mark Dredze. 2019. Phenotyping of Clinical Notes with Improved Document Classification Models Using Contextualized Neural Language Models. *ArXiv*, abs/1910.13664.

Beau Norgeot, Kathleen Muenzen, Thomas A Peterson, Xuancheng Fan, Benjamin S Glicksberg, Gundolf Schenk, Eugenia Rutenberg, Boris Oskotsky, Marina Sirota, Jinoos Yazdany, et al. 2020. Protected Health Information filter (Philter): accurately and securely de-identifying free-text clinical notes. *NPJ digital medicine*, 3(1):1–8.

Pierangela Samarati and Latanya Sweeney. 1998. Protecting privacy when disclosing information: k-anonymity and its enforcement through generalization and suppression.

Guergana K Savova, James J Masanz, Philip V Ogren, Jiaping Zheng, Sunghwan Sohn, Karin C Kipper-Schuler, and Christopher G Chute. 2010. Mayo clinical Text Analysis and Knowledge Extraction System (cTAKES): architecture, component evaluation and applications. *Journal of the American Medical Informatics Association*, 17(5):507–513.

Chaitanya Shivade. 2019. MedNLI — A Natural Language Inference Dataset For The Clinical Domain (version 1.0.0). *PhysioNet*.

Saku Sugawara, Pontus Stenetorp, Kentaro Inui, and Akiko Aizawa. 2020. Assessing the benchmarking capacity of machine reading comprehension datasets. In *Proceedings of the AAAI Conference on Artificial Intelligence*, volume 34, pages 8918–8927.

Özlem Uzuner. 2009. Recognizing Obesity and Comorbidities in Sparse Data. *Journal of the American Medical Informatics Association*, 16(4):561–570.

Özlem Uzuner, Ira Goldstein, Yuan Luo, and Isaac Kohane. 2008. Identifying Patient Smoking Status from Medical Discharge Records. *Journal of the American Medical Informatics Association*, 15(1):14–24.

Özlem Uzuner, Brett R South, Shuying Shen, and Scott L DuVall. 2011. 2010 i2b2/VA challenge on concepts, assertions, and relations in clinical text. *Journal of the American Medical Informatics Association*, 18(5):552–556.

Thomas Vakili, Anastasios Lamproudis, Aron Henriksson, and Hercules Dalianis. 2022. Downstream task performance of bert models pre-trained using automatically de-identified clinical data. In *Proceedings of the Thirteenth International Conference on Language Resources and Evaluation (LREC 2022)*.

Yanshan Wang, Sunyang Fu, Feichen Shen, Sam Henry, Ozlem Uzuner, and Hongfang Liu. 2020. The 2019 n2c2/OHNLP track on clinical semantic textual similarity: overview. *JMIR Medical Informatics*, 8(11):e23375.

Zheming Zuo, Matthew Watson, David Budgen, Robert Hall, Chris Kennelly, Noura Al Moubayed, et al. 2021. Data Anonymization for Pervasive Health Care: Systematic Literature Mapping Study. *JMIR medical informatics*, 9(10):e29871.

Automatic Dialog Flow Extraction and Guidance

Patrícia Ferreira
CISUC, Univ. Coimbra
DEI, Univ. Coimbra
patriciaf@dei.uc.pt

Abstract

Today, human assistants are often replaced by chatbots, designed to communicate via natural language, however, some disadvantages are notorious with this replacement. This PhD thesis project consists of researching, implementing, and testing a solution for guiding the action of a human in a contact center. It will start with the discovery and creation of datasets in Portuguese. Next, it will go through three main components: Extraction for processing dialogs and using the information to describe interactions; Representation for discovering the most frequent dialog flows represented by graphs; Guidance for helping the agent during a new dialog. These will be integrated in a single framework. In order to avoid service degradation resulting from the adoption of chatbots, this work aims to explore technologies in order to increase the efficiency of the human's job without losing human contact.

1 Introduction

In the past, a consumer's only option for customer service was to speak directly with a service employee. Now, many customer interactions are handled by automated systems powered by artificial intelligence called chatbots (Tran et al., 2021).

During the last few years, there has been a growing interest in text-based chatbots. However, despite the market's enthusiastic predictions, chatting with this type of agent raises some technological limitations, directly involving the human side of the interaction (Rapp et al., 2021).

That said, this thesis project proposes to prevent call-center service degradation and customer dissatisfaction through the use of chatbots, taking advantage of technologies that can make a human's job more efficient without losing human contact.

This work consists of researching, implementing and testing a solution to aid communication between participants, suggesting appropriate responses, thus anticipating their interventions. This guidance can be supported by the history of interactions, where information is extracted from and frequent dialog flows are discovered, which may then be used for guiding humans engaging in new dialogs of the same kind. The approaches will be applied to task-oriented dialog transcriptions (e.g. call center), providing a more efficient and facilitated service.

It begins by identifying, collecting and annotating dialogs written in Portuguese to be used in the experimentation and make available to the community. We plan to tackle the problem with a three-component pipeline: Extraction, for processing dialogs, extracting information from them and classifying interactions; Representation of the most frequent dialog flows, by graphs of interaction classes; Guidance, for assisting a human agent during a new dialog. All components are often tackled in the scope of Dialog Modelling (DM) (Budzianowski et al., 2018) to allow the reproduction of aspects of a natural conversation. Research in the area of dialogs is currently booming, with interest in chatbots, but most systems are developed for English. Instead, this work has innovative potential in the area because it is targeted for Portuguese.

In the next section, important concepts for understanding this research are introduced and an overview of related work is given. It includes an introduction to Portuguese datasets, research work on chatbots and its limitations, with the remaining subsections divided according to the three components of the project. In section 3, the research proposal and the intended methodologies are presented. Finally, section 4 presents some preliminary experiments, using NLP tools and related extraction tasks.

2 Background and Related Work

This section starts with the presentation of a Portuguese dataset, then it is checked how chatbots and human-based customer service can be so different,

Proceedings of the 17th Conference of the European Chapter of the Association for Computational Linguistics: Student Research Workshop, pages 112–122
May 2-4, 2023 ©2023 Association for Computational Linguistics

and finally it is divided into the three components of the project where concepts and related work for each are found.

2.1 Datasets

One of the first objectives of this work is the identification or creation of datasets in Portuguese.

There are several dialog datasets, of different natures, mainly for English (Oliveira et al., 2022), however, this work will focus on Portuguese, where dialog datasets are scarce and thus it is possible to explore approaches for low resource scenarios.

Existing resources for Portuguese are composed of audios containing only read and prepared speeches, and there is a lack of datasets that include spontaneous speeches, essential in different applications. An exception is a new dataset in Portuguese designated as CORAA (Junior et al., 2021) that is composed of five different corpora of European and Brazilian Portuguese conversations. They tried to bridge the gap of lack of spontaneity and formal speech by having only real conversations.

2.2 Human agents and chatbots

Chatbots are the result of advances in Artificial intelligence (AI), in order to interact and respond with suggestions appropriate to certain needs (Shum et al., 2018).

Human-chatbot communication has notable differences in content and quality compared to human-human. The crucial difference is empathy, as chatbots are less capable of conversational understanding than humans. However, chatbots are gradually becoming more aware of their interlocutor's feelings (Adamopoulou and Moussiades, 2020).

The first known chatbot, developed in 1966, was Eliza [1] (Weizenbaum, 1966). Its purpose was to behave like a psychologist. It used simple patterns and user sentences returned in the form of a question. Its conversational ability was not very good, but it was enough to start the development of other chatbot systems (Bradeško and Mladenić, 2012).

Most chatbots tend to respond with the same message, have a very limited vocabulary, and often provide wrong information. To demonstrate the lack of language capabilities of chatbots, a comparison was made between chatbots responses and human responses (Feine et al., 2020), by analyzing an existing human chat dialog analyzed from the Conversational Intelligence Challenge 2 (ConvAI2[2]), where the lexical diversity was analyzed of all chatbot and human messages, through Part of Speech (PoS) and counted the adjectives, adverbs and verbs that are relevant for expressing emotion which is an inherently human ability. The results indicate that human users used 75% more adjectives, 65% more adverbs, and 76% more verbs than the ConvAI2 chatbots. Therefore, this work reveals that human language use is far from superior in terms of lexical and emotional diversity.

There are several solutions on the market that allow the development of chatbots such as DialogFlow (Sabharwal and Agrawal, 2020), Amazon Lex (Sreeharsha et al., 2022), Rasa (Sharma and Joshi, 2020), etc. Using one of these solutions, it is possible to develop a chatbot, through dialog flows for selecting responses or actions based on the identification of expressions that the agent should recognize, also called intents. However, these are limited to maintaining a dialog based on flows that are created manually. The limitations of chatbots motivate the need for human involvement.

2.3 Knowledge Extraction from Dialog

The extraction component should start by processing transcripts of real dialogs between humans, using an NLP pipeline (Tenney et al., 2019). This pipeline starts by segmenting the text into tokens and using a set of parsing processes such as Information Extraction (IE) (Grishman, 2019) or Semantic Parsing (Berant et al., 2013), the latter being the task of deriving a representation of meaning from the language sufficient for a given task, since IE of the text can be characterized as representing a certain level of semantic parsing.

It is also necessary to clean up the transcriptions used from what is not relevant to the creation of the dialog flow and segment it into individual utterances, from the two interlocutors, linking them together to create an objective dialog line. This process can be implemented using contextual models, based on Sentence Embeddings (Reimers and Gurevych, 2019), created from Deep Learning approaches (Li et al., 2018), and also from approaches for Intent Classification (Chen et al., 2019), which allow transforming words into vector representations and, thus, mapping the words used into known concepts or intentions.

It is also fundamental to identify entities, through Named Entity Recognition (NER) (Mo-

[1] http://psych.fullerton.edu/mbirnbaum/psych101/eliza.htm

[2] https://paperswithcode.com/dataset/convai2

hit, 2014), an IE task that consists in identifying and classifying only some types of information elements, called Named Entity (NE). DM (Bai et al., 2021) is a subarea of NLP that covers tasks aimed at learning how humans use this language to interact with each other, and exploiting it in computational applications. This typically includes intent recognition (Sukthankar et al., 2014), which maps utterances with responses or actions that the system has to perform, and can be used for dialog summarization (Goo and Chen, 2018; Liu et al., 2019), human assistance (De et al., 2021) in communication, prediction of the next interactions (Ritter et al., 2011) of a human user with a dialog system, among others.

Dialogues are sequences of utterances, commonly classified according to: intents, which represent the end-user's intents; or DAs, which represent the action performed by the speaker (Austin, 1962) and can be seen as more generic intents.

DAs function as action labels for the utterances in a given conversation (e.g., ask, explain, speak, request, etc.), thus helping to characterize intents and enabling a better understanding of conversations (Hoxha et al., 2016). On the other hand, an intent categorizes an end-user's intent for one conversation turn (Truong et al., 2004) and is usually more specific, depending on the given scenario. Thus, DAs recognition can be accomplished by identifying the function-related DAs of a single utterance or segment, unrelated to a specific domain or task. This is relevant during an ongoing conversation, as it allows for interpretation or knowledge extraction taking into account the intent and simplifies the identification of related segments in the dialog history. A dialog representation is a sequence of DAs that are useful for their interpretation by humans, conversational systems, or computational methods and for summarizing the conversation or predicting future utterances (Hoxha et al., 2016).

Dialog Act Classification (DAC) is useful for identifying patterns and extracting common flows in dialogs. Several approaches have been developed for automatic DAC. Most adopt a supervised approach, with models trained on dialog corpus where DAs are manually annotated (Bangalore et al., 2008). Some use traditional methods of classification considering the context of the dialog, using previous interactions, and capturing hierarchical relationships between tasks. In Sordoni et al. (2015) they formulate a neural network architecture for data-driven response generation trained from social conversations, in which the generation of responses is constrained by dialog utterances that provide contextual information.

Others methods adopt learning by considering utterances in isolation. However, since there may be a dependency between the current interaction and previous ones, that is, between consecutive utterances (e.g., usually after a question comes an answer) DAC should be approached as a sequential classification problem and not as a simple classification problem.

Hidden Markov Models (HMMs) (Stolcke et al., 2000) present time intervals, where the process evolves from one state to another, depending only on its last state. The hidden states of the model are the DA labels that generate the sequence of words. Another widely used alternative path to HMMs to address DAC as a sequence labeling problem is the use of neural network models associated with a Conditional Random Field (CRF) (Zimmermann, 2009; Kim et al., 2010) as the last layer. The CRF implements dialog state management to keep track of conversation history and current state in order to decide on the next conversation step and models the conditional probability of the DA label sequence given the input sequence. Long Short Term Memory (LSTM) (Yu et al., 2019; Barahona et al., 2016) is an artificial replay of the neural network (ANN) (Diehl et al., 2016) that can process not only single data points (such as images) but also entire sequences of data.

Statements provide knowledge that can be extracted in pairs, such as questions and their corresponding answers. Thus, in order to learn through dialogues, an agent must be able to identify what these statements are, and thus DAs must be identified by automatically recognizing the generic DAs conveyed by each segment (Searle, 1969). For this, it will be useful to recognize the communicative functions defined by ISO 24617-2 for the annotation of DAs (Bunt et al., 2012, 2017), which are hierarchically organized and feature a specific branch for knowledge-providing functions.

As the dialog progresses, some systems maintain a state representation in a process called Dialog State Tracking (DST) (Henderson et al., 2014), thus representing the user's intentions, which involves filling in predefined slot values.

Currently, most NLP tasks use Transformer neural network-based models which is an encoder-decoder architecture that allows the model to focus on the relevant parts of input sequences, especially long sequences such as sentences and paragraphs. Improvements can be achieved if utterances are encoded by a transformer network-based (BERT) (Devlin et al., 2018).

Since manually creating the dialog flows used by conversational agents is complex and time-consuming, there are academic works focused on automatic extraction of dialog flows. One of the identified works presents structure extraction in task-oriented dialogs by representing the dialog flow with probabilistic transitions between different states of the flow, based on HMMs (Stolcke et al., 2000). A still preliminary work (Negi et al., 2009) presents the identification of dialog flows for use in chatbots, using clustering of similar expressions and their sequencing. These works are only some parts of the process we intend to develop, and most of them focus on specific domains, with narrow scope and scale, so they are not applicable to dialogs in a generic way, and therefore their use is not feasible in a real environment. Thus, there is a need to study and develop a suitable framework to guide humans in a dialog, and represent knowledge extracted from past interactions.

A supervised approach (Bangalore et al., 2008) was exploited based on a dataset of annotated dialogs, exploited the id and the speaker's word trigrams of the current utterance. In a first attempt to incorporate context, for DAC only, the previous statements were considered. DAs were discovered from open domain Twitter conversations (Ritter et al., 2010). Each post in a conversation is represented by a bag of words. DAs will correspond to clusters of statements, representing their sequential behavior, which is captured by an HMM. In addition, to separate between content words and dialog indicators, the HMM is combined with a Latent Dirichlet Allocation (LDA) topic model. The clusters have to be inspected manually. Negi et al. (Negi et al., 2009) were based on initiated conversations by replacing named entities with their type. Clustering was applied to similar utterances based on frequent words. When these clusters are discovered, calls are represented by sequences of clusters and subtasks are discovered based on sequences of frequent utterances.

2.4 Representation of Dialog

In order to create a single representation that integrates all dialog flows and their variations, we must first study the best approach to aggregate the expressions that represent the same intent, information, or action. In this way, we can apply approaches to dialogs, such as Topic Modeling (Vayansky and Kumar, 2020) and Automatic Summarization (Gupta et al., 2009), to reveal high-level topics covered in dialogs and compress their content, or use Text Clustering (Aggarwal and Zhai, 2012), which allows the clustering of similar utterances. Since DAs are less tied to the scenario or domain than intentions, this is also a better representation for recognizing common patterns in dialogs. DA Identification (Omuya et al., 2013) may help in a more abstract representation of the flow, by classifying the various interactions into different types.

DAs and transition graphs allow the discovery of different types of interactions and the most common dialog flows that will be useful for classifying the current dialog and recommending the next interactions. Automatic response generation techniques are based on sequence-to-sequence models (Yuan and Yu, 2019) learned from large collections of dialogs. One of the problems with such models is that they are not able to model the context and history of the dialog. To solve this, the model can be extended with a latent representation of the dialog history or encapsulated in a hierarchical dialog model (Sordoni et al., 2015; Lowe et al., 2017).

If annotated data is unavailable, clustering of utterances can be done, in the expectation of grouping them according to DAs or intents. Human intervention is required for interpretation, which involves looking at the utterances in each of the clusters.

The flow can be represented by a graph where the nodes represent an expression of the dialog and the arcs, directed between nodes, represent the different expressions that can follow. A single tree can encapsulate the task structure (domain and precedence relations between tasks), the DA structure (sequences of DAs), and the linguistic structure of utterances. We can also represent the probability associated with each of the possible transitions between expressions (Ritter et al., 2010), as well as the conditions, based on the extracted context, that make each transition possible or impossible.

There are annotation schemes designed for open domain human-machine conversations, such as Midas (Yu and Yu, 2019). This has a hierarchical structure, including a semantic and functional ordering tree, and supports multi-label annotations. Since dialogs in a large collection are represented by sequences of tasks (Bangalore et al., 2008) or DAs, hierarchical relationships between the latter can be discovered from common patterns and represented by trees or graphs that are friendly for human analysis, including transition probabilities.

Young et al. (2010) described a dialog manager *Hidden Information State System* (HIS) where each utterance is a DA and is designed for information retrieval tasks. However, compared to simple slot-filling systems, it supports a richer set of user goal representations based on tree-like structures built from classes that represent related values and sub types that are specific variants of a class.

To be used as the input of most of the previous approaches, textual utterances need to be represented in a vector space where semantically similar words or utterances are closer to each other. This is typically done at preprocessing and may resort to models of vector semantics. For instance, when performing intent classification, Hashemi et al. (Hashemi et al., 2016) used pretrained models of word embeddings, such as word2vec (Mikolov et al., 2013), for representing utterances. Park et al. (Park et al., 2022) obtains various intent clustering results with different embeddings, namely the Sentence Transformer's MiniLM-L6 and MiniLM-L12 models. More recent efforts obtain sentence embeddings from available transformers fine-tuned in sentence similarity tasks (e.g., (Vulić et al., 2022; Park et al., 2022)). An alternative to using pretrained embeddings is to learn embeddings and part of the training process (e.g., first layer of the neural network) (Firdaus et al., 2021).

2.5 Call Guidance

The orientation component will take advantage of past dialogs, represented according to the previously defined, to identify the recommendations it should provide to the agent during a new interaction. Dialogs represented as a sequence or a graph of DAs can be exploited in live conversations, either to guide dialog systems that may include automatic response generation, or to guide human agents in a call. The system can be useful for classifying utterances according to specific goals as quickly as possible. The call can be redirected to a different agent that has access to different knowledge bases and/or different streams. For example, Gunrock (Chen et al., 2018), a social bot, maps users' intentions to a topic, selects the most appropriate module for the topic, and advances the user's request to this module. In addition to the topic or goal, the current DA can be classified in real time using approaches already described, allowing the anticipation of the next dialog with different probabilities, which can be used to narrow down the automatically generated responses.

It is important to use approaches such as Semantic Textual Similarity (Cer et al., 2017), using techniques that consider the words used and their relevance, such as TF-IDF or more comprehensive models based on embeddings.

Therefore, it is necessary to look at approaches such as Recommender Systems (RS) (Resnick and Varian, 1997) that help users find items of interest and can be based on past behavior.

The design of flows is especially relevant for task-oriented dialogue systems and can steer the conversation in specific directions, avoiding purely reactive responses to what the user says (Grassi et al., 2022). It encompasses the definition of task-specific intents and training phrases, among other decisions, and generally ends up being created manually, often with the help of tools like Google's DialogFlow[3], Microsoft Luis[4], or the open source platform Rasa[5].

As the dialogue progresses, the recommendation system accumulates the user's information and builds his profile. Thus, it can provide a recommendation based on user preferences reflected in the conversation. A recommendation system can be based on conventional collaborative filtering algorithms (Resnick et al., 1994; Sarwar et al., 2001) or based on neural networks (Wang et al., 2018; He et al., 2017; Ying et al., 2018).The generated graphs can be used in a recommendation or guidance system.

3 Research Proposal

The main goal of this PhD thesis is the research and development of approaches to help communication between interlocutors in a dialog, in Portuguese, guiding the operator's action that can be supported by previous interactions. Information is to be automatically extracted and frequent dialog flows are identified, allowing their representation to guide the

[3]https://cloud.google.com/dialogflow/
[4]https://www.luis.ai/
[5]https://rasa.com/

human in how to respond. To this extent, we define five specific objectives to be achieved throughout the development of the research work:

1. Collection and creation of a corpus of dialogs in Portuguese that can be used in the project.
2. Studying, developing and experimenting with approaches for extracting structured dialog information from the various interactions.
3. Studying, developing and experimenting with approaches for representing interactions and flows extracted from those interactions.
4. Studying, developing and experimenting with approaches for guiding the human by exploiting the knowledge extracted from dialogs, interactions, and common flows.
5. Evaluation on data collected and created, using automated and manual metrics.

To achieve the five defined objectives presented above, the following tasks were defined:

1. Deepen the study of the state of the art to understand important concepts for research;
2. Collection or creation of the data to be used;
3. Approaches for IE;
4. Approaches for representing dialog flows;
5. Approaches for dialog guidance;
6. Framework with approaches explored;
7. Tests and final evaluation;
8. Writing of the thesis and scientific articles.

We intend to explore generalized approaches applied to different types of task-oriented dialogues, where one contribution will be to increase the efficiency of call centers.

The experiments will be focused with data in Portuguese, which will be a differentiating factor. They will also be limited to written text, i.e., written conversations or transcripts of oral communication.

Several alternatives will be explored to obtain the data: Following the WOZ paradigm (Green et al., 2004), where a conversation is held between two interlocutors in which one is assigned a certain task and to accomplish this task, this user must interact, using natural language, with another who will have access to more information about the domain (for example, a database or a service such as Booking[6]) and will be able to provide appropriate answers. Interaction can be done through any chat application, such as Slack or Microsoft Teams; Transcripts of existing dialogs in Portuguese, such as CORAA (Junior et al., 2021); Customer support services on social networks, such as conversations with telecom operators on Twitter[7]; Movie subtitles (Lison and Tiedemann, 2016); Translation of English datasets (e.g. DailyDialogue (Li et al., 2017) or MultiWOz (Budzianowski et al., 2018)) into Portuguese, from which it will be possible to import existing annotations.

The data will be used in the development of a framework consisting of three components:

- Extraction - Process transcripts of dialogs and extract information;
- Representation - Discovery of the most frequent dialog flows, represented by graphs;
- Guidance - will take advantage of the flow representation to guide the human.

The first component processes real dialog transcripts and extract useful information from them to represent the interactions, such as keywords, entities or actions. The extraction of some of these items may resort to an NLP pipeline (Tenney et al., 2019), but some additional development may be required, considering the language (Portuguese) and the type of text (dialog).

The extracted information can be used to better describe utterances, classifying intentions and filling slots. However, performing these tasks is usually based on supervised learning, which involves data annotation, something to consider during data definition. It can also be used to group similar utterances, using clustering. This process can make use of sentence embedding techniques (Reimers and Gurevych, 2019) to represent utterances. During the extraction process, it is necessary to remove from the text private information about the client in order to ensure the confidentiality of the data.

In Figure 1, we show an example of a dialog in which the customer requests the cancellation of an order he previously placed.

Sometimes, the information found in knowledge bases is not organized in a way that facilitate its use

[6]http://www.booking.com

[7]http://www. twitter.com

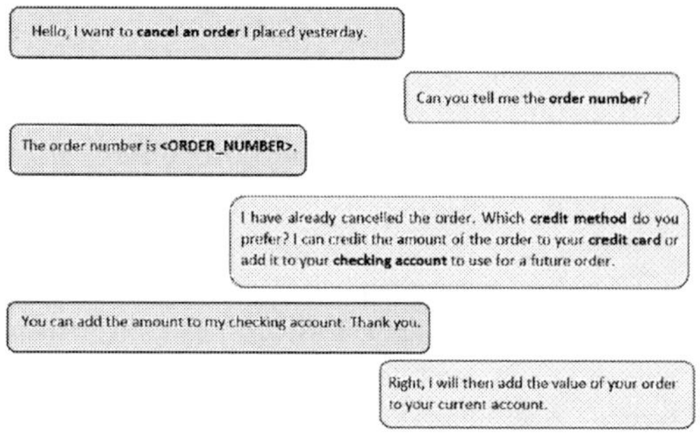

Figure 1: Example of a dialog flow created by the extraction component

by the agent in a conversation (Taylor et al., 2002). Therefore, the project to be developed will answer the question of how to improve the organization and representation of information that supports the agent's assistance during a conversation.

Interactions with customers are dependent on need and context. Even if the information is up to date, we need to make sure that we effectively map the need expressed by the possible solutions and use the context to ensure that we choose the solution that best fits that specific case. To this end, the project will be able to answer the question of how to find the best solution for customer's need and how to ensure that this solution fits its context.

The second component will aim to discover the most frequent dialog flows, represented by graphs, where the vertices represent speech classes or groupings, and the arcs represent transitions between them, with probabilities. In this component one can apply the classification of interactions into more generic classes (DAs) or, if there is a lack of data to make the system less domain-dependent, perform a grouping that approximates these acts. To facilitate human interpretation, it will be important to have a way to describe the groupings/classes through relevant n-grams or verb phrases. Figure 2 shows an example of a dialog graph, generated from the previous dialog flow.

Finally, the guidance component will take advantage of the representation of flows to guide the human.

The ability to take into account the previous statements is key to building dialog systems that can keep conversations active and engaging (Sordoni et al., 2015). Past interactions are an important source of information about customers and how their needs are met by agents, however, due to

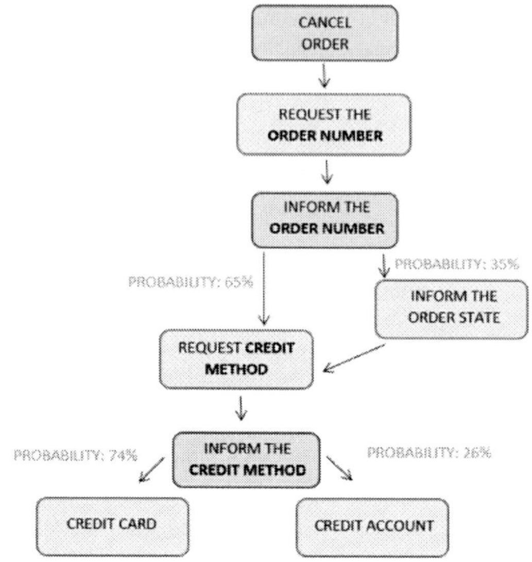

Figure 2: Example of a dialog graph created by the representation component

the complexity of working with past interactions, they are generally ignored. We aim to find the best approaches to extract from past interactions the knowledge needed to guide agents on how to respond to customer needs.

In each interaction, previous interactions will be considered to suggest responses, while anticipating the next interactions. It will function as a RS (Resnick and Varian, 1997) in the sense that we want to recommend speech and/or actions. Figure 3 shows an example of a user interface with expressions used in dialog and the recommendations provided by the guidance component.

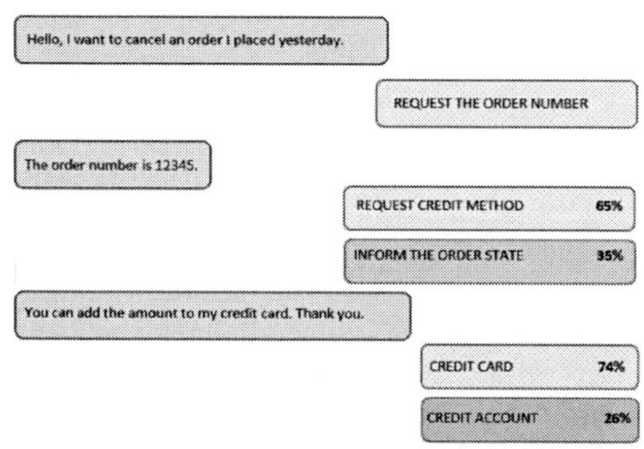

Figure 3: Example of user interface - recommendations are provided to the agent by the guidance component

The approaches resulting from tasks 3, 4, and 5 will be evaluated independently but a final evaluation of their integration into the framework is required. In this way, the approaches will be evaluated on the data collected and created using metrics for classification, used when annotations are produced, or metrics for clustering when this is not the case. Due to the subjectivity of the quality of the flows identified and the guidance produced, a subjective evaluation based on human opinions using the resulting framework is imperative, as well as an objective evaluation where a control group that uses the node-generated graphs and a group that does not is selected and the average success rates and response times are then compared.

4 Preliminary Experiments

The exploration of some NLP tools, through the spaCy [8] library such as PoS Tagging considering verbal syntagma, NER and coreference resolution was performed and DAC, taking into account different vector representations, was done for these tasks in order to generalize utterances.

Given that DAs can be seen as generic intents, a possible representation of dialog flows is through a graph of DAs. Transitions between DAs may further have assigned probabilities, computed from the dialogue history. This can be see as a Markov chain, and its inspection may further enable the identification of communication patterns.

For illustrative purposes, we generated such a representation for the Mastodon dataset (Cerisara et al., 2018) and its annotated DAs, with the help of the NetworkX [9] package. The flow can be visualized in Figure 4, where nodes were also included for the start (SOD) and end (EOD) of dialog. Transitions with probability below 0.05 were ignored.

5 Conclusion

This research proposal aims to improve the customer/human experience when contacting a call-center, by improving the responsiveness of human agents in conversations, guided by intelligent methods and NLP about the current context and about previous interactions with customers. To achieve this goal, the project is organized into three components: extraction, representation and guidance. One of the challenges involved is that this project will be focused on Portuguese, a language for which there is little work in this area.

[8]https://spacy.io/

[9]https://networkx.org/

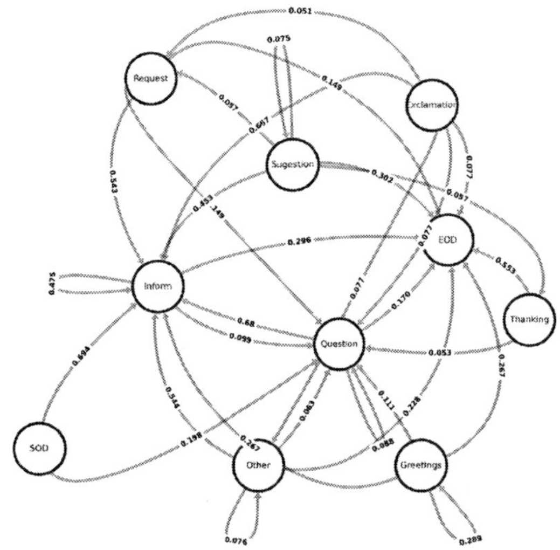

Figure 4: DAs transitions in Mastodon

The existing work for the automatic extraction of dialog flows is still underdeveloped and has been applied in a small scope and scale. Furthermore, this work is usually referenced in the context of application to chatbots, and its application is not oriented towards human agents.

The development of the proposed solution allows for the automatic extraction of dialog flows from past interactions, guiding human agents, and may represent a breakthrough in the state of the art in this area, answering the question of how to find the best solution for the customer's needs and how to ensure that this solution fits the customer's context.

Thus, the use of chatbots is increasingly present, however, we believe that human agents have a relevant role in contact centers, since they can handle situations with a level of complexity that is not yet within the reach of any chatbot and there is no distance between customers and human interlocutors. All relevant findings and results will be published in reports, articles and scientific papers, in addition to the resulting doctoral thesis.

Acknowledgements This work was financially supported by the project FLOWANCE (POCI-01-0247-FEDER-047022), cofinanced by FEDER, through PT2020, and by COMPETE 2020; and by national funds through FCT, within the scope of the project CISUC (UID/CEC/00326/2020) and by European Social Fund, through the Regional Operational Program Centro 2020. I would like to thank my supervisors Hugo Gonçalo Oliveira, Ana Alves, and Catarina Silva for all their support and to the mentor assigned by the EACL organization, Maria Jung Barrett, for her availability and help.

References

Eleni Adamopoulou and Lefteris Moussiades. 2020. Chatbots: History, technology, and applications. *Machine Learning with Applications*, 2:100006.

Charu C Aggarwal and ChengXiang Zhai. 2012. A survey of text clustering algorithms. In *Mining text data*, pages 77–128. Springer.

John Langshaw Austin. 1962. *How to do things with words: the William James lectures delivered at Harvard University in 1955*. Oxford University Press, New York.

Xuefeng Bai, Yulong Chen, Linfeng Song, and Yue Zhang. 2021. Semantic representation for dialogue modeling. *arXiv preprint arXiv:2105.10188*.

Srinivas Bangalore, Giuseppe Di Fabbrizio, and Amanda Stent. 2008. Learning the structure of task-driven human–human dialogs. *IEEE Transactions on Audio, Speech, and Language Processing*, 16(7):1249–1259.

Lina M Rojas Barahona, Milica Gasic, Nikola Mrkšić, Pei-Hao Su, Stefan Ultes, Tsung-Hsien Wen, and Steve Young. 2016. Exploiting sentence and context representations in deep neural models for spoken language understanding. *arXiv preprint arXiv:1610.04120*.

Jonathan Berant, Andrew Chou, Roy Frostig, and Percy Liang. 2013. Semantic parsing on freebase from question-answer pairs. In *Proceedings of the 2013 conference on empirical methods in natural language processing*, pages 1533–1544.

Luka Bradeško and Dunja Mladenić. 2012. A survey of chatbot systems through a loebner prize competition. In *Proceedings of Slovenian language technologies society eighth conference of language technologies*, pages 34–37. Institut Jožef Stefan Ljubljana, Slovenia.

Paweł Budzianowski, Tsung-Hsien Wen, Bo-Hsiang Tseng, Inigo Casanueva, Stefan Ultes, Osman Ramadan, and Milica Gašić. 2018. Multiwoz–a large-scale multi-domain wizard-of-oz dataset for task-oriented dialogue modelling. *arXiv preprint arXiv:1810.00278*.

Harry Bunt, Volha Petukhova, David Traum, and Jan Alexandersson. 2017. Dialogue act annotation with the iso 24617-2 standard. In *Multimodal interaction with W3C standards*, pages 109–135. Springer.

HC Bunt, J Alexandersson, J Choe, C Alex, K Hasida, VV Petukhova, A Popescu-Belis, and D Traum. 2012. Iso 246170-2: A semantically-based standard for dialogue annotation. In *Proceedings of the 8th International Conference on Language Resources and Evaluation, Istanbul, Turkey*, page 8. ELRA.

Daniel Cer, Mona Diab, Eneko Agirre, Inigo Lopez-Gazpio, and Lucia Specia. 2017. Semeval-2017 task 1: Semantic textual similarity-multilingual and cross-lingual focused evaluation. *arXiv preprint arXiv:1708.00055*.

Christophe Cerisara, Somayeh Jafaritazehjani, Adedayo Oluokun, and Hoa Le. 2018. Multi-task dialog act and sentiment recognition on mastodon. *arXiv preprint arXiv:1807.05013*.

Chun-Yen Chen, Dian Yu, Weiming Wen, Yi Mang Yang, Jiaping Zhang, Mingyang Zhou, Kevin Jesse, Austin Chau, Antara Bhowmick, Shreenath Iyer, et al. 2018. Gunrock: Building a human-like social bot by leveraging large scale real user data. *Alexa Prize Proceedings*.

Qian Chen, Zhu Zhuo, and Wen Wang. 2019. Bert for joint intent classification and slot filling. *arXiv preprint arXiv:1902.10909*.

Abir De, Nastaran Okati, Ali Zarezade, and Manuel Gomez Rodriguez. 2021. Classification under human assistance. In *Proceedings of the AAAI Conference on Artificial Intelligence*, volume 35, pages 5905–5913.

Jacob Devlin, Ming-Wei Chang, Kenton Lee, and Kristina Toutanova. 2018. Bert: Pre-training of deep bidirectional transformers for language understanding. *arXiv preprint arXiv:1810.04805*.

Peter U Diehl, Guido Zarrella, Andrew Cassidy, Bruno U Pedroni, and Emre Neftci. 2016. Conversion of artificial recurrent neural networks to spiking neural networks for low-power neuromorphic hardware. In *2016 IEEE International Conference on Rebooting Computing (ICRC)*, pages 1–8. IEEE.

Jasper Feine, Stefan Morana, and Alexander Maedche. 2020. A chatbot response generation system. In *Proceedings of the Conference on Mensch und Computer*, pages 333–341.

Mauajama Firdaus, Hitesh Golchha, Asif Ekbal, and Pushpak Bhattacharyya. 2021. A deep multi-task model for dialogue act classification, intent detection and slot filling. *Cognitive Computation*, 13:626–645.

Chih-Wen Goo and Yun-Nung Chen. 2018. Abstractive dialogue summarization with sentence-gated modeling optimized by dialogue acts. In *2018 IEEE Spoken Language Technology Workshop (SLT)*, pages 735–742. IEEE.

Lucrezia Grassi, Carmine Tommaso Recchiuto, and Antonio Sgorbissa. 2022. Knowledge-grounded dialogue flow management for social robots and conversational agents. *International Journal of Social Robotics*, 14(5):1273–1293.

Anders Green, Helge Huttenrauch, and K Severinson Eklundh. 2004. Applying the wizard-of-oz framework to cooperative service discovery and configuration. In *RO-MAN 2004. 13th IEEE International Workshop on Robot and Human Interactive Communication (IEEE Catalog No. 04TH8759)*, pages 575–580. IEEE.

Ralph Grishman. 2019. Twenty-five years of information extraction. *Natural Language Engineering*, 25(6):677–692.

Vishal Gupta, Gurpreet S Lehal, et al. 2009. A survey of text mining techniques and applications. *Journal of emerging technologies in web intelligence*, 1(1):60–76.

Homa B Hashemi, Amir Asiaee, and Reiner Kraft. 2016. Query intent detection using convolutional neural networks. In *International conference on web search and data mining, workshop on query understanding*.

Xiangnan He, Lizi Liao, Hanwang Zhang, Liqiang Nie, Xia Hu, and Tat-Seng Chua. 2017. Neural collaborative filtering. In *Proceedings of the 26th international conference on world wide web*, pages 173–182.

Matthew Henderson, Blaise Thomson, and Jason D Williams. 2014. The second dialog state tracking challenge. In *Proceedings of the 15th annual meeting of the special interest group on discourse and dialogue (SIGDIAL)*, pages 263–272.

Julia Hoxha, Praveen Chandar, Zhe He, James Cimino, David Hanauer, and Chunhua Weng. 2016. Dream: Classification scheme for dialog acts in clinical research query mediation. *Journal of biomedical informatics*, 59:89–101.

Arnaldo Candido Junior, Edresson Casanova, Anderson Soares, Frederico Santos de Oliveira, Lucas Oliveira, Ricardo Corso Fernandes Junior, Daniel Peixoto Pinto da Silva, Fernando Gorgulho Fayet, Bruno Baldissera Carlotto, Lucas Rafael Stefanel Gris, et al. 2021. Coraa: a large corpus of spontaneous and prepared speech manually validated for speech recognition in brazilian portuguese. *arXiv preprint arXiv:2110.15731*.

Su Nam Kim, Lawrence Cavedon, and Timothy Baldwin. 2010. Classifying dialogue acts in one-on-one live chats. In *Proceedings of the 2010 Conference on Empirical Methods in Natural Language Processing*, pages 862–871.

Ruizhe Li, Chenghua Lin, Matthew Collinson, Xiao Li, and Guanyi Chen. 2018. A dual-attention hierarchical recurrent neural network for dialogue act classification. *arXiv preprint arXiv:1810.09154*.

Yanran Li, Hui Su, Xiaoyu Shen, Wenjie Li, Ziqiang Cao, and Shuzi Niu. 2017. Dailydialog: A manually labelled multi-turn dialogue dataset. *arXiv preprint arXiv:1710.03957*.

Pierre Lison and Jörg Tiedemann. 2016. Opensubtitles2016: Extracting large parallel corpora from movie and tv subtitles. *European Language Resources Association*.

Chunyi Liu, Peng Wang, Jiang Xu, Zang Li, and Jieping Ye. 2019. Automatic dialogue summary generation for customer service. In *Proceedings of the 25th ACM SIGKDD International Conference on Knowledge Discovery & Data Mining*, pages 1957–1965.

Ryan Lowe, Nissan Pow, Iulian Vlad Serban, Laurent Charlin, Chia-Wei Liu, and Joelle Pineau. 2017. Training end-to-end dialogue systems with the ubuntu dialogue corpus. *Dialogue & Discourse*, 8(1):31–65.

Tomas Mikolov, Ilya Sutskever, Kai Chen, Greg Corrado, and Jeffrey Dean. 2013. Distributed representations of words and phrases and their compositionality. In *Proceedings of the 26th International Conference on Neural Information Processing Systems - Volume 2*, NIPS'13, page 3111–3119, Red Hook, NY, USA. Curran Associates Inc.

Behrang Mohit. 2014. Named entity recognition. In *Natural language processing of semitic languages*, pages 221–245. Springer.

Sumit Negi, Sachindra Joshi, Anup K Chalamalla, and L Venkata Subramaniam. 2009. Automatically extracting dialog models from conversation transcripts. In *2009 Ninth IEEE International Conference on Data Mining*, pages 890–895. IEEE.

Hugo Oliveira, Patrícia Ferreira, Daniel Martins, Catarina Silva, and Ana Alves. 2022. A brief survey on textual dialogue corpora. *Proceedings of the 13th International Conference on Language Resources and Evaluation (LREC 2022)*.

Adinoyi Omuya, Vinodkumar Prabhakaran, and Owen Rambow. 2013. Improving the quality of minority class identification in dialog act tagging. In *Proceedings of the 2013 Conference of the North American Chapter of the Association for Computational Linguistics: Human Language Technologies*, pages 802–807.

Jeiyoon Park, Yoonna Jang, Chanhee Lee, and Heuiseok Lim. 2022. Analysis of utterance embeddings and clustering methods related to intent induction for task-oriented dialogue. *arXiv preprint arXiv:2212.02021*.

Amon Rapp, Lorenzo Curti, and Arianna Boldi. 2021. The human side of human-chatbot interaction: A systematic literature review of ten years of research on text-based chatbots. *International Journal of Human-Computer Studies*, 151:102630.

Nils Reimers and Iryna Gurevych. 2019. Sentence-bert: Sentence embeddings using siamese bert-networks. *arXiv preprint arXiv:1908.10084*.

Paul Resnick, Neophytos Iacovou, Mitesh Suchak, Peter Bergstrom, and John Riedl. 1994. Grouplens: An open architecture for collaborative filtering of netnews. In *Proceedings of the 1994 ACM conference on Computer supported cooperative work*, pages 175–186.

Paul Resnick and Hal R Varian. 1997. Recommender systems. *Communications of the ACM*, 40(3):56–58.

Alan Ritter, Colin Cherry, and Bill Dolan. 2010. Unsupervised modeling of twitter conversations. *North American Chapter of the Association for Computational Linguistics (HLT-NAACL)*.

Alan Ritter, Colin Cherry, and Bill Dolan. 2011. Data-driven response generation in social media. In *Empirical Methods in Natural Language Processing (EMNLP)*.

Navin Sabharwal and Amit Agrawal. 2020. Introduction to google dialogflow. In *Cognitive virtual assistants using Google Dialogflow*, pages 13–54. Springer.

Badrul Sarwar, George Karypis, Joseph Konstan, and John Riedl. 2001. Item-based collaborative filtering recommendation algorithms. In *Proceedings of the 10th international conference on World Wide Web*, pages 285–295.

John R Searle. 1969. *Speech acts: An essay in the philosophy of language*, volume 626. Cambridge university press.

Rakesh Kumar Sharma and Manoj Joshi. 2020. An analytical study and review of open source chatbot framework, rasa. *International Journal of Engineering Research and*, 9(06).

Heung-Yeung Shum, Xiao-dong He, and Di Li. 2018. From eliza to xiaoice: challenges and opportunities with social chatbots. *Frontiers of Information Technology & Electronic Engineering*, 19(1):10–26.

Alessandro Sordoni, Michel Galley, Michael Auli, Chris Brockett, Yangfeng Ji, Margaret Mitchell, Jian-Yun Nie, Jianfeng Gao, and Bill Dolan. 2015. A neural network approach to context-sensitive generation of conversational responses. *arXiv preprint arXiv:1506.06714*.

ASSK Sreeharsha, Sai Mohan Kesapragada, and Sai Pratheek Chalamalasetty. 2022. Building chatbot using amazon lex and integrating with a chat application. *International Journal of Scientific Research in Engineering and Management (IJSREM)*, 6(04).

Andreas Stolcke, Klaus Ries, Noah Coccaro, Elizabeth Shriberg, Rebecca Bates, Daniel Jurafsky, Paul Taylor, Rachel Martin, Carol Van Ess-Dykema, and Marie Meteer. 2000. Dialogue act modeling for automatic tagging and recognition of conversational speech. *Computational linguistics*, 26(3):339–373.

Gita Sukthankar, Christopher Geib, Hung Bui, David Pynadath, and Robert P Goldman. 2014. *Plan, activity, and intent recognition: Theory and practice*. Newnes.

Phil Taylor, Gareth Mulvey, Jeff Hyman, and Peter Bain. 2002. Work organization, control and the experience of work in call centres. *Work, employment and society*, 16(1):133–150.

Ian Tenney, Dipanjan Das, and Ellie Pavlick. 2019. Bert rediscovers the classical nlp pipeline. *arXiv preprint arXiv:1905.05950*.

Anh D Tran, Jason I Pallant, and Lester W Johnson. 2021. Exploring the impact of chatbots on consumer sentiment and expectations in retail. *Journal of Retailing and Consumer Services*, 63:102718.

Khai N Truong, Elaine M Huang, and Gregory D Abowd. 2004. Camp: A magnetic poetry interface for end-user programming of capture applications for the home. In *UbiComp 2004: Ubiquitous Computing: 6th International Conference, Nottingham, UK, September 7-10, 2004. Proceedings 6*, pages 143–160. Springer.

Ike Vayansky and Sathish AP Kumar. 2020. A review of topic modeling methods. *Information Systems*, 94:101582.

Ivan Vulić, Iñigo Casanueva, Georgios Spithourakis, Avishek Mondal, Tsung-Hsien Wen, and Paweł Budzianowski. 2022. Multi-label intent detection via contrastive task specialization of sentence encoders. In *Proceedings of the 2022 Conference on Empirical Methods in Natural Language Processing*, pages 7544–7559, Abu Dhabi, United Arab Emirates. Association for Computational Linguistics.

Xiting Wang, Yiru Chen, Jie Yang, Le Wu, Zhengtao Wu, and Xing Xie. 2018. A reinforcement learning framework for explainable recommendation. In *2018 IEEE international conference on data mining (ICDM)*, pages 587–596. IEEE.

Joseph Weizenbaum. 1966. Eliza—a computer program for the study of natural language communication between man and machine. *Communications of the ACM*, 9(1):36–45.

Rex Ying, Ruining He, Kaifeng Chen, Pong Eksombatchai, William L Hamilton, and Jure Leskovec. 2018. Graph convolutional neural networks for web-scale recommender systems. In *Proceedings of the 24th ACM SIGKDD international conference on knowledge discovery & data mining*, pages 974–983.

Steve Young, Milica Gašić, Simon Keizer, François Mairesse, Jost Schatzmann, Blaise Thomson, and Kai Yu. 2010. The hidden information state model: A practical framework for pomdp-based spoken dialogue management. *Computer Speech & Language*, 24(2):150–174.

Dian Yu and Zhou Yu. 2019. Midas: A dialog act annotation scheme for open domain human machine spoken conversations. *arXiv preprint arXiv:1908.10023*.

Yong Yu, Xiaosheng Si, Changhua Hu, and Jianxun Zhang. 2019. A review of recurrent neural networks: Lstm cells and network architectures. *Neural computation*, 31(7):1235–1270.

Lin Yuan and Zhou Yu. 2019. Abstractive dialog summarization with semantic scaffolds. *arXiv preprint arXiv:1910.00825*.

Matthias Zimmermann. 2009. Joint segmentation and classification of dialog acts using conditional random fields. In *Tenth Annual Conference of the International Speech Communication Association*.

Diverse Content Selection for Educational Question Generation

Amir Hadifar **Semere Kiros Bitew** **Johannes Deleu**
Veronique Hoste **Chris Develder** **Thomas Demesteer**
firstname.lastname@ugent.be

Abstract

Question Generation (QG) systems have shown promising results in reducing the time and effort required to create questions for students. Typically, a first step in QG is to select the content to design a question for. In an educational setting, it is crucial that the resulting questions cover the most relevant/important pieces of knowledge the student should have acquired. Yet, current QG systems either consider just a single sentence or paragraph (thus do not include a selection step), or do not consider this educational viewpoint of content selection. Aiming to fill this research gap with a solution for educational document-level QG, we thus propose to select contents for QG based on relevance and topic diversity. We demonstrate the effectiveness of our proposed content selection strategy for QG on 2 educational datasets. In our performance assessment, we also highlight limitations of existing QG evaluation metrics in light of the content selection problem.[1]

1 Introduction

Over the past few years, educational institutes have increasingly embraced digital tools and solutions to extend the purely classroom-based setting and enable wider access to high-quality education. An essential component of digital educational tools is the ability to test the learners' progress in acquiring the knowledge offered in a course. Indeed, subjecting learners to such tests triggers reflection on and consolidation of the information they have consumed (Rickards, 1979; DeAngelo et al., 2009). Yet, creating high-quality questions that comprehensively and accurately evaluate a learner's knowledge and/or skills is quite challenging due to the extensive human domain knowledge required. Current automatic Question Generation (QG) solutions have already shown significant progress in reducing the time and effort to phrase suitable questions. However, a common weakness is that they do not employ an education-oriented approach when processing full documents or book chapters (Le et al., 2014; Mostow and Chen, 2009). This implies human intervention is required to either select the input or filter suitable output questions afterwards. Note that the latter likely implies a significant computational overhead associated with the generation of questions for each and every possible paragraph/sentence.

In this research, we take one step back and focus on one of the earliest stages of developing a test called *content identification* or *content selection*, the process of reducing the amount of text in a chapter or document to its most meaningful subparts suitable for constructing questions (Kurdi et al., 2020; Davis, 2009). Content selection is a crucial and challenging step in any assessment system. It is crucial because decisions regarding which content to include or exclude can significantly influence the inferences teachers make about their students' understanding of key concepts in the considered course material. More importantly, in some settings such as self-assessment and self-learning environments, leaving the content selection to users is not feasible (Kurdi et al., 2020). It is challenging because numerous trade-offs have to be considered, such as the type of exam (e.g., low stakes vs. high stakes), the subject (e.g., mathematics vs. history), and instructor preferences, among others (Davis, 2009).

Although natural language processing has been extensively employed in educational environments (Kurdi et al., 2020; Laban et al., 2022), only a few researchers have investigated content selection for generating educational questions. Some studies (Chen et al., 2019; Rüdian et al., 2020) used summarization techniques to identify important contents. However, because these methods aim to select sentences that maximize content coverage, they may not be suitable for generating questions

[1]Code will be available at: https://github.com/hadifar/content_selection

Proceedings of the 17th Conference of the European Chapter of the Association for Computational Linguistics: Student Research Workshop, pages 123–133
May 2-4, 2023

in the context of education, as such sentences can be incoherent and complex (Kumar et al., 2015). Steuer et al. (Steuer et al., 2021) utilized a binary classifier trained on definitions from scientific textbooks to prioritize worthy over non-worthy content. This study, however, was limited to the definition of named entities or concepts rather than general pedagogical contents. Related to our method is (Kumar et al., 2015), that ranked sentences based on topic distributions obtained from a topic model for fill-the-gaps (cloze) questions. However, unlike our proposed method, the notion of relevance of contents to teachers is ignored. Other methods (Du and Cardie, 2017; Kumar et al., 2019; Nakanishi et al., 2019; Back et al., 2021) jointly optimized content selection and QG in an end-to-end fashion. Most of the previous studies validated their methodologies by evaluating QG performance using n-gram metrics (e.g., Papineni et al. (BLEU; 2002), Banerjee and Lavie (METEOR; 2005)) instead of directly evaluating the content selection method. We will show (§4) how these metrics are inadequate to evaluate this task.

We frame *content selection* as a ranking problem that maximizes both relevance and topic diversity. The topic diversity is motivated by test development studies (Webb, 2006; Haladyna and Downing, 1989; Haladyna and Rodriguez, 2013), that suggest reliable inference regarding students' understanding of contents is tied to the number of questions that cover main topics. This hypothesis is implicitly held by teachers during question construction (Fig. 1). To this end, we propose a ranking model that assigns a score to each content (i.e., all paragraphs or sentences in a textbook), allowing us to prioritize relevant candidates. Furthermore, we introduce a re-ranker that encourages topic diversity. Our empirical results (§4) not only show that our model leads to an improved content ranking compared to existing methods on two recently released educational datasets but also reveal difficulties in measuring ranking quality through evaluation of the question generation end task.

2 Methodology

This section describes our strategy for obtaining a suitable ranking of a document's sentences or paragraphs. Since optimizing relevance and diversity at the same time is an NP-hard problem (Agrawal et al., 2009), heuristic approaches are typically used (Carbonell and Goldstein, 1998; Santos et al., 2010), which we propose for our setting as well. After an initial ranking purely based on estimated relevance, we apply an iterative diversity-aware reranking.

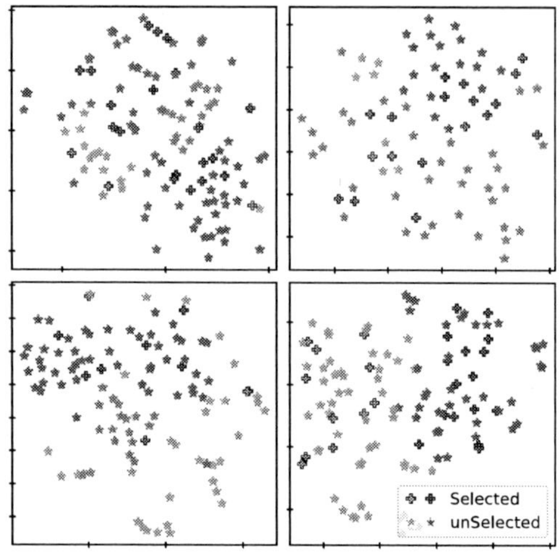

Figure 1: 2D visualization of the pooled hidden-state representations of the RoBERTa (Liu et al., 2019) on all paragraphs for four randomly sampled chapters of EduQG (Hadifar et al., 2023) using t-SNE (van der Maaten and Hinton, 2008). Each color stands for a different topic assigned by the Gaussian clustering model, while the marker types represent the selected vs. unselected paragraphs by teachers.

Relevance-based ranking: We assume that the considered educational content involves textual documents D (e.g., course book chapters), each represented as a set of N content elements $D = \{s_0, s_1, s_2, ..., s_{N-1}\}$. These elements s_i can be, for example, the document's sentences or paragraphs (and will be referred to as the sentences). In our datasets, an associated question is available for a selection of the sentences, created by a teacher. Although different teachers would likely not agree on which sentences are relevant (i.e., to create questions from) given the same document, we consider the sentences associated with the available questions as a good proxy. As such, we train a classifier to predict for each sentence whether it is relevant or not. In our experiments, this is achieved by training a logistic regression classifier on top of a pre-trained language model's representation (Liu et al., 2019), similar to the approach in Nogueira and Cho (2019). At inference, after ranking all sentences according to decreasing relevance scores as predicted by that model, each sentence s_i is represented by the *relevance score* $R_i = 1 - \rho_i/N$, with ρ_i its rank (i.e., the highest ranked sentence is scored 1, and the lowest one $1/N$).

Diversity-aware reranking: Next, all sentences s_i are iteratively reranked by combining the relevance-based score R_i with a score that promotes *topic-related diversity*, in line with educational insights (Davis, 2009). The following paragraphs outline this procedure.

First, topics are identified through a Gaussian clustering model, fit to all (language model-based) sentence representations $x_i = RoBERTa(s_i)$. The likelihood $p(s_i)$ of a sentence s_i over all topics is written as $p(s_i) = \sum_z p(z)\, p(s_i|z)$, with the topic probability $p(z)$ and the gaussian mixture component $p(s_i|z) = \mathcal{N}(\mathbf{x}_i; \mu_z, \Sigma_z)$ (with mean vector μ_z and covariance matrix Σ_z).After obtaining a fit for the topic probabilities and gaussian component parameters, the topic distribution for each sentence can be readily obtained as $p(z|s_i) = p(s_i, z)/\sum_{z'} p(s_i, z')$. Next, we initialize the final sentence ranking S with the sentence that received the highest relevance-oriented rank R_i. We then iteratively add sentence by sentence, by combining their relevance score and a diversity score that measures topic diversity with respect to the sentences already present in S. During every considered iteration, the diversity scores $D(s_i|S)$ are calculated as follows, for any sentence $s_i \notin S$:

$$D(s_i|S) = \sum_z p(z)\Big(p(s_i, z) \prod_{s_j \in S} \big(1 - p(s_j, z)\big)\Big)$$

which can be interpreted as the expectation over all topics, that a given topic would occur with s_i *and* with none of the sentences already ranked in S (if the considered sentences were independent, strictly speaking). The quantities $p(s_i, z)$ are approximated as $p(s_i, z) \approx R_i\, p(z|s_i)$, substituting the prior probability of sentence s_i by the relevance score R_i. For each sentence s_i not yet ranked in S, the relevance and diversity scores are combined into the score $\lambda R_i + (1-\lambda) D(s_i|S)$, with a weighting coefficient λ. The highest scoring sentence is then added to S, and the next iteration starts.

The method described above is inspired by a well-known technique for query reformulation for web search results diversification (Santos et al., 2010). It would likely work with alternative topic models as well. Note that in our experiments, we do not predefine the number of topics, which is estimated through the bayesian information criterion (Schwarz, 1978). However, a teacher could alter the number of topics manually, depending on the desired level of granularity in the topics.

3 Experimental Setup

Datasets. Most existing QG datasets are neither educational (e.g., SQuAD (Rajpurkar et al., 2016)) or do not provide an explicit link between questions and course content (e.g., LearningQ (Chen et al., 2018)) making it impossible to evaluate content selection methods directly. To the best of our knowledge, the only educational datasets that allow for such evaluation are EduQG (Hadifar et al., 2023) and TQA-A (Steuer et al., 2022). EduQG contains questions (i.e., phrased in cloze or close-ended form) and correct answers that are sentence-level aligned to source documents. TQA-A contains question-answer pairs where answers are annotated at the span level. We evaluate our content selection methods at the paragraph and sentence levels, respectively, for EduQG and TQA-A (an example entry of each dataset is presented in Appendix §A).

Baselines. We compare different content selection baselines including: ORACLE (a perfect retrieval system), LEXRANK (Erkan and Radev, 2004), SVM (Cortes and Vapnik, 1995), *Overgeneration and Rank* (OVR; Heilman and Smith, 2009). The baselines are compared against OUR methodology (§2) for some selected λ values. The T5 model (Raffel et al., 2020) has been fine-tuned to function as the QG model for the baselines. We devised a fixed QG model for all content selection strategies in each dataset, in order to obtain a fair evaluation regarding diversity and generation quality (see Appendix §B for further details).

Evaluation. To measure the content ranking performance, we report Recall (R) and Mean Average Precision (MAP) for the top 10 candidates. Diversity, for the selected sentences/paragraphs as well as among the generated questions, is measured by Average cosine Distance between Candidates (ADC; Belém et al., 2013), Self-BLEU (SBLEU; Zhu et al., 2018), and distinct-unigram (DIST1; Li et al., 2015). We also report BLEU and METEOR to measure the quality of the generated questions (more details in Appendix §C).

Table 1: Summary of our results on EduQG and TQA-A datasets.

		Retrieval		Content-diversity			Question-diversity			Generation	
	Method	R	MAP	ADC	SBLEU$\downarrow^{(*)}$	DIST1	ADC	SBLEU$\downarrow$	DIST1	BLEU	METEOR
EduQG	Oracle	100	100	67.5	7.8	37.1	65.8	49.0	36.3	35.6	46.7
	LexRank	20.0	37.2	50.7	13.9	34.4	54.6	54.4	31.8	33.3	45.0
	SVM	28.5	46.3	63.9	9.2	32.8	66.4	50.8	35.7	33.3	45.4
	OvR	-	-	-	-	-	67.1	**48.0**	36.9	31.0	39.8
	Our (λ=1.0)	**32.7**	**51.6**	64.5	8.7	33.8	66.5	49.2	37.0	**33.7**	**45.8**
	Our (λ=0.01)	23.6	40.3	75.2	7.1	38.5	**73.6**	48.6	**37.8**	31.8	43.3
	Our (λ=0.0)	12.2	43.2	**76.1**	**6.0**	**44.1**	70.6	**46.7**	37.3	31.8	42.5
TQA-A	Oracle	100	100	57.6	66.1	40.3	48.2	65.4	49.1	7.4	19.4
	LexRank	20.7	31.7	51.7	74.1	35.4	45.5	69.1	46.5	7.1	**19.5**
	SVM	20.2	32.6	56.7	72.2	38.5	48.7	67.8	47.3	7.8	18.6
	OvR	-	-	-	-	-	**70.2**	**26.5**	**79.9**	6.0	17.3
	Our (λ=1.0)	**26.2**	**39.7**	57.3	63.7	41.0	51.3	57.5	53.2	**8.2**	19.1
	Our (λ=0.01)	22.9	38.0	**61.7**	49.2	45.3	64.3	34.1	60.6	7.6	19.2
	Our (λ=0.0)	19.6	32.9	60.8	**42.9**	**48.5**	61.2	37.2	59.2	7.1	18.6

($*$) Lower is better as it indicates higher diversity.

4 Results and Discussion

Table 1 presents a summary of our results on both datasets. The transformer-based relevancy estimator, Our ($\lambda = 1.0$), obtains the highest retrieval scores. However, this high recall or MAP does not neccessary translate into better BLEU or METEOR score (see column 'Generation'). For example, LexRank leads to almost the same overall QG quality. This phenomenon was already present in previous studies (Chen et al., 2019; Mahdavi et al., 2020), although not explicitly addressed. In addition, not even the generation scores based on perfect rankings (Oracle) are consistently better than those from predicted rankings (See Appendix E for some generated examples). This implies that the current QG evaluation metrics are incapable of evaluating the content selection step, given the QG quality of present-day competitive models like our tuned T5, and these two tasks must be evaluated separately. Alternatively, asking experts to review the quality of generated questions or content selection as done in previous studies (Steuer et al., 2022; Huang and He, 2016) is not reproducible.

We can see a clear correlation between Content-diversity and Question-diversity columns. For instance, Our ($\lambda = 0.0$) selection leads to the highest content diversity and, consequently, the highest question diversity. A higher degree of diversity can be obtained by decreasing λ, at the expense of retrieval effectiveness. The correlation between content diversity and question diversity further supports our suggestion to split up the evaluation of content selection and question generation.

The OvR strategy gets better diversity scores on TQA-A. We observed the ranker prioritize cloze questions over "wh" questions. Our hypothesis is that the lower word overlap on "wh" words in the highest ranked questions leads to the observed higher diversity. In EduQG, we do not observe this behavior, since all questions have the same format. In fact, We believe that selecting content first and then generating questions is a better strategy compared to OvR. This aligns more closely with how teachers typically create questions and is also more computationally efficient.[2], and in terms of quality of the resulting question set (cf. higher generation scores for Our models than OvR).

Summarized, our experiments lead to the following insights: (i) Our proposed model is able to outperform all baselines in terms of retrieval metrics. (ii) It allows control over the trade-off between retrieval quality and diversity (through the parameter λ). (iii) Content-diversity and question-diversity do correlate (which is less than surprising), but neither retrieval nor diversity seems to correlate well with established metrics to evaluate generated questions.

5 Conclusion

This paper describes an educational-oriented strategy for content selection from educational documents to support question generation, using a ranker and a topic-wise diversifier. Our empirical

[2]Note that when using content selection, we only generate a limited set of questions, rather than all possible ones for a chapter, as we do with the OvR strategy. Based on our analysis, the inference time for question generation using T5-base is an order of magnitude higher than ranking with RoBERTa-base (288.69 vs. 14.29 milliseconds for a single inference pass).

evaluations of two educational QG datasets demonstrate the effectiveness of the proposed model. However, we found that current ngram-based evaluation metrics of the generated questions, given the current level of generation quality, do not carry sufficient signal to evaluate the content selection problem.

Limitations

We believe the current study can improve in at least two ways: (i) The limitations of existing QG evaluation metrics in light of the content selection problem are highlighted in this study, however, a promising next step is to annotate topics/subtopics and evaluate the diversity of generated contents and questions by more sophisticated metrics such as α-NDCG (Clarke et al., 2008) or ERR-AI (Chapelle et al., 2009). (ii) A human study on content selection and question generation will be insightful. For example, the analysis of question diversity and its impact on students' learning allows us to understand the necessity of diversification better.

References

Rakesh Agrawal, Sreenivas Gollapudi, Alan Halverson, and Samuel Ieong. 2009. Diversifying search results. In *Proceedings of WSDM*.

Seohyun Back, Akhil Kedia, Sai Chetan Chinthakindi, Haejun Lee, and Jaegul Choo. 2021. Learning to generate questions by learning to recover answer-containing sentences. In *Proceedings of ACL-IJCNLP*.

Satanjeev Banerjee and Alon Lavie. 2005. METEOR: An automatic metric for MT evaluation with improved correlation with human judgments. In *Proceedings of WS*.

Fabiano Belém, Eder Martins, Jussara Almeida, and Marcos Gonçalves. 2013. Exploiting novelty and diversity in tag recommendation. In *Proceedings of ECIR*, pages 380–391.

Jaime Carbonell and Jade Goldstein. 1998. The use of MMR, diversity-based reranking for reordering documents and producing summaries. In *Proceedings of the SIGIR*.

Olivier Chapelle, Donald Metlzer, Ya Zhang, and Pierre Grinspan. 2009. Expected reciprocal rank for graded relevance. In *Proceedings of CIKM*.

Guanliang Chen, Jie Yang, and Dragan Gasevic. 2019. A comparative study on question-worthy sentence selection strategies for educational question generation. In *Proceedings of AIED*.

Guanliang Chen, Jie Yang, Claudia Hauff, and Geert-Jan Houben. 2018. LearningQ: a large-scale dataset for educational question generation. In *Proceedings of AAAI*.

Charles LA Clarke, Maheedhar Kolla, Gordon V Cormack, Olga Vechtomova, Azin Ashkan, Stefan Büttcher, and Ian MacKinnon. 2008. Novelty and diversity in information retrieval evaluation. In *Proceedings of SIGIR*.

Corinna Cortes and Vladimir Vapnik. 1995. Support-vector networks. *Machine learning*, 20(3).

Barbara Gross Davis. 2009. *Tools for teaching*. John Wiley & Sons.

Linda DeAngelo, Sylvia Hurtado, John H Pryor, Kimberly R Kelly, Jose Luis Santos, and William S Korn. 2009. The american college teacher: National norms for the 2007-2008 HERI faculty survey. *Los Angeles: Higher Education Research Institute, UCLA*.

Xinya Du and Claire Cardie. 2017. Identifying where to focus in reading comprehension for neural question generation. In *Proceedings of EMNLP*.

Günes Erkan and Dragomir R Radev. 2004. LexRank: Graph-based lexical centrality as salience in text summarization. *Journal of artificial intelligence research*, 22.

Amir Hadifar, Semere Kiros Bitew, Johannes Deleu, Chris Develder, and Thomas Demeester. 2023. EduQG: A multi-format multiple choice dataset for the educational domain. *IEEE Access*.

Thomas M Haladyna and Steven M Downing. 1989. A taxonomy of multiple-choice item-writing rules. *Applied measurement in education*, 2(1).

Thomas M Haladyna and Michael C Rodriguez. 2013. *Developing and validating test items*. Routledge.

Michael Heilman and Noah A Smith. 2009. Question generation via overgenerating transformations and ranking. Technical report, Carnegie-Mellon University Pittsburgh - language technologies institute.

Yan Huang and Lianzhen He. 2016. Automatic generation of short answer questions for reading comprehension assessment. *Natural Language Engineering*, 22(3):457–489.

Girish Kumar, Rafael E Banchs, and Luis Fernando D'Haro. 2015. Revup: Automatic gap-fill question generation from educational texts. In *Proceedings of SIGEDU*.

Vishwajeet Kumar, Ganesh Ramakrishnan, and Yuan-Fang Li. 2019. Putting the horse before the cart: A generator-evaluator framework for question generation from text. In *Proceedings of CoNLL*.

Ghader Kurdi, Jared Leo, Bijan Parsia, Uli Sattler, and Salam Al-Emari. 2020. A systematic review of automatic question generation for educational purposes. *International Journal of Artificial Intelligence in Education*, 30(1).

Philippe Laban, Chien-Sheng Wu, Lidiya Murakhovs'ka, Wenhao Liu, and Caiming Xiong. 2022. Quiz design task: Helping teachers create quizzes with automated question generation. In *Proceedings of NAACL*.

Nguyen-Thinh Le, Tomoko Kojiri, and Niels Pinkwart. 2014. Automatic question generation for educational applications–the state of art. In *Proceedings of ICCSAMA*.

Jiwei Li, Michel Galley, Chris Brockett, Jianfeng Gao, and Bill Dolan. 2015. A diversity-promoting objective function for neural conversation models. In *Proceedings of NAACL-HLT*.

Yinhan Liu, Myle Ott, Naman Goyal, Jingfei Du, Mandar Joshi, Danqi Chen, Omer Levy, Mike Lewis, Luke Zettlemoyer, and Veselin Stoyanov. 2019. RoBERTa: A robustly optimized BERT pretraining approach. *arXiv preprint arXiv:1907.11692*.

Sedigheh Mahdavi, Aijun An, Heidar Davoudi, Marjan Delpisheh, and Emad Gohari. 2020. Question-worthy sentence selection for question generation. In *Proceedings of CANAI*.

Jack Mostow and Wei Chen. 2009. Generating instruction automatically for the reading strategy of self-questioning. In *Proceedings of AIED*.

Mao Nakanishi, Tetsunori Kobayashi, and Yoshihiko Hayashi. 2019. Towards answer-unaware conversational question generation. In *Proceedings of MRQA*.

Rodrigo Nogueira and Kyunghyun Cho. 2019. Passage re-ranking with BERT. *arXiv preprint arXiv:1901.04085*.

Kishore Papineni, Salim Roukos, Todd Ward, and Wei-Jing Zhu. 2002. BLEU: a method for automatic evaluation of machine translation. In *Proceedings of ACL*.

Colin Raffel, Noam Shazeer, Adam Roberts, Katherine Lee, Sharan Narang, Michael Matena, Yanqi Zhou, Wei Li, Peter J Liu, et al. 2020. Exploring the limits of transfer learning with a unified text-to-text transformer. *Journal of Machine Learning Research*, 21(140).

Pranav Rajpurkar, Jian Zhang, Konstantin Lopyrev, and Percy Liang. 2016. SQuAD: 100,000+ questions for machine comprehension of text. In *Proceedings of EMNLP*.

John P Rickards. 1979. Adjunct postquestions in text: A critical review of methods and processes. *Review of Educational Research*, 49(2).

Sylvio Rüdian, Alexander Heuts, and Niels Pinkwart. 2020. Educational text summarizer: Which sentences are worth asking for? *Fachtagung Bildungstechnologien der Gesellschaft für Informatik*.

Rodrygo LT Santos, Craig Macdonald, and Iadh Ounis. 2010. Exploiting query reformulations for web search result diversification. In *Proceedings of WWW*.

Gideon Schwarz. 1978. Estimating the dimension of a model. *The annals of statistics*.

Tim Steuer, Anna Filighera, Tobias Meuser, and Christoph Rensing. 2021. I do not understand what I cannot define: Automatic question generation with pedagogically-driven content selection. *arXiv preprint arXiv:2110.04123*.

Tim Steuer, Anna Filighera, and Thomas Tregel. 2022. Investigating educational and noneducational answer selection for educational question generation. *IEEE Access*.

Laurens van der Maaten and Geoffrey Hinton. 2008. Visualizing data using t-SNE. *Journal of Machine Learning Research*, 9.

Norman L Webb. 2006. Identifying content for student achievement tests. *Handbook of test development*.

Ruqing Zhang, Jiafeng Guo, Lu Chen, Yixing Fan, and Xueqi Cheng. 2021. A review on question generation from natural language text. *ACM Transactions on Information Systems*, 40(1).

Yaoming Zhu, Sidi Lu, Lei Zheng, Jiaxian Guo, Weinan Zhang, Jun Wang, and Yong Yu. 2018. TexyGen: A benchmarking platform for text generation models. In *Proceedings of SIGIR*.

Appendices

A Datasets

An example of a randomly selected chapter and corresponding question(s) for EduQG and TQA-A is presented in Table 3 and Table 4 respectively. As can be seen in the tables, the length of the chapter in TQA-A is significantly shorter than in EduQG.

B Baselines

In this section, we provide more details about our baselines presented in §3. As mentioned, we compare different baselines including: (i) ORACLE: a perfect retrieval system that simulates teachers' behaviors for selecting suitable sentences or paragraphs. We operated under the assumption that the ORACLE is flawless and exactly retrieves the same number of content as teachers. (ii) LEXRANK (Erkan and Radev, 2004): the graph-based automatic text summarizer from (Chen et al., 2019),[3] (iii) SVM (Cortes and Vapnik, 1995): a pointwise ranking that is comparable to the feature-based strategy from (Mahdavi et al., 2020).[4] We fine-tuned the T5-base (Raffel et al., 2020) (see Appendix §D for the configurations) in answer-agnostic mode (Zhang et al., 2021) on our datasets and used it as the QG model for all of our content selection baselines. The greedy decoding is employed because other strategies have minimal impact on final results.

As a final baseline, we apply the fundamentally different strategy called overgeneration, a highly popular technique in the educational QG literature (Kurdi et al., 2020). First, all possible questions are generated ('overgeneration') and ranked, after which the exam designers decide which questions to select. Similar to *Overgeneration and Rank* (OvR) (Heilman and Smith, 2009), we generated all possible questions in a chapter and trained a ranker to select the most important questions. However, we replaced their rule-based QG and linear regression ranker with our T5-based QG model and new RoBERTa-base question ranker for a fair comparison with the other baselines. We utilized a similar setup for sorting questions (pointwise-ranker with cross-entropy loss). The above baselines are compared against OUR methodology (§2) for various values of λ.

C Evaluation metrics

To evaluate different retrieval strategies, we feed the selected contents (sentences or paragraphs) to the finetuned T5 and evaluate the effectiveness of strategies with automatic diversity and quality metrics. The diversity of the selected sentences/paragraphs, as well as among the generated questions is measured[5] by Average cosine Distance between Candidates (ADC) (Belém et al., 2013), Self-BLEU (SBLEU) (Zhu et al., 2018), and distinct-ngram (DIST1, $n = 1$ in our case) (Li et al., 2015). ADC calculates the average cosine distance dissimilarity between the representations of all pairs. Similar to ADC, SBLEU, computes the average BLEU score (Papineni et al., 2002) between one instance and others by considering the instance as a hypothesis and the other as references. The lower SBLEU score indicates the higher diversity. Distinct ngram computes the proportion of unique n-grams out of the total number of n-grams in a set of generated questions.

The generation quality assessed by BLEU and METEOR scores.[6] BLEU relies on the maximum n-grams for counting the co-occurrences between the generated question by the generative model (i.e., T5), and a set of ground truth reference questions constructed by a teacher. The final score is derived from the average of BLEU scores through all examples. METEOR is calculated similarly by considering stemming and synonymy into account.

D Hyperparameters

Both datasets comes with a predefined train-test split. For all tasks (i.e., ranking and generation), we hold out 10% of the data for validation, while the remaining part is used for training. T5 was fine-tuned separately for both datasets from pretrained 'base' version[7] with the following hyperparameter settings in an answer agnostic[8] way:

```
batch_size=8
total_epochs=10
max_source_length=512
max_target_length=64
optimizer=AdamW
weight_decay=0.1
adam_epsilon=1e-08
max_grad_norm=1.0
lr_scheduler=linear
learning_rate=5e-05
warmup_steps=500
gradient_accumulation_steps=4
```

The presented λ for OUR methodology in Table 1 selected carefully to illustrate its effect across the datasets. Figure 2 shows different values of lambda and corresponding ADC metrics in EduQG and TQA-A.

E Example Generations

In this section, we provide some examples to illustrate the limitation of the existing metrics to evaluate content selection methods. Table 2 provides a set of generated questions based on different retrieval strategies presented in §4 for a chapter in

[3] `https://github.com/crabcamp/lexrank`

[4] `https://scikit-learn.org`

[5] α-NDCG (Clarke et al., 2008) or other popular metrics for retrieval diversity have not been reported, by lack of ground-truth topic annotations.

[6] We used an existing implementation from `https://www.nltk.org/`

[7] `https://huggingface.co/docs/transformers`

[8] Note that assuming access to the answer during inference time is not always a valid option in real-world applications.

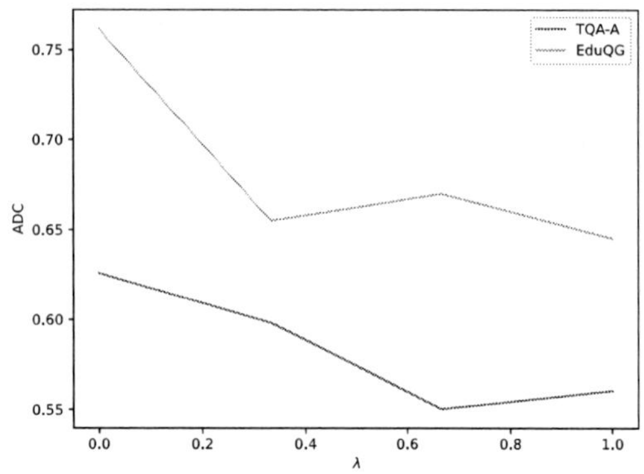

Figure 2: The effect of λ values on diversity of contents (in terms of the Average Distance between Candidate (ADC) metric).

the EduQG dataset. In addition to generated questions based on different retrieval strategies, we also show questions that were originally constructed by a teacher for the chapter (denoted by REFERENCE). It also should be noted that the difference between REFERENCE and ORACLE arises from the fact that generated questions from ORACLE were produced by the T5 model rather than a teacher. We also report BLEU and METEOR scores for these strategies.

As can be seen in the table, the top two performing retrieval systems, ORACLE and OUR ($\lambda = 1.0$), for the EduQG dataset in our experiments (§4) lead to the lower BLEU scores compared to the weaker baselines (in terms of MAP score) such as SVM or OUR ($\lambda = 0.0$). This issue arises from the fact that the BLEU score heavily penalizes examples that have no tri-gram or 4-gram overlap. As an example, the last two questions in ORACLE blocks (**Q5** and **Q6**) obtained BLEU scores of 0.76 and 0.63, respectively (almost zero). Although these questions seem reasonable, the last two questions in SVM block received much better scores, 25.96 and 30.21, due to the 4-gram overlap with REFERENCE set. Therefore, ORACLE retrieval receives a lower score compared to SVM despite its perfect recall and MAP.

Method	Questions	BLEU	METEOR
REFERENCE	**Q1** The study of nutrient cycling through the environment is an example of which of the following? **Q2** Understory plants in a temperate forest have adaptations to capture limited which of the following? **Q3** Which of the following biomes is characterized by abundant water resources? **Q4** Which of the following biomes is characterized by short growing seasons? **Q5** What is a key feature of estuaries? **Q6** Which of the following natural forces is responsible for the release of carbon dioxide and other atmospheric gases?	100.0	100.0
ORACLE	**Q1** Which of the following is correct about the Arctic tundra? **Q2** Which of the following is a natural driver of climate change? **Q3** What are plants that grow on other plants that are not harmed? **Q4** Which of the following is an example of a barren habitat? **Q5** What is the ecosystem composed of? **Q6** What is the seasonality of tropical wet forests?	18.92	29.23
LEXRANK	**Q1** Which of the following is not a characteristic of freshwater biomes? **Q2** What are freshwater biomes? **Q3** Water is a source of drinking water for the city. **Q4** Which of the following is correct about the spring and fall turnover? **Q5** What happens to the lake's surface water when it cools to 4 degrees C? **Q6** Climate change is a term used to describe changes in weather patterns that have become increasingly evident over	10.52	27.74
SVM	**Q1** Which of the following is not found in the neritic zone? **Q2** Which of the following is correct about the spring and fall turnover? **Q3** Which of the following is correct about the intertidal zone? **Q4** Which of the following is correct about the Little Ice Age? **Q5** Which of the following is not a characteristic of the chaparral? **Q6** Which of the following is correct about temperate grasslands?	25.56	37.94
OUR ($\lambda = 1.0$)	**Q1** Which of the following is correct about the Challenger Deep? **Q2** Which of the following is correct about the intertidal zone? **Q2** What are environments in which the soil is permanently or periodically saturated with water? **Q4** What is the amount of organic matter available as food called? **Q5** Which of the following is correct about the deepest part of the ocean? **Q6** Which of the following is not a characteristic of the deepwater region of the ocean?	16.21	32.23
OUR ($\lambda = 0.01$)	**Q1** Which of the following is correct about the Challenger Deep? **Q2** In which of the following regions would you expect to find photosynthetic organisms? **Q3** Which of the following is correct about the Milankovitch cycles? **Q4** Which of the following is correct about subtropical deserts? **Q5** What are lakes and ponds? **Q6** Which of the following is an endemic species?	23.25	33.51
OUR ($\lambda = 0.0$)	**Q1** Which of the following is correct about the Challenger Deep? **Q2** Which of the following is correct about abiotic forces? **Q3** Which of the following is not a marine biome? **Q4** Which of the following is correct about the environment? **Q5** What is the net primary productivity of boreal forests? **Q6** Which of the following is correct about coral reefs?	25.55	39.75

Table 2: A set of generated questions based on different retrieval strategies for a cherry-picked chapter in the EduQG dataset.

[Begining of the chapter is truncated due to the length limit]
Socialism is an alternative economic system. In socialist societies, the means of generating wealth, such as factories, large farms, and banks, are owned by the government and not by private individuals. The government accumulates wealth and then redistributes it to citizens, primarily in the form of social programs that provide such things as free or inexpensive health care, education, and childcare. In socialist countries, the government also usually owns and controls utilities such as electricity, transportation systems like airlines and railroads, and telecommunications systems. In many socialist countries the government is an oligarchy : only members of a certain political party or ruling elite can participate in government. For example, in China, the government is run by members of the Chinese Communist Party. However, socialist countries can have democratic forms of government as well, such as Sweden. Although many Americans associate socialism with tyranny and a loss of individual liberties, this does not have to be the case, as we see in Sweden.
In the United States, the democratic government works closely together with its capitalist economic system. The interconnectedness of the two affects the way in which goods and services are distributed. The market provides many goods and services needed by Americans. For example, food, clothing, and housing are provided in ample supply by private businesses that earn a profit in return. These goods and services are known as private goods . 1 People can purchase what they need in the quantity in which they need it. This, of course, is the ideal. In reality, those who live in poverty cannot always afford to buy ample food and clothing to meet their needs, or the food and clothing that they can afford to buy in abundance is of inferior quality. Also, it is often difficult to find adequate housing; housing in the most desirable neighborhoods—those that have low crime rates and good schools—is often too expensive for poor or working-class (and sometimes middle-class) people to buy or rent.
Thus, the market cannot provide everything (in enough quantity or at low enough costs) in order to meet everyone's needs. Therefore, some goods are provided by the government. Such goods or services that are available to all without charge are called public goods. Two such public goods are national security and education. It is difficult to see how a private business could protect the United States from attack. How could it build its own armies and create plans for defense and attack? Who would pay the men and women who served? Where would the intelligence come from? Due to its ability to tax, draw upon the resources of an entire nation, and compel citizen compliance, only government is capable of protecting the nation.
Similarly, public schools provide education for all children in the United States. Children of all religions, races and ethnicities, socioeconomic classes, and levels of academic ability can attend public schools free of charge from kindergarten through the twelfth grade. It would be impossible for private schools to provide an education for all of the nation's children. Private schools do provide some education in the United States; however, they charge tuition, and only those parents who can afford to pay their fees (or whose children gain a scholarship) can attend these institutions. Some schools charge very high tuition, the equivalent to the tuition at a private college. If private schools were the only educational institutions, most poor and working-class children and many middle-class children would be uneducated. Private schooling is a type of good called a toll good . Toll goods are available to many people, and many people can make use of them, but only if they can pay the price. They occupy a middle ground between public and private goods. All parents may send their children to public schools in the United States. They can choose to send their children to a private school, but the private school will charge them. On the other hand, public schools, which are operated by the government, provide free education so all children can attend school. Therefore, everyone in the nation benefits from the educated voters and workers produced by the public school system. Another distinction between public and private goods is that public goods are available to all, typically without additional charge.
[Rest of the chapter is truncated due to the length limit]

Reference Question:
Q1 What goods are available to all without direct payment?
a) private goods b) public goods c) common goods d) toll goods

[Rest of the questions are truncated due to the length limit]

Table 3: An example of a randomly selected chapter in the EduQG dataset with a reference question. The highlighted paragraph indicates the selected content or the grounding answer.

Dust storms like the one in Figure 10.20 are more common in dry climates. The soil is dried out and dusty. Plants may be few and far between. Dry, bare soil is more easily blown away by the wind than wetter soil or soil held in place by plant roots.
Like flowing water, wind picks up and transports particles. Wind carries particles of different sizes in the same ways that water carries them. You can see this in Figure 10.21. Tiny particles, such as clay and silt, move by suspension. They hang in the air, sometimes for days. They may be carried great distances and rise high above the ground. Larger particles, such as sand, move by saltation. The wind blows them in short hops. They stay close to the ground. Particles larger than sand move by traction. The wind rolls or pushes them over the surface. They stay on the ground. Did you ever see workers sandblasting a building to clean it? Sand is blown onto the surface to scour away dirt and debris. Wind-blown sand has the same effect. It scours and polishes rocks and other surfaces. Wind-blown sand may carve rocks into interesting shapes. You can see an example in Figure 10.22. This form of erosion is called abrasion. It occurs any time rough sediments are blown or dragged over surfaces. Can you think of other ways abrasion might occur? Like water, when wind slows down it drops the sediment its carrying. This often happens when the wind has to move over or around an obstacle. A rock or tree may cause wind to slow down. As the wind slows, it deposits the largest particles first. Different types of deposits form depending on the size of the particles deposited. When the wind deposits sand, it forms small hills of sand. These hills are called sand dunes. For sand dunes to form, there must be plenty of sand and wind. Sand dunes are found mainly in deserts and on beaches. You can see examples of sand dunes in Figure 10.23. What causes a sand dune to form? It starts with an obstacle, such as a rock. The obstacle causes the wind to slow down. The wind then drops some of its sand. As more sand is deposited, the dune gets bigger. The dune becomes the obstacle that slows the wind and causes it to drop its sand. The hill takes on the typical shape of a sand dune, shown in Figure 10.24. Once a sand dune forms, it may slowly migrate over the land. The wind moves grains of sand up the gently sloping side of the dune. This is done by saltation. When the sand grains reach the top of the dune, they slip down the steeper side. The grains are pulled by gravity. The constant movement of sand up and over the dune causes the dune to move along the ground. It always moves in the same direction that the wind usually blows. Can you explain why? When the wind drops fine particles of silt and clay, it forms deposits called loess. Loess deposits form vertical cliffs. Loess can become a thick, rich soil. Thats why loess deposits are used for farming in many parts of the world. You can see an example of loess in Figure 10.25. Its very important to control wind erosion of soil. Good soil is a precious resource that takes a long time to form. Covering soil with plants is one way to reduce wind erosion. Plants and their roots help hold the soil in place. They also help the soil retain water so it is less likely to blow away. Planting rows of trees around fields is another way to reduce wind erosion. The trees slow down the wind, so it doesnt cause as much erosion. Fences like the one in Figure 10.26 serve the same purpose. The fence in the figure is preventing erosion and migration of sand dunes on a beach.

Reference Questions:
Q1 Wind drops the sediment it is carrying when it ...
a) slows down. b) is very moist. c) arrives at a beach. d) reaches a certain altitude.

Q2 A sand dune migrates because wind keeps
a) reversing its direction. b) blowing sand up and over the dune. c) causing longshore drift. d) none of the above

Q3 Deposits called loess
a) form vertical cliffs. b) have thick rich soil. c) are deposited by wind. d) all of the above

Q4 Loess deposits consist of
a) sand and silt. b) silt and clay. c) clay and gravel. d) gravel and sand.

Table 4: An example of a randomly selected chapter in the TQA-A dataset with reference questions. The highlighted sentences indicate the selected contents or the grounding answers.

Towards Automatic Grammatical Error Type Classification for Turkish

Harun Uz and **Gülşen Eryiğit**
İTÜ NLP Research Group
Faculty of Computer & Informatics
Istanbul Technical University
İstanbul, Türkiye
[uz20, gulsen.cebiroglu]@itu.edu.tr

Abstract

Automatic error type classification is an important process in both learner corpora creation and evaluation of large-scale grammatical error correction systems. Rule-based classifier approaches such as ERRANT have been widely used to classify edits between correct-erroneous sentence pairs into predefined error categories. However, the used error categories are far from being universal yielding many language specific variants of ERRANT. In this paper, we discuss the applicability of the previously introduced grammatical error types to an agglutinative language, Turkish. We suggest changes on current error categories and discuss a hierarchical structure to better suit the inflectional and derivational properties of this morphologically highly rich language. We also introduce ERRANT-TR, the first automatic error type classification toolkit for Turkish. ERRANT-TR currently uses a rule-based error type classification pipeline which relies on word level morphological information. Due to unavailability of learner corpora in Turkish, the proposed system is evaluated on a small set of 106 annotated sentences and its performance is measured as 77.04% $F_{0.5}$ score. The next step is to use ERRANT-TR for the development of a Turkish learner corpus. The code will be made publicly available.[1]

1 Introduction

Automatic error type classification is the task of assigning error type classes to predetermined grammatical errors. The Building Educational Applications (BEA) 2019 Shared Task on Grammatical Error Correction (GEC) (Bryant et al., 2019) emphasizes the importance of error correcting systems for educational applications. A total of 24 teams have developed GEC systems for the task and ERRANT (Bryant et al., 2017) (a rule-based error type classifier) was used for automatic evaluation of these systems on 5 different datasets. Automatic evaluation in GEC is the process of error classification on parallel data consisting of erroneous and correct sentence pairs. Automatic error classification is an important process while evaluating GEC systems, since the direct approach of exact match precision and recall scores is not intuitive enough to correctly analyze the strengths and weaknesses of these systems.

Due to the advances in deep learning based language processing in recent years, considerable performance improvements have been observed in GEC systems. In parallel with this, the need for bigger and labeled datasets increased even more. Usually, learner corpora[2] are used to create GEC datasets since foreign-language learners are the ones who make such grammatical errors the most. For resource-rich languages like English, there exist many such corpora; e.g., Cambridge Learner Corpus (Nicholls, 2003), NUCLE (Dahlmeier et al., 2013) and W&I+LOCNESS (Bryant et al., 2019). Collecting and annotating learner corpora are pretty costly and time-consuming tasks. The erroneous sentences need to be corrected by professionals, and the inter-annotator agreement should be high (annotators should use a universal set of error categories as much as possible) so that a sufficient amount of useful samples could be obtained. The challenges of creating a learner corpus have also led researchers to find alternative data resources such as extracting edit history of comments from the web (Chen et al., 2019). ERRANT-like systems help professionals annotate a vast amount of data quickly in a semi-automatic way.

Although there exist no prior complete GEC tools nor datasets for Turkish, there exist some related works (e.g., datasets related to social media errors of native speakers (Eryiğit and Torunoğlu-

[1] https://github.com/harunuz/erranttr.git

[2] Learner corpora are electronic collections of language data produced by L2 learners (second or foreign-language learners).

Proceedings of the 17th Conference of the European Chapter of the Association for Computational Linguistics: Student Research Workshop, pages 134–142
May 2-4, 2023 ©2023 Association for Computational Linguistics

Selamet, 2017) or to some specific error type (Arikan et al., 2019)). These datasets are not directly usable in a general GEC system since they mostly focus on social media specific error types such as intentional repetition of the same characters for exclamation purposes or misuse of diacritics due to wrong keyboard choices.

Text normalization and spelling correction methods which have been developed with these datasets are evaluated according to the exact match scores. However, due to the rich morphological properties of Turkish, the exact match does not provide much insight on the type of errors where the system produces good and bad results. In Turkish, most of grammatical errors occur in suffixes as the learners tend to make inflectional and derivational errors Başak Karakoç Öztürk (2017). And in theory, since Turkish is a highly agglutinative language, it is possible to apply some derivations recursively and result in an infinite number of possible word derivations in Turkish. A single word in Turkish contains more syntactic information compared to English and corresponds to several English words most of the time. Therefore, while evaluating a Turkish GEC system output, a simple surface form matching approach loses more valuable information than it would in English.

In this paper, we discuss the applicability of the previously introduced ERRANT's grammatical error types to an agglutinative language, Turkish. We suggest changes on current error categories and discuss a hierarchical structure to better suit the inflectional and derivational properties of this morphologically highly rich language. The paper introduces ERRANT-TR, the first automatic error type classification toolkit for Turkish. ERRANT-TR currently uses a rule-based error type classification pipeline which relies on word level morphological information. Due to unavailability of learner corpora in Turkish, the proposed system is evaluated on a small set of 106 annotated sentences and its performance is measured as 77.04% $F_{0.5}$ score.

2 Related Work

Automatic error annotation has been a popular topic in computational linguistics for a long time (Wang et al., 2020; Bryant et al., 2022). Researchers tried to come up with standard error categories to cover possible error types in mono or multilingual settings and tried to develop automatic annotator systems. However, it is a challenging problem to come up with a unified solution and error categories due to the big structural differences between languages. There have been many attempts to develop ERRANT-like algorithms for different languages such as Greek (Korre et al., 2021), Czech (Náplava et al., 2022), German (Boyd, 2018), Spanish (Davidson et al., 2020), Russian (Katinskaia et al., 2022) and Korean (Yoon et al., 2022). Each work considers the original error types (Bryant et al., 2017) for the corresponding language and update them according to new needs. The need for developing particular annotation methods, even for languages that fall under the same language families, proves the ongoing challenge of developing a universal error annotation scheme.

Learner corpora have been the main focus when it comes to creating a GEC learning dataset recently. Synthetically generated data has been used prior to learner corpora and are still being used as additional data during the development of GEC systems (Kaneko et al., 2020; Kiyono et al., 2019; Zhao et al., 2019; Rothe et al., 2021; Omelianchuk et al., 2020; Lichtarge et al., 2019; Grundkiewicz et al., 2019). There has been other semi-automatic alternatives for creating learning datasets such as extracting Wikipedia edits (Grundkiewicz and Junczys-Dowmunt, 2014) as correct-erroneous sentence pairs. Both synthetically generated and semi-automatic datasets can be found in large amounts. However, they do not contain the natural distribution of real world errors. Therefore, learner corpora have become the de-facto data source for GEC systems, and many works focused on collecting and annotating these corpora (Katinskaia et al., 2022; Davidson et al., 2020; Boyd, 2018; Náplava et al., 2022). English has been the main subject of learner corpora studies as the language with the highest number of foreign students from all over the world. However for many other languages, these resources are still missing.

For Turkish, by the time of this writing, there is an ongoing research on collecting and manually annotating the first Turkish learner corpus. In the future, we plan on evaluating our system on this corpus when the data is publicly available.

3 ERRANT-TR

In this section, we present the first version of ERRANT-TR which relies on original ERRANT error categories described in Bryant et al. (2017). We explain how we discover these error types from the morphological structure of Turkish. There are 25 error types introduced with ERRANT. The list of categories and possible examples can be seen in Table 1.

In order to categorize the error types, we make use of the morphological information obtained through an automatic morphological analyzer and disambiguator (Akın and Akın, 2007). After the disambiguation process, we extract POS tags for each word from its morphological properties. The edits between correct and erroneous sentences can be grouped under 3 main categories at token level and the error types can be prefixed with "R", "M" and "U" labels, indicating "Replacement", "Missing" and "Unnecessary" errors respectively: A necessary token may be **M**issing or an **U**nnecessary token may be added in the erroneous sentence. But the most common, correct token(s) are **R**eplaced with erroneous token(s). Thus, not all error types are paired with "M" and "U". The possible combinations of labels can be seen in Bryant et al. (2017)'s Table 9. There can also be one-to-many or many-to-one alignments.

3.1 Edit Extraction

The first step to classify error types is to align the erroneous parts of the corrupt sentence with the correct parts of the correct sentence. ERRANT uses an edit extraction method introduced by Felice et al. (2016). It uses a modified Damerau-Levenshtein algorithm enhanced with linguistic features (POS tags, lemmas etc.) to extract the potential edits and merges some of them with predefined rules. In our experiments, with Turkish POS tag information added, it produced good results, therefore we used it as is.

3.2 Error Type Classification

The error type classification for each edit is done with a set of rules. The main information source for an edit classification is the morphological analysis and the POS tag of tokens in the correct sentence. An edit that does not contain an original token (an unnecessary token is used in the erroneous sentence) is difficult to identify as the only clue for the error type is the corrupt token(s). An edit that does not contain a corrupt token indicates a missing token error and the output purely relies on the success of the morphological analysis of the correct token(s). An edit that contains both correct and corrupt tokens is the most common alignment type and can have the most diverse set of error types.

Since in agglutinative languages most of the syntactic information resides at morphology level, the inflections are very rich and alignment at word level is not enough to specify the error types: one needs to align the morphemes (between correct and corrupt tokens) in order to specifically determine the error category (Yoon et al., 2022). As stated in Section-3.1, we use the default ERRANT aligner for word-level alignment. However, we use morphological features annotated at morpheme level in order to first align the morphemes and then specify the error types during error classification. Morphemes are aligned only if they are similar types (tense, mood, person, number etc.) or the similarity score for their surface forms exceeds a predefined threshold which is set to 0.85 by default. A sample output from the used morphological analyzer is provided below. The first line provides the correct and erroneous words respectively. The second line provides the morphological analysis of the correct word. The third line provides the aligned morphemes of the erroneous word. The word lemma is "*git*" but a probable stem "*gid*" is also provided by the used tool. Upon morpheme level alignment, we can observe that the tense suffix of the verb is produced erroneously:

```
gidiyorum   -> gidiyirum
git/gid(Verb)  iyor(Pres)  um(A1sg)
gid            iyir        um
 +              X           +
```

We used 50 erroneous sentences from Kurt (2020), Şahin (2013) and Fidan (2019) during the development of the classifier to validate the rules. The sentences were labeled by a linguist according to the error types in Table-1. The system tries to classify edits with the rules described in this section and assigns the discussed error types.

WO, ORTH and PUNCT errors (Table 1) are independent from morphological analysis and can be checked before the main decision mechanism. In order to classify these, we use ERRANT's methods as they are. Contractions (CONTR) in English combine a pronoun/noun and a verb, or a verb and the word "not", in a shorter form. CONTR errors are not common in Turkish. The words *"daha" (more)* and *"en" (the most)* are used before an adjective for comparative and superlative respectively, but differing from English, the adjective form itself is not affected with these constructions. Therefore, ADJ:FORM errors are also not common in Turkish.

Error Code	Meaning	Example
ADJ	Wrong choice of adjective	*büyük -> küçük*
ADJ:FORM	Wrong usage of comparative or superlative adjective	-
ADV	Wrong choice of adverb	*önce -> sonra*
CONJ	Wrong choice of conjunction	*ama -> belki*
CONTR	Wrong choice of contraction	-
DET	Wrong choice of determiner	*bu* elma -> *o* elma
MORPH	Tokens have the same lemma but nothing else in common	-
NOUN	Wrong choice of nouns	*kalem -> silgi*
NOUN:INFL	Count-mass noun errors	-
NOUN:NUM	Wrong usage of noun number	*elma -> elmalar*
NOUN:POSS	Wrong usage of noun possessive	*hastalarının ilaçları -> hastaların ilaçları*
ORTH	Case and/or whitespace errors	*herşey -> her şey*
OTHER	Errors that do not fall into any other category	-
PART	Wrong choice of particle	-
PREP	Wrong choice of preposition	*gibi -> için*
PRON	Wrong usage of pronoun	*sen -> ben*
PUNCT	Wrong usage of punctuation	*? -> !*
SPELL	Misspelling	*broblem -> problem*
UNK	A detected but not corrected error	-
VERB	Wrong choice of verbs	*geldim -> gittim*
VERB:FORM	Infinitives, gerunds and participles	gitmek, gitme, giden
VERB:INFL	Wrong usage of tense morphology	*(biz) yaptız -> (biz) yaptık*
VERB:SVA	Subject-verb agreement	*sen geliyorum -> sen geliyorsun*
VERB:TENSE	Wrong choice of inflectional and periphrastic tense, modal verbs and passivization	*geliyorum -> gelmiştim*
WO	Word order	*elma kırmızı -> kırmızı elma*

Table 1: Error code, description and examples. A dash indicates that the category has no example for being either too wide or not useful for Turkish. The original table is introduced in Bryant et al. (2017).

Both particles and prepositions (and postpositions as well) are considered as "edat" in Turkish. "Edat"s have a much broader scope and they may appear as either standalone words (e.g. *ile (with), için (for)*), or as suffixes (e.g. *-le (with)*) or as both suffix and a word (e.g. *-a kadar (until)*). Therefore we find it useful to use one type, PREP, for all "edat" errors. "Edat" as suffix is classified with morphological analysis. Word level PREP, DET, CONJ and PRON categories are simply classified with the help of POS tags and a predefined vocabulary for each type. MORPH category is too wide to cover any error type in Turkish. Therefore, we decide to discard this category and distribute its coverage to other, mainly :INFL, sub-categories.

In order to catch morphological errors, we need morphological analysis and POS tags of the words. "NOUN", "ADJ" and "ADV" tags are the main concerns as they may be derived from either a verb stem or a noun stem. The nouns, adjectives and adverbs that are derived from a verb (Infinitive, Participle and Gerund) may have the same suffixes as the ones inflected from a noun. ADJ, ADV and NOUN categories are assigned if the correct and erroneous tokens' lemmas are different but their morphological properties are the same as it means that the choice of word is wrong but the inflections are correct. The sub-categories (:INFL, :POSS, :NUM) are assigned if the word lemma is the same for both correct and erroneous tokens but possessive, numeral or other inflections are wrong.

VERB error types are classified similar to NOUN types. If the inflection is the same for both correct and erroneous verbs but the lemmas are different, this means that the choice of verb is wrong.

The :SVA sub-category is detected if the correct and erroneous verb contains different *personal suffixes*. Though it might be an inflection error as the error may be caused by the inflection inability rather than the wrong choice of "personal suffix". The :TENSE sub-category is assigned if the verb lemmas are the same but the chosen tense is wrong although the produced word is a valid verb. The :INFL sub-category is the other inflection errors that do not fall into neither :TENSE nor :SVA.

4 Experimental Results

4.1 Dataset

We collect 106 erroneous and corrected sentences [3] from academic studies discussing the errors made by foreign learners of Turkish; İltar (2021), Çelik (2019), Altintop (2018) and Dizeli and Sonkaya (2021). The mentioned studies categorizes some of the sentences under error types different from Table 1; e.g., diacritics usage errors, usage of dialects in writings, wrong usage of noun cases and wrong usage of noun number suffix. We map these types to the closest ERRANT types such as SPELL, NOUN:INFL.

In order to evaluate the proposed system, the error types have been reviewed by another linguist and the edits are labeled according to the discussed error types. The distribution and the number of error types can be seen in Table-2. It can be seen that the inflection sub-categories (:INFL) have much more samples than other morphological error types. This is due to the inflectional richness of Turkish and there are many sub-categories under :INFL.

4.2 Evaluation

We use M^2 file format (Dahlmeier and Ng, 2012) and measure the system performance using ERRANT's default scorer to compare the system output and the gold reference. The default scorer calculates span-based correction precision, recall and $F_{0.5}$ scores between two annotated M^2 files (Bryant et al., 2019).

We evaluate ERRANT-TR's error type classifier on manually annotated 106 parallel sentences. We consider the edit labels, which were reviewed by a linguist, as the ground truth and compare them to the system's output. ERRANT-TR achieves an average 77.04% $F_{0.5}$ score of span-based correction score. In order to better understand the system's strengths and weaknesses, we provide the $F_{0.5}$ scores per error type which can be seen in Table 2. Some inflection errors are classified as SPELL due to limited morphological analysis of an erroneous token. However, the overall $F_{0.5}$ score of the classifier is 77.04%. There are not many studies which compares their ERRANT implementation with gold standard data as we do. Only Korre et al. (2021) measured it this way and reported a maximum $F_{0.5}$ score of 43.50% on one dataset and 86.28% on another.

[3] The collected dataset is publicly available from https://github.com/harunuz/erranttr.git

5 Discussion

In this work, we developed the first error annotation tool for Turkish using the error types introduced in ERRANT. Even though the main purpose of these types is meant to cover the most common error types in a parallel corpus, during the development of ERRANT-TR and the annotation of the validation dataset, we observed that they are not completely applicable to agglutinative languages like Turkish. Some common errors in Turkish are not exactly covered with these types and some error types (e.g. MORPH, VERB:INFL) are too wide. Especially the morphological ones need to be expanded to cover a wide range of inflectional and derivational errors. On the other hand, the advantage of an agglutinative language is that the suffixes are usually added to a word stem in an order (see Good and Alan (1999) and Part 2 of Göksel and Kerslake (2004) for the case of Turkish). This phenomenon helps to classify error types into hierarchical classes and makes it relatively easier to implement a decision making algorithm.

Bryant et al. (2017) proposed a hierarchical relationship between error types. For instance, a NOUN:POSS error is also a NOUN error or a VERB:TENSE error is also a VERB error. Knowing these relationships prior to developing a classifier will help in classifying sub-types and will provide more information during the test phase. In Turkish, even more detailed hierarchical relationship between error types can be established due to the rich derivational morphology. To further illustrate this, we provide a simple example:

```
yap (VERB)
    -tık(ğ) (PastPart+A3sg+Noun)
        -ın (P2sg)
            -ı (Acc)
```

The verb lemma *yap-* has the following transformations: it is derived to a participle (an adjective-verb); the modified noun (third person singular) is dropped and the participle becomes a noun; then it is inflected with a second person singular possessive; lastly it is inflected with an accusative case.

Error Type	Number of Occurrence	Percentage of Occurrence (%)	P	R	$F_{0.5}$
ADJ	2	1.02	0.4	1.0	0.45
ADJ:FORM	0	0	-	-	-
ADV	5	2.55	1.0	0.8	0.95
CONJ	1	0.51	1.0	1.0	1.0
CONTR	0	0	-	-	-
DET	0	0	-	-	-
MORPH	0	0	-	-	-
NOUN	1	0.51	0.1	1.0	0.12
NOUN:INFL	43	21.93	0.88	0.86	0.87
NOUN:NUM	20	10.20	0.73	0.95	0.76
NOUN:POSS	17	8.67	0.87	0.41	0.71
ORTH	10	5.10	1.0	0.9	0.97
OTHER	16	8.16	0.52	0.68	0.55
PART	0	0	-	-	-
PREP	3	1.53	1.0	1.0	1.0
PRON	0	0	-	-	-
PUNCT	6	3.06	1.0	0.83	0.96
SPELL	38	19.38	0.82	0.73	0.80
UNK	0	0	-	-	-
VERB	8	4.08	0.75	0.75	0.75
VERB:FORM	0	0	-	-	-
VERB:INFL	16	8.16	0.6	0.27	0.48
VERB:SVA	3	1.53	1.0	1.0	1.0
VERB:TENSE	5	2.55	1.0	1.0	1.0
WO	2	1.02	1.0	1.0	1.0
Total / Micro Average	196	~100.00	0.77	0.77	0.77

Table 2: (Left) Error code, the number of occurrences and the percentage in the dataset. Note that each sentence may have more than one error. (Right) Precision, recall and $F_{0.5}$ scores of ERRANT-TR on the dataset for each error type.

Let us suppose that the learner made an error in possessive and used a third person singular possessive suffix *"-ı"*. Classifying this error as a NOUN:POSS type loses a valuable information of a common possessive error case in *participles* (İltar, 2021). Moreover, knowing that a verb can not be inflected with a possessive suffix, even though the lemma of the word is a verb we can safely discard the VERB and its sub-types while classifying this error. Therefore, a more precise classification system and an improved labeling scheme can be created by establishing hierarchical relationships among error types in a more intricate manner.

For nouns and verbs, "INFL" sub-categories mostly cover other sub-categories. For example, a "NOUN:NUM" or a "NOUN:POSS" error in Turkish can also be considered a "NOUN:INFL" error as the *number* and *possessive* properties are provided with inflectional suffixes. Furthermore, in the specific case of Turkish, a possessive error can also be considered a *genitive construction* error. As can be seen in the example below, a possession suffix *-ı* is appended to the head (modified noun) in a genitive construction and the modifier is appended with a *tamlayan (modifier)* suffix *-ın*.

```
Kitabın kapağı -> Kitab-ın kapağ-ı

(The book's cover)
```

Despite technically being a possession, errors in this type of phrase may also fall under the category of "genitive construction" errors due to frequent inflectional errors made by non-native Turkish learners in such phrases, even though they use possessives correctly in other contexts

5.1 Uncovered Turkish Specific Cases

Although it is not a grammatical error, the usage of Turkish specific characters (diacritics) could be non trivial for some learners. In addition to that, specifically on social media, some people choose to write with ASCII characters rather than their Turkish correspondents. The usage of *dialects* in written text is also the result of either a genuine mistake or a preference (Eryiğit and Torunoğlu-Selamet, 2017). Therefore, both *accent* and *diacritics* error types might be considered to take into account while developing Turkish GEC systems.

In Turkish, passivization, reciprocal verbs and the meaning of *making somebody do something* are all done with inflectional suffixes that are appended to a verb. The errors on these inflections are common enough to be considered standalone error categories.

6 Future Work

In this section, we aim to address the issues concerning the labeling and classification of grammatical error types that we have discussed earlier. We also outline possible areas for further research and suggest potential enhancements for ERRANT-TR.

Categorizing certain errors based solely on morphological analysis can be difficult, particularly when dealing with multi-token edits. Nonetheless, supplementing morphological analysis with dependency parsing can assist in precisely aligning and categorizing multi-token errors. Our intention is to use these techniques to enhance the system's performance on existing error types and address the Turkish-specific errors discussed in Section-5.1.

The evaluation of an automatic annotation toolkit (detection, alignment and classification capabilities) is a time and resource consuming process. One needs a big amount of already-annotated parallel data with high inter-annotator agreement. As we did not possess such data we only evaluated the classifier. In this work, the ground truth data is considered properly aligned and corrected. Therefore, the evaluation process has still room for improvement. We plan to test the system on a real world learner corpus which is being collected at the moment as part of an ongoing research.

Error type classification relies on the accuracy of the morphological analysis and disambiguation. Therefore, a potential mistake in these steps may yield incorrect classifications. In order to improve the system in the future, a better morphological analyzer can be used. There is also a room for improvement in the decision making pipeline of the classifier. The detection of certain error types is not trivial with only the morphological analysis as discussed earlier.

7 Conclusion

In this paper, we introduced ERRANT-TR a grammatical error annotation and automatic evaluation toolkit for Turkish. It automatically annotates the error types in a parallel corpus. We designed a decision making pipeline for Turkish based on morphological analysis information and hand-crafted specific vocabularies (for CONJ, PREP, PRON, DET types). We discussed and proposed potential changes to the error categories (which have been introduced mainly for English) in order to cover inflectional and derivational properties of Turkish, an agglutinative language.

We created a small evaluation dataset consisting of 106 erroneous-corrected sentence pairs collected from academic studies. ERRANT-TR achieves an average 77.04% $F_{0.5}$ score on this dataset. We discussed the strengths and weaknesses of the system based on this evaluation. In the future, we will evaluate and improve the system on the first Turkish learner corpus.

ERRANT-TR will also help learners and teachers by being used as a semi-automatic annotation toolkit while annotating erroneous-correct sentence pairs and reduce the time required to create parallel corpora drastically.

Limitations

The used morphological analyzer does not provide morpheme and POS tag lists compatible with Universal Postags (de Marneffe et al., 2021). Therefore, there might be issues with adapting this work in other languages while using the system as is.

Although the computational power requirements for the system are low, it does not work well with parallel computing. Thus a large amount of data might take long time to be processed.

Lastly, the proposed classifier system has been developed and evaluated with publicly available, limited samples from academic studies in linguistics. The data does not represent real world scenarios well enough. Therefore, we will test the system on real data only after the first Turkish learner corpus (which is mentioned at the end of the Section 5) is available.

References

Ahmet Afsin Akın and Mehmet Dündar Akın. 2007. Zemberek, an open source NLP framework for Turkic languages. *Structure*, 10(2007):1–5.

Esra Altintop. 2018. Yabancı dil olarak Türkçe öğrenen öğrencilerin kompozisyonlarındaki ek yanlışları ve nedenleri.

Ugurcan Arikan, Onur Gungor, and Suzan Uskudarli. 2019. Detecting clitics related orthographic errors in Turkish. In *Proceedings of the International Conference on Recent Advances in Natural Language Processing (RANLP 2019)*, pages 71–76, Varna, Bulgaria. INCOMA Ltd.

B. Erdem Dağıstanlıoğlu Başak Karakoç Öztürk. 2017. Yabancı dil olarak Türkçe öğrenen öğrencilerin yazdıkları öyküleyici metinlerdeki yazım sorunları: Bir hata analizi örneği. *Uluslararası 2. Sosyal Bilimler Sempozyumu (Asos Congress).*

Adriane Boyd. 2018. Using Wikipedia edits in low resource grammatical error correction. In *Proceedings of the 2018 EMNLP Workshop W-NUT: The 4th Workshop on Noisy User-generated Text*, pages 79–84, Brussels, Belgium. Association for Computational Linguistics.

Christopher Bryant, Mariano Felice, Øistein E. Andersen, and Ted Briscoe. 2019. The BEA-2019 shared task on grammatical error correction. In *Proceedings of the Fourteenth Workshop on Innovative Use of NLP for Building Educational Applications*, pages 52–75, Florence, Italy. Association for Computational Linguistics.

Christopher Bryant, Mariano Felice, and Ted Briscoe. 2017. Automatic annotation and evaluation of error types for grammatical error correction. In *Proceedings of the 55th Annual Meeting of the Association for Computational Linguistics (Volume 1: Long Papers)*, pages 793–805, Vancouver, Canada. Association for Computational Linguistics.

Christopher Bryant, Zheng Yuan, Muhammad Reza Qorib, Hannan Cao, Hwee Tou Ng, and Ted Briscoe. 2022. Grammatical error correction: A survey of the state of the art. *arXiv preprint arXiv:2211.05166*.

Aslı Çelik. 2019. İkinci/yabancı dil olarak Türkçe öğrenenlerin sözel hatalarına ilişkin öğretici tercihleri ve tutumları.

Jhih-Jie Chen, Yi-Dong Wu, Yu-Chuan Tai, Ching-Yu Yang, Hai-Lun Tu, and Jason S. Chang. 2019. Extracting grammatical error corrections from wikipedia revision history. In *2019 IEEE International Conference on Big Data (Big Data)*, pages 6016–6018.

Daniel Dahlmeier and Hwee Tou Ng. 2012. Better evaluation for grammatical error correction. In *Proceedings of the 2012 Conference of the North American Chapter of the Association for Computational Linguistics: Human Language Technologies*, pages 568–572, Montréal, Canada. Association for Computational Linguistics.

Daniel Dahlmeier, Hwee Tou Ng, and Siew Mei Wu. 2013. Building a large annotated corpus of learner English: The NUS corpus of learner English. In *Proceedings of the Eighth Workshop on Innovative Use of NLP for Building Educational Applications*, pages 22–31, Atlanta, Georgia. Association for Computational Linguistics.

Sam Davidson, Aaron Yamada, Paloma Fernandez Mira, Agustina Carando, Claudia H. Sanchez Gutierrez, and Kenji Sagae. 2020. Developing NLP tools with a new corpus of learner Spanish. In *Proceedings of the Twelfth Language Resources and Evaluation Conference*, pages 7238–7243, Marseille, France. European Language Resources Association.

Marie-Catherine de Marneffe, Christopher D. Manning, Joakim Nivre, and Daniel Zeman. 2021. Universal Dependencies. *Computational Linguistics*, 47(2):255–308.

Merve Dizeli and Zeynep Zeliha Sonkaya. 2021. Birinci ve ikinci yabancı dil olarak Türkçe öğrenen öğrencilerin yaptıkları dilbilimsel hatalar. *Türkiye Sosyal Araştırmalar Dergisi*, 25(1):225 – 234.

Gülşen Eryiğit and Dilara Torunoğlu-Selamet. 2017. Social media text normalization for Turkish. *Natural Language Engineering*, 23:1–41.

Mariano Felice, Christopher Bryant, and Ted Briscoe. 2016. Automatic extraction of learner errors in ESL sentences using linguistically enhanced alignments. In *Proceedings of COLING 2016, the 26th International Conference on Computational Linguistics: Technical Papers*, pages 825–835, Osaka, Japan. The COLING 2016 Organizing Committee.

Mehmet Fidan. 2019. Türkçe öğrenen yabancı öğrencilerin yazılı anlatım metinlerinin yazım ve noktalama kuralları yönünden değerlendirilmesi. *EKEV Akademi Dergisi*, 0(77):253 – 266.

Aslı Göksel and Celia Kerslake. 2004. *Turkish: A comprehensive grammar.* Routledge.

Jeff Good and CL Alan. 1999. Affix-placement variation in Turkish. In *Annual Meeting of the Berkeley Linguistics Society*, volume 25, pages 63–74.

Roman Grundkiewicz and Marcin Junczys-Dowmunt. 2014. The wiked error corpus: A corpus of corrective wikipedia edits and its application to grammatical error correction. In *Advances in Natural Language Processing*, pages 478–490, Cham. Springer International Publishing.

Roman Grundkiewicz, Marcin Junczys-Dowmunt, and Kenneth Heafield. 2019. Neural grammatical error correction systems with unsupervised pre-training on synthetic data. In *Proceedings of the Fourteenth Workshop on Innovative Use of NLP for Building Educational Applications*, pages 252–263, Florence, Italy. Association for Computational Linguistics.

Masahiro Kaneko, Masato Mita, Shun Kiyono, Jun Suzuki, and Kentaro Inui. 2020. Encoder-decoder models can benefit from pre-trained masked language models in grammatical error correction. In *Proceedings of the 58th Annual Meeting of the Association for Computational Linguistics*, pages 4248–4254, Online. Association for Computational Linguistics.

Anisia Katinskaia, Maria Lebedeva, Jue Hou, and Roman Yangarber. 2022. Semi-automatically annotated learner corpus for Russian. In *Proceedings of the Thirteenth Language Resources and Evaluation Conference*, pages 832–839, Marseille, France. European Language Resources Association.

Shun Kiyono, Jun Suzuki, Masato Mita, Tomoya Mizumoto, and Kentaro Inui. 2019. An empirical study of incorporating pseudo data into grammatical error correction. In *Proceedings of the 2019 Conference on Empirical Methods in Natural Language Processing and the 9th International Joint Conference on Natural Language Processing (EMNLP-IJCNLP)*, pages 1236–1242, Hong Kong, China. Association for Computational Linguistics.

Katerina Korre, Marita Chatzipanagiotou, and John Pavlopoulos. 2021. ELERRANT: Automatic grammatical error type classification for Greek. In *Proceedings of the International Conference on Recent Advances in Natural Language Processing (RANLP 2021)*, pages 708–717, Held Online. INCOMA Ltd.

Berker Kurt. 2020. Yabancı dil olarak Türkçe öğrenenlerin konuşmada yaptıkları dilsel hatalar ve iletişim stratejileri üzerine fenomenolojik bir çalışma. *International Journal of Languages Education*, 8.1:51–70.

Jared Lichtarge, Chris Alberti, Shankar Kumar, Noam Shazeer, Niki Parmar, and Simon Tong. 2019. Corpora generation for grammatical error correction. In *Proceedings of the 2019 Conference of the North American Chapter of the Association for Computational Linguistics: Human Language Technologies, Volume 1 (Long and Short Papers)*, pages 3291–3301, Minneapolis, Minnesota. Association for Computational Linguistics.

Diane Nicholls. 2003. The cambridge learner corpus: Error coding and analysis for lexicography and ELT. In *Proceedings of the Corpus Linguistics 2003 conference*, volume 16, pages 572–581.

Jakub Náplava, Milan Straka, Jana Straková, and Alexandr Rosen. 2022. Czech Grammar Error Correction with a Large and Diverse Corpus. *Transactions of the Association for Computational Linguistics*, 10:452–467.

Kostiantyn Omelianchuk, Vitaliy Atrasevych, Artem Chernodub, and Oleksandr Skurzhanskyi. 2020. GECToR – grammatical error correction: Tag, not rewrite. In *Proceedings of the Fifteenth Workshop on Innovative Use of NLP for Building Educational Applications*, pages 163–170, Seattle, WA, USA → Online. Association for Computational Linguistics.

Sascha Rothe, Jonathan Mallinson, Eric Malmi, Sebastian Krause, and Aliaksei Severyn. 2021. A simple recipe for multilingual grammatical error correction. In *Proceedings of the 59th Annual Meeting of the Association for Computational Linguistics and the 11th International Joint Conference on Natural Language Processing (Volume 2: Short Papers)*, pages 702–707, Online. Association for Computational Linguistics.

Esin Yağmur Şahin. 2013. Yabancı dil olarak Türkçe öğrenen öğrencilerin yazılı anlatımlarındaki ek yanlışları. *Tarih Okulu Dergisi*, 2013(XV).

Yu Wang, Yuelin Wang, Jie Liu, and Zhuo Liu. 2020. A comprehensive survey of grammar error correction. *arXiv preprint arXiv:2005.06600*.

Soyoung Yoon, Sungjoon Park, Gyuwan Kim, Junhee Cho, Kihyo Park, Gyu Tae Kim, Minjoon Seo, and Alice Oh. 2022. Towards standardizing Korean grammatical error correction: Datasets and annotation.

Wei Zhao, Liang Wang, Kewei Shen, Ruoyu Jia, and Jingming Liu. 2019. Improving grammatical error correction via pre-training a copy-augmented architecture with unlabeled data. In *Proceedings of the 2019 Conference of the North American Chapter of the Association for Computational Linguistics: Human Language Technologies, Volume 1 (Long and Short Papers)*, pages 156–165, Minneapolis, Minnesota. Association for Computational Linguistics.

Latif İltar. 2021. Türkçeyi yabancı dil olarak öğrenenlerin C1 yazma sınavındaki dil bilgisi hatalarının düzeylere göre dağılımı. *Bayburt Eğitim Fakültesi Dergisi*, 16(Özel Sayı):129 – 147.

Theoretical Conditions and Empirical Failure of Bracket Counting on Long Sequences with Linear Recurrent Networks

Nadine El-Naggar **Pranava Madhyastha** **Tillman Weyde**
City, University of London
United Kingdom
{nadine.el-naggar,pranava.madhyastha,t.e.weyde}@city.ac.uk

Abstract

Previous work has established that RNNs with an unbounded activation function have the capacity to count exactly. However, it has also been shown that RNNs are challenging to train effectively and generally do not learn exact counting behaviour. In this paper, we focus on this problem by studying the simplest possible RNN, a linear single-cell network. We conduct a theoretical analysis of linear RNNs and identify conditions for the models to exhibit *exact* counting behaviour. We provide a formal proof that these conditions are necessary and sufficient. We also conduct an empirical analysis using tasks involving a Dyck-1-like Balanced Bracket language under two different settings. We observe that linear RNNs generally do not meet the necessary and sufficient conditions for counting behaviour when trained with the standard approach. We investigate how varying the length of training sequences and utilising different target classes impacts model behaviour during training and the ability of linear RNN models to effectively approximate the indicator conditions.

1 Introduction

Recurrent Neural Networks (RNNs) have a long history of being used to solve a wide range of tasks involving sequential data. They were the most common choice for natural language processing, but have since been largely replaced by transformers in recent years. However, there has been a recent resurgence of interest in the theoretical aspects of RNNs, as seen in studies such as Merrill et al. (2020). Another study found that RNNs with squashing and non-squashing (i.e. unbounded) activation functions exhibit qualitative differences in their counting abilities (Weiss et al., 2018). This, along with the findings of El-Naggar et al. (2022), suggests that even RNNs with unbounded activation functions struggle to learn accurate counting on very long sequences. It is therefore crucial to understand why RNNs, despite having the capacity, often fail to accurately count in practice.

In this study, we examine the behaviour of the simplest form of RNNs: a linear single-cell RNN. Our goals are to: a) theoretically identify the necessary conditions for a linear RNN to have the ability to count, and b) explore how these conditions relate to the empirical behaviour of trained linear RNN models. The primary contributions of this paper are: a) we identify two conditions that indicate counting behaviour in linear RNNs; b) we prove that these indicator conditions are necessary and sufficient for exact counting behaviour to be achieved in linear RNNs; c) we then show empirically that linear RNNs generally do not learn exact counting and do not meet the indicator conditions; and finally, d) we show empirical relationships between the length of the training sequences and the indicator value distributions.

2 Related Work

The success of deep learning sparked a renewed interest in research into the understanding of the theoretical properties of neural networks. It has been known for long that RNNs are Turing-complete (Siegelmann and Sontag, 1992). However, Weiss et al. (2018) showed that there are different classes of RNN architectures with respect to counting capacity when using finite precision states. The relationship between RNNs and automata and formal languages has been investigated by Merrill (2019) and a formal hierarchy of counter machines has been developed by Merrill et al. (2020). This analysis is often based on "saturating" the network, i.e. replacing sigmoids with step functions, so that neural activations become binary, allowing for simpler analysis.

In practice however, activations in neural networks use a wide variety of values and systematic behaviour like counting or even parsing is often not observed, which has been discussed for

Proceedings of the 17th Conference of the European Chapter of the Association for Computational Linguistics: Student Research Workshop, pages 143–148
May 2-4, 2023

over 30 years since Fodor and Pylyshyn (1988). More recently, Lake and Baroni (2017) identified a specific lack of systematic behaviour and devised SCAN, a synthetic language processing task that standard RNNs fail on. A traditional approach for processing the hierarchical structure of language is to use a stack and a number of neural stack versions have been introduced, such as those by Joulin and Mikolov (2015), Grefenstette et al. (2015) and Chen et al. (2020), which performed well on SCAN. Suzgun et al. (2019b) use stack-augmented RNNs to learn Dyck-2 languages. Mali et al. (2021) developed methods to achieve more stable behaviour of neural stacks, achieving good, but not perfect, performance on longer sequences up to 160 tokens.

The generalisation of formal language tasks to very long sequences is not often addressed, as it requires an exact or near exact behaviour of the neural network in order avoid accumulation of errors, e.g. when counting. Suzgun et al. (2019a) claims that LSTMs can learn to count, but did not test for sequences of length greater than 100. Weiss et al. (2018) reported that ReLU RNNs, which were generally hard to train, and even LSTMs which are easier to train on counting tasks, did fail for sequences of several hundred tokens. Similarly, in our previous work (El-Naggar et al., 2022) we show that almost all ReLU RNNs and LSTMs fail on sequences of length 1000.

These studies generally indicate that RNNs do not reach a configuration that enables exact counting. It is not clear what the general conditions are for an RNN to perform exact counting, which is necessary for developing a deeper understanding of the behaviour of RNNs. We start to address this question here by studying the case of a linear single-cell RNN.

3 Counting Behaviour in Linear RNNs

In this section we formally define the Balanced Bracket Language, Balanced Bracket Counter and Linear Recurrent Network and we identify conditions for the network weights that indicate that the Linear Recurrent Network will behave as a Balanced Bracket Counter. We base our counter definitions on the General Counter Machine (GCM) as defined by Merrill (2020), which we also listed for convenience in Appendix A.

The GCM is defined by a vocabulary Σ, finite set of states Q, initial state q_0, counter update function u, state update function δ, and acceptance mask F. Some components, such as states, can be empty. The counter computation also uses a zero check function. An input string x is processed by the counter one token x_t at a time. The counter update function u is used to update the counter value **c** with integer increments $(+m)$. The counter updates are dependent on the current input token, the current state, and a finite mask of the current state. In our setting, a counter machine is said to accept a sequence if $\mathbf{c} = 0$ after the whole sequence is has been processed. A counter machine M is said to accept a language L if M accepts $s \iff s \in L$.

We focus on sequences consisting of one type of bracket: $\Sigma = \{$'(', ')'$\}$.

Definition 1. (Balanced Bracket Language BB) The Balanced Bracket Language BB is defined as

$$BB = \{s \in \Sigma^* | \text{ count(`(', } s) = \text{count( `)', } s)\}.$$

The order of the opening and closing brackets does not matter for the BB language, only that the number of opening and closing brackets in a sequence is equal overall. Dyck-1 sequences are a special case of BB sequences where the number of closing brackets is never greater than the number of opening brackets at any point in the sequence, i.e. for all prefixes.

Our focus is on the counting abilities of single-cell linear RNNs. These networks do not have the capacity to accept Dyck-1 sequences from the universe of all possible sequences, because they would need to treat negative counts differently from positive activations to distinguish correctly ordered from incorrectly ordered bracket sequences. However, that is not possible with a single linear neuron, and additional mechanisms would be needed to fully accept a Dyck-1 language from the entire universe of possible sequences.

Previous work, such as Suzgun et al. (2019a), who train their single-cell RNN models to learn Dyck-1 languages only use valid Dyck-1 sequences in their datasets, where there are never any excess closing brackets at any point in the sequences. This seems unnecessarily limiting, however. Therefore, we use the BB language which can be fully accepted using a single-cell linear RNN.

Definition 2. (Balanced Bracket Counter) A General Counter Machine is a Balanced Bracket Counter iff it accepts BB.

Definition 3. (Linear Recurrent Network) A Linear Recurrent Network (LRN) is a network which receives an input x_t at every timestep t, which is used along with the activation from the previous timestep h_{t-1} and weights W, U, and W_b to produce activation h_t, which is then passed on to the next timestep with the update function:

$$h_t = Wx_t + Uh_{t-1} + W_b.$$

Here, x_t is a one-hot-encoded input token, an LRN is similar to a stateless counter machine if we apply a zero check z function to h_t after processing the last input. A counter based on the LRN deviates from the definition by Merrill (2020) in that:

- The counter value **c** corresponds to h_t (it is the only value that propagates from one time step to the next), which is real instead of integer,
- The results of the update function ($+m$ in the Counter Machine) are real numbers, specifically:

$$a = Wx_t + W_b \text{ if } x_t = \text{'('} \text{ , and}$$
$$b = Wx_t + W_b \text{ if } x_t = \text{')'} \text{ .}$$

We use a single-cell LRN for bracket counting. As a result, W is a vector of the same dimensionality as x_t and U and W_b are scalars, as well as m, **c**, and h_t.

In Theorem 1, we relate Balanced Bracket Counter behaviour of a LRN to specific conditions on its *weights*. We define two indicator conditions and show that they are necessary and sufficient for exact counting behaviour to be achieved in a LRN.

Theorem 1. (Linear RNN Counting Indicators) The following two indicator conditions are necessary and sufficient for a Linear Recurrent Network to accept the Balanced Bracket Language BB.

1. $\frac{a}{b} = -1$ (AB ratio)
2. $U = 1$ (recurrent weight).

Proof 1. We prove that the counting indicator conditions in Theorem 1 are necessary and sufficient to accept the Balanced Bracket Language with a Linear Recurrent Network. We first prove that the conditions are necessary (Part 1) and then that they are sufficient (Part 2).

Part 1: We prove that the counting indicator conditions in Theorem 1 are satisfied if a Linear Recurrent Network accepts the Balanced Bracket Language by using different input sequences (Table 1), from which we derive the indicator conditions. If a Linear Recurrent Network accepts the Balanced Bracket Language, then equal numbers of opening and closing brackets result in an output activation $h_t = 0$, otherwise, $h_t \neq 0$. This is equivalent to zero check function $z(h_t)$ yielding 0 or 1. Therefore, we will not include the zero-check function in the following derivation.

Case	Input	Output (h)	Findings
1	'('	$h_1 \neq 0$	$a \neq 0$
2	')'	$h_1 \neq 0$	$b \neq 0$
3	'()'	$h_2 = 0$	$b = -Ua$ and $U \neq 0$
4	'(('	$h_2 \neq 0$	$U \neq -1$
5	'(())'	$h_4 = 0$	$b + Ub + U^2a + U^3a = 0$
6	'()()'	$h_4 = 0$	$b + Ua + U^2b + U^3a = 0$

Table 1: Input sequences used to derive the indicator conditions from Theorem 1.

Case 1: $seq =$'(', $h_0 = 0, h_1 \neq 0$
$h_1 = a + Uh_0 = a$
$\therefore a \neq 0$

Case 2: $seq =$')', $h_0 = 0, h_1 \neq 0$
$h_1 = b + Uh_0 = b$
$\therefore b \neq 0$

Case 3: $seq =$ '()', $h_2 = 0$
$h_2 = b + Ua$
$b + Ua = 0$
From cases 1,2: $a \neq 0$ and $b \neq 0$
$\therefore b = -Ua$, and $U \neq 0$

Case 4: $seq =$'((', $h_2 \neq 0$
$h_2 = a + Ua$
$a + Ua \neq 0$
$\therefore U \neq -1$

Case 5: $seq =$'(())', $h_4 = 0$
$h_3 = b + Uh_2 = b + U(a + Ua)$
$h_4 = b + Uh_3 = b + U(b + U(a + Ua))$
$\therefore h_4 = b + Ub + U^2a + U^3a = 0$

Case 6: $seq =$'()()', $h_4 = 0$
$h_3 = a + Uh_2 = a + U(b + Ua)$
$h_4 = b + Uh_3 = b + U(a + U(b + Ua))$
$\therefore h_4 = b + Ua + U^2b + U^3a = 0$

Combine the findings from cases 5 and 6.
$b + Ub + U^2a + U^3a = b + Ua + U^2b + U^3a$

Subtract $b + U^3a$ from both sides and divide both sides by U
$b + Ua = a + Ub$

Rearrange and factorise
$b - a = U(b - a)$

As a result, we get 2 possible situations:

(a) $U = 1$, which implies $a = -b$ by case 3

(b) $a = b$, where by cases 1 and 2 we know $a \neq 0$ and $b \neq 0$, and $U = -1$ follows from case 3, which contradicts case 4

$\therefore U = 1$ and $a = -b$, i.e., the counter indicator conditions listed in Theorem 1 hold, if a Linear Recurrent Network accepts the Balanced Bracket Language.

Part 2: We prove by induction that if the counting indicator conditions listed in Theorem 1 hold, a Linear Recurrent Network accepts the Balanced Bracket Language.

Each sequence consists of n opening brackets and m closing brackets, and the input token x_k is either '(' or ')'.

Base Case: $k = 1$

- $x_1 =$'(', $n = 1$ and $m = 0$:
  $h_1 = a + Uh_0$
  $h_1 = a$
- $x_1 =$')', $n = 0$ and $m = 1$:
  $h_1 = -a + Uh_0$
  $h_1 = -a$

For n opening and m closing brackets, the following equation satisfies the base case, and is therefore our induction hypothesis:

$$h_k = (n - m) \times a$$

We assume that this is true for sequences of length k consisting of n opening brackets and m closing brackets. We prove by induction that if this holds for sequences of length k tokens, it holds for sequences of length $k + 1$ tokens. In our induction step, we use once $x_{k+1} =$'(' and once $x_{k+1} =$')'.

Induction Step:

- If $x_{k+1} =$'(':
  $h_{k+1} = ((n + 1) - m) \times a$
- If $x_{k+1} =$')':
  $h_{k+1} = (n - (m + 1)) \times a$

From the premise, we can derive that:
$h_k = a+Uh_{k-1}$ if $x_k =$'(', and $h_k = -a+Uh_{k-1}$ if $x_k =$')'

- If $x_{k+1} =$'(':
  $h_{k+1} = a + h_k$
  Substitute $h_k = (n - m) \times a$
  $h_{k+1} = a + ((n - m) \times a)$
  $\therefore h_{k+1} = ((n + 1) - m) \times a$
- If $x_{k+1} =$')':
  $h_{k+1} = -a + h_k$
  Substitute $h_k = (n - m) \times a$
  $h_{k+1} = -a + ((n - m) \times a)$
  $\therefore h_{k+1} = (n - (m + 1)) \times a$

Therefore, we prove that if the counting indicator conditions listed in Theorem 1 are satisfied in a Linear Recurrent Network, it accepts the Balanced Bracket Language. □

4 Counting in Linear RNNs in Practice

We conduct experiments to analyse the models and whether or not they satisfy the conditions defined in the previous section in training. We use 2 classification tasks to evaluate our models.

4.1 Task 1: Binary Classification

We use the same task and model as in our previous work (El-Naggar et al., 2022), i.e., a linear RNN without biases with a single output neuron with sigmoid activation to classify the bracket difference of the sequence as > 0 or ≤ 0 (binary). The absence of a trainable bias reduces the degrees of freedom in the model, and is equivalent to having a bias (W_b) value that is fixed to 0, hence simplifying the learning task. We also use the same models with trainable biases. The models are trained with sequences of lengths 2, 4 and 8 tokens for 100 epochs in 10 runs. The initial count value (h_0) has a value of 0 for every sequence. We inspect the weights of our models and plot the distribution of the indicator values (a/b,U) of the trained models for each training set size in Figure 1. We observe that the models do not fulfill the indicator conditions, but they do approach the conditions as the length of the training sequences increases. We observe that the distributions of the a/b indicator have mean values above -1 but less so for longer training sequences.

4.2 Task 2: Ternary Classification

We also apply a ternary classification: > 0, $= 0$ or < 0. We use the same model as in Task 1, except that instead of a single output neuron with a sigmoid output activation, we use 3 output neurons and a softmax output layer with bias, which is the minimal configuration that can achieve this task. We also use the same models with trainable biases.

The initial count value (h_0) has a value of 0 for every sequence and the models are trained in the same manner as the models from Task 1. The ternary classification accuracy is slightly lower as

Classification Experiment	Train Length	Train Avg(Min/Max)	20 Tokens Avg(Min/Max)	50 Tokens Avg(Min/Max)
Binary (without bias)	2	100 (100/100)	69.2 (6.04/77.3)	69.0 (66.7/72.7)
Binary (without bias)	4	100 (100/100)	94.8 (94.7/95.3)	89.3 (88.7/90.0)
Binary (without bias)	8	100 (100/100)	96.9 (94.0/100)	92.7 (78.7/98.0)
Ternary (without bias)	2	90 (33.3/100)	55.6 (33.3/64.4)	51.4 (33.3/60.0)
Ternary (without bias)	4	100 (100/100)	79.5 (65.8/94.7)	67.2 (66.7/68.0)
Ternary (without bias)	8	100 (100/100)	94.4 (67.1/100)	85.7 (66.7/100)
Binary (with bias)	2	100 (100/100)	73.4 (63.3/100)	72.4 (60.0/93.3)
Binary (with bias)	4	100 (100/100)	95.3 (92.7/98.0)	86.0 (77.3/90.7)
Binary (with bias)	8	100 (100/100)	95.2 (85.3/100)	87.9 (70.0/98.0)
Ternary (with bias)	2	88.3 (66.7/100)	58.0 (38.2/67.6)	54.4 (43.6/67.5)
Ternary (with bias)	4	97.9 (79.2/100)	81.5 (64.4/100)	68.0 (65.3/73.3)
Ternary (with bias)	8	100 (100/100)	95.9 (83.6/100)	76.5 (65.3/100)

Table 2: Accuracy metrics of our previous binary classification experiments without bias (El-Naggar et al., 2022), ternary classification experiments without bias, and binary and ternary classification experiments with bias.

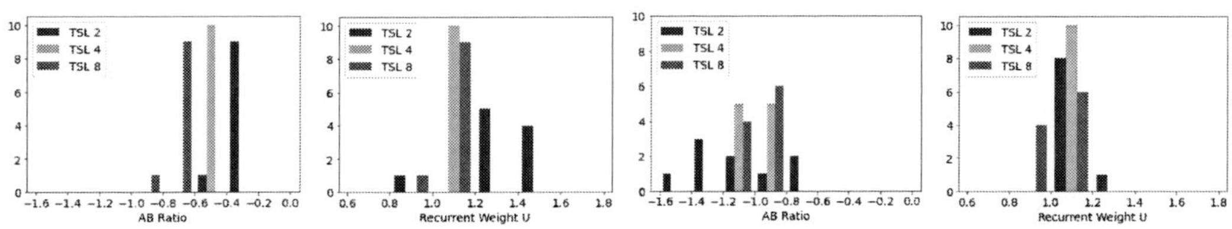

(a) AB ratio binary (no bias) (b) U value binary (no bias) (c) AB ratio ternary (no bias) (d) U value ternary (no bias)

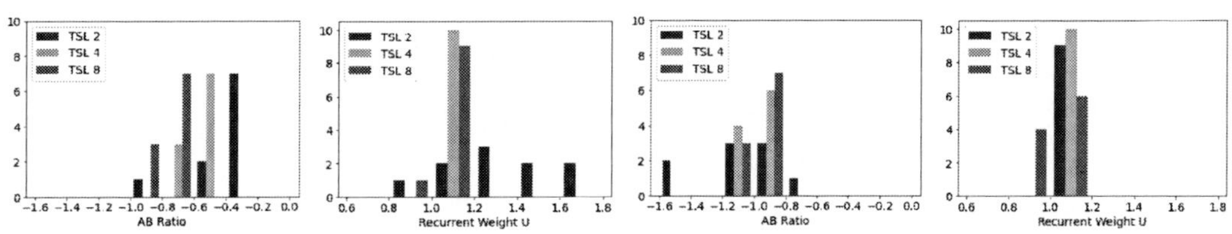

(e) AB ratio binary (bias) (f) U value binary (bias) (g) AB ratio ternary (bias) (h) U value ternary (bias)

Figure 1: Indicators after training on binary and ternary classification without biases (top) and with biases (bottom) with different Training Sequence Lengths (TSL).

can be expected with more classes. For shorter training sequences, this may be related to the larger number of model parameters relative to the data points. The accuracy improves with longer training sequences. Ternary classification does not show a mean of a/b above -1 as can be seen in Figure 1.

5 Conclusions and Future Work

Although linear RNNs have the theoretical capacity for counting behaviour, previous research has shown that these models often struggle to effectively generalise counting behaviour to long sequences. In this study, we present a set of necessary and sufficient conditions that indicate counting behaviour in linear RNNs and provide proof that meeting these conditions is equivalent to counting behaviour. To investigate the extent to which these conditions are met, we examine the parameters of models trained on sequences of varying lengths for classification tasks. We use both binary and ternary classification tasks and find that the models do not fully meet these conditions, but do approach them and get closer as the sequence length increases.

There are several potential areas for future work based on these findings. One possible research direction is to extend this approach to ReLU RNNs, and LSTMs as far as possible. Another option is to devise methods to ensure that the indicator conditions we have identified are met during training in order to improve the generalisation abilities of our models.

References

Xinyun Chen, Chen Liang, Adams Wei Yu, Dawn Song, and Denny Zhou. 2020. Compositional generalization via neural-symbolic stack machines. *arXiv preprint arXiv:2008.06662*.

Nadine El-Naggar, Pranava Madhyastha, and Tillman Weyde. 2022. Experiments in learning dyck-1 languages with recurrent neural networks. In *Proceedings of the 3rd Human-Like Computing Workshop (HLC 2022) co-located with the 2nd International Joint Conference on Learning and Reasoning (IJCLR 2022), Windsor, United Kingdom, September 28-30th, 2022*, volume 3227 of *CEUR Workshop Proceedings*, pages 24–28. CEUR-WS.org.

Nadine El-Naggar, Pranava Madhyastha, and Tillman Weyde. 2022. Exploring the long-term generalization of counting behavior in rnns. In *I Can't Believe It's Not Better Workshop: Understanding Deep Learning Through Empirical Falsification*.

Jerry A Fodor and Zenon W Pylyshyn. 1988. Connectionism and cognitive architecture: A critical analysis. *Cognition*, 28(1-2):3–71.

Edward Grefenstette, Karl Moritz Hermann, Mustafa Suleyman, and Phil Blunsom. 2015. Learning to transduce with unbounded memory. In *Advances in neural information processing systems*, pages 1828–1836.

Armand Joulin and Tomas Mikolov. 2015. Inferring algorithmic patterns with stack-augmented recurrent nets. *Advances in neural information processing systems*, 28.

Brenden M Lake and Marco Baroni. 2017. Generalization without systematicity: On the compositional skills of sequence-to-sequence recurrent networks. *arXiv preprint arXiv:1711.00350*.

Ankur Mali, Alexander Ororbia, Daniel Kifer, and Lee Giles. 2021. Investigating backpropagation alternatives when learning to dynamically count with recurrent neural networks. In *International Conference on Grammatical Inference*, pages 154–175. PMLR.

William Merrill. 2019. Sequential neural networks as automata. In *Proceedings of the Workshop on Deep Learning and Formal Languages: Building Bridges*, pages 1–13.

William Merrill. 2020. On the linguistic capacity of real-time counter automata. *CoRR*, abs/2004.06866.

William Merrill, Gail Weiss, Yoav Goldberg, Roy Schwartz, Noah A Smith, and Eran Yahav. 2020. A formal hierarchy of rnn architectures. In *Proceedings of the 58th Annual Meeting of the Association for Computational Linguistics*, pages 443–459.

Hava T. Siegelmann and Eduardo D. Sontag. 1992. On the computational power of neural nets. In *Proceedings of the Fifth Annual Workshop on Computational Learning Theory*, COLT '92, page 440–449, New York, NY, USA. Association for Computing Machinery.

Mirac Suzgun, Sebastian Gehrmann, Yonatan Belinkov, and Stuart M Shieber. 2019a. Lstm networks can perform dynamic counting. *arXiv preprint arXiv:1906.03648*.

Mirac Suzgun, Sebastian Gehrmann, Yonatan Belinkov, and Stuart M Shieber. 2019b. Memory-augmented recurrent neural networks can learn generalized dyck languages. *arXiv preprint arXiv:1911.03329*.

Gail Weiss, Yoav Goldberg, and Eran Yahav. 2018. On the practical computational power of finite precision rnns for language recognition. In *Proceedings of the 56th Annual Meeting of the Association for Computational Linguistics, ACL 2018, Melbourne, Australia, July 15-20, 2018, Volume 2: Short Papers*, pages 740–745. Association for Computational Linguistics.

A General Counter Machine

This definition is from Merrill (2020).

Definition 4. (General Counter Machine) A k-Counter is a tuple $\langle \Sigma, Q, q_0, u, \delta, F \rangle$ with:

1. A finite alphabet Σ
2. A finite set of states Q
3. An initial state q_0
4. A counter update function
$$u : \Sigma \times Q \times \{0,1\}^k \to (\{+m : m \in \mathbb{Z}\} \cup \{\times 0\})^k$$
5. A state transition function
$$\delta : \Sigma \times Q \times \{0,1\}^k \to Q$$
6. An acceptance mask
$$F \subseteq Q \times \{0,1\}$$

The counter machine computation is formalised in Definition 5. The finite mask of the current state is created using a zero-check function $z(\mathbf{v})$ for a vector v, where:

$$z(\mathbf{v})_i = \begin{cases} 0, & \text{if } v_i = 0 \\ 1, & \text{otherwise} \end{cases} \quad (1)$$

Definition 5. (Counter Machine Computation) Let $\langle q, \mathbf{c} \rangle \in Q \times \mathbb{Z}^k$ be a configuration of machine M. Upon reading input $x_t \in \Sigma$, we define the transition

$$\langle q, \mathbf{c} \rangle \to_{x_t} \langle \delta(x_t, q, z(\mathbf{c})), u(x_t, q, z(\mathbf{c}))(\mathbf{c}) \rangle$$

Addressing Domain Changes in Task-oriented Conversational Agents through Dialogue Adaptation

Tiziano Labruna
Fondazione Bruno Kessler - Trento, Italy and Free University of Bozen-Bolzano, Italy
tlabruna@fbk.eu

Bernardo Magnini
Fondazione Bruno Kessler - Trento, Italy
magnini@fbk.eu

Abstract

Recent task-oriented dialogue systems are trained on annotated dialogues, which, in turn, reflect certain domain information (e.g., restaurants or hotels in a given region). However, when such domain knowledge changes (e.g., new restaurants open), the initial dialogue model may become obsolete, decreasing the overall performance of the system. Through a number of experiments, we show, for instance, that adding 50% of new slot-values reduces of about 55% the dialogue state-tracker performance. In light of such evidence, we suggest that automatic adaptation of training dialogues is a valuable option for re-training obsolete models. We experimented with a dialogue adaptation approach based on fine-tuning a generative language model on domain changes, showing that a significant reduction of performance decrease can be obtained.

1 Introduction

Most of the recent approaches in task-oriented dialogue systems (McTear, 2020) assume that each component is trained using annotated dialogues. Such data-driven approaches are common both for intent detection and slot filling (Louvan and Magnini, 2020a) and for dialogue state tracking (Balaraman and Magnini, 2021). In this paper, we deal with the situation where we have a conversational dataset, i.e., a collection of annotated dialogues for a certain domain (e.g., booking a restaurant), and then the domain changes (e.g., new restaurants open, or some restaurants change food or price). We investigate to what extent dialogue models trained on the initial dialogues are adequate for the occurred changes, and whether those dialogues can be automatically adapted to domain changes. Being able to manage domain changes is highly relevant for practical purposes, as the process of data collection (in the order of several thousand dialogues for a medium-size domain) for an application domain is both rather complex (e.g., Wizard of Oz (Kelley, 1984)) and very expensive. On the other side, automatic adaptation of training dialogues (Labruna and Magnini, 2021a,b) such that they reflect domain changes, is still a challenging research goal. In the paper, we first provide a definition for the domain changes we are interested in. Second, we set an experimental framework, including evaluation metrics, where we can simulate how the performance of current dialogue models is sensitive to different kinds and amounts of domain changes. Finally, a relevant contribution of the paper is the design and experimentation of unsupervised approaches for training dialogue models from synthetically adapted dialogues.

To be more concrete, Figure 1 presents an example of the situation we are addressing. On the left side we have an initial knowledge base (a) for the restaurant booking domain, and, below it, we show a reservation dialogue (c) between a user and a system. We assume that this dialogue has been human-generated (e.g., through Wizard of Oz) and that it is coherent with the content of the knowledge base. Then, we assume that the knowledge base changes (reported on the right side of Figure 1 (b)), as a new restaurant has opened offering a new kind of food, and one restaurant closed. According to these changes, the initial dialogue is no more consistent with the new domain.

Our intuition is that an adapted dialogue should preserve as much as possible the dialogic structure (e.g., user communicative goals, order of turns, conversation style) of the original dialogue, while it should be adapted to changes occurred in the domain knowledge. In principle, both the user requests and the system responses might be affected by domain changes. On one side the user might be (partially) aware of changes, and adapt its goals and requests (e.g., in Figure 1 the user might be aware of a new restaurant with Poke food, and ask about it). On the other side we assume that the system is fully aware of domain changes and that, in

Proceedings of the 17th Conference of the European Chapter of the Association for Computational Linguistics: Student Research Workshop, pages 149–158
May 2-4, 2023

Name	Food	Price	Area
Oak Bistro	British	moderate	centre
One Seven	British	expensive	centre
Fitxbillies	British	expensive	centre

(a) Original Knowledge Base

Name	Food	Price	Area
Poke House	Poke	cheap	centre
One Seven	British	expensive	centre
Fitxbillies	British	expensive	centre

(b) Adapted Knowledge Base

USER: I am seeking a restaurant that serves **British** food in the centre.
SYSTEM: I have **3** different options for you. Do you have a price range in mind?
USER: I 'd like a **moderately priced** one.
SYSTEM: **The Oak Bistro** matches your needs.

(c) Original Dialogue

USER: I am seeking a restaurant that serves **Poke** food in the centre.
SYSTEM: I have **one** option for you. Do you have a price range in mind?
USER: I 'd like a **cheap** one.
SYSTEM: **Poke House** matches your needs.

(d) Adapted Dialogue

Figure 1: Domain Dialogue Adaptation. (a) shows the initial situation of the KB, with 3 British restaurants in the center. In (b) the first instance is removed and a new instance is added. (c) is the original dialogue, consistent with the KB, and (d) is the adapted dialogue, according to the changes in the new KB.

order to provide correct information to the user, its responses have to be coherent with such changes. In this context, dialogue adaptations are well defined changes of an original dialogue that make the dialogue coherent with a new domain knowledge. Such adaptation include changing the name of a slot value (e.g., *Poke* in place of *British* in Figure 1), change number of instances (e.g., *one* in place of *3*), change name of instances (e.g., *Poke House* in place of *The Oak Bistro*). Overall, the structure of the initial dialogue has been as much as possible preserved, while modifications aim at reflecting the occurred changes and reconstructing consistency with the new domain.
Although the long-term perspective of our research is to fully automatize dialogue adaptation, the goal of this paper is limited to an investigation of the main issues behind it, following the research directions mentioned above. Particularly, we are interested in two aspects: first, assessing the impact of domain changes in current dialogue state tracking models; second taking advantage of the generative capacity of large pre-trained language models (e.g., (Chen et al., 2019) (Raffel et al., 2020) (Li et al., 2022)) to provide appropriate dialogue adaptations.

More specifically, Section 2 presents the relevant background on task-oriented dialogues, particularly on dialogue state tracking and dialogue manager. Sections 3.1 and 3.2 face domain changes due to, respectively, slot-value and instance alterations, showing their impact on dialogue models. Section 4 introduces dialogue adaptation, which is put into practice with some initial experiments presented in Section 5 and corresponding results, which are discussed in Section 6. Finally, Section 7 presents dialogue adaptation in the context of recent work in the field.

2 Background on Task-oriented Dialogues

This section provides background on task-oriented dialogues, with a focus on how domain knowledge is represented, data-driven approaches, dialogue state tracking and dialogue manager.

2.1 Domain Knowledge

According to most of the recent literature (Budzianowski et al., 2018; Bordes et al., 2017; Mrkšić et al., 2017), we consider a task-oriented dialogue between a system and a user as composed of a sequence of turns $\{t_1, t_2, ...t_n\}$. The goal of the dialogue system is to retrieve a set of entities (possibly empty) in a domain knowledge base (KB) that satisfy the user's needs. A domain ontology O provides a schema for the KB and typically represents entities (e.g., RESTAURANT, HOTEL, MOVIE) according to a pre-defined set of slots S (e.g., FOOD, AREA, PRICE, for the RESTAURANT domain), and values that a certain slot can assume (e.g., EXPENSIVE, MODERATE and CHEAP, for the slot PRICE).
On the basis of the entities defined in the domain ontology, the KB is then populated with instances of such entities. As in most of the literature, we distinguish *informable slots*, which the user can use to constraint the search (e.g., AREA), and *requestable slots* (e.g., PHONENUMBER), whose values are typ-

ically asked only when a certain entity has been retrieved through the dialogue. At each turn in the dialogue, both the user and the system may refer to facts in the KB, the user with the goal of retrieving entities matching his/her needs, and the system to propose entities that can help the user to achieve the dialogue goals.

2.2 Dialogue State Tracking

In a task-oriented system, the Dialogue State Tracker (DST) is responsible for maintaining a record of all information exchanged throughout the entire dialogue history, up to the current step. A dialogue state d_i for a turn t_i is typically represented as a set of slot and slot-value pairs, such as {PRICE=MODERATE, FOOD=ITALIAN}, meaning that at t_i the system assumes that the user is looking for an Italian restaurant with a moderate price. A common method for collecting task-oriented conversational data-sets is through the Wizard of Oz technique. This approach involves two individuals: one person plays the role of a user who asks for information on a particular topic, while the other person acts as a system and provides the requested information. After being collected through Wizard of Oz, the turns of each dialogue are annotated with the corresponding *dialogue state*, consisting of an intent and a set of slot and slot-value pairs. The following is an example of the annotation provided in MultiWOZ 2.1 (Budzianowski et al., 2018):

USER: I would like a moderately priced restaurant in the west part of town.
INFORM(PRICE=MODERATE, AREA=WEST)

SYSTEM: There are three moderately priced restaurants in the west part of town. Do you prefer Indian, Italian or British?
REQUEST(FOOD)

USER: Can I have the address and phone number of the Italian location?
INFORM(PRICE=MODERATE, AREA=WEST, FOOD=ITALIAN)
REQUEST(ADDRESS,PHONE-NUMBER)

Evaluating dialogue state tracking. The most common metric for dialogue state tracking is the Joint Goal Accuracy (JGA), which measures the proportion of correct dialogue states predictions at each dialogue turn. A prediction is considered correct if the slot-values v_i for all slots s_i in the dialogue turn are correctly predicted. Assuming that we have n slot-values in the utterance, the JGA for a single dialogue turn t can be defined as follows (Kumar et al., 2020):

$$JGA(t) = \mathbb{1}_{((\sum_{i=1}^{n} \mathbb{1}_{y_i=\hat{y}_i})=n)} \quad (1)$$

where y_i is the ground truth slot-value, $\hat{y}_i$ is the predicted slot-value and $\mathbb{1}_{x=y}$ is a variable that takes the value of 1 if $x = y$, 0 otherwise.

2.3 Dialogue Manager

Given a certain dialogue state, the goal of the Dialogue Manager (DM) component (Kwan et al., 2022; Liu and Lane, 2017) is to decide the best action to take next, which typically consists of an intent and a list of slot-value pairs. As an example, an output action for the DM can be RESTAURANT-INFORM (FOOD_TYPE=ITALIAN, AREA=CENTER), where the system decides to return a response message with intent RESTAURANT-INFORM and ITALIAN and CENTER as slot values for the slot names FOOD_TYPE and AREA. Then, a generation component will be in charge of actually generating responses, like *We have several Italian restaurants in the city centre.*

Evaluating dialogue manager. Dialogue manager is typically evaluated in terms of effectiveness of suggested dialogue actions to achieve the user's goals (Papangelis et al., 2012). Evaluation is carried out in a reinforcement learning setting with rewards, either through interactions with users or, more frequently, using a dialogue simulator (El Asri and Trischler, 2017). For the purposes of our investigation, we are not interested in measuring action effectiveness. Rather, we aim at estimating the impact of domain changes on the dialogue manager behaviour. According to this perspective, we evaluate the correctness of the system responses provided by the DM, given the dialogue history (i.e., the dialogue states). A response is judged as correct if the information it conveys is consistent with the current knowledge base of the dialogue system. For instance, in the example reported in Figure 1, the response *I have 3 different options for you.* is correct if in the knowledge base there are three restaurants that serve British food and they are located in the centre, otherwise, this response is considered as incorrect. We check the system's utterance correctness considering both the case where the system presents instances whose slot-values do not correspond in the KB, and cases where the number of instances in the response does not match with the KB. Accordingly, we define the dialogue manager correctness DMC as follows:

$$DMC = (\sum_{i=1}^{n} \mathbb{1}_{C(u_i)})/n \qquad (2)$$

where n is the total number of utterances in the dialogue, $\mathbb{1}_{\mathbb{x}}$ is equal to 1 if $\mathbb{x}$ is True, 0 otherwise. $C(u)$ is True if the utterance u is evaluated as correct with respect to the current KB, False if at least one of the domain information in the utterance is evaluated as incorrect with respect to the KB.

3 Domain Changes

In this section we define a number of domain changes that will be investigated in the paper.

3.1 Changing Slot-values

The first type of domain change is *slot-value change*. This occurs every time a slot-value v used to describe an existing instance in the initial knowledge base is changed with another slot-value (see Figure 1 for an example). This change may involve an already existing slot-value (e.g., a certain restaurant moved from INDIAN to PIZZA food, assuming that PIZZA was already used for other instances), or a new slot-value (e.g., moving from INDIAN to MEDITERRANEAN, which was never used before). An important side effect of slot-value changes is that they modify the distribution of slot-values through instances. For example, after some changes, it might be the case that the initial distribution (e.g., 30% INDIAN restaurants and 10% PIZZA restaurants) is significantly modified (e.g., 20% INDIAN and 20% PIZZA). This is relevant because we need to reflect the same distribution in the test dialogues. As it will be clarified in section 4, this is achieved by substituting occurrences of the initial slot-value (e.g., INDIAN) with occurrences of the new slot-value (e.g., PIZZA) till the domain distribution is reached.

3.2 Changing Instances

The second type of domain change is *changing instances*, where a new instance (e.g., a new restaurant) is added to the domain knowledge, or an existing instance is removed. Adding a new instance implies that the KB slot-value distribution varies, as it has been already noted in Section 3.1, and we assume that its impact follows a similar pattern. However, changing instances may also affect the system's responses, as the dialogue in Figure 1 illustrates. Here, in the initial dialogue, there are three restaurants in the KB that satisfy the user query (FOOD=BRITISH, AREA=CENTER), while in the new KB one restaurant has been removed, and therefore the same query would require a different response from the system. Particularly, assuming that such responses have to be consistent with the KB, the initial dialogue should be adapted so as to be consistent with instance changes.

4 Dialogue Adaptation

In this section, we provide a definition for the *dialogue adaptation* task, as well as its main features.

4.1 Task Definition

Dialogue adaptation consists in modifying a task-oriented dialogue D_0, collected for a certain knowledge base KB_0, with the goal of reflecting a modified knowledge base KB_1, where KB_0 and KB_1 share the same domain ontology O (i.e., they share domain entities and thier slots). The resulting dialogue D_1 is adapted to KB_1 if: (i) D_1 is still a coherent dialogue; (ii) D_1 is consistent with the domain KB_1. We distinguish between initial and adapted training dialogues (notated, respectively, with D_0_train and D_1_train), and initial and adapted test dialogues (D_0_test and D_1_test). Although our definition is neutral with respect to how D_0 is collected, we assume that D_0 are human-generated dialogues, and that the adapted D_1 should maintain the main characteristics of human-human dialogues. We will detail those requirements in the next sections.

4.2 Maintaining Dialogue Coherence

As a first requirement, dialogue adaptations need to maintain the internal coherence of a dialogue, meaning that if an entity is mentioned in a portion of a dialogue, then appropriate references have to be maintained in the rest of the dialogue. As an example of dialogue coherence, in Figure 1(c) the user is looking for *British* food in the *centre*, the system asks for the price range, and the user indicates *moderate* as his/her preference; finally, the system proposes a restaurant that is consistent to all the requests made throughout the dialogue. If the system proposed a *Poke* restaurant instead, the dialogue coherence would not have been maintained. An automatic adaptation procedure should preserve the coherence of all turns of the dialogue.

4.3 Preserve Domain Adherence

A second requirement for dialogue adaptation is the need to preserve consistency with domain knowledge. Here there are two aspects to consider: adaptation of the system's responses and adaptation of the user's queries. As for the system's responses, the assumption is that the system has complete knowledge of the domain, and adaptations are necessary so that the training dialogues contain responses based on correct information, this way allowing correct training of the DM component. As for user utterance adaptation, users may be partially aware of the domain, and of the changes that may have occurred (e.g., a new popular type of food is served in many restaurants). This means that the user goals may also change, and this fact has to be reflected through dialogue adaptation.

4.4 Maintaining Language Variability

Dialogue adaptations should preserve as much as possible the language variability of human-like dialogues. This is relevant both for maintaining the naturalness of dialogues and for favouring the robustness of the models that are trained. There are several aspects of language variability that need to be considered, including lexical variability, e.g., semantically related expressions, like synonyms, and syntactic variability, e.g., passive forms, or left dislocation. In terms of automatic adaptation procedures, rule-based adaptation (e.g., based on patterns) is likely to produce repetitive dialogues with low variability, while approaches based on generative language models may work better.

4.5 Respect Morpho-Syntactic Constraints

A quite obvious requirement is that adaptation should respect morpho-syntactic constraints of the language, such as the agreement for genre and number, and tense for verbs. As an example, in Figure 1, dialogue adaptation has involved changing the plural *options* into the singular *option*, to respect the agreement with, respectively, *three* and *one*.

5 Experiments

We now define an experimental framework for simulating domain changes in a conversational system. We have two main goals: (i) investigate the impact of the domain changes defined in section 3 on a model trained on D_0_train dialogues and tested on D_1_test adapted dialogues; (ii) simulate the use of a model trained on adapted D_1_train dialogues and tested on D_1_test adapted dialogues. For the first goal, we consider both a DST model (for slot-value changes) and a DM model (for instance changes), while for the second goal we carry on a comparison on a DST model.

5.1 General Experimental Setting

We assume the availability of a data-set of annotated training and test dialogues, mostly following the MultiWOZ (Budzianowski et al., 2018) style. We also assume that such dialogues reflect the information described in the knowledge base of the dialogue system (cfr. Section 2.1), in the sense that the system responses should be as much as possible coherent with the domain knowledge. The experiments presented in the paper are all carried out on MultiWOZ 2.3 (Eric et al., 2020). For all the experiments we consider four incremental amount of changes (25%, 50%, 75%, and 100%), randomly selected from the different domains (e.g., RESTAURANT, HOTEL, ATTRACTION) of the MultiWOZ 2.3 knowledge base, and from their slots (e.g., FOOD, PRICE, DESTINATION).

As for training DST models, we used two well-known approaches: TRADE and TripPy.

TRADE (Wu et al., 2019) consists of three components: an utterance encoder based on bidirectional GRU, responsible for transforming the utterance into a fixed-size vector; a slot gate, which determines whether a slot-value appears in the utterance; a state generator, which predicts the slot that is triggered by the dialogue. The model shares all parameters across multiple domains, being able to perform few-shot and zero-shot learning for the DST task.

TripPy (Heck et al., 2020) is a DST model based on a triple copy strategy that, in order to select the best slot-value for its predictions, performs the following operations: copying the value from user utterances, copying values from system utterances, inferring new values from values that are already present in the dialogue state. It involves BERT as the front-end context encoder and it is equipped with a slot gate for each domain-slot pair.

As for dialogue manager (DM), we employ

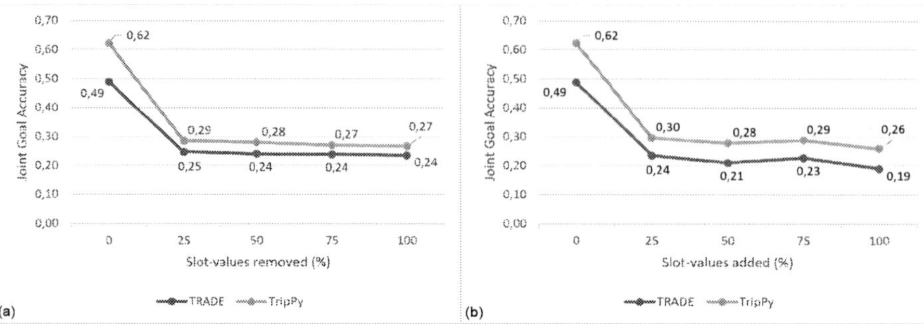

Figure 2: Impact on DST. TRADE and TripPy JGA when trained on D_0_train and tested on adapted D_1_test, with (a) increasing percentages of slot-values removed, and (b) increasing percentages of slot-values added.

a simple algorithm that, given the intent and the slot-values predicted for a user's message, queries the KB and returns the best action based on the query results (e.g. if no entities are found in the KB, it returns the action NO-RESULTS).

5.2 Impact of Slot-value Changes

In the following experiments a DST model is first trained on D_0_train dialogues, and then tested on adapted D_1_test dialogues, in order to assess the impact of slot-value changes. D_1_test dialogues for both Experiment1 and Experiment2 are automatically produced through a dialogue adaptation procedure based on a large pre-trained language model.

Dialogue adaptation procedure. We have adopted a dialogue adaptation strategy based on the method proposed in (Labruna and Magnini, 2022). There are three steps:

- (i) Modify KB_0 introducing a specified amount of changes, i.e., introducing or removing slot-values and instances.
- (ii) From the resulting KB_1, using a set of manually defined patterns, we extract a corpus of about 100K textual sentences; this corpus is used to fine-tune a pre-trained language model (we use BERT (Devlin et al., 2019)).
- (iii) Once BERT has been fine-tuned on KB_1, we use the resulting model (i.e., $BERT_{KB_1}$) to predict slot-values to be substituted in D_0_test test dialogues. We prompt $BERT_{KB_1}$ masking all the slot-values in D_0_test, and, in order to maximize the slot-value language variability, we randomly select from the top ten predictions returned by the model.

The resulting D_1_test has exactly the same amount of dialogues of the original D_0_test provided by MultiWOZ 2.3. More specific details of this procedure are presented in the next paragraphs. As an example, the following user utterance from D_0 dialogues: "I'm looking for an **Indian** restaurant in the **north** part of town" will first be masked as follows:
"I'm looking for an **[MASK]** restaurant in the **[MASK]** part of town"
and finally, we will ask $BERT_{KB_1}$ to predict the substitutions to the masks, which will produce something like:
"I'm looking for an **English** restaurant in the **northwest** part of town"
which populates D_1_test dialogues. Note that the substitutions are produced sequentially from left to right, therefore the first prediction will condition the subsequent ones.

Generating the fine-tuning patterns. In order to fine-tune BERT on our domain, we select a number of utterances - both from user and system - randomly taken from the original MultiWOZ dataset. Then, we mechanically substitute the slot-values in the utterance with all the possible slot-values from KB_1 (the target domain) that have the same slot as the original one. For example, in the utterance "I'm looking for an **Indian** restaurant" the value INDIAN is substituted with all values with the slot RESTAURANT-FOOD in KB_1.

Experiment1: Removing slot-values. Here the goal is to quantify the impact of removing existing slot-values on a DST model. We have defined four versions of modified KB_1 (25%, 50%, 70%, 100%), where we have removed increasing amounts of slot-values from KB_0, randomly substituting them with values that are not removed.

Percentages refer to the proportion between the slot-values that are removed and those kept (e.g., 100% means that the same number of slot-values are removed and kept). In order to choose which slot-values are to be removed, we used an algorithm that minimizes the difference between the actual percentage of removed values and the desired percentage. Note that, after removing, the number of instances in KB_0 and KB_1 is exactly the same, although the slot-value distribution is changed. As for evaluation, we use adapted D_1_test dialogues generated by the dialogue adaptation procedure described in this section, applied on the four versions of KB_1.

Experiment 2: Introducing new slot-values. Here the goal is to quantify the impact of introducing new slot-values (unseen in KB_0) on a DST model. We have defined four versions of modified KB_1 (25%, 50%, 70%, 100%), where we have added an increasing amount of slot-values from KB_0. The percentages refer to the proportion between the new slot-values and the old ones (e.g. 100% means that the number of the new values is the same as the old ones). The new slot-values where taken from a number of different databases, taking care to preserve the domain affinity with respect to each slot. After the addition, the number of instances in KB_0 and KB_1 is exactly the same, although the slot-value distribution is changed. As for the evaluation, we use adapted D_0_test dialogues, generated by the dialogue adaptation procedure described in this section, on the four versions of KB_1.

5.3 Assessing the impact of Instance Changes

We now aim at assessing the impact on the dialogue manager (DM) component caused by introducing or removing domain instances. We start from the MultiWOZ KB_0 and randomly simulated variations both increasing and reducing the number of instances, to obtain KB_1. We consider only the RESTAURANT domain since it is the most complete and well-representative of all domains. The dialogue manager is evaluated checking whether its responses on the D_0_test MultiWOZ dialogues are consistent with the modified KB_1. The intuition is that as new instances are added or removed, the DM capacity to correctly predict the next action would correspondingly decrease. As evaluation metric we used dialog manager correctness (DMC), introduced in Section 2.3.

Experiment 3: Increasing the number of instances. In the increasing setting, we considered five incremental percentages of instance addition (10, 20, 30, 40 and 50). Each new instance was created by selecting random slot-values from those already in KB_0 (no new slot-value is added).

Experiment 4: Decreasing the number of instances. In the reduction setting, we used the same percentages for deciding how many instances have to be randomly removed at each variation of KB_0. Each of the modified KBs was then compared to the original MultiWOZ dialogue and the corresponding DMC correctness is assessed.

5.4 Training on Adapted Dialogues

In this experiment we apply dialogue adaptation on D_0_train dialogues, build a DST model on top of such adapted D_1_train dialogues, and evaluate the resulting model against adapted D_1_test test dialogues. The goal is to investigate whether automatic dialogue adaptation on D_0_train can reduce the decrease in performance of the DST model.

Experiment 5: Training on adapted slot-values. This is similar to Experiment 2 in Section 5.2, introducing new slot-values, with the difference that now, instead of training DST on D_0_train, it is trained on adapted D_1_train dialogues. To produce D_1_train we apply the same procedure used in Experiment 2 to produce D_1_test and defined in this Section. Note that, although the same dialogue adaptation procedure is applied to both training and test data, being independently run on D_0_train and D_0_test, the resulting adaptations may still differ, and slot-values that are present in D_1_train may not appear in D_1_test.

6 Results and Discussion

In this section we present the results obtained on the five experiments introduced in Section 5.

6.1 Impact of Slot-value Changes

As for Experiment 1, Figure 2(a) plots the variation of TRADE and TripPy global joint accuracy at different slot-value removing rates. We observe that removing slot-values in the dialogues brings a massive impact on the degradation of the DST models. Both models show a similar degradation pattern, with TripPy having better scores in general. In both cases, however, the JGA shows a decrease

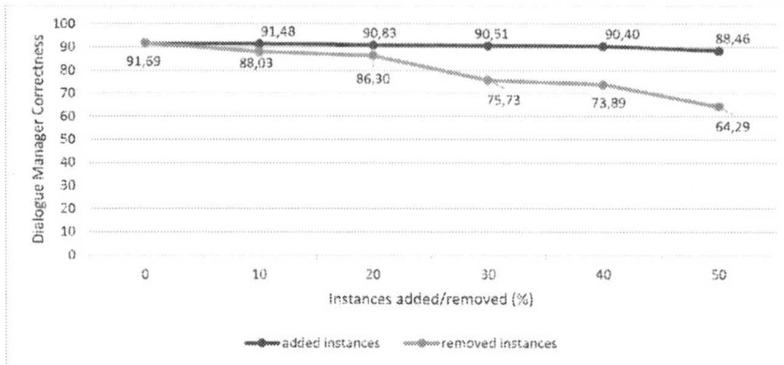

Figure 3: Impact on DM. Correctness when different amounts of instances are added or removed.

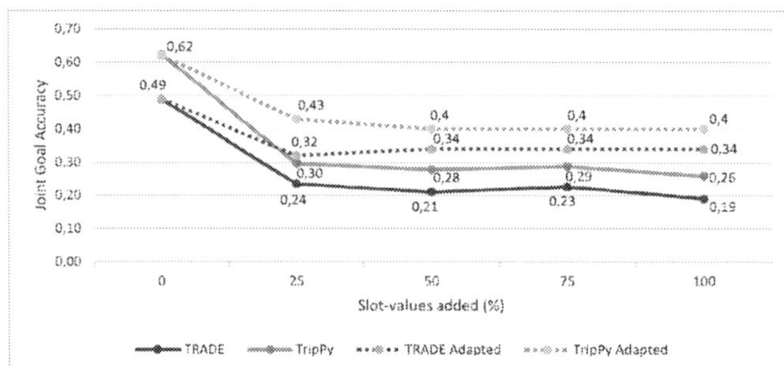

Figure 4: Performances (JGA) of DST models when trained on non-adapted dialogues (continuous line) and adapted dialogues (dotted line) for incremental additions of slot-values.

of about 50% with respect to the zero-change situation.

As for Experiment 2, Figure 2(b) plots the variation of TRADE and TripPy when we incrementally introduce the new slot-values. We note that, again, TripPy scores slightly better than Trade, with both models showing similar degradation rates. As for Experiment 1, the JGA decreases of around 50% with respect to the zero-change situation, showing that the two DST models are poorly robust to the domain changes we have introduced.

For both experiments, the JGA difference among increasing changes is minimal, with a loss of a couple of points in the adding situation, and about 5 points in the removing situation. This can be explained because the current dialogue adaptation procedure does not guarantee that all the changes in KB_0 are actually reflected in D_1_test after BERT fine-tuning.

6.2 Impact of Instance Changes

Figure 3 plots the variation of DM correctness (DMC) when we incrementally add new instances, or reduce them (Experiments 3 and 4). Here, reducing instances comes with a more significant degradation, while adding instances brings the score down by only 3 points. This is due to the fact that cutting off pieces of knowledge, until halving it, has a much stronger impact on the system responses in the dialogues, rather than adding new knowledge, which leaves all previous information untouched. For instance, if the system provides information on a specific restaurant, DMC is not affected by the number of new restaurants that have been introduced; on the other hand, a system presenting to the user information on a restaurant that is not present anymore in the KB, will lead to a failure situation. This is very clear in the plot, with the DMC decreasing by up to 27 points when the reduction rate is set to 50%.

6.3 Training on Adapted Slot-values

As for Experiment 5, Figure 4 compares the DST models when trained without any dialogue adaptation (i.e., using the original MultiWOZ training) and with dialogue adaptation. We see that the automatic adaptation results in a significant improvement with respect to the no-adaptation situation. For instance, adding 100% of the slot values, TripPy gains 35% JGA (from .26 to .40) when trained on automatically adapted D_1_train. On the other side, the performance degradation from the initial no-change situation is about 51% for both models. This is because, while the original dataset was collected manually, the adapted dataset uses values automatically generated by the fine-tuned BERT, which still introduces noise values.

7 Related Work

This section presents relevant work related to dialogue adaptation. Although the idea of adapting dialogues to reflect domain changes is, to the best of our knowledge, original, there have been numerous attempts to modify or extend training data in order to make models more robust to unseen dialogue phenomena.

Delexicalization. The most similar approach to dialogue adaptation is delexicalization, which consists of substituting the slot-values in the dialogue with their corresponding slots (e.g., *"I'm looking for Italian food"* with *"I'm looking for* FOOD-TYPE *food"*), or other placeholders (Wen et al., 2016; Wang et al., 2022). Although the idea is that the dialogue model can generalize enough for recognising different slots for similar KBs, delexicalization, in practice, does not achieve good performance. On the MultiWOZ data-set, a Trade DST model trained on delexicalized slot-values has a Joint accuracy of 0.014, with a significant decrease in performance.

Data augmentation. The idea behind data augmentation in dialogue modeling (Louvan and Magnini, 2020b,c) is to automatically create new training data by applying changes to existing data, without altering their fundamental characteristics. In the case of a conversational data-set, new utterances are created substituting every slot-value with a different value taken from the values for the same slot (e.g., from the utterance *I want to go to the north*, we can create new utterances substituting "south", "west" and "east" to "north").

8 Conclusion

Dialogue adaptation is useful when collecting and annotating new dialogues for certain domain changes becomes too costly, and a cheap solution is preferable. The idea is that domain changes (e.g., new slot-values, new instances) are reflected in training dialogues through corresponding automatic adaptations. We have provided empirical evidence that current dialogue models, both dialogue state tracking and dialogue manager, are strongly affected by domain changes, with a significant decrease in performance. We discussed a number of issues that make automatic dialogue adaptation a challenging task. As for future work, the main goal is to improve dialogue adaptation techniques. While the use of pre-trained generative language models fine-tuned to the specific domain changes is promising, the amount of generated noise is still high, and more work is necessary to better constraint the slot-value generation to achieve human-like performance.

References

Vevake Balaraman and Bernardo Magnini. 2021. Domain-aware dialogue state tracker for multi-domain dialogue systems. *IEEE/ACM Transactions on Audio, Speech, and Language Processing*, 29:866–873.

Antoine Bordes, Y-Lan Boureau, and Jason Weston. 2017. Learning end-to-end goal-oriented dialog. In *ICLR*. OpenReview.net.

Paweł Budzianowski, Tsung-Hsien Wen, Bo-Hsiang Tseng, Iñigo Casanueva, Stefan Ultes, Osman Ramadan, and Milica Gašić. 2018. MultiWOZ - a large-scale multi-domain Wizard-of-Oz dataset for task-oriented dialogue modelling. In *Proceedings of the 2018 Conference on Empirical Methods in Natural Language Processing*, pages 5016–5026, Brussels, Belgium. Association for Computational Linguistics.

Qian Chen, Zhu Zhuo, and Wen Wang. 2019. Bert for joint intent classification and slot filling. *arXiv preprint arXiv:1902.10909*.

Jacob Devlin, Ming-Wei Chang, Kenton Lee, and Kristina Toutanova. 2019. BERT: Pre-training of deep bidirectional transformers for language understanding. In *Proceedings of the 2019 Conference of the North American Chapter of the Association for Computational Linguistics: Human Language Technologies, Volume 1 (Long and Short Papers)*, pages 4171–4186, Minneapolis, Minnesota. Association for Computational Linguistics.

Layla El Asri and Adam Trischler. 2017. Safe evaluation of dialogue management. In *Proceedings of WiNLP*.

Mihail Eric, Rahul Goel, Shachi Paul, Abhishek Sethi, Sanchit Agarwal, Shuyang Gao, Adarsh Kumar, Anuj Goyal, Peter Ku, and Dilek Hakkani-Tur. 2020. MultiWOZ 2.1: A consolidated multi-domain dialogue dataset with state corrections and state tracking baselines. In *Proceedings of the 12th Language Resources and Evaluation Conference*, pages 422–428, Marseille, France. European Language Resources Association.

Michael Heck, Carel van Niekerk, Nurul Lubis, Christian Geishauser, Hsien-Chin Lin, Marco Moresi, and Milica Gasic. 2020. Trippy: A triple copy strategy for value independent neural dialog state tracking. In *Proceedings of the 21th Annual Meeting of the Special Interest Group on Discourse and Dialogue, SIGdial 2020, 1st virtual meeting, July 1-3, 2020*, pages 35–44. Association for Computational Linguistics.

John F. Kelley. 1984. An iterative design methodology for user-friendly natural language office information applications. *ACM Trans. Inf. Syst.*, 2(1):26–41.

Adarsh Kumar, Peter Ku, Anuj Goyal, Angeliki Metallinou, and Dilek Hakkani-Tur. 2020. Ma-dst: Multi-attention-based scalable dialog state tracking. In *Proceedings of the AAAI Conference on Artificial Intelligence*, volume 34, pages 8107–8114.

Wai-Chung Kwan, Hongru Wang, Huimin Wang, and Kam-Fai Wong. 2022. A survey on recent advances and challenges in reinforcement learningmethods for task-oriented dialogue policy learning. *arXiv preprint arXiv:2202.13675*.

Tiziano Labruna and Bernardo Magnini. 2021a. Addressing slot-value changes in task-oriented dialogue systems through dialogue domain adaptation. In *Proceedings of RANLP 2021*.

Tiziano Labruna and Bernardo Magnini. 2021b. From cambridge to pisa: A journey into cross-lingual dialogue domain adaptation for conversational agents. *CLiC-it 2021*.

Tiziano Labruna and Bernardo Magnini. 2022. Finetuning bert for generative dialogue domain adaptation. In *Text, Speech, and Dialogue*, pages 490–501.

Changye Li, David Knopman, Weizhe Xu, Trevor Cohen, and Serguei Pakhomov. 2022. GPT-D: Inducing dementia-related linguistic anomalies by deliberate degradation of artificial neural language models. In *Proceedings of the 60th Annual Meeting of the Association for Computational Linguistics (Volume 1: Long Papers)*, pages 1866–1877, Dublin, Ireland. Association for Computational Linguistics.

Bing Liu and Ian Lane. 2017. Iterative policy learning in end-to-end trainable task-oriented neural dialog models. In *2017 IEEE Automatic Speech Recognition and Understanding Workshop (ASRU)*, pages 482–489. IEEE.

Samuel Louvan and Bernardo Magnini. 2020a. Recent neural methods on slot filling and intent classification for task-oriented dialogue systems: A survey. In *Proceedings of the 28th International Conference on Computational Linguistics*, pages 480–496, Barcelona, Spain (Online). International Committee on Computational Linguistics.

Samuel Louvan and Bernardo Magnini. 2020b. Simple data augmentation for multilingual nlu in task oriented dialogue systems.

Samuel Louvan and Bernardo Magnini. 2020c. Simple is better! lightweight data augmentation for low resource slot filling and intent classification. *arXiv preprint arXiv:2009.03695*.

Michaael McTear. 2020. *Conversational AI: Dialogue Systems, Conversational Agents, and Chatbots*. Morgan and Claypool Publishers.

Nikola Mrkšić, Diarmuid Ó Séaghdha, Tsung-Hsien Wen, Blaise Thomson, and Steve Young. 2017. Neural belief tracker: Data-driven dialogue state tracking. In *Proceedings of the 55th Annual Meeting of the Association for Computational Linguistics (Volume 1: Long Papers)*, pages 1777–1788. Association for Computational Linguistics.

Alexandros Papangelis, Vangelis Karkaletsis, and Fillia Makedon. 2012. Evaluation of online dialogue policy learning techniques. In *Proceedings of the Eighth International Conference on Language Resources and Evaluation (LREC'12)*, pages 1410–1415.

Colin Raffel, Noam Shazeer, Adam Roberts, Katherine Lee, Sharan Narang, Michael Matena, Yanqi Zhou, Wei Li, and Peter J. Liu. 2020. Exploring the limits of transfer learning with a unified text-to-text transformer. *Journal of Machine Learning Research*, 21(140):1–67.

Weizhi Wang, Zhirui Zhang, Junliang Guo, Yinpei Dai, Boxing Chen, and Weihua Luo. 2022. Task-oriented dialogue system as natural language generation. In *Proceedings of the 45th International ACM SIGIR Conference on Research and Development in Information Retrieval*, pages 2698–2703.

Tsung-Hsien Wen, Milica Gasic, Nikola Mrksic, Lina M Rojas-Barahona, Pei-Hao Su, David Vandyke, and Steve Young. 2016. Multi-domain neural network language generation for spoken dialogue systems. *arXiv preprint arXiv:1603.01232*.

Chien-Sheng Wu, Andrea Madotto, Ehsan Hosseini-Asl, Caiming Xiong, Richard Socher, and Pascale Fung. 2019. Transferable multi-domain state generator for task-oriented dialogue systems. In *Proceedings of the 57th Annual Meeting of the Association for Computational Linguistics*, pages 808–819, Florence, Italy. Association for Computational Linguistics.

Author Index

Association for Computational Linguistics
209 N. Eighth Street
Stroudsburg, Pennsylvania 18360

ISBN 978-1-7138-7376-1

CURRAN ASSOCIATES INC.
proceedings.com